FRONT-END DEVELOPMENT PROJECTS WITH VUE.JS

Learn to build scalable web applications and dynamic user interfaces with Vue 2

Raymond Camden, Hugo Di Francesco, Clifford Gurney,
Philip Kirkbride, and Maya Shavin

FRONT-END DEVELOPMENT PROJECTS WITH VUE.JS

Authors: Raymond Camden, Hugo Di Francesco, Clifford Gurney, Philip Kirkbride, and Maya Shavin

Reviewers: Dániel Ernő Szabó and Akshit Sharma

Managing Editors: Prachi Jain and Priyanka Sawant

Acquisitions Editors: Royluis Rodrigues, Sneha Shinde, Anindya Sil, and Alicia Wooding

Production Editor: Shantanu Zagade

Editorial Board: Megan Carlisle, Samuel Christa, Mahesh Dhyani, Heather Gopsill, Manasa Kumar, Alex Mazonowicz, Monesh Mirpuri, Bridget Neale, Dominic Pereira, Shiny Poojary, Abhishek Rane, Brendan Rodrigues, Erol Staveley, Ankita Thakur, Nitesh Thakur, and Jonathan Wray

First published: November 2020

Production reference: 2081220

ISBN: 978-1-83898-482-3

Published by Packt Publishing Ltd.

Livery Place, 35 Livery Street

Birmingham B3 2PB, UK

Table of Contents

Chapter 2: Working with Data   71

Chapter 8: The State of Vue.js State Management   367

Chapter 9: Working with Vuex – State, Getters, Actions, and Mutations 411

Chapter 10: Working with Vuex – Fetching Remote Data 441

Chapter 11: Working with Vuex – Organizing Larger Stores 457

Chapter 12: Unit Testing 477

Chapter 13: End-to-End Testing 531

Chapter 14: Deploying Your Code to the Web 579

Appendix 637

Index 743

PREFACE

ABOUT THE BOOK

Are you looking to use Vue 2 for web applications, but don't know where to begin? *Front-End Development Projects with Vue.js* will help build your development toolkit and get ready to tackle real-world web projects. You'll get to grips with the core concepts of this JavaScript framework with practical examples and activities.

Through the use-cases in this book, you'll discover how to handle data in Vue components, define communication interfaces between components, and handle static and dynamic routing to control application flow. You'll get to grips with Vue CLI and Vue DevTools, and learn how to handle transition and animation effects to create an engaging user experience. In chapters on testing and deploying to the web, you'll gain the skills to start working like an experienced Vue developer and build professional apps that can be used by other people.

You'll work on realistic projects that are presented as bitesize exercises and activities, allowing you to challenge yourself in an enjoyable and attainable way. These mini projects include a chat interface, a shopping cart and price calculator, a to-do app, and a profile card generator for storing contact details.

By the end of this book, you'll have the confidence to handle any web development project and tackle real-world front-end development problems.

ABOUT THE AUTHORS

Raymond Camden is a developer advocate for IBM. His work focuses on the MobileFirst platform, Bluemix, hybrid mobile development, Node.js, HTML5, and web standards in general. He is a published author and presents at conferences and user groups on a variety of topics. Raymond can be reached at his blog, on Twitter, or via email. He is the author of many development books, including Apache Cordova in Action and Client-Side Data Storage.

Hugo Di Francesco is a software engineer who has worked extensively with JavaScript. He holds a MEng degree in mathematical computation from University College London (UCL). He has used JavaScript across the stack to create scalable and performant platforms at companies such as Canon and Elsevier. He is currently tackling problems in the retail operations space with Node.js, React, and Kubernetes while running the eponymous Code with Hugo website. Outside of work, he is an international fencer, in the pursuit of which he trains and competes across the globe.

Clifford Gurney is a solution-focused and results-oriented technical lead at a series-A funded startup. A background in communication design and broad exposure to leading digital transformation initiatives enriches his delivery of conceptually designed front-end solutions using Vue JS. Cliff has presented at the Vue JS Melbourne meetups and collaborates with other like-minded individuals to deliver best in class digital experience platforms.

Philip Kirkbride has over 5 years of experience with JavaScript and is based in Montreal. He graduated from a technical college in 2011 and since then he has been working with web technologies in various roles.

Maya Shavin is a senior frontend developer, speaker, blogger, Storefront UI core member, and the founder and organizer of VueJS Israel Meetups.

WHO THIS BOOK IS FOR

This book is for developers who are just getting started with Vue.js and are looking to gain a basic understanding of **Single-Page Application** (**SPA**) patterns and learn how to create scalable enterprise applications using Vue.js. You'll also find this book useful if you already use React or Angular and want to start learning Vue.js. To understand the concepts explained in this book, you must be familiar with basic HTML, CSS, JavaScript (such as objects, scopes, this contexts, and values versus references), and **Node Package Manager** (**NPM**).

ABOUT THE CHAPTERS

Chapter 1, Starting Your First Vue Project, sees you creating Vue components immediately. You'll learn the basics of Vue.js as well as understand reactivity in JavaScript applications.

Chapter 2, Working with Data, provides information on more component building blocks using computed data props, observing state changes with watchers, and utilizing asynchronous APIs.

Chapter 3, Vue CLI, is a deep dive into Vue's quality-of-life toolkit. You'll understand how to use the Vue CLI and browser DevTools.

Chapter 4, Nesting Components (Modularity), looks at approaches to passing data across components to modularize them.

Chapter 5, Global Component Composition, dives deep into ways to share component functionality across a Vue.js code base.

Chapter 6, Routing, covers the use of standard and dynamic routing with Vue. You'll learn how to create an SPA with complex multi-page applications in Vue.

Chapter 7, Animations and Transitions, covers the built-in animations and transitions that come with Vue as well as using external JavaScript libraries for Vue. We'll create custom animations to be used in a demo app.

Chapter 8, The State of Vue.js State Management, provides a view into different approaches for Vue.js state management.

Chapter 9, Working with Vuex – State, Getters, Actions, and Mutations, introduces you to the Vuex library for state management in Vue.

Chapter 10, Working with Vuex – Fetching Remote Data, discusses how to use Vuex and remote APIs.

Chapter 11, Working with Vuex – Organizing Larger Stores, helps you organize and manage large Vuex stores.

Chapter 12, Unit Testing, looks at testing individual pieces of a Vue.js application, including components, filters, and mixins.

Chapter 13, End-to-End Testing, introduces Cypress, which is used for writing end-to-end tests for a Vue.js application.

Chapter 14, Deploying Your Code to the Web, looks at modern best practices in continuous integration/continuous deployment and considers how to deploy a Vue.js application to multiple hosting providers.

CONVENTIONS

Code words in text, database table names, folder names, filenames, file extensions, path names, dummy URLs, user input, and Twitter handles are shown as follows:

"A **panic()** function accepts an empty interface."

Words that you see on the screen, for example, in menus or dialog boxes, also appear in the same format.

A block of code is set as follows:

```
<template>
    <div>
        Vue Template Code
    </div>
</template>
```

New terms and important words are shown like this: "These behaviors are collectively called **method sets**."

Reference to other chapters and images are shown like this: "*Figure 2.15* displays the output generated by the preceding code."

Key parts of code snippets are highlighted as follows:

```
<input
    id="phone"
    type="tel"
    name="phone"
    v-model="phone"
    class="border-2 border-solid border-blue-200 rounded
        px-2 py-1"
/>
```

Long code snippets are truncated, and the corresponding names of the code files on GitHub are placed at the top of the truncated code. The permalinks to the entire code are placed below the code snippet. It should look as follows:

Exercise1-12.vue

```
17 <script>
18 export default {
19   data() {
20     return {
21       list: [
22         'Apex Legends',
23         'A Plague Tale: Innocence',
24         'ART SQOOL',
25         'Baba Is You',
26         'Devil May Cry 5',
27         'The Division 2',
28         'Hypnospace Outlaw',
29         'Katana ZERO',
30       ],
31     }
32   },
33   methods: {
34     deleteItem(value) {
35       this.list = this.list.filter(item => item !== value)
36     },
37   },
38 ...
```

The complete code for this step is available at https://packt.live/3pJGLvO.

BEFORE YOU BEGIN

Every great journey begins with a humble step. Our upcoming adventure with Vue.js is no exception. Before we can do awesome things using Vue, we need to be prepared with a productive environment. In the following short sections, we shall see how to do that.

MINIMUM HARDWARE RECOMMENDATIONS FOR RUNNING NODE.JS APPLICATIONS

To be able to run all the recommended tools used in the book, it's recommended that you have the following:

- 1 GHz or faster desktop processor

- 512 MB of RAM (at a minimum; more is better)

- Windows 32/64 bit, macOS 64 bit, Linux ARMv7/v8

INSTALLING NODE.JS

Node.js is required to be installed on your computer in order for Vue.js to run. Download the latest LTS version by following the instructions for Windows, macOS, and Linux at https://nodejs.org/en/download/. Node.js is free to install and use.

INSTALLING GIT

Node.js applications use the version control tool Git to install extra tools and code. You can find the installation instructions for Windows, macOS, and Linux at https://git-scm.com/book/en/v2/Getting-Started-Installing-Git. Git is free to install and use.

INSTALLING YARN

Some exercises will use the Yarn dependency manager to install and run Vue.js applications. You can find the instructions to download and install Yarn for Windows, macOS, and Linux at https://classic.yarnpkg.com/en/docs/install. Yarn is free to install and use.

INSTALLING VUE.JS CLI (THE VUE COMMAND-LINE INTERFACE)

Some exercises will require you to use the Vue.js CLI. You can find the instructions to download and install the Vue.js CLI at https://cli.vuejs.org/guide/installation.html.

INSTALLING VISUAL STUDIO CODE (EDITOR/IDE)

You need something in which to write your Vue source code. This tool is called an editor or an **Integrated Development Environment** (**IDE**). If you already have an editor you like, you can use it with this book if you'd like to.

If you don't already have an editor, we recommend you use the free Visual Studio Code editor. You can download the installer from https://code.visualstudio.com:

1. After it is downloaded, open Visual Studio Code.

2. From the top menu bar, select **View**.

3. From the list of options, select **Extensions**. A panel should appear on the left side. At the top is a search input box.

4. Type **Vetur**. The first option should be an extension called **Vetur** by **Pine Wu**.

5. Click the **Install** button on that option. Wait for a message that says it's successfully installed.

INSTALLING THE CODE BUNDLE

Download the code files from GitHub at https://packt.live/3nOX2xE. Refer to these code files for the complete code bundle.

GET IN TOUCH

Feedback from our readers is always welcome.

General feedback: If you have any questions about this book, please mention the book title in the subject of your message and email us at **customercare@packtpub.com**.

Errata: Although we have taken every care to ensure the accuracy of our content, mistakes do happen. If you have found a mistake in this book, we would be grateful if you could report this to us. Please visit www.packtpub.com/support/errata and complete the form.

Piracy: If you come across any illegal copies of our works in any form on the Internet, we would be grateful if you could provide us with the location address or website name. Please contact us at **copyright@packt.com** with a link to the material.

If you are interested in becoming an author: If there is a topic that you have expertise in and you are interested in either writing or contributing to a book, please visit authors.packtpub.com.

PLEASE LEAVE A REVIEW

Let us know what you think by leaving a detailed, impartial review on Amazon. We appreciate all feedback – it helps us continue to make great products and help aspiring developers build their skills. Please spare a few minutes to give your thoughts – it makes a big difference to us.

1

STARTING YOUR FIRST VUE PROJECT

OVERVIEW

In this chapter, you will learn the key concepts of Vue.js and why you should consider Vue.js for your next project. You will learn how to run Vue projects from the command line; describe the Vue.js project architecture; create Vue single file components using various styling and HTML syntax flavors; and also write Vue methods and data objects and control HTML templates competently.

By the end of this first chapter, you will be able to describe the basics of Vue lifecycle hooks and expressions.

INTRODUCTION

Developers in the industry are required to resolve frontend development problems quickly with minimal impact on existing workflows or backend architecture. In many cases, the UI is overlooked completely until the end of a project, which can happen because of a lack of resources, ever-evolving product requirements, or the existing attitude that the frontend is the easy bit. However, companies such as Apple and Google have proven that design thinking on the frontend is key to a solid product or platform that will excite and engage users leading to a higher return on investment and a more successful business.

If you have found Vue.js, you may have also come across other frontend frameworks that, at face value, solve the same problems such as Ember, Angular, or React. At the surface level, they all attempt to make reactive frontend development more reliable and introduce patterns that make this easier to do. However, there are some critical differences in how a Vue project might play out compared to an Angular or React project. Let's look into them.

ANGULAR VERSUS VUE

Angular is a **Model-View-ViewModel** (**MVVM**) framework built by Google that, generally, enterprise companies in the past tended to favor because of Google's backing and the fact that from the ground up, Angular was created to be used alongside TypeScript. The ecosystem supporting Angular includes **Ahead of Time** (**AoT**) rendering, and router and CLI management, but fails to deliver a simplified global state management system; developers would need to learn and use **Flux** or adopt **NgRx**. Vue takes Angular's core ideas of robustness and reliability and improves the development experience with its agnostic approach to development by removing the restrictiveness of an enforced code style for developers. Simplifying familiar Angular patterns such as HTML directives and dependency injection for modularity with Vue's single-file component system benefits developers by removing the necessity to learn and remember a variety of structures (injectables, components, pipes, modules, and so on). Vue has excellent support for TypeScript and typing without the drawbacks that Angular can have with its enforced coding language and development style. React and Vue share a focus on component-driven development, which reduces the amount of time and effort needed to uptake a new framework.

REACT VERSUS VUE

The driving force behind React's popularity and large development community is attributed to Facebook's dedicated engineers and its 2013 open source release at a time when Angular 2+ was nowhere to be seen. React's JSX pattern (a way of writing HTML and CSS in JavaScript) introduces with it a heightened learning curve for new developers who are both required to learn another language and also wrap their heads around component-based architecture. Components allow developers to build applications in a modular way; individual components describe their own piece of functionality and lifecycle, where they can be instantiated when they are required and destroyed when they are not used. Vue takes these core concepts of modular coding and enables developers to build these components using either JSX or writing HTML, CSS, and JavaScript as you would a traditional web application in a single file. Vue's separation of concerns in a single-file component simplifies this modular structure for developers.

ADVANTAGES OF USING VUE FOR YOUR PROJECT

Vue has a gentle learning curve and a vibrant ecosystem. This benefits teams of any size by not requiring a huge amount of overhead to educate teams of developers on how to use the Vue.js framework.

- Vue.js is another example of a pattern in development that is easy to learn but hard to master. A key benefit of Vue is its *approachability for both new and veteran developers*.

- Out of the box, developers can use a *well-optimized* and performant framework on which to build dynamic frontend applications of any size.

- The **single-file component (SFC)** pattern offers a modular and flexible blueprint to simplify the development process and provides an *enjoyable experience* for developers of all levels, bringing order to component chaos. Single-file components allow Vue to be genuinely *versatile*, where you can implement basic functionality and incrementally adopt pieces of a static site into Vue rather than overhauling your entire website.

- Official global state management support should come as a relief to any developer who is familiar with the **Redux** and **NgRx** patterns. As powerful as these libraries can be when used well, **Vuex** is a great middle-ground for creating *robust global state patterns* that are flexible to meet most development needs.

For those developers who are looking to get off the ground quickly, do not reinvent the wheel by building a custom reactive pattern unless individual use cases require it. You can save time and money by using Vue as a framework because it is already performant and officially supports libraries that are necessary to build an end-to-end app, which include **vue-router**, Vuex state management, dev tools, and more.

In this chapter, we will start by introducing the Vue architecture before familiarizing you with Vue's unique SFC pattern and HTML template syntax sugar. You will learn how to work with the Vue-specific template syntax and coding patterns that include Vue bindings, directives, lifecycle hooks, scopes, and the local state. Out of the Vue ecosystem of official plugins, we will primarily be focusing on the core Vue libraries. First, let's look at Vue's project architecture.

THE VUE INSTANCE IN A SIMPLE VUE APPLICATION

One of the easiest ways to get started with Vue is to import the Vue package through a **Content Distribution Network** (**CDN**). By doing this you can create a Vue instance with the **Vue** function. Each Vue application consists of one root Vue instance that is created using the **new Vue** function. All corresponding Vue components that are created are also defined using the same syntax, however, are considered as nested Vue instances that can contain their own options and properties:

```
var vm = new Vue({
  // options
})
```

> **NOTE**
>
> **vm** is a term commonly used to refer to a **View Model**, which is an abstraction of the view that describes the state of the data in the model. Binding a Vue instance to **vm** helps you to keep track of your Vue instance in a block of code.

In this example, we import Vue using the **jsdelivr** CDN, which will allow you to utilize the Vue functions:

```
<!DOCTYPE html>
<html>
<head>
    <title>Vue.js CDN</title>
    <script src="https://cdn.jsdelivr.net/npm/vue/dist/vue.js">
```

```
    </script>
  </head>
</html>
```

Declare an element in the **<body>** tag using a class, ID, or data attribute. Vue is known for its ability to declaratively render data to the DOM using simple template syntax such as double curly braces to specify reactive content, for example, **{{ text }}**:

```
<!DOCTYPE html>
<html>
<head>
    <title>Vue.js CDN</title>
    <script src="https://cdn.jsdelivr.net/npm/vue/dist/vue.js">
    </script>
</head>

<body>
    <div>
        <p class="reactive-text">{{ text }}</p>
    </div>
</body>

</html>
```

In the **<head>** tag, we see some vanilla JavaScript code that fires off when the DOM loads. This constructs a Vue component bound to the element with **class .reactive-text**. The data property labeled **text** will replace the curly brace placeholder with the string defined as **Start using Vue.js today!**:

```
<head>
    <title>Vue.js CDN</title>
    <script src="https://cdn.jsdelivr.net/npm/vue/dist/vue.js">
    </script>
    <script>
        document.addEventListener('DOMContentLoaded', function () {
            new Vue({
                el: '.reactive-text',
                data: {
                    text: "Start using Vue.js today!"
                }
            })
```

```
        })
    </script>
</head>

<body>
    <div>
        <p class="reactive-text">{{ text }}</p>
    </div>
</body>

</html>
```

In the preceding script, you bind the **<p>** element with the **reactive-text** class to the new Vue instance. So, now that Vue understands this HTML element you can use the **{{ text }}** syntax to output the data property **text** inside of the **<p>** element.

The output of the preceding code will be as follows:

```
Start using Vue.js today!
```

While a CDN is a very portable way to start including Vue.js in your projects, using package managers is the recommended installation method for Vue, which is compiled by webpack, because it allows you to control third-party library versions easily. You can access it here: https://vuejs.org/v2/guide/installation.html. We will explore what a webpack example looks like next.

A WEBPACK VUE APPLICATION

Vue projects are structured similarly to a lot of modern node-based apps that contain a **package.json** file and a **node_modules** folder in the root of your project. Various other configuration files are usually contained at the root level, such as **babel.config.js** and **.eslintrc.js**, since they will generally have an effect across your whole project. The following screenshot displays a default Vue app folder structure:

Figure 1.1: Default Vue application folder structure

The Vue project structure follows a pattern where most of your source code is managed within the **/src** directory. You can subdivide your Vue files into various folders, for example, using a **components** folder to store reusable Vue components. By default, Vue will create assets and a **components** folder to code split the default files. For beginners, it is good to follow this pattern until you get more comfortable with splitting up your code in ways that make sense for your application:

Figure 1.2: Default Vue application src folder structure

The **public** folder is a special directory for containing files that need to be transferred directly to the output location. The following screenshot displays how this folder will look:

Figure 1.3: Default Vue application public folder

By default, the **public** folder will contain an **index.html** file that serves as a placeholder for loading the Vue application. The **index.html** file can be modified to include header and footer scripts as required, such as Google Fonts or third-party JavaScript libraries that are not included as a part of your webpack bundle.

VUE SINGLE-PAGE COMPONENTS

Components are the building blocks of most modern frameworks. Generally splitting your work into smaller chunks not only makes your code much easier to interpret but functionally follows the principles of **Don't Repeat Yourself** (**DRY**). One of the most unique patterns for Vue users with arguably one of the most benefits is the **Single File Component** (**SFC**) pattern. SFCs centralize the responsibility of both appearance and behavior into a single file, often simplifying the architecture of your project and making the development process simpler being able to refer to your HTML, CSS, and JavaScript logic without switching files. Your default .vue file structure will be as follows:

```
<template>
  <div>
    <!-- Write HTML syntax here -->
  </div>
</template>

<script>
  export default {
    // Write javascript here
  }
</script>

<style>
  /* Write styling here */
</style>
```

Figure 1.4: Default .vue file structure

A trap that a lot of new Vue developers fall into is writing mega Vue files of over 500 lines of code, just for the HTML itself. Usually, what this means is that you could break this long component down into some smaller ones; however, we will cover file importing and code splitting in future chapters.

For example, in the header of your application, you may have a reusable logo element that needs to remain consistent on other pages. You would create a component such as **logo.vue**:

```
// logo.vue

<template>
     <img src="myLogo.png" />
</template>
```

You can import it into your header component named **header.vue**:

```
// header.vue

<template>
    <header>
      <a href="mywebsite.com"><logo /></a>
    </header>
</template>

<script>
    import logo from 'components/logo.vue'

    export default {
        components: {
          logo
        }
    }
</script>
```

Very soon, you will have lots of these semantically structured files, which use these small chunks of reusable syntax that your team can implement across various areas of your application.

In the next section, we will gain an understanding of data properties.

DATA PROPERTIES (PROPS)

One of the most used terms and reactive elements used when constructing Vue components is data property. These manifest themselves within the data function of a Vue instance:

```
<template>
    <div>{{color}}</div>
</template>
<script>
    export default {
        data() {
            return {
                color: 'red'
            }
        }
    }
</script>
```

You can use data property to essentially store any information you want to use within your Vue templates. When this data property is updated or is changed, it will reactively update in the corresponding template.

EXERCISE 1.01: BUILDING YOUR FIRST COMPONENT

In this exercise, we are going to build our first component inside of a Vue project. In this context, components are imported using **ES6**. We will require Node.js and **yarn** to be installed. These will be covered in the *Preface*. By the end of the exercise, you will be able to confidently create new Vue components using Vetur and import them into your project.

To access the code files for this exercise, refer to https://packt.live/35Lhycl.

1. Open a command-line terminal and navigate into the **Exercise 1.01** folder and run the following commands in order:

```
> cd Exercise1.01/
> code .
> yarn
> yarn serve
```

Go to **https://localhost:8080.**

> **NOTE**
>
> Your app will hot reload when you save new changes, so you can see them instantly.

2. In **VSCode** (which will have opened when you ran the **code .** command), go into the **src/App.vue** directory and delete everything in that file and save.

3. In your browser, everything should be blank a clean slate to start working from.

4. The three primary components that make up a single-file component are the **<template>**, **<script>**, and **<style>** blocks. If you installed the Vetur extension from the *Preface*, write **vue** and press *Tab* to choose the first selection of the prompt. This is the quickest way to set up your default code blocks as displayed in the following screenshot:

```
1│   vue
```
```
▼  <vue> with default.vue 🖑              default.vue  | ...>
🖥  <template> html.vue 🖑
🖥  <template> pug.vue 🖑
🖥  <style> css-scoped.vue 🖑
🖥  <style> css.vue 🖑
🖥  <style> less-scoped.vue 🖑
🖥  <style> less.vue 🖑
🖥  <style> postcss-scoped.vue 🖑
🖥  <style> postcss.vue 🖑
🖥  <style> sass-scoped.vue 🖑
🖥  <style> sass.vue 🖑
🖥  <style> scss-scoped.vue 🖑
```

Figure 1.5: VSCode Vetur

The following is the code generated after pressing *Tab* when using Vetur:

```
// src/App.vue
<template>
</template>
<script>
export default {
}
</script>
<style>
</style>
```

5. Create another file in the **components** folder called **Exercise1-01.vue** and repeat the same step for scaffolding the Vue blocks using Vetur:

```
// src/components/Exercise1-01.vue
<template>
</template>
<script>
export default {
}
</script>
<style>
</style>
```

6. Within our **Exercise1-01.vue** component, compose a set of **<div>** tags, with an **<h1>** element and a heading inside the **<template>** tags:

```
<template>
  <div>
    <h1>My first component!</h1>
  </div>
</template>
```

7. Inside the **<style>** block, add some styling as follows:

```
<template>
  <div>
    <h1>My first component!</h1>
  </div>
</template>
<style>
  h1 {
    font-family: 'Avenir', Helvetica, Arial, sans-serif;
    text-align: center;
    color: #2c3e50;
    margin-top: 60px;
  }
</style>
```

8. Import our component into the **App.vue** by using the ES6 **import** method and defining the component inside the **components** object in the **<script>** block. We can now reference this component inside the HTML by using its name in **camelCase** or **kebab-case** (both will work):

```
<template>
  <Exercise />
</template>

<script>
import Exercise from './components/Exercise1-01'
export default {
  components: {
    Exercise,
  }
}
</script>
```

When you press **Save**, **https://localhost:8080** should reload and display the following output:

My first component!

Figure 1.6: Localhost output for Exercise 1.01

In this exercise, we saw how to structure Vue components using template tags, scaffold basic Vue components using **Vetur**, output HTML, and use ES6 syntax to import the **Exercise1-01** component into **App.vue**.

> ### NOTE
>
> You can only have one root HTML element inside **<template>** tags. Complex components should be wrapped in a containing HTML tag of your choice. **<div>**, **<article>**, and **<section>** are all semantic HTML component wrappers.

DATA BINDING SYNTAX USING INTERPOLATION

Interpolation is the insertion of something of a different nature into something else. In the Vue.js context, this is where you would use *mustache* syntax (double curly braces) to define an area where you can inject data into a component's HTML template.

Consider the following example:

```
new Vue({
    data() {
        title: 'Vue.js'
    },
    template: '<span>Framework: {{ title }}</span>'
})
```

The data property **title** is bound to Vue.js reactive data and will update on the fly depending on state changes to the UI and its data. We will go into more depth about how to use interpolation and how to bind it to data properties in the next exercise.

EXERCISE 1.02: INTERPOLATION WITH CONDITIONALS

When you want to output data into your template or make elements on a page be reactive, interpolate data into the template by using curly braces. Vue can understand and replace that placeholder with data.

To access the code files for this exercise, refer to https://packt.live/3feLsJ3.

1. Open a command-line terminal and navigate into the **Exercise 1.02** folder and run the following commands in order:

```
> cd Exercise1.02/
> code .
> yarn
> yarn serve
```

Go to **https://localhost:8080**.

2. Inside of the **Exercise1-02.vue** component, let's add data within the **<script>** tags by adding a function called **data()** and return a key called **title** with your heading string as the value:

```
<script>
export default {
  data() {
    return {
      title: 'My first component!',
    }
  },
}
</script>
```

3. Reference the data **title** by replacing your **<h1>** text with the interpolated value **{{ title }}**:

```
<template>
  <div>
    <h1>{{ title }}</h1>
  </div>
</template>
```

When you save this document, the data title will now appear inside your **h1** tag.

4. In Vue, interpolation will resolve any JavaScript inside curly braces. For example, you can transform your text inside the curly braces using the **toUpperCase()** method:

```
<template>
  <div>
    <h1>{{ title.toUpperCase() }}</h1>
  </div>
</template>
```

You should see an output like the following screenshot:

MY FIRST COMPONENT!

Figure 1.7: Save the file—you should now have an uppercased title

5. In addition to parsing JavaScript methods, interpolation can handle conditional logic. Inside the data object, add a Boolean key-value pair **isUppercase: false**:

```
<template>
  <div>
    <h1>{{ isUppercase ? title.toUpperCase() : title }}</h1>
  </div>
</template>
<script>
export default {
  data() {
    return {
      title: 'My first component!',
      isUppercase: false,
    }
  },
}
</script>
```

The preceding code will generate the following output:

My first component!

Figure 1.8: Exercise 1.02 output after including the inline conditional statement

6. Add this condition to the curly braces, and when you save you should see the non-uppercased title. Play around with this value by changing **isUppercase** to **true**:

```
<script>
export default {
  data() {
    return {
      title: 'My first component!',
      isUppercase: true,
    }
  },
}
</script>
```

The following screenshot displays the final output generated upon running the preceding code:

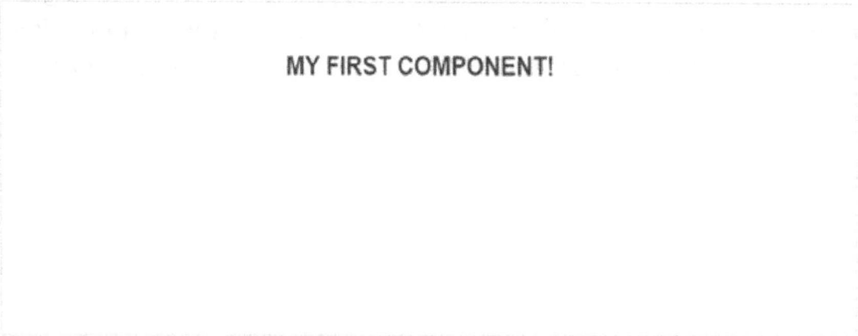

MY FIRST COMPONENT!

Figure 1.9: Final Exercise 1.02 output

In this exercise, we were able to use inline conditionals inside the interpolated tags (curly braces) by using a Boolean variable. This allows us to modify what data is displayed inside of our component without overly complicated conditions, which can be useful in certain use cases.

We will now learn about how to style components using a variety of methods.

STYLING COMPONENTS

When using Vue components, the webpack compiler allows you to use almost any frontend templating language style you prefer. For example, there are several ways to compose CSS, either directly or with pre-processing. The easiest way to enable these expressive languages in your Vue templates is to install them when you set up your project ahead of time using the Vue CLI.

When using the **style** tag inside of a Vue component, you have the option to specify a language, provided you have installed the appropriate webpack loader. In **Exercise 1.01**, if you chose to install the SCSS preprocessor, you can add the **lang="scss"** attribute to the **style** tag to begin using SCSS.

For example, if you chose to install the Stylus preprocessor, you can add the **lang="stylus"** attribute to the **style** tag to begin using Stylus:

```
<style lang="stylus">
ul
  color: #2c3e50;
  > h2
  color: #22cc33;
</style>
```

Vue scoping is a handy way to stop individual components from inheriting styles from the virtual DOM head. Add the scoped attribute to your **style** tag and write some component-specific styles that will override any other CSS rules from the global sheet. The general rule is to not scope global styles. A common method for defining global styling is to separate these styles into another style sheet and import them into your **App.vue**.

EXERCISE 1.03: IMPORTING SCSS INTO A SCOPED COMPONENT

In this exercise, we will be utilizing the **style** tag to add SCSS preprocessed styles to a component and importing external stylesheets.

To access the code files for this exercise, refer to https://packt.live/3nBBZyl.

1. Open a command-line terminal and navigate into the **Exercise1.03** folder and run the following commands in order:

```
> cd Exercise1.03/
> code .
> yarn
> yarn serve
```

   Go to **https://localhost:8080**.

2. Inside of the exercise file, let's write some HTML that can be styled using SCSS. Let's keep practicing the interpolation method:

```
// src/components/Exercise1-03.vue

<template>
  <div>
    <h1>{{ title }}</h1>
    <h2>{{ subtitle }}</h2>
    <ul>
      <li>{{ items[0] }}</li>
      <li>{{ items[1] }}</li>
      <li>{{ items[2] }}</li>
    </ul>
  </div>
</template>

<script>
export default {
  data() {
    return {
      title: 'My list component!',
      subtitle: 'Vue JS basics',
      items: ['Item 1', 'Item 2', 'Item 3']
```

```
        }
    },
}
</script>
```

3. Add the **lang** property to the **style** tag and add the value **scss** to enable SCSS syntax inside the **style** block:

```
<style lang="scss"></style>
```

4. Create a folder inside the **src/** directory called **styles**. Inside this new folder create a file called **typography.scss**:

```
src/styles/typography.scss
```

5. Inside **typography.scss**, add some styling for the template you composed in your component:

```scss
/* typography.scss */
$color-green: #4fc08d;
$color-grey: #2c3e50;
$color-blue: #003366;
h1 {
    margin-top: 60px;
    text-align: center;
    color: $color-grey;

    + h2 {
        text-align: center;
        color: $color-green;
    }
}

ul {
    display: block;
    margin: 0 auto;
    max-width: 400px;
    padding: 30px;
    border: 1px solid rgba(0,0,0,0.25);

    > li {
```

```
    color: $color-grey;
    margin-bottom: 4px;
  }
}
```

> **NOTE**
>
> In SCSS, you can use standard CSS selectors to select elements in your component.
>
> **ul > li** will select every **<li>** element inside of a **<ul>** element for styling. Similarly, using the addition symbol **+** means the elements placed after the first element will be styled if they match the condition. For example, **h1 + h2** will dictate that all **H2** elements after **H1** will be styled in a way, but **H3** will not. You can understand this better through the following example.

In CSS, you would present this code as follows:

```
h1 + h2 {
    /* Add styling */
}
ul > li {
    /* Add styling */
}
```

In SCSS, the same code can be represented as follows:

```
h1 {
    + h2 {
      // Add styling
    }
}
ul {
    > li {
      // Add styling
    }
}
```

6. In your component, import these styles by using the SCSS `@import` method:

```
<style lang="scss">
@import '../styles/typography';
</style>
```

This will generate an output as follows:

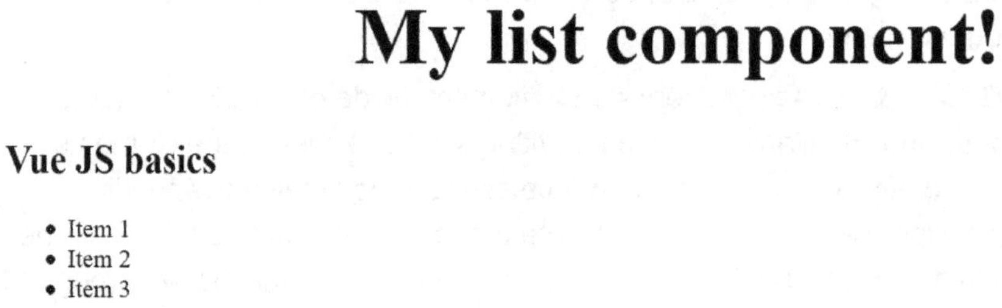

My list component!

Vue JS basics

- Item 1
- Item 2
- Item 3

Figure 1.10: When you save and reload, your project should have the style imported

7. Add the **scoped** attribute to your **<style>** tag to only apply these styles to this component instance. Use the variable from the imported stylesheet **$color-blue**:

```
<style lang="scss" scoped>
@import '../styles/typography';
h1 {
  font-size: 50px;
  color: $color-blue; // Use variables from imported stylesheets
}
</style>
```

The output of the preceding code is as follows:

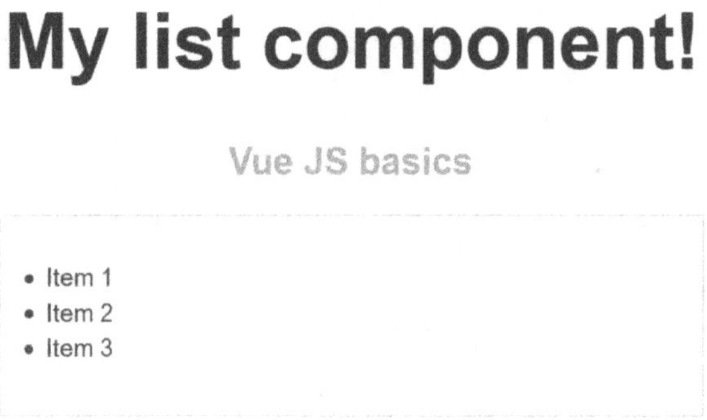

My list component!

Vue JS basics

- Item 1
- Item 2
- Item 3

Figure 1.11: The outcome of scoping styles

Inspect the DOM and you will notice that at run-time, that scoping has applied **v-data-*** attributes to your DOM elements specifying these specific rules. Our **typography.scss**, which we are scoping to our component, references an HTML tag that does not live within the scope of our component. When Vue adds data attributes to the scoped component, it generates the style if the **<body>** tag exists within the component. In our case, it does not.

The **Elements** tab of your browser dev tools will show the following after expanding the **<head>** and **<style>** tags:

```
▼<style type="text/css">
  h1[data-v-da42e8b2] {
    margin-top: 60px;
    text-align: center;
    color: #2c3e50;
  }
  h1 + h2[data-v-da42e8b2] {
    text-align: center;
    color: #4fc08d;
  }
  ul[data-v-da42e8b2] {
    display: block;
    margin: 0 auto;
    max-width: 400px;
    padding: 30px;
    border: 1px solid rgba(0, 0, 0, 0.25);
  }
  ul > li[data-v-da42e8b2] {
    color: #2c3e50;
    margin-bottom: 4px;
  }
  h1[data-v-da42e8b2] {
    font-size: 50px;
    color: #003366;
  }
</style>
<style type="text/css">body {
  font-family: "Avenir", Helvetica, Arial, sans-serif;
  margin: 0;
}</style>
</head>
▼<body data-gr-c-s-loaded="true">
  ▶<noscript>…</noscript>
  ▼<div data-v-da42e8b2>
    <h1 data-v-da42e8b2>My list component!</h1>
    <h2 data-v-da42e8b2>Vue JS basics</h2>
```

Figure 1.12: Observe how the virtual DOM uses data attributes to assign scoped styles

8. Create a new style sheet called **global.scss** in the **styles** folder:

```
/* /src/styles/global.scss */
body {
    font-family: 'Avenir', Helvetica, Arial, sans-serif;
    margin: 0;
}
```

9. Import this stylesheet into your **App.vue**:

```
<style lang="scss">
@import './styles/global';
</style>
```

Our app should now be back to normal, with a mixture of globally defined styling and properly scoped styles for this component, as follows:

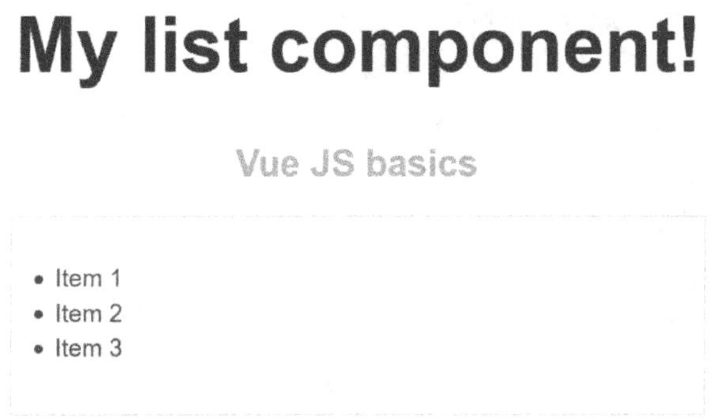

My list component!

Vue JS basics

- Item 1
- Item 2
- Item 3

Figure 1.13: Properly scoped styles for Exercise 1.03

In this exercise, we interpolated data that originated from an array, then styled our component using forms of scoped SCSS, which can both exist inside the **<style>** tag or be imported from another directory in our project.

CSS MODULES

A recent pattern that has become popular in the reactive framework world is CSS modules. Frontend development has always had to face the issue of conflicting CSS class names, ill-structured BEM code, and confusing CSS file structures. Vue components help to solve this by being modular and allowing you to compose CSS that, at compile time, will generate unique class names for the specific component that it was composed for. You can even have the exact same class names across components; however, they will be uniquely identified using a randomly generated string attached to the end.

To enable this feature in Vue, you will need to add the module attribute to the **style** block, and reference classes using JavaScript syntax:

```
<template>
    <div :class="$style.container">CSS modules</div>
</template>
<style lang="scss" module>
.container {
  Width: 100px;
    Margin: 0 auto;
    background: green;
}
</style>
```

In the preceding example, if you inspected the DOM tree that class will be called something like **.container_ABC123**. If you were to create multiple components that had a semantic class name like **.container** but used CSS modules, you would never run into style conflicts again.

EXERCISE 1.04: STYLE VUE COMPONENTS USING CSS MODULES

In this exercise, you will utilize CSS modules to style a **.vue** component. By using the **$style** syntax inside of a **:class** bind, you refer to the Vue instance's **this.$style** scope. Vue will generate random class names based on the components at run or build time ensuring the style will not overlap with any other classes in your project.

To access the code files for this exercise, refer to https://packt.live/36PPYdd.

1. Open a command-line terminal, navigate into the **Exercise1.04** folder, and run the following commands in order:

```
> cd Exercise1.04/
> code .
> yarn
> yarn serve
```

Go to **https://localhost:8080**.

2. Inside of **Exercise1-04.vue**, compose the following code:

```
<template>
  <div>
    <h1>{{ title }}</h1>
```

```
    <h2>{{ subtitle }}</h2>
  </div>
</template>
<script>
export default {
  data() {
    return {
      title: 'CSS module component!',
      subtitle: 'The fourth exercise',
    }
  },
}
</script>
```

3. Add the **<style>** block with the SCSS language and add **module** as an attribute instead of **scoped**:

```
<style lang="scss" module>
h1,
h2 {
    font-family: 'Avenir', Helvetica, Arial, sans-serif;
    text-align: center;
}
.title {
    font-family: 'Avenir', Helvetica, Arial, sans-serif;
    color: #2c3e50;
    margin-top: 60px;
}
.subtitle {
    color: #4fc08d;
    font-style: italic;
}
</style>
```

4. To use CSS modules in your template, you need to bind them to your HTML elements by using **:class** syntax, which is the same as the **v-bind:class** directive:

```
<h1 :class="$style.title">{{ title }}</h1>
<h2 :class="$style.subtitle">{{ subtitle }}</h2>
```

When you save, your project should look something like this:

CSS module component!

The fourth exercise

Figure 1.14: Exercise 1.04 output using CSS modules

If you inspect the virtual DOM, you will see how it has applied unique class names to the bound elements:

```
⌖   ⬡ Inspector   ⊡ Console   ⬠ Debugger   ↑↓ Network   {} Style Edit

🔍 Search HTML
<!DOCTYPE html>
<html lang="en"> event
▶ <head> ••• </head>
▼ <body>
    ▶ <noscript> ••• </noscript>
    ▼ <div>
        <h1 class="Exercise1-04_title_1YRtW">CSS module component!</h1>
        <h2 class="Exercise1-04_subtitle_29CJ5">The fourth exercise</h2>
    </div>
    <!--built files will be auto injected-->
    <script type="text/javascript" src="/js/chunk-vendors.js"></script>
    <script type="text/javascript" src="/js/app.js"></script>
</body>
</html>
```

Figure 1.15: The virtual DOM tree's generated CSS module class

In this exercise, we saw how to use CSS modules in your Vue components and how it works differently to CSS scoping. In the next exercise, we will learn how to write a template in **PUG (HAML)**.

> **NOTE**
>
> In combination with file splitting and importing SCSS, CSS modules are the preferred method of scoping component styling here. This safely ensures that individual component styles and business rules do not risk overriding each other and do not pollute global styling and variables with component-specific styling requirements. Readability is important. The class name also hints to the component name as opposed to the **v-data** attribute, which can be good when debugging large projects.

EXERCISE 1.05: WRITING A COMPONENT TEMPLATE IN PUG (HAML)

With the right loader enabled you can use HTML abstractions such as PUG and HAML to template your Vue components instead of writing HTML.

To access the code files for this exercise, refer to https://packt.live/2IOrHvN.

1. Open a command-line terminal and navigate into the **Exercise1.05** folder and run the following commands in order:

```
> cd Exercise1.05/
> code .
> yarn
```

   Go to **https://localhost:8080**.

2. If Vue is running in the command line, press *Ctrl + C* to stop the instance. Then run the following command:

```
vue add pug

yarn serve
```

3. Inside of **Exercise1-05.vue**, compose the following code and specify the **lang** attribute **pug** on the **<template>** tag:

```
<template lang="pug">
  div
    h1(class='title') {{ title }}
```

```
    </template>

    <script>
    export default {
      data() {
        return {
          title: 'PUG component!',
        }
      },
    }
    </script>

    <style lang="scss">
    .title {
      font-family: 'Avenir', Helvetica, Arial, sans-serif;
      text-align: center;
      color: #2c3e50;
      margin-top: 60px;
    }
    </style>
```

The preceding code will generate the following output:

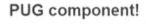

Figure 1.16: Output for the PUG exercise

In this exercise, we saw how to use other HTML languages for templating and to interpolate data in **PUG** format. After installing the Vue.js **PUG** plugin you can write your component syntax inside of these template tags using **PUG** by adding the **lang** attribute with the value **pug**.

VUE DIRECTIVES

Vue's templating language allows you to interpolate the HTML code with JavaScript expressions and Vue directives. This templating pattern is often referred to as syntax sugar because it does not change how the code itself works, just how you use it. Syntax sugar allows you to clearly define template-specific logic inside of your HTML without the need to abstract this logic elsewhere in your project or return copious amounts of HTML directly from your JavaScript code. All Vue based directives are prefixed with **v-***, which indicates that it is a Vue specific attribute:

- **v-text**: The **v-text** directive has the same reactivity interpolation does, except you reference the same piece of data inside of a directive. Interpolation (curly braces) **{{ }}** is more performant than the **v-text** directive; however, you may find yourself in situations where you have pre-rendered text from a server and want to override it once your Vue application has loaded. For example, you can predefine static placeholder text while the DOM waits for the **data** and **v-text** attributes to eventually replace it.

- **v-once**: As a directive, this is unique in that you pair it with other directives to augment how they function. Passing data via **v-text** or interpolated curly braces into the HTML element this attribute is added to will stop the Vue instance from reloading the element with new data, removing the reactivity of the element. This is handy for situations where you want to render decorative elements using data, but do not want them to update when the data changes after the initial render.

- **v-html**: This directive will render valid HTML in your data string inside of the HTML element it has been bound to. This directive is a heavier operation than the other directives, so limited usage is recommended when other options are not otherwise available.

> **NOTE**
>
> **<script>** tags can be run in this directive. Only render content originating from secure or trusted sources.

- **v-bind**: This directive is one of the most widely used directives in Vue. Throughout Vue, you will be binding reactive data to HTML attributes and passing data into props using this directive's **:attr** shortcut instead of **v-bind:attr**.

- **v-if**: To control the display state of HTML elements inside the template, you will often use **v-if** to completely remove elements from the DOM tree. So far, you have seen how to interpolate conditionals like this **{{ isTrue ? 'Show this': 'Not this' }}**. With the **v-if** directive, you can control entire blocks of HTML syntax. **v-else-if** can be used like **else if** statements and finish with **v-else**, which is the equivalent to the **catch { ... }** declaration of an **else { ... }** statement in traditional JavaScript.

- **v-show**: You can control the visible state of HTML elements by using **v-show**, which, instead of removing the element from the DOM tree, will apply a **display: none** style. The difference between a **v-if** and **v-show** is that **v-show** will remain as a block element in the DOM tree but will be hidden with **css** instead of being removed from the DOM tree. You also cannot chain **v-show** with **v-else** or **v-else-if**.

- **v-for**: Apply this to an element you want to repeat or iterate on. This directive requires an additional prop called **:key** to allow it to properly reactively render; it can be as simple as a unique number.

  Consider an example where we iterate over the list element five times. Each list item will render its count (1, 2... 5):

  ```
  <ul><!-- do not apply v-for to this <ul> element -->
      <li v-for="n in 5" :key="n">{{ n }}</li>
  </ul>
  ```

Now let's look at how some of the basic directives work.

EXERCISE 1.06: BASIC DIRECTIVES (V-TEXT, V-ONCE, V-HTML, V-BIND, V-IF, V-SHOW)

More complicated components will use multiple directives to achieve the desired outcome. In this exercise, we will construct a component that uses several directives to bind, manipulate, and output data to a template view.

To access the code files for this exercise, refer to https://packt.live/3fdCNqa.

1. Open a command-line terminal, navigate into the **Exercise1.06** folder, and run the following commands in order:

   ```
   > cd Exercise1.06/
   > code .
   > yarn
   > yarn serve
   ```

   Go to **https://localhost:8080**.

2. Compose the following syntax inside of **Exercise1-06.vue**. This uses the interpolation method that we have used in previous exercises and that will be very familiar by this point:

```
<template>
  <div>
    <h1>{{ text }}</h1>
  </div>
</template>

<script>
export default {
  data() {
    return {
      // v-text
      text: 'Directive text',
    }
  },
}
</script>
<style lang="scss" scoped>
h2 {
  margin: 40px 0 0;
  font-weight: normal;
}
</style>
```

3. Replace the interpolation with the **v-text** attribute. You will notice the output will not change:

```
<template>
  <div>
    <h1 v-text="text">Loading...</h1>
  </div>
</template>

<script>

export default {
  data() {
    return {
```

```
        // v-text
      text: 'Directive text',
    }
  },
}
</script>
```

Figure 1.17 displays the output of the preceding code:

Directive text

Figure 1.17: The v-text directive output works very similarly to the interpolation method

4. Add the **v-once** directive on the same element. This will force this DOM element to only load the **v-text** data once for as long as it exists in the page:

```
<template>
  <div>
    <h1 v-once v-text="text">Loading...</h1>
  </div>
</template>

<script>

export default {
  data() {
    return {
      // v-text
      text: 'Directive text',
    }
  },
}
```

```
</script>

...
```

5. Underneath the **h1** element, include a new **h2** element, which uses the **v-html** attribute. Add a new data key called **html**, which contains a string with HTML formatting in it like the following:

```
<template>
  <div>
    <h1 v-once v-text="text">Loading...</h1>
    <h2 v-html="html" />
  </div>
</template>
<script>
export default {
  data() {
    return {
      // v-text
      text: 'Directive text',
      // v-html
      html: 'Stylise</br>HTML in<br/><b>your data</b>',
    }
  },
}
</script>

...
```

Running the preceding code will generate an output as follows:

Directive text

Stylize
HTML in
your data

Figure 1.18: Output on rendering the HTML elements

6. Add a new **link** object to the **data** object that contains a bunch of information such as URL, target, title, and tab index. Inside the template, add a new anchor HTML element and bind the **link data** object to the HTML element using the colon syntax, for example, **:href="link.url"**:

```
<template>
  <div>
    <h1 v-once v-text="text">Loading...</h1>
    <h2 v-html="html" />
  </div>
</template>
<script>
export default {
  data() {
    return {
      // v-text
      text: 'Directive text',
      // v-html
      html: 'Stylise</br>HTML in<br/><b>your data</b>',
    }
  },
}
</script>
...
```

The following screenshot displays the output:

Directive text

Stylize
HTML in
your data

Go to Google

Figure 1.19: Output on binding the reactive data from
the Vue instance to any HTML attribute

7. Apply **v-if="false"** to the **h1** element, **v-else-if="false"** to **h2**, and **v-else** to the **a** tag like this:

```
<template>
  <div>
    <h1 v-if="false" v-once v-text="text">Loading...</h1>

    <h2 v-else-if="false" v-html="html" />

    <a
      v-else
      :href="link.url"
      :target="link.target"
      :tabindex="link.tabindex"
      v-text="link.title"
    />
  </div>
</template>
```

You should only see the **<a>** tag in the page since we have set the conditional statements to **false**.

The **v-else** condition will display as follows:

Go to Google

Figure 1.20: False v-if statements hiding the whole HTML element from the DOM

8. Change the template to use **v-show** instead of the **v-if** statements:

```
<template>
  <div>
    <h1 v-show="true" v-once v-text="text">Loading...</h1>

    <h2 v-show="false" v-html="html" />

    <a
      :href="link.url"
      :target="link.target"
      :tabindex="link.tabindex"
      v-text="link.title"
    />
  </div>
</template>
```

The output of the preceding code will be as follows:

Directive text

Go to Google

Figure 1.21: Changing v-show to true will display the element

When you open the **Elements** tab of your browser dev tools, you should be able to observe the **h2** display state set to **none**, as follows:

```
<!DOCTYPE html>
<html lang="en">
▶ <head>…</head>
▼ <body data-gr-c-s-loaded="true">
   ▶ <noscript>…</noscript>
   ▼ <div data-v-d9ee5bac>
       <h1 data-v-d9ee5bac>Directive text</h1>
···    ▶ <h2 data-v-d9ee5bac style="display: none;">…</h2> == $0
       <a data-v-d9ee5bac href="https://google.com" target="_blank"
       tabindex="0">Go to Google</a>
     </div>
     <!-- built files will be auto injected -->
     <script type="text/javascript" src="/js/chunk-vendors.js">
     </script>
     <script type="text/javascript" src="/js/app.js"></script>
   </body>
</html>
```

Figure 1.22: h2 displaying "display: none" for false condition

If **v-show** results in a **true** Boolean, it will leave the DOM element as is. If it resolves as **false**, it will apply **display: none** styling to the element.

In this exercise, we learned about the core Vue directives to control, bind, show, and hide HTML template elements without requiring any JavaScript outside of adding new data objects to your local state.

In the next section, we will learn how to achieve a two-way binding with the help of Vue's **v-model**.

TWO-WAY BINDING USING V-MODEL

Vue has simplified the way to achieve two-way data binding by creating a directive that specifically watches a data property inside of your Vue component. The Vue directive **v-model** will reactively change when the bound data property that Vue is watching changes. This directive is usually useful for HTML form elements that need to both display the data and modify it reactively, for example, input, textarea, radio buttons, and so on.

Two-way binding is achieved by adding the **v-model** directive to the element you want bound and referring to a data prop:

```
<template>
    <input v-model="name" />
</template>
<script>
    export default {
        data() {
            return {
                name: ''
            }
        }
    }
</script>
```

Figure 1.23 represents the output generated by running the preceding code:

Figure 1.23: Output for the v-model example

Be careful using this directive as binding a huge amount of data in this way can affect the performance of your application. Consider your UI and split these into different Vue components or views. Vue data in the local state is not immutable and can be redefined anywhere in the template.

EXERCISE 1.07: TWO-WAY BINDING USING V-MODEL

We are going to build a component using Vue's two-way data binding attribute v-model. Consider what it means to bind a piece of data in two ways. The context for this form of data model is usually forms, or where you expect both input and output data. By the end of the exercise, we should be able to utilize the v-model attribute in a form context.

To access the code files for this exercise, refer to https://packt.live/2IILld8.

1. Open a command-line terminal, navigate into the **Exercise1.07** folder, and run the following commands in order:

```
> cd Exercise1.07/
> code .
> yarn
> yarn serve
```

Go to **https://localhost:8080**.

2. Start by composing an HTML label and input element bound to the **name** data prop using **v-model** inside the template area:

```
<div class="form">
    <label>
      Name
        <input type="text" v-model="name" />
    </label>
</div>
```

3. Finish binding the text input by returning a reactive data prop called **name** in the **<script>** tag:

```
<script>
export default {
  data() {
    return {
      name: '',
    }
  },
}
</script>
```

4. Compose a label and selectable HTML list bound to the data prop **language** using **v-model** inside of the template area:

```
<div class="form">
  <label>
    Name
    <input type="text" v-model="name" />
  </label>
  <label>
    Preferred javascript style
    <select name="language" v-model="language">
      <option value="Javascript">JavaScript</option>
      <option value="TypeScript">TypeScript</option>
      <option value="CoffeeScript">CoffeeScript</option>
      <option value="Dart">Dart</option>
    </select>
  </label>
</div>
```

5. Finish binding the select input by returning a reactive data prop called **language** in the **<script>** tag:

```
<script>
export default {
  data() {
    return {
      name: '',
      language: '',
    }
  },
}
</script>
```

6. Below the form fields, output the name and language inside of an unordered list structure (**<ul>** and **<li>**) by using curly braces, for example, **{{ name }}**:

> **NOTE**
>
> Wrap the form and the display area within another tag such as a **<section>** tag, as only one HTML element can be at the root of a template.

Your code should look as follows:

```
<template>
  <section>
    <div class="form">
      <label>
        Name
        <input type="text" v-model="name" />
      </label>
      <label>
        Preferred javascript style
        <select name="language" v-model="language">
          <option value="Javascript">JavaScript</option>
          <option value="TypeScript">TypeScript</option>
          <option value="CoffeeScript">CoffeeScript</option>
          <option value="Dart">Dart</option>
        </select>
      </label>
    </div>
    <ul class="overview">
      <li><strong>Overview</strong></li>
      <li>Name: {{ name }}</li>
      <li>Preference: {{ language }}</li>
    </ul>
  </section>
</template>
```

7. Add styling inside the **<style>** tag at the bottom of the component, and set the **lang** attribute to **scss**:

Exercise1-07.vue

```scss
37 <style lang="scss">
38 .form {
39   display: flex;
40   justify-content: space-evenly;
41   max-width: 800px;
42   padding: 40px 20px;
43   border-radius: 10px;
44   margin: 0 auto;
45   background: #ececec;
46 }
47
48 .overview {
49   display: flex;
50   flex-direction: column;
51   justify-content: space-evenly;
52   max-width: 300px;
53   margin: 40px auto;
54   padding: 40px 20px;
55   border-radius: 10px;
56   border: 1px solid #ececec;
57
58   > li {
59     list-style: none;
60     + li {
61       margin-top: 20px;
62     }
63   }
64 }
65 </style>
```

The complete code for this step is available at https://packt.live/36NiNXH.

Your output should look as follows:

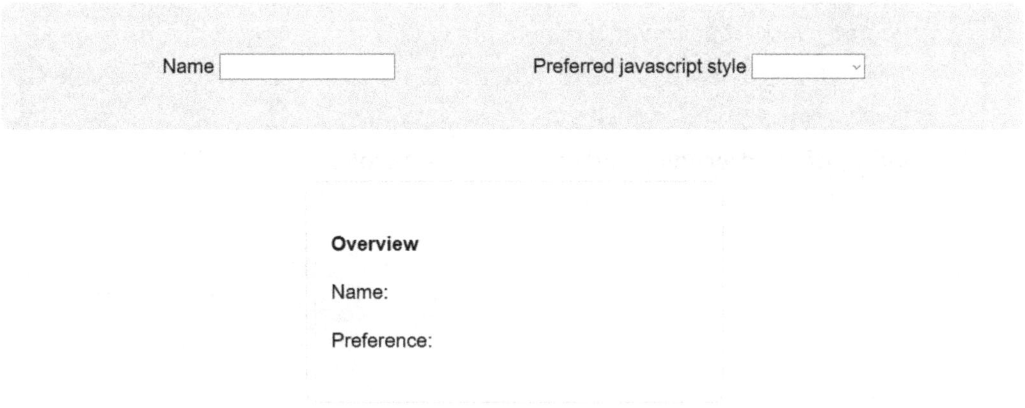

Name _____   Preferred javascript style _____ ⌄

Overview

Name:

Preference:

Figure 1.24: Displaying the final form after the data is updated

Your form should look something like this. When you update the data in the form, it should also update the overview area synchronously.

In this exercise, we used the **v-model** directive to bind the name and JavaScript-style drop-down selection to our local state's data. When you change the data, it will reactively update the DOM elements we output this bound data to.

ANONYMOUS LOOPS

To loop over HTML elements in Vue, you utilize the **v-for** loop directive. When Vue renders the component, it will iterate the HTML element you have added the directive to in order to use the data being parsed into the directive. **Anonymous loops** can be performed using this directive, where you can define a number X and the loop will iterate that many times, which can be handy in situations where you can more strictly control how many loops you iterate on or for placeholder content. All loops require an iterator **:key**. When the key or the content bound to the key changes, Vue knows that it needs to reload the content inside the loop. If you have multiple loops in one component, randomize the key with extra characters or context-related strings to avoid **:key** duplication conflicts.

Anonymous loops are demonstrated below; note that you can use quotation marks or backticks (`) to describe strings:

```
            <div v-for="n in 2" :key="'loop-1-' + n">
        {{ n }}
    </div>


    <!-- Backticks -->
    <div v-for="n in 5" :key="`loop-2-${n}`">
        {{ n }}
    </div>
```

The output of the preceding code should look as follows.

Figure 1.25: Output of anonymous loops example

Understanding loops is key to not only working with Vue but also with JavaScript in general. Now that we have covered how to handle loops by using the **v-for** syntax and the importance of binding the **:key** property to add reactivity to the content being looped, we will utilize this function in the next exercise.

EXERCISE 1.08: USING V-FOR TO LOOP OVER AN ARRAY OF STRINGS

In this exercise, we are going to perform an anonymous loop using Vue's **v-for** directive. This will be familiar to those who have used **for** or **foreach** loops in JavaScript before.

To access the code files for this exercise, refer to https://packt.live/390SO1J.

Perform the following steps to complete the exercise:

1. Open a command-line terminal, navigate into the **Exercise1.08** folder, and run the following commands in order:

```
> cd Exercise1.08/
> code .
> yarn
> yarn serve
```

Go to **https://localhost:8080**.

2. Compose the following syntax inside of **Exercise1-08.vue** by adding an **<h1>** title to your component and a **<ul>** element with an **<li>** tag which will have the **v-for** directive, which has the value of **n** as **5**:

Exercise1-08.vue

```
1 <template>
2   <div>
3     <h1>Looping through arrays</h1>
4     <ul>
5       <li v-for="n in 5" :key="n">
6         {{ n }}
7       </li>
8     </ul>
```

The complete code for this step is available at https://packt.live/3pFAtgB.

This will generate an output as follows:

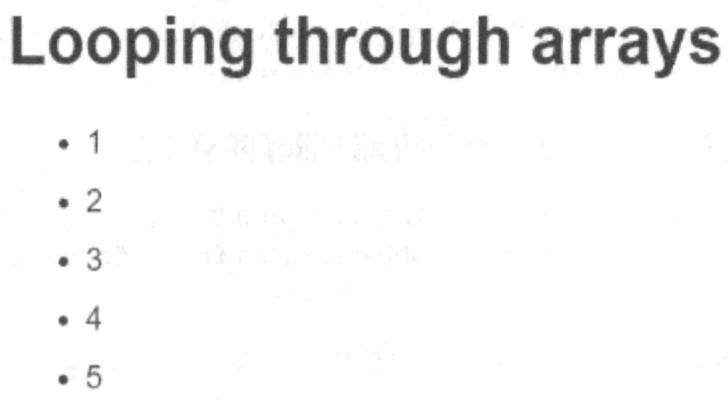

Looping through arrays

- 1
- 2
- 3
- 4
- 5

Figure 1.26: Iterating over arbitrary numbers will also allow you to output the index

3. Now let's loop through an array of strings and count the iteration of our array with **n**. Prepare an array of your personal interests in the **data()** function. By looking for (**item, n**) inside the **interests** array, **item** outputs the string of the array, and **n** is the loop index:

```
<template>
  <div>
    <h1>Looping through arrays</h1>
    <ul>
      <li v-for="(item, n) in interests" :key="n">
        {{ item }}
      </li>
    </ul>
  </div>
</template>

<script>
export default {
  data() {
    return {
      interests: ['TV', 'Games', 'Sports'],
    }
  },
}
</script>
```

The following output is generated upon running the preceding code:

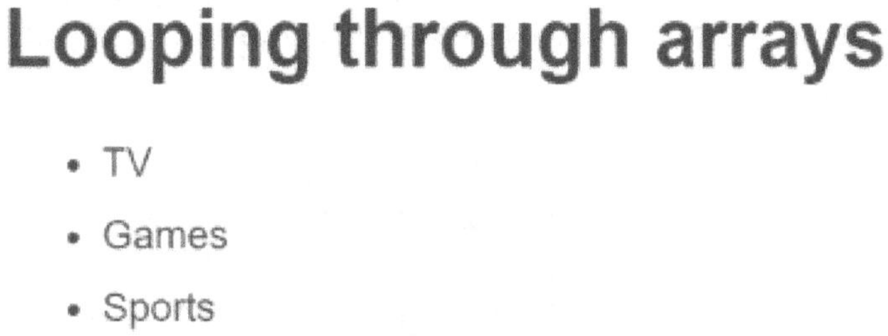

Looping through arrays

- TV
- Games
- Sports

Figure 1.27: Iterating over an array of strings

In this exercise, we learned how to iterate over both an arbitrary number and a specific array of strings, outputting the string value or index of an array. We also learned that the key attribute needs to be unique to avoid DOM conflicts and forces the DOM to re-render the component properly.

ITERATING OVER OBJECTS

When requesting data from an API, you will often be iterating over an array of objects that contains both logic and raw content. Vue makes it easy to control the data's various states through its directive syntax. Conditional directives control the display state of DOM elements in Vue. The HTML syntax provides clear visibility when it comes to the display rules set in your component.

EXERCISE 1.09: USING A V-FOR LOOP OVER AN ARRAY OF OBJECTS AND USING THEIR PROPERTIES FOR V-IF CONDITIONS

In this exercise, we will be controlling a Vue data array and iterating over the objects inside of it.

To access the code files for this exercise, refer to https://packt.live/32YokKa.

1. Open a command-line terminal, navigate into the **Exercise1.09** folder, and run the following commands in order:

```
> cd Exercise1.09/
> code .
> yarn
> yarn serve
```

Go to **https://localhost:8080**.

2. Compose the following syntax inside **Exercise1-09.vue** and create a data

object that contains a **title** string, and a **favorite** array of strings. We will loop over the **interests** object similarly to the array of strings; however, you will need to refer to the **title** key inside the **interests** object:

```
<template>
  <div>
    <h1>Looping through array of objects</h1>
    <ul>
      <li v-for="(item, n) in interests" :key="n">
        {{ item.title }}
      </li>
    </ul>
  </div>
</template>
```

The output of the preceding code will be as follows:

Looping through array of objects

TV

Games

Sports

Figure 1.28: You should see a list of titles now in the frontend

3. Let's create a second **v-for** loop to iterate over your favorites list. Note that we use different keys— **fav** and **m**—for our nested loop. This is because you can still use the values **item** and **n** inside the nested loop context:

```
<template>
  <div>
    <h1>Looping through array of objects</h1>
    <ul>
      <li v-for="(item, n) in interests" :key="n">
        {{ item.title }}

        <ol>
          <li v-for="(fav, m) in item.favorite" :key="m">
            {{ fav }}</li>
```

```
        </ol>
      </li>
    </ul>
  </div>
</template>
```

Figure 1.29 displays an output where looping is performed through an array of objects:

Figure 1.29: Nested ordered list detailing your favorites

4. To optimize the DOM tree, we can use the **v-if** conditional directive from **Exercise 1.09** to hide unnecessary DOM elements:

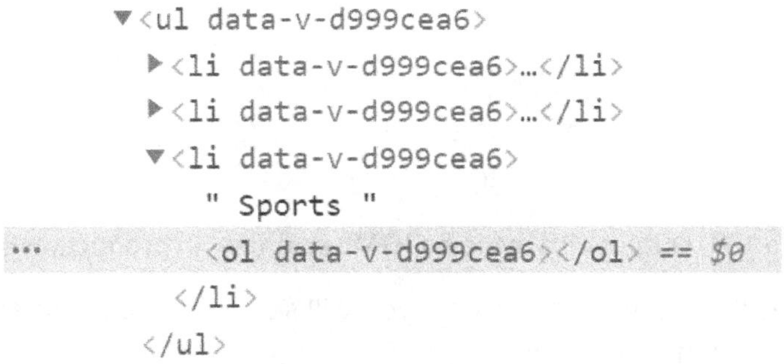

```
▼<ul data-v-d999cea6>
  ▶<li data-v-d999cea6>…</li>
  ▶<li data-v-d999cea6>…</li>
  ▼<li data-v-d999cea6>
    " Sports "
      <ol data-v-d999cea6></ol> == $0
  </li>
</ul>
```

Figure 1.30: Displaying empty DOM elements in your virtual DOM

5. We will check whether there are more than **0** items in the array to display the ordered list HTML element. Add a **v-if** directive to the **<ol>** with the condition **item.favorite.length > 0**:

```
// src/components/Exercise1-09.vue
<template>
  <div>
    <h1>Looping through array of objects</h1>
    <ul>
      <li v-for="(item, n) in interests" :key="n">
        {{ item.title }}

        <ol v-if="item.favorite.length > 0">
          <li v-for="(fav, m) in item.favorite" :key="m">
            {{ fav }}</li>
        </ol>
      </li>
    </ul>
  </div>
</template>
```

This won't make a difference in the visuals of your page, but when you inspect the virtual DOM tree in your browser, you'll notice an HTML comment in dev mode allowing you to understand where a **v-if** statement might be **false**. When you build for production, these HTML comments won't be in your DOM.

```
▼<li data-v-d999cea6>
    " Sports "
...    <!----> == $0
  </li>
</ul>
```

Figure 1.31: Output displaying no HTML comment in production builds

By using the **v-if** directive in dev mode, you will see an HTML comment. These will not exist in production builds.

In this exercise we have been able to iterate over complex arrays of objects, outputting these objects' nested keys and controlling the view state of DOM elements based on length conditions.

METHODS IN VUE

Vue methods are defined inside the **methods** object within the Vue instance and can be written like normal JavaScript functions where you define a piece of logic that is executed. When you use JavaScript functions, normally, you would either return a value or simply perform a global action. The primary difference between writing functions and Vue methods is that the Vue method is scoped to your Vue component and can be run from anywhere inside the component it was written inside. Since the methods are scoped to your component's Vue instance, you can reference them inside of event directives easily in the HTML template. When binding events to HTML elements in Vue, you would use the @ symbol; for example, **v-on:click** is equivalent to **@click**.

EXERCISE 1.10: TRIGGERING METHODS

In this exercise, we are going to build a component that uses Vue's methods API. Consider how similar these Vue methods can be written like your own named functions in JavaScript, as they behave in a very similar way. By the end of the exercise, we should be able to use methods and trigger them from the HTML template.

To access the code files for this exercise, refer to https://packt.live/3kMTWs5.

1. Open a command-line terminal and navigate into the **Exercise1.10** folder and run the following commands in order:

```
> cd Exercise1.10/
> code .
> yarn
> yarn serve
```

Go to **https://localhost:8080**.

2. Let's loop over a method trigger and pass its number to a method. Set up an anonymous **v-for** loop on an HTML list and add an anchor element inside of the list element. Set the loop to iterate **5** times:

```
<template>
  <div>
    <h1>Triggering Vue Methods</h1>
    <ul>
      <li v-for="n in 5" :key="n">
```

```
        <a href="#">Trigger</a>
    </li>
  </ul>
 </div>
</template>
```

3. Add the @**click** directive referencing a method called **triggerAlert** and pass the value of **n** as an argument. Output the value **n** into the anchor element using curly braces:

```
<template>
  <div>
    <h1>Triggering Vue Methods</h1>
    <ul>
      <li v-for="n in 5" :key="n">
        <a href="#" @click="triggerAlert(n)">Trigger {{ n }}</a>
      </li>
    </ul>
  </div>
</template>
```

4. Inside the **methods** object, add the **triggerAlert(n)** key with the **n** argument. Inside this method, add an **alert** function, which will output the value **n** plus some static text:

```
<script>
export default {
  methods: {
    triggerAlert(n) {
      alert(`${n} has been clicked`)
    },
  },
}
</script>
```

5. Add styling inside the **<style>** tag at the bottom of the component, and set the **lang** attribute to **scss**:

Exercise1-10.vue

```
22 <style lang="scss" scoped>
23 ul {
24   padding-left: 0;
25 }
26 li {
27   display: block;
28   list-style: none;
29
30   + li {
31     margin-top: 10px;
32   }
33 }
34
35 a {
36   display: inline-block;
37   background: #4fc08d;
38   border-radius: 10px;
39   color: white;
40   padding: 10px 20px;
41   text-decoration: none;
42 }
43 </style>
```

The complete code for this step is available at https://packt.live/374yKZZ.

6. Your page should feature a list of buttons that when clicked, trigger an alert with a message that contains the button number you clicked as follows:

Triggering Vue Methods

Trigger 1

Trigger 2

Trigger 3

Trigger 4

Trigger 5

Figure 1.32: Output a list of triggers

The following prompt is displayed when a trigger is clicked:

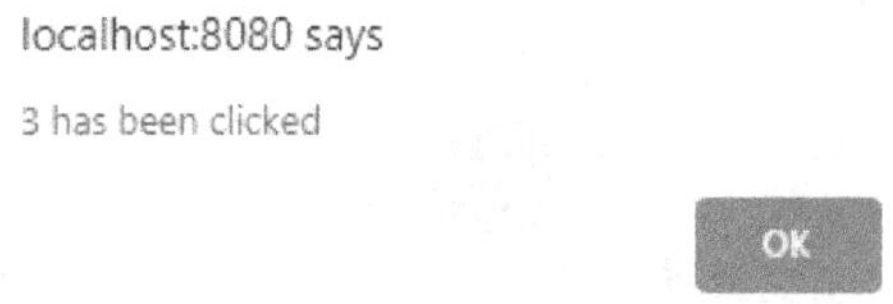

localhost:8080 says

3 has been clicked

OK

Figure 1.33: Displaying a browser alert with the index number in it

> **NOTE**
>
> While you can add an event directive to any HTML element, a suggestion would be applying them to native HTML interactive elements such as anchor tags, form input, or buttons to help with browser accessibility.

In this exercise, we were able to utilize the Vue methods API to define and trigger methods from the HTML template, and parse arguments into each method dynamically.

EXERCISE 1.11: RETURNING DATA USING VUE METHODS

In this exercise, we are going to learn how to use Vue methods as a function to return data in the Vue instance and inside of the template.

Often in a web application, we want elements to appear on the page depending on whether a condition is met or not. For instance, if our product is not in stock, our page should display the fact that it is out of stock.

So, let's figure out how could we conditionally render these elements, depending on whether our product is in stock or not.

To access the code files for this exercise, refer to https://packt.live/3pHWCeh.

1. Open a command-line terminal, navigate into the **Exercise1.11** folder, and run the following commands in order:

```
> cd Exercise1.11/
> code .
> yarn
> yarn serve
```

Go to **https://localhost:8080**.

2. Let's iterate over a random amount and trigger an **addToCart** method. Set up two data objects, **totalItems** and **totalCost**, which will be updated when a user clicks on our shop buttons. Next, refer to data objects inside the **script** block of Vue by specifying **this**. For example, in the **template** block, we refer to **totalItems** as **{{ totalItems }}**, but in the **script** block, we will refer to it as **this.totalItems**. The same pattern is used for methods where **addToCart** would be referred to as **this.addToCart** within another method:

```
<template>
  <div>
    <h1>Returning Methods</h1>

    <div>Cart({{ totalItems }}) {{ totalCost }} </div>

    <ul>
      <li v-for="n in 5" :key="n">
        <a href="#" @click="addToCart(n)">Add {{ n }}</a>
      </li>
    </ul>
  </div>
</template>

<script>
export default {
  data() {
    return {
      totalItems: 0,
      totalCost: 0,
    }
  },
  methods: {
    addToCart(n) {
      this.totalItems = this.totalItems + 1
      this.totalCost = this.totalCost + n
    },
  },
}
</script>
```

```scss
<style lang="scss" scoped>
ul {
  padding-left: 0;
}
li {
  display: block;
  list-style: none;

  + li {
    margin-top: 10px;
  }
}

a {
  display: inline-block;
  background: rgb(235, 50, 50);
  border-radius: 10px;
  color: white;
  padding: 10px 20px;
  text-decoration: none;
}
</style>
```

This will generate an output as follows:

Returning Methods

Cart(0) 0

Figure 1.34: Pressing any of the buttons will demonstrate the cart logic

When you click the buttons, the items counter should increment by **1**, but the cost will increment by the **n** value, which should demonstrate normal cart functionality (clicking **Add 2**, then **Add 5**):

Returning Methods

Cart(2) 7

Add 1

Add 2

Add 3

Add 4

Add 5

Figure 1.35: Output displaying Returning Methods after increments

3. Let's talk money. We can use methods to perform logical operations that augment or format strings based on events. Create a method called **formatCurrency**, which accepts one argument. We will return the same value after giving it two decimal points and a **$** symbol. To use this method in the template, simply add it to the interpolated curly braces and pass the value that was there as an argument inside the method instead:

```
<template>
  <div>
    <h1>Returning Methods</h1>

    <div>Cart({{ totalItems }}) {{ formatCurrency(totalCost) }}
      </div>

    <ul>
      <li v-for="n in 5" :key="n">
        <a href="#" @click="addToCart(n)">Add
          {{ formatCurrency(n) }}</a>
      </li>
    </ul>
  </div>
```

```
</template>

<script>
export default {
  data() {
    return {
      totalItems: 0,
      totalCost: 0,
    }
  },
  methods: {
    addToCart(n) {
      this.totalItems = this.totalItems + 1
      this.totalCost = this.totalCost + n
    },
    formatCurrency(val) {
      return `$${val.toFixed(2)}`
    },
  },
}
</script>
```

The following screenshot displays the output of the preceding code:

Returning Methods

Cart(0) $0.00

Add $1.00

Add $2.00

Add $3.00

Add $4.00

Add $5.00

Figure 1.36: Now all the values are expected to look like currency, while retaining the cart counter

In this exercise, we were able to utilize Vue's methods API to parse arguments into methods, return modified values, and use methods to update the local data state in a life-like scenario.

VUE LIFECYCLE HOOKS

The Vue component lifecycle events include the following:

- **beforeCreate**: Runs when your component has been initialized. **data** has not been made reactive and events are not set up in your DOM.

- **created**: You will be able to access reactive data and events, but the templates and DOM are not mounted or rendered. This hook is generally good to use when requesting asynchronous data from a server since you will more than likely want this information as early as you can before the virtual DOM is mounted.

- **beforeMount**: A very uncommon hook as it runs directly before the first render of your component and is not called in **Server-Side Rendering**.

- **mounted**: Mounting hooks are among the most common hooks you will use since they allow you to access your DOM elements so non-Vue libraries can be integrated.

- **beforeUpdate**: Runs immediately after a change to your component occurs, and before it has been re-rendered. Useful for acquiring the state of reactive data before it has been rendered.

- **updated**: Runs immediately after the **beforeUpdate** hook and re-renders your component with new data changes.

- **beforeDestroy**: Fired directly before destroying your component instance. The component will still be functional until the destroyed hook is called, allowing you to stop event listeners and subscriptions to data to avoid memory leaks.

- **destroyed**: All the virtual DOM elements and event listeners have been cleaned up from your Vue instance. This hook allows you to communicate that to anyone or any element that needs to know this was completed.

EXERCISE 1.12: USING VUE LIFECYCLES FOR CONTROLLING DATA

In this exercise, we will be learning how and when to use Vue's lifecycle hooks, and when they trigger by using JavaScript alerts. By the end of the exercise, we will be able to understand and use multiple Vue lifecycle hooks.

To access the code files for this exercise, refer to https://packt.live/36N42nT.

1. Open a command-line terminal, navigate into the **Exercise1.12** folder, and run the following commands in order:

```
> cd Exercise1.12/
> code .
> yarn
> yarn serve
```

Go to **https://localhost:8080**.

> **NOTE**
>
> Feel free to swap the alert for **console.log()**.

2. Start by creating an array of data to iterate over in a list element, set the key to **n**, and output the value **{{item}}** inside of the **<li>** element using curly braces:

```
<template>
  <div>
    <h1>Vue Lifecycle hooks</h1>
    <ul>
      <li v-for="(item, n) in list" :key="n">
        {{ item }}
      </li>
    </ul>
  </div>
</template>

<script>
export default {
  data() {
    return {
      list: [
        'Apex Legends',
```

```
        'A Plague Tale: Innocence',
        'ART SQOOL',
        'Baba Is You',
        'Devil May Cry 5',
        'The Division 2',
        'Hypnospace Outlaw',
        'Katana ZERO',
      ],
    }
  }
}
</script>
```

3. Add **beforeCreated()** and **created()** as functions below the **data()** function. Set an alert or console log inside these hooks so that you can see when they are being triggered:

```
<script>
export default {
  ...

  beforeCreate() {
    alert('beforeCreate: data is static, thats it')
  },
  created() {
    alert('created: data and events ready, but no DOM')
  },
}
</script>
```

When you refresh your browser, you should see both alerts before you can see your list load on the page:

Figure 1.37: Observe the beforeCreate() hook alert first

The following screenshot displays the **created()** hook alert after the **beforeCreate()** hook:

Figure 1.38: Observe the before() hook alert after the beforeCreate() hook

4. Add **beforeMount()** and **mounted()** as functions below the **created()** hook. Set an alert or console log inside of these hooks so you can see when they are being triggered:

```
<script>
export default {
...

  beforeMount() {
    alert('beforeMount: $el not ready')
  },
  mounted() {
    alert('mounted: DOM ready to use')
  },
}
</script>
```

When you refresh your browser, you should also see these alerts before you can see your list load on the page:

Figure 1.39: Observe the beforeMount() hook alert after the create() hook

The following screenshot displays the **mounted()** hook alert after the **beforeMount()** hook:

Figure 1.40: Observe alert mounted() hook alert after the beforeMount() hook

5. Add a new anchor element inside your **<li>** element that sits next to the item output. Use a **@click** directive to bind this button to a method called **deleteItem** and pass the **item** value as an argument:

```
<template>
  <div>
    <h1>Vue Lifecycle hooks</h1>
    <ul>
      <li v-for="(item, n) in list" :key="n">
        {{ item }} <a @click="deleteItem(item)">Delete</a>
      </li>
    </ul>
  </div>
</template>
```

6. Add a method called **deleteItem** into a **methods** object above your hooks, but below the **data ()** function. Inside this function, pass **value** as an argument and filter out items from the list array that do not match the value, then replace the existing list with the new list:

Exercise1-12.vue

```
17 <script>
18 export default {
19   data() {
20     return {
21       list: [
22         'Apex Legends',
23         'A Plague Tale: Innocence',
24         'ART SQOOL',
25         'Baba Is You',
26         'Devil May Cry 5',
27         'The Division 2',
28         'Hypnospace Outlaw',
29         'Katana ZERO',
30       ],
31     }
32   },
33   methods: {
34     deleteItem(value) {
35       this.list = this.list.filter(item => item !== value)
36     },
37   },
```

The complete code for this step is available at https://packt.live/3pJGLvO.

7. Add styling inside the **<style>** tag at the bottom of the component, and set the **lang** attribute to **scss**:

```
<style lang="scss" scoped>
ul {
  padding-left: 0;
}
li {
  display: block;
  list-style: none;

  + li {
    margin-top: 10px;
  }
}
```

```
a {
    display: inline-block;
    background: rgb(235, 50, 50);
    padding: 5px 10px;
    border-radius: 10px;
    font-size: 10px;
    color: white;
    text-transform: uppercase;
    text-decoration: none;
}
</style>
```

8. Add **beforeUpdate()** and **updated()** as functions below the **mounted()** hook and set an alert or console log inside these hooks so that you can see when they are being triggered:

```
<script>
export default {
    ...
    beforeUpdate() {
        alert('beforeUpdate: we know an update is about to
          happen, and have the data')
    },
    updated() {
        alert('updated: virtual DOM will update after you click OK')
    },
}
</script>
```

When you delete a list item by clicking the delete button in your browser, you should see these alerts.

9. Add **beforeDestroy()** and **destroyed()** as functions below the
   updated() hook. Set an alert or console log inside these hooks so that you can
   see when they are being triggered:

```
<script>
export default {
  ...

  beforeDestroy() {
    alert('beforeDestroy: about to blow up this component')
  },
  destroyed() {
    alert('destroyed: this component has been destroyed')
  },
}
</script>
```

10. Add a new item to your **list** array:

```
<script>
export default {
  data() {
    return {
      list: [
        'Apex Legends',
        'A Plague Tale: Innocence',
        'ART SQOOL',
        'Baba Is You',
        'Devil May Cry 5',
        'The Division 2',
        'Hypnospace Outlaw',
        'Katana ZERO',
      ],
    }
  },
```

You should also see the destroy alerts after the update alerts are shown in your browser after you have saved this change with localhost running. This will generate the following output:

Vue Lifecycle hooks

Apex Legends DELETE
A Plague Tale: Innocence DELETE
ART SQOOL DELETE
Baba Is You DELETE
Devil May Cry 5 DELETE
The Division 2 DELETE
Hypnospace Outlaw DELETE
Katana ZERO DELETE

Add a new item in the list array and save while running localhost to preview the destroy hooks

Figure 1.41: Output displaying Vue Lifecycle hooks

11. Alerts will run at each lifecycle hook. Try deleting elements, adding new ones in the list array, and refreshing the page to see when each of these hooks occurs. This will generate an output as follows:

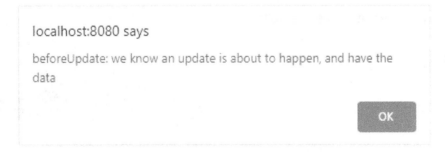

localhost:8080 says

beforeUpdate: we know an update is about to happen, and have the data

OK

Figure 1.42: Displaying a message on every trigger

An alert will trigger every time you manipulate something on the page, demonstrating each available Vue lifecycle.

> **NOTE**
>
> **Mounted** and **created** lifecycle hooks will run every time a component loads. If this is not the desired effect, consider running the code you want to run once from the parent component or view, such as the **App.vue** file.

In this exercise, we learned what Vue lifecycle hooks are and when they trigger. This will be useful in combination with triggering methods and controlling data within your Vue components.

ACTIVITY 1.01: BUILDING A DYNAMIC SHOPPING LIST APP USING VUE.JS

In this activity, we will build a dynamic shopping list app that will test your knowledge of Vue by using all the basic functions of an SFC, such as expressions, loops, two-way binding, and event handling.

This application should let users create and delete individual list items and clear the total list in one click.

The following steps will help you complete the activity:

1. Build an interactive form in one component using an input bound to **v-model**.

2. Add one input field that you can add shopping list items to. Allow users to add items by using the *Enter* key by binding a method to the @**keyup.enter** event.

3. Users can expect to clear the list by deleting all the items or removing them one at a time. To do so, you can use a **delete** method that can pass the array position as an argument, or simply overwrite the whole shopping list data prop to be an empty array **[]**.

The expected outcome is as follows:

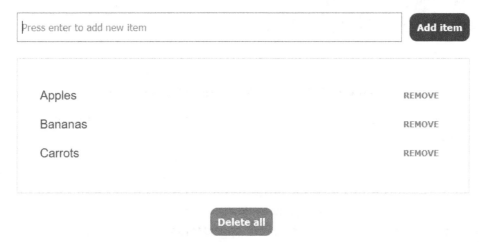

Figure 1.43: Final output

> **NOTE**
>
> The solution for this activity can be found on page 638.

SUMMARY

In this chapter, you have learned how to run a Vue project using the command prompt and to create basic Vue components. Within these Vue components, you can scaffold template that use Vue's unique directives and HTML syntax sugar to loop over data or control DOM states with conditional statements. Key concepts of reactive data through the use of data props and the **v-model** binding were explored and made useful in real-life examples that utilized Vue.js methods and lifecycles.

In the next chapter, we will learn about more advanced reactive data concepts that will build upon this first chapter: using computed props and watchers and fetching asynchronous data from an external source.

2

WORKING WITH DATA

OVERVIEW

In this chapter, you will expand on what you learned in the previous chapter by introducing more ways to control data inside Vue components. You will learn how to set up advanced watchers to observe data changes inside your components, and utilize Vue's powerful reactive data feature, computed data properties, to concisely output just the data you need in your template. You will also be able to utilize asynchronous methods to fetch data for your Vue components.

By the end of this chapter, you will be able to watch, manage, and manipulate data from various sources in your Vue.js components.

INTRODUCTION

In the previous chapter, you were introduced to the concepts of single-file components and the Vue API, which provides access to methods, directives, and data properties. Building on these foundations, we will be introducing computed properties, which, like data properties, are reactive in the UI but can perform powerful calculations, and their results are cacheable, increasing the performance of your project. When building e-commerce stores, you will usually want to calculate pricing and cart items reactively as users interact with your UI, which in the past would need to be achieved without a page reload using something like **jQuery**. Vue.js makes short work of these common frontend tasks by introducing computed properties that react immediately to frontend user input.

Let's begin by introducing reactive data that can be computed on the fly and understanding how to call and manipulate asynchronous data.

COMPUTED PROPERTIES

Computed properties are a unique data type that will reactively update when source data used within the property is updated. They may look like a Vue method, but they are not. In Vue, we can track changes to a data property by defining them as a computed property, add custom logic within this property, and use it anywhere within the component to return a value. Computed properties are cached by Vue, making them more performant for returning data than a data prop or using a Vue method.

Instances where you may use a computed property include but are not limited to:

- **Form validation**:

    In this example, an error message will appear when the **total** data property is less than **1**. The computed property for **total** will update every time a new piece of data is added to the **items** array:

```
<template>
    <div>{{errorMessage}}</div>
</template>
<script>
    export default {
        data() {
            return {
                items: []
            }
        },
```

```
        computed: {
            total() {
                return this.items.length
            },
            errorMessage() {
                if (this.total < 1) {
                    return 'The total must be more than zero'
                } else {
                    return ''
                }
            }
        }
    }
</script>
```

This will generate the following output:

```
The total must be more than zero
```

- **Combining data props**:

  In the following example, you can use computed props to combine two pieces of data into one returnable string, **formalName**, that can be used within your component:

```
<template>
    <div>{{ formalName }}</div>
</template>
<script>
    export default {
        data() {
            return {
                title: 'Mr.',
                surname: 'Smith'
            }
        },
        computed: {
            formalName() {
                return this.title + ' ' + this.surname
            }
        }
    }
</script>
```

This will generate the following output:

```
Mr. Smith
```

- **Outputting complex information into the Vue template**:

In this more complicated example, we use computed properties to break down the large data object called **post**. You will use the simplified and semantic computed properties to output the information into your components template. The computed properties in this example make it easier to identify and use the author's full name, see how many posts they have produced, and have the data to display their featured post:

```
<template>
    <div>
        <p>{{ fullName }}</p>
        <p>{{ totalPosts }}</p>
        <p>{{ featuredPosts }}</p>
    </div>
</template>
<script>
    export default {
        data() {
            return {
                post: {
                    fields: {
                        author: {
                            firstName: 'John',
                            lastName: 'Doe'
                        },
                        entries: [{
                                title: "Entry 1",
                                content: "Entry 1's content",
                                featured: true
                            },
                            {
                                title: "Entry 2",
                                content: "Entry 2's content",
                                featured: false
                            }
                        ]
                    }
```

```
                    }
                }
            },
            computed: {
                fullName() {
                    // Return string
                    return this.post.fields.author.firstName + ' ' +
                        this.post.fields.author.lastName
                },
                totalPosts() {
                    // Return number
                    return this.post.fields.entries.length
                },
                featuredPosts() {
                    // Return string
                    return this.post.fields.entries.filter(entry => {
                        // If featured is true, return the entry title
                        if (entry.featured) {
                            return entry
                        }
                    })
                }
            }
        }
</script>
```

This will generate the following output:

John Doe

2

[{ "title": "Entry 1", "content": "Entry 1's content", "featured": true }]

Figure 2.1: The computed name output

Computed properties are very valuable to a Vue developer when creating performant components. In the next exercise, we will explore how to use this inside of a Vue component.

EXERCISE 2.01: IMPLEMENTING COMPUTED DATA INTO A VUE COMPONENT

In this exercise, you will use a computed property to help cut down the amount of code you need to write inside your Vue templates by concisely outputting basic data. To access the code files for this exercise, refer to https://packt.live/3n1fQZY.

1. Open a command-line terminal, navigate into the **Exercise 2.01** folder, and run the following commands in order:

```
> cd Exercise2.01/
> code .
> yarn
> yarn serve
```

   Go to **https://localhost:8080**.

2. Create an input field for the first name, use **v-model** to bind the data prop **firstName** to this field:

```
<input v-model="firstName" placeholder="First name" />
```

3. Create a second input field for the last name, and use **v-model** to bind the data prop **lastName** to this field:

```
<input v-model="lastName" placeholder="Last name" />
```

4. Include these new **v-model** data props in the Vue instance by returning them in the **data()** function:

```
data() {
    return {
        firstName: '',
        lastName: '',
    }
},
```

5. Create a computed data variable called **fullName**:

```
computed: {
    fullName() {
        return `${this.firstName} ${this.lastName}`
    },
},
```

6. Underneath your input fields, using **heading** tags, output the computed data:

```
<h3 class="output">{{ fullName }}</h3>
```

This will generate the following output:

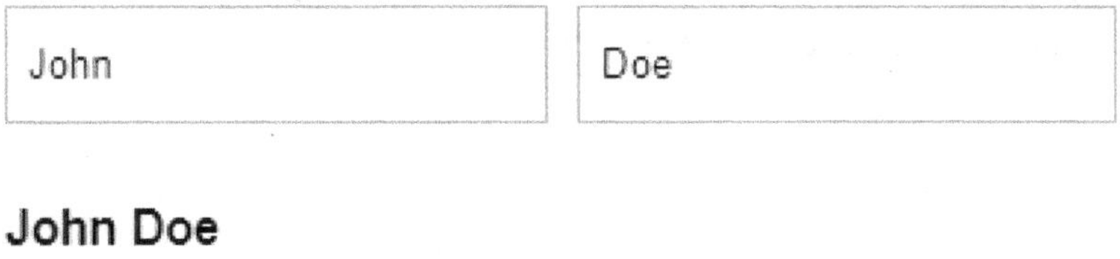

John	Doe

John Doe

Figure 2.2: Output of the computed data will show the first and last name

In this exercise, we saw how we can write an expression inside a computed data property using data from the **v-model** and combine the first name and last name into a single output variable that can be reused.

COMPUTED SETTERS

In the last exercise, you saw how to write maintainable and declarative computed properties that are reusable and reactive and can be called anywhere within your component. In some real-world cases when a computed property is called, you may need to call an external API to correspond with that UI interaction or mutate data elsewhere in the project. The thing that performs this function is called a setter.

Computed setters are demonstrated in the following example:

```
data() {
  return {
    count: 0
  }
},
computed: {
    myComputedDataProp: {
      // getter
      get() {
        return this.count + 1
      },
      // setter
      set(val) {
        this.count = val - 1
        this.callAnotherApi(this.count)
      },
    },
  },
}
```

By default, computed data is a getter only, which means it will only output the outcome of your expression. In this example, the computed **myComputedDataProp** data prop will output **1** in your Vue component:

```
get() {
  return this.count + 1
},
```

Then, using a setter in a computed property allows you to reactively listen to data and run a callback (setter) that contains the returned value from the getter, which can optionally be used in the setter.

In this example, the setter will update the data prop count to its new value (reflected in the getter) and then call a method within the component called **callAnotherApi**. Here, we pass in the count data prop to mimic sending this information somewhere useful:

```
set(val) {
  this.count = val - 1
  this.callAnotherApi(this.count)
},
```

You will find out exactly how to use computed data as both getters and setters in the following exercise.

EXERCISE 2.02: USING COMPUTED SETTERS

In this exercise, you will use a computed prop as a setter and a getter, which will both output expressions and set data when triggered by a user's input.

To access the code files for this exercise, refer to https://packt.live/2GwYapA.

1. Open a command-line terminal, navigate into the **Exercise 2.02** folder, and run the following commands in order:

```
> cd Exercise2.02/
> code .
> yarn
> yarn serve
```

Go to **https://localhost:8080**.

2. Create an input field with a **v-model** value bound to a computed data value called **incrementOne**, return the value of a Vue data variable called **count** in the getter, and set the **count** variable in the setter:

```
<template>
  <div class="container">
    <input type="number" v-model="incrementOne" />
    <h3>Get input: {{ incrementOne }}</h3>
  </div>
</template>

<script>
export default {
  data() {
    return {
      count: -1,
    }
  },
  computed: {
    incrementOne: {
      // getter
      get() {
        return this.count + 1
      },
      // setter
      set(val) {
        this.count = val - 1
      },
    },
  },
}
</script>
```

The output of the preceding code will be as follows:

```
123
```

Get input: 123

Figure 2.3: First steps of a computed setter and getter

3. Next, let's utilize the setter again. We will divide whatever the new **val** argument is by **2**, and save that to a new data variable called **divideByTwo**:

```
<template>
  <div class="container">
```

```
        <input type="number" v-model="incrementOne" />
        <h3>Get input: {{ incrementOne }}</h3>
        <h5>Set division: {{ divideByTwo }}</h5>
    </div>
</template>

<script>
export default {
    data() {
        return {
            count: -1,
            divideByTwo: 0,
        }
    },
    ...
</script>
    ...
```

4. Update the setter to divide **val** by **2**, and bind this new value to the **divideByTwo** variable:

```
        set(val) {
            this.count = val - 1
            this.divideByTwo = val / 2
        },
```

The output of the **divideByTwo** value should generate an outcome from the value entered in the input field, as follows:

Get input: 1000

Set division: 500

Figure 2.4: The outcome of the divideByTwo value

In this exercise, we saw how we can use computed data to both get and set data reactively in our template by binding computed variables to the **v-model**.

WATCHERS

Vue **watchers** programmatically observe component data and run whenever a particular property changes. Watched data can contain two arguments: **oldVal** and **newVal**. This can help you when writing expressions to compare data before writing or binding new values. Watchers can observe objects as well as **string**, **number**, and **array** types. When observing objects, it will only trigger the handler if the whole object changes.

In *Chapter 1, Starting Your First Vue Project*, we introduced life cycle hooks that run at specific times during a component's lifespan. If the **immediate** key is set to **true** on a watcher, then when this component initializes it will run this watcher on creation. You can watch all keys inside of any given object by including the key and value **deep: true** (default is **false**) To clean up your watcher code, you can assign a handler argument to a defined Vue method, which is best practice for large projects.

Watchers complement the usage of computed data since they can passively observe values and cannot be used like normal Vue data variables, while computed data must always return a value and can be looked up. Remember not to use arrow functions unless you do not require the Vue context of **this**.

The following watcher example demonstrates the **immediate** and **deep** optional keys; if any key inside of the **myDataProperty** object were to change it would trigger a console log:

```
watch: {
    myDataProperty: {
        handler: function(newVal, oldVal) {
          console.log('myDataProperty changed:', newVal, oldVal)
        },
        immediate: true,
        deep: true
    },
}
```

Now, let's set some new values with the help of watchers.

EXERCISE 2.03: USING WATCHERS TO SET NEW VALUES

In this exercise, you will use watcher arguments to watch data properties for changes, then use this watcher to set variables via a method.

To access the code files for this exercise, refer to https://packt.live/35OORI4.

1. Open a command-line terminal, navigate into the **Exercise 2.03** folder, and run the following commands in order:

```
> cd Exercise2.03/
> code .
> yarn
> yarn serve
```

Go to **https://localhost:8080**.

2. Set up the document by adding a discount and an **oldDiscount** data variable with some styling:

```
<template>
  <div class="container">
    <h1>Shop Watcher</h1>

    <div>
      Black Friday sale
      <strike>Was {{ oldDiscount }}%</strike>
      <strong> Now {{ discount }}% OFF</strong>
    </div>

  </div>
</template>

<script>
export default {
  data() {
    return {
      oldDiscount: 0,
      discount: 5,
    }
  },
}
```

```
</script>

<style lang="scss" scoped>
.container {
  margin: 0 auto;
  padding: 30px;
  max-width: 600px;
  font-family: 'Avenir', Helvetica, sans-serif;
  margin: 0;
}
a {
  display: inline-block;
  background: rgb(235, 50, 50);
  border-radius: 10px;
  font-size: 14px;
  color: white;
  padding: 10px 20px;
  text-decoration: none;
}
</style>
```

3. Observe the **discount** property by adding it to the **watch** object. Trigger a method called **updateDiscount**. Inside the method, set the **oldDiscount** data prop to be **this.discount + 5**:

```
watch: {
  discount(newValue, oldValue) {
    this.oldDiscount = oldValue
  },
},
```

4. Include a method that will augment the **discount** variable and trigger the watcher:

```
methods: {
  updateDiscount() {
    this.discount = this.discount + 5
  },
},
```

Now add a line break, and an anchor element with the @**click** directive bound to the **updateDiscount** method:

```
<br />

<a href="#" @click="updateDiscount">Increase Discount!</a>
```

The output of the preceding command will be as follows:

Shop Watcher

Black Friday sale ~~Was 145%~~ **Now 150% OFF**

Increase Discount!

Figure 2.5: A shop watcher page should look something like this

In this exercise, we saw how we can use watchers to observe and reactively manipulate data when data is changed by other methods in the Vue component.

In the next section, we will learn about deep watching concepts.

DEEP WATCHING CONCEPTS

When using Vue.js to watch a data property, you can purposefully observe keys inside an object for changes, rather than changes to the object itself. This is done by setting the optional **deep** property to **true**:

```
data() {
  return {
    organization: {
      name: 'ABC',
      employees: [
          'Jack', 'Jill'
      ]
    }
  }
},
watch: {
  organization: {
    handler: function(v) {
      this.sendIntercomData()
    },
```

```
    deep: true,
    immediate: true,
  },
},
```

This example will watch all available keys inside the organization data object for changes, so if the **name** property inside the organization changes, the organization watcher will trigger.

If you do not need to observe every key inside of an object, it can be more performant to just watch a specific key inside an object for changes by specifying it as a **myObj.value** string. For example, you may allow a user to edit their company name and have that data sent to an API only when that key has been modified.

In the following example, the watcher is specifically observing the **name** key of the **organization** object.

```
data() {
  return {
    organization: {
      name: 'ABC',
      employees: [
          'Jack', 'Jill'
      ]
    }
  }
},
watch: {
    'organization.name': {
      handler: function(v) {
        this.sendIntercomData()
      },
      immediate: true,
    },
  },
```

We saw how deep watching works. Now, let's try the next exercise and watch the nested properties of a data object.

EXERCISE 2.04: WATCHING NESTED PROPERTIES OF A DATA OBJECT

In this exercise, you will use watchers to observe keys within an object, which will update when a user triggers a method within the UI.

To access the code files for this exercise, refer to https://packt.live/353m59N.

1. Open a command-line terminal, navigate to the **Exercise 2.04** folder, and run the following commands in order:

```
> cd Exercise2.04/
> code .
> yarn
> yarn serve
```

Go to **https://localhost:8080**.

2. Start by defining a **product** object that contains a **price** and **label** and a **discount** key. Output these values into the template:

```
<template>
  <div class="container">
    <h1>Deep Watcher</h1>

    <div>
        <h4>{{ product.label }}</h4>
        <h5>${{ product.price }} (${{ discount }} Off)</h5>
    </div>
  </div>
</template>

<script>
export default {
  data() {
    return {
      discount: 0,
      product: {
        price: 25,
        label: 'Blue juice',
      },
    }
  },
}
```

```
</script>

<style lang="scss" scoped>
.container {
  margin: 0 auto;
  padding: 30px;
  max-width: 600px;
  font-family: 'Avenir', Helvetica, sans-serif;
  margin: 0;
}
a {
  display: inline-block;
  background: rgb(235, 50, 50);
  border-radius: 10px;
  font-size: 14px;
  color: white;
  padding: 10px 20px;
  text-decoration: none;
}
</style>
```

3. Set up a button that will modify the price of the product. Do this by adding a button element with a **click** event bound to an **updatePrice** method that decrements the value of price:

```
<template>
...
    <a href="#" @click="updatePrice">Reduce Price!</a>
...
</template>
<script>
...
  methods: {
    updatePrice() {
      if (this.product.price < 1) return
      this.product.price--
    },
  },
...
</script>
```

When you click the button, it should reduce the price as seen in the following screenshot:

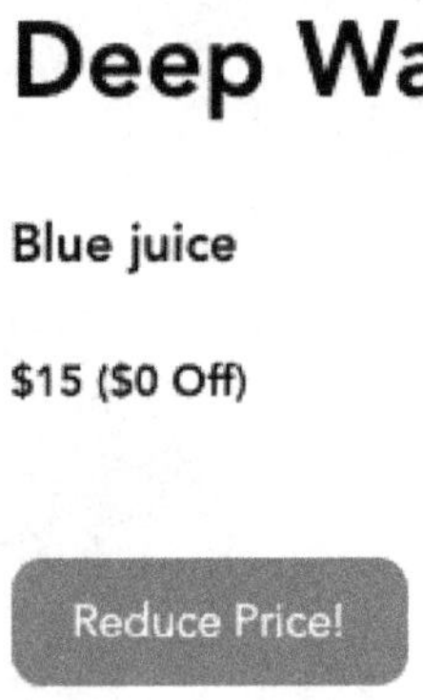

Deep Watcher

Blue juice

$15 ($0 Off)

Reduce Price!

Figure 2.6: Screen displaying the reduced price of Blue juice

4. Time for the nested watcher. We will watch the **product** object's **price**, and increment the **discount** data prop:

```
watch: {
  'product.price'() {
    this.discount++
  },
},
```

Now, as you reduce the **price**, the **discount** value will go up because of the watcher:

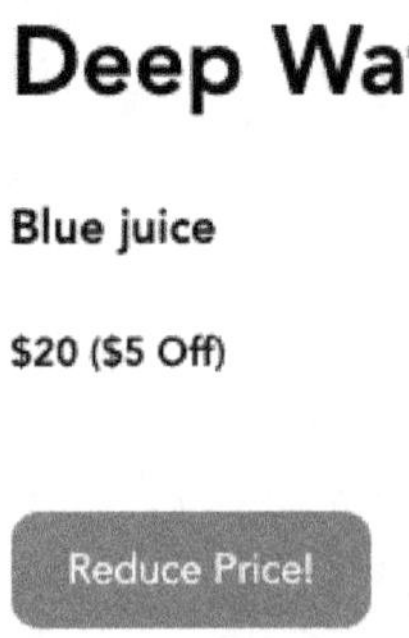

Deep Watcher

Blue juice

$20 ($5 Off)

Reduce Price!

Figure 2.7 Output displaying an increased discount value

In this exercise, we used watchers to observe a key inside an object and then set new data with or without using the optional arguments parsed by the watcher.

METHODS VERSUS WATCHERS VERSUS COMPUTED PROPS

In the Vue.js toolbox, we have access to methods, watchers, and computed properties. When should you use one or the other?

Methods are best used to react to an event occurring in the **DOM**, and in situations where you would need to call a function or perform a call instead of reference a value, for example, **date.now()**.

In Vue, you would compose an action denoted by **@click**, and reference a method:

```
<template>
    <button @click="getDate">Click me</button>
</template>
<script>
export default {
    methods: {
        getDate() {
            alert(date.now())
        }
    }
}
</script>
```

Computed props are best used when reacting to data updates or for composing complicated expressions for us in your template. In this instance, if the **animalList** data changes, the **animals** computed prop will also update by slicing the second item from the array and returning the new value:

```
<template>
    <div>{{ animals }}</div>
</template>
<script>
export default {
    data() {
        return {
            animalList: ['dog', 'cat']
        }
    },
    computed: {
        animals() {
            return this.animalList.slice(1)
        }
```

```
    }
}
</script>
```

Their reactive nature makes computed properties perfect for composing new data variables from existing data, such as when you are referencing specific keys of a larger, more complicated object, helping to simplify readability of your template. In this example, we output the authors twice in two different ways. However, notice in the **authorName** computed prop, you can compose conditional logic cleanly without bloating the HTML template:

```
<template>
    <div>
        <p id="not-optimal">{{ authors[0].bio.name }}</p>
        <p id="optimal">{{ authorName }}</p>
    </div>
</template>
<script>
export default {
    data() {
        return {
            authors: [
                {
                    bio: {
                        name: 'John',
                        title: 'Dr.',
                    }
                }
            ]
        }
    },
    computed: {
        authorName () {
            return this.authors ? this.authors[0].bio.name :
                'No Name'
        }
    }
}
</script>
```

Data watchers should be used when you need to listen to a data property change or a specific data property inside an object, and then perform an action. Because of the unique **newVal** and **oldVal** arguments of a watcher, you can watch a variable until a certain value is reached, and only then perform an action:

```
<template>
    <div>
        <button @click="getNewName()">Click to generate name
            </button>
        <p v-if="author">{{ author }}</p>
    </div>
</template>
<script>
    export default {
        data() {
            return {
                data: {},
                author: '',
            }
        },
        watch: {
            data: function(newVal, oldVal) {
                this.author = newVal.first
                alert(`Name changed from ${oldVal.first} to
                    ${newVal.first}`)
            }
        },
        methods: {
            async getNewName() {
                await fetch('https://randomuser.me/api/').
                    then(response => response.json()).then(data => {
                        this.data = data.results[0].name
                    })
            },
        },
    }
</script>
```

With this in mind, we will build a simple search functionality using a method, computed props, and a watcher to achieve a similar outcome and demonstrate the ability of each method.

EXERCISE 2.05: HANDLING SEARCH FUNCTIONALITY USING A VUE METHOD, A WATCHER, AND COMPUTED PROPS

In this exercise, you will create a component that allows users to search data arrays using three different methods in Vue. By the end of the exercise, you will be able to see firsthand how each different method works.

To access the code files for this exercise, refer to https://packt.live/32iDJVe.

1. Open the command-line terminal, navigate to the **Exercise 2.05** folder, and run the following commands in order:

```
> cd Exercise2.05/
> code .
> yarn
> yarn serve
```

Go to **https://localhost:8080**.

2. In the **data** object, add a list of frameworks in an array, assigned to the **frameworkList** value. Include an empty string with the key to input and an empty array with a key of **methodFilterList**:

```
<script>
export default {
  data() {
    return {
      // Shared
      frameworkList: [
        'Vue',
        'React',
        'Backbone',
        'Ember',
        'Knockout',
        'jQuery',
        'Angular',
      ],

      // Method
      input: '',
      methodFilterList: [],
    }
  },
```

```
    }
  </script>
```

3. In the template, include a **div** container, a **title**, and a **column** container. Inside this **column** container, create an input that is bound to the **v-model** input, and bind the **keyup** event on the input to the **searchMethod** method:

```
<template>
  <div class="container">
    <h1>Methods vs watchers vs computed props</h1>

    <div class="col">
      <input
        type="text"
        placeholder="Search with method"
        v-model="input"
        @keyup="searchMethod"
      />

      <ul>
        <li v-for="(item, i) in methodFilterList" :key="i">
          {{ item }}</li>
      </ul>
    </div>
  </div>
</template>

<script>
export default {
  data() {
    return {
      // Shared
      frameworkList: [
        'Vue',
        'React',
        'Backbone',
        'Ember',
        'Knockout',
        'jQuery',
        'Angular',
      ],
```

```
      // Method
      input: '',
      methodFilterList: [],
    }
  },
  methods: {
    searchMethod(e) {
     console.log(e)
    },
  },
}
</script>

<style lang="scss" scoped>
.container {
  margin: 0 auto;
  padding: 30px;
  max-width: 600px;
  font-family: 'Avenir', Helvetica, Arial, sans-serif;
}
.col {
  width: 33%;
  height: 100%;
  float: left;
}
input {
  padding: 10px 6px;
  margin: 20px 10px 10px 0;
}
</style>
```

The output of the preceding code will be as follows:

Figure 2.8: Console should output the key input

4. Inside our **searchMethod** method, write a filter expression that binds the **methodFilterList** data prop to a filtered **frameworkList** array based on the input value. Trigger **searchMethod** on the **created()** life cycle hook so that when the component loads, a list is present:

```
<script>
export default {
  ...
  created() {
    this.searchMethod()
  },
  methods: {
    searchMethod() {
      this.methodFilterList = this.frameworkList.filter(item =>
        item.toLowerCase().includes(this.input.toLowerCase())
      )
    },
  },
}
</script>
```

On running the preceding code, you will be able to filter the list as shown in *Figure 2.9*:

Methods vs watchers vs computed props

- Backbone
- Ember

Figure 2.9: You should now be able to filter the list using a Vue method

5. Let's make a filter using computed props. Include a new data prop called **input2** and create a **computed** prop called **computedList** that returns the same filter as the **searchMethod** but does not need to bind to another data prop:

```
<template>
  <div class="container">

    . . .

    <div class="col">
      <input type="text" placeholder="Search with computed"
        v-model="input2" />

      <ul>
        <li v-for="(item, i) in computedList" :key="i">
          {{ item }}</li>
      </ul>
    </div>

    . . .

  </div>
</template>

<script>
export default {
  data() {
    return {

      . . .
      // Computed
      input2: '',
      . . .


    }
  },
  . . .
  computed: {
    computedList() {
      return this.frameworkList.filter(item => {
        return item.toLowerCase().includes(this.input2.
          toLowerCase())
```

```
      })
    },
  },
  ...


}
</script>
```

You should now be able to filter the second column of frameworks with the help of computed props, as shown in the following screenshot:

Methods vs watchers vs computed props

- React
- Backbone
- Angular

- Backbone
- Ember

Figure 2.10: Filtering the second column of frameworks using computed props

6. Finally, let's filter the same list using a watcher. Include an **input3** prop with an empty string and **watchFilterList** prop with an empty array. Also create a third column **div**, which contains an input bound to the **input3 v-model**, and a list outputting the **watchFilterList** array:

```
<template>
  <div class="container">


    ...


    <div class="col">
      <input type="text" placeholder="Search with watcher"
        v-model="input3" />

      <ul>
        <li v-for="(item, i) in watchFilterList" :key="i">
          {{ item }}</li>
```

```
        </ul>
      </div>
    </div>
  </template>

<script>
export default {
  data() {
    return {
      ...
      // Watcher
      input3: '',
      watchFilterList: [],
    }
  },
  ...
</script>
```

7. Create a watcher that watches the **input3** prop for changes and binds the result of the **frameworkList** filter to the **watchFilterList** array. Set the immediate key of **input3** to **true** so it will run when the component is created:

```
<script>
export default {
...
  watch: {
    input3: {
      handler() {
        this.watchFilterList = this.frameworkList.filter(item =>
          item.toLowerCase().includes(this.input3.toLowerCase())
        )
      },
      immediate: true,
    },
  },
  ...
}
</script>
```

With the help of a watcher, you should now be able to filter the third column, as shown in the following screenshot:

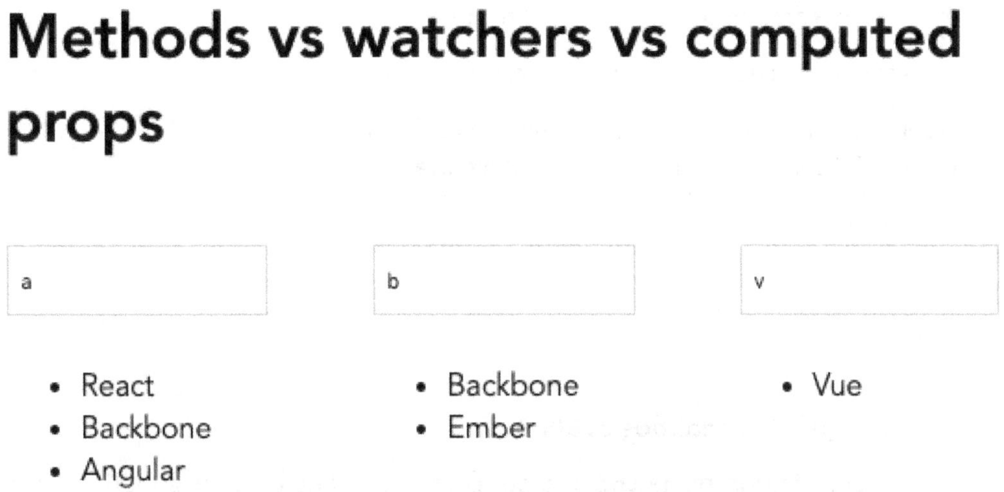

Methods vs watchers vs computed props

a	b	v

- React
- Backbone
- Angular

- Backbone
- Ember

- Vue

Figure 2.11: Filtering the list using a watcher in the third column

In this exercise, we have seen how we can achieve a filtered list using a method, computed props, and a watcher. Each has their own pros, cons, and use cases depending on what you are trying to achieve in your application.

ASYNC METHODS AND DATA FETCHING

Asynchronous functions in JavaScript are defined by the async function syntax and return an **AsyncFunction** object. These functions operate asynchronously via the event loop, using an implicit promise, which is an object that may return a result in the future. Vue.js uses this JavaScript behavior to allow you to declare asynchronous blocks of code inside methods by including the **async** keyword in front of a method. You can then chain **then()** and **catch()** functions or try the **{ }** syntax inside these Vue methods and return the results.

Axios is a popular JavaScript library that allows you to make external requests for data using Node.js. It has wide browser support making it a versatile library when doing **HTTP** or API requests. We will be using this library in the next exercise.

EXERCISE 2.06: USING ASYNCHRONOUS METHODS TO RETRIEVE DATA FROM AN API

In this exercise, you will asynchronously fetch data from an external API source and display it in the frontend using computed props.

To access the code files for this exercise, refer to https://packt.live/353md9h.

1. Open a command-line terminal, navigate to the **Exercise 2.06** folder, and run the following commands to install **axios**:

```
> cd Exercise2.06/
> code .
> yarn
> yarn add axios
> yarn serve
```

Go to **https://localhost:8080**.

2. Let's start by importing **axios** into our component and creating a method called **getApi()**. Use **axios** to call a response from https://api.adviceslip.com/advice and **console.log** the result. Include a button that has a **click** event bound to the **getApi()** call:

```
<template>
  <div class="container">
    <h1>Async fetch</h1>
    <button @click="getApi()">Learn something profound</button>
  </div>
</template>

<script>
import axios from 'axios'

export default {
  methods: {
    async getApi() {
      return   axios.get('https://api.adviceslip.com/advice').
        then((response) => {
        console.log(response)
      })
    },
  },
}
```

```
</script>

<style lang="scss" scoped>
.container {
  margin: 0 auto;
  padding: 30px;
  max-width: 600px;
  font-family: 'Avenir', Helvetica, Arial, sans-serif;
}
blockquote {
  position: relative;
  width: 100%;
  margin: 50px auto;
  padding: 1.2em 30px 1.2em 30px;
  background: #ededed;
  border-left: 8px solid #78c0a8;
  font-size: 24px;
  color: #555555;
  line-height: 1.6;
}
</style>
```

The output of the preceding code will be as follows:

Figure 2.12: Screen displaying a very large object in the console

3. We are only interested in the data object inside the **response** object. Assign this data object to a Vue data prop called **response** that we can reuse:

```
export default {
  data() {
    return {
```

```
        axiosResponse: {},
      }
    },
    methods: {
      async getApi() {
        return axios.get('https://api.adviceslip.com/advice').
          then(response => {
          this.axiosResponse = response.data
        })
      },
    },
}
```

4. Output the **quote** from inside the **response** prop object using a computed prop that will update every time the **response** prop changes. Use a ternary operator to perform a conditional statement to check whether the **response** prop contains the **slip** object to avoid errors:

```
<template>
  <div class="container">
    <h1>Async fetch</h1>
    <button @click="getApi()">Learn something profound</button>

    <blockquote v-if="quote">{{ quote }}</blockquote>
  </div>
</template>

<script>
import axios from 'axios'

export default {
  data() {
    return {
      axiosResponse: {},
    }
  },
  computed: {
    quote() {
      return this.axiosResponse && this.axiosResponse.slip
        ? this.axiosResponse.slip.advice
        : null
    },
```

```
    },
    methods: {
      async getApi() {
        return axios.get('https://api.adviceslip.com/advice').
          then(response => {
          this.axiosResponse = response.data
        })
      },
    },
  }
</script>
```

Figure 2.13 displays the output generated by the preceding code:

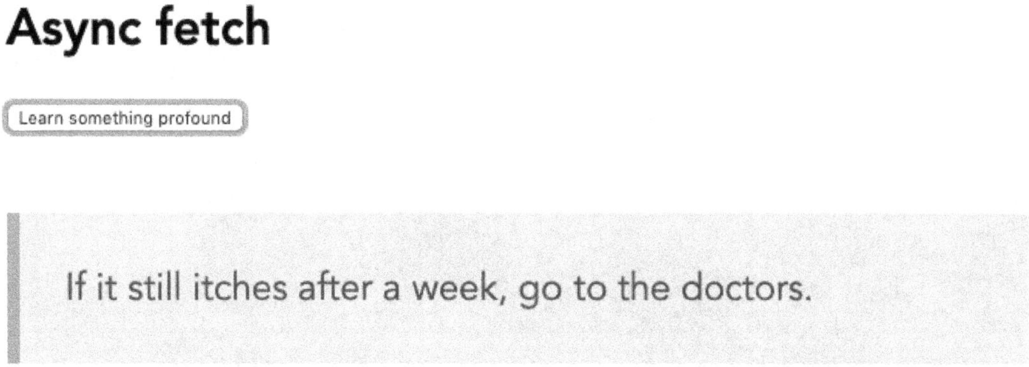

Async fetch

Learn something profound

If it still itches after a week, go to the doctors.

Figure 2.13: Screen displaying the quote output in your template

5. As a final touch, include a **loading** data prop so the user can see when the UI is loading. Set **loading** to **false** by default. Inside the **getApi** method, set **loading** to **true**, and in the **then()** chain, set it back to **false** after 4 seconds using the **setTimeout** function. You can use a ternary operator to change the button text between the loading state and its default state:

```
<template>
  <div class="container">
    <h1>Async fetch</h1>

    <button @click="getApi()">{{
      loading ? 'Loading...' : 'Learn something profound'
    }}</button>

    <blockquote v-if="quote">{{ quote }}</blockquote>
  </div>
```

```
</template>

<script>
import axios from 'axios'

export default {
  data() {
    return {
      loading: false,
      axiosResponse: {},
    }
  },
  computed: {
    quote() {
      return this.axiosResponse && this.axiosResponse.slip
        ? this.axiosResponse.slip.advice
        : null
    },
  },
  methods: {
    async getApi() {
      this.loading = true
      return axios.get('https://api.adviceslip.com/advice').
        then(response => {
        this.axiosResponse = response.data

        setTimeout(() => {
          this.loading = false
        }, 4000);
      })
    },
  },
}
</script>
```

The output of the preceding code will be as follows:

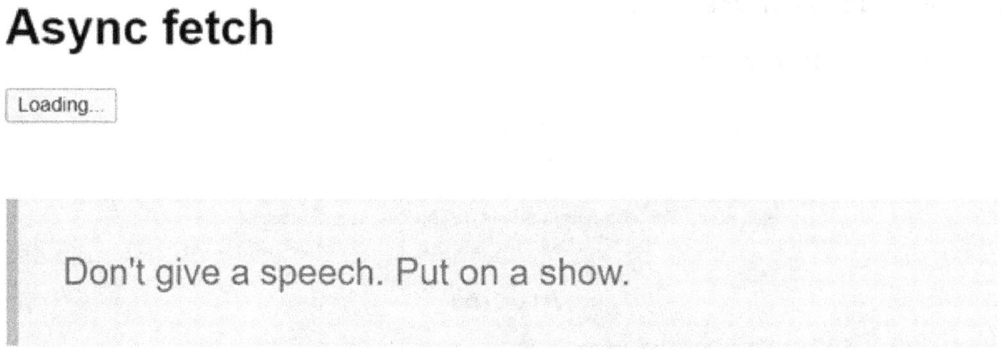

Async fetch

Loading...

Don't give a speech. Put on a show.

Figure 2.14: Screen displaying the loading button state output in your template

In this exercise, we saw how we can fetch data from an external source, assign it to a computed prop, display it in our template, and apply a loading state to our content.

ACTIVITY 2.01: CREATING A BLOG LIST USING THE CONTENTFUL API

In this activity, we will build a blog that lists articles from an API source. This will test your knowledge of Vue by using all the basic functions of a **Single-File Component (SFC)** and `async` methods to fetch remote data from an API and use computed properties to organize deep nested object structures.

`Contentful` is a headless **content management system** (CMS) that allows you to manage content separately to your code repository. You can consume this content using the API inside as many code repositories as you need. For example, you may have a blog website that acts as a primary source of information, but your clients want a standalone page on a different domain that only pulls in the most recent featured articles. Using a headless CMS inherently allows you to develop these two separate code bases and use the same updated data source.

This activity will be using the headless CMS `Contentful`. The access keys and endpoints will be listed in the solution.

The following steps will help you complete the activity:

1. Use the Vue CLI to create a new project that uses `babel` presets.

2. Install the `contentful` dependency into your project.

3. Use computed properties to output the deeply nested data from the API response.

4. Use **data** props to output the user's **name**, **job title**, and **description**.

5. Use **SCSS** to style the page.

The expected outcome is as follows:

John Doe
Web Developer

Research and recommendations for modern stack websites.

Articles

MON DEC 30 2019

Hello world

Your very first content with Contentful, pulled in JSON format using the Content Delivery API.

SUN DEC 01 2019

Automate with webhooks

Webhooks notify you, another person or system when resources have changed by calling a given HTTP endpoint.

THU AUG 01 2019

Static sites are great

Worry less about security, caching, and talking to the server. Static sites are the new thing.

Figure 2.15: Expected outcome with Contentful blog posts

> **NOTE**
>
> The solution for this activity can be found on page 646

After the activity has been completed, you should be able to use **async** methods to pull remote data from an API source into your Vue components. You will find that computed props are a sophisticated way of breaking down the information into smaller chunks of reusable data.

SUMMARY

In this chapter, you were introduced to Vue.js computed and watch properties, which allow you to observe and control reactive data. You also saw how to use methods to asynchronously fetch data from an API using the **axios** library and how to flatten the data to be more usable within the Vue template using computed props. The differences between using methods and computed and watch properties were demonstrated by building search functionality using each method.

The next chapter will cover the Vue CLI and show you how to manage and debug your Vue.js applications that use these computed properties and events.

3

VUE CLI

OVERVIEW

This chapter introduces Vue CLI, including the Vue-UI and Vue.js DevTools, which are used when developing Vue applications for production. The Vue-UI allows you to create, develop, and manage Vue projects through an accompanying graphical user interface. Vue.js DevTools is a standalone app and browser extension for debugging Vue.js applications. We go into the details of the use cases and benefits of using Vue CLI features, which will teach you how to utilize these Vue commands. In addition to the command-line controls, we will set up and run Vue projects utilizing the new Vue GUI. We will combine the knowledge accrued in previous chapters to create new Vue applications that use v-model directives and two-way binding concepts. We will then dive into how to prototype Vue components. We will also learn how to build a Vue prototype for production and serve it locally. As we proceed, you will see how to set up and debug your Vue app and showcase its features.

By the end of this chapter, you will have a firm grasp of how to use Vue CLI's features, prototype Vue components, and utilize Vue.js DevTools.

INTRODUCTION

In the previous chapter, we covered how to manage and manipulate data reactively in our component templates using Vue.js. In this chapter, we will be looking at how to support the development of such templates using Vue CLI. Vue.js takes advantage of the **npm** and webpack ecosystem, as seen in *Chapter 1, Starting Your First Vue Project*, in the *The Vue Instance in a Simple Vue Application* example. These tools help developers to quickly scaffold and build great web applications. Notable patterns inside of Vue.js are **vue.config** (which allows you to add webpack rules without directly editing the webpack file itself), **two-way data binding**, and **single file components (SFCs)**, as seen in *Chapter 1, Starting Your First Vue Project*, in the *Two-Way Binding Using V-Model* example.

Webpack projects instantiated using the **Vue command-line interface (Vue CLI)** will come with hot reloading already installed. Hot reloading is a frontend development pattern where your app in the browser will automatically update when code changes are detected. The reason you want this is so that you do not lose any of your browser state and changes made in your code are immediately reflected in the browser, which is useful when working on a **user interface (UI)**. Occasionally, a full-page reload will be necessary because JavaScript is a very stateful language.

Vue CLI is a core tool for Vue development, as it allows programmers to maintain their projects much more comfortably with a set of descriptive and pre-configured commands. An often-overlooked process in development projects is code linting, which is a process where a program will flag potential errors or problems in your code, which can be quite difficult to add to an existing project. When using Vue CLI, your webpack project will come with linting so long as you choose it as an option when you create a Vue CLI project.

We are going to configure a Vue project using Vue CLI and run each basic command so that you can understand the tool you need to build your Vue applications. Out of the box, Vue CLI has support for **Babel**, **TypeScript**, **ESLint**, **PostCSS**, **PWAs**, **testing**, and more.

USING VUE CLI

Projects created using the Vue CLI tool have access to common tasks that will help you **serve** (run a project in your browser locally), **build** (compile files for production), and **lint** (examine code for errors) your project. The Vue CLI service development dependency packages are installed automatically with a new project and allow you to run the following commands:

- `npm run serve` or `yarn serve` – Runs your project code on `localhost:8080` with hot reloading. The port number **8080** is arbitrarily assigned, as it is above the well-known port numbers **1–1023** used in other areas of computing. If you have multiple Vue projects running at the same time, they will have incremental port numbers such as `:8080`, `:8081`, and so on.

- `npm run build` or `yarn build` – Runs a production build that reduces the file size of your project and can be served from a host.

- `npm run lint` or `yarn lint` – Runs the process of linting, which will highlight code errors or warnings, making your code more consistent.

Now that you understand what Vue CLI is, and the commands available to you, we will learn how to set up Vue.js projects from scratch using Vue CLI.

EXERCISE 3.01: SETTING UP A PROJECT USING VUE CLI

In this exercise, you will create your first Vue.js webpack project using the Vue CLI commands. But, first, ensure you have followed the *Preface* guide to install **Node** and **Vue CLI 4**. It is recommended that you use **iTerm2** on OS X as it is very customizable for your development flow. If you are using Windows, it is recommended that you use **PowerShell** as it can be more performant than the default Command Prompt and GIT bash.

To access the code files for this exercise, refer to https://packt.live/3ph2xXt.

1. Open Command Prompt. Your window should look as follows:

Figure 3.1: A blank Command Prompt window

2. Run the command **vue --version**. Ensure you are on the latest version of Vue CLI, as the following instructions will not work in versions of Vue CLI 2 or below.

After the preceding command, your screen should look as follows:

Figure 3.2: Command Prompt when checking the Vue version

Your @**vue/cli** version should be at least 4.1.2.

3. Run the following Vue CLI command:

```
vue create my-app
```

Upon running the preceding command, you should see a list of saved presets, as shown in the following screenshot:

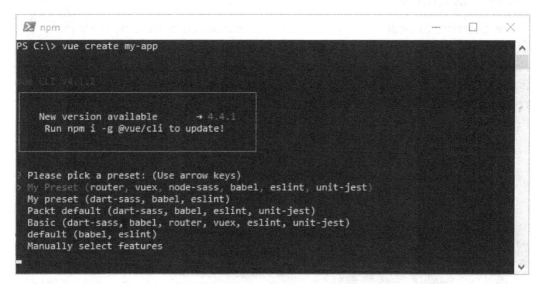

Figure 3.3: Displaying the list of saved presets

4. Choose the last selection **Manually select features** by pressing the *Down arrow key* once and then pressing *Enter* to select:

```
? Please pick a preset: (Use arrow keys)
  default (babel, eslint)
> Manually select features
```

5. You will notice features with an asterisk in brackets. Each feature represents a preset that you can enable in your app. It does not matter if you do not know what each of these represents. For now, we will choose **Babel**, **CSS Pre-processors**, and **Linter/Formatter** by navigating with the arrow keys, pressing the spacebar on each option, then pressing *Enter* to proceed:

```
? Check the features needed for your project:
 (*) Babel
 ( ) TypeScript
 ( ) Progressive Web App (PWA) Support
 ( ) Router
 ( ) Vuex
 (*) CSS Pre-processors
>(*) Linter / Formatter
 ( ) Unit Testing
 ( ) E2E Testing
```

6. Because you chose to enable a preprocessor, you now have a choice of which CSS preprocessor you prefer. In this exercise, we will use **Sass/SCSS (with dart-scss)**:

```
? Pick a CSS pre-processor (PostCSS, Autoprefixer and CSS Modules
are supported by default): (Use arrow keys)
> Sass/SCSS (with dart-sass)
  Sass/SCSS (with node-sass)
  Less
  Stylus
```

> **NOTE**
>
> **dart-scss** is a pure JavaScript compilation of the **Sass** library, making it a much smaller dependency compared to **node-sass** (which is a wrapper on the C++ implementation of SCSS), and it does not require rebuilding between Node upgrade versions.

7. We will now choose the **Eslint + Prettier** option, which automatically formats the code in a consistent manner:

> **NOTE**
>
> **Prettier** is an opinionated code formatter, which makes code development easier and more efficient by automatically formatting your code in a consistent way. Aligning the developers on your team should increase productivity and remove the need to debate code styling.

```
? Pick a linter / formatter config: (Use arrow keys)
  ESLint with error prevention only
  ESLint + Airbnb config
  ESLint + Standard config
> ESLint + Prettier
```

8. To automatically format your code when you save your work, choose the option to **Lint on Save**:

```
? Pick additional lint features: (Press <space> to select, <a>
to toggle all, <i> to invert selection)
 >(*) Lint on save
  (*) Lint and fix on commit
```

> **NOTE**
>
> **Lint on save** is a useful tool to format your code as you go. Choose both linting options in *Step 8* to make sure that all your work is linted as you go, in turn making your code more readable and consistent.

9. Next, we will choose the **In dedicated config files** option to place the configurations as per our preference:

```
? Where do you prefer placing config for Babel, PostCSS,
  ESLint, etc.? (Use arrow keys)
  > In dedicated config files
  In package.json
```

> **NOTE**
>
> An argument for **package.json** is to keep all configurations consistently formatted in JSON and in one file. For smaller projects, this would be acceptable, however, large projects will tend to produce a very long **package.json** file. This is where file splitting would be preferable. Splitting configurations into separate files both reduces the amount of cognitive load when editing these options and places greater emphasis on what is being changed in your commit logs. For example, when you edit the **babelrc** file, you know the changes relate to the Babel config, as opposed to **package.json** changes, where it could be anything.

10. Choose the **Save preset (y)** option to save your preset.

    You can call the preset by any name. In the example, it will be called **My preset**.

    Next time you want to install this preset, try running **vue create favourite -p "My preset"** (using the general command-line syntax of **vue create [project-name] -p [preset-name]**):

    ```
    ? Save this as a preset for future projects? Yes
    ? Save preset as: My preset
    ```

11. Run the package installer. If the installer does not start automatically, run the **yarn install** command:

    ```
    yarn install v1.16.0
    info No lockfile found.
     [1/4] Resolving packages...
    ```

12. Once the package installer has completed, **serve** your project to compile your code and serve it on **http://localhost:8080**:

    ```
    yarn serve
    ```

    If port **8080** is taken already by another application, use the **--port** flag to specify another port, such as **9000**:

    ```
    yarn serve --port 9000
    ```

Running the preceding command, we'll see a default Vue project screen, as shown in *Figure 3.4*:

Welcome to Your Vue.js App

For a guide and recipes on how to configure / customize this project,
check out the vue-cli documentation.

Installed CLI Plugins

babel   eslint

Essential Links

Core Docs   Forum   Community Chat   Twitter   News

Ecosystem

vue-router   vuex   vue-devtools   vue-loader   awesome-vue

Figure 3.4: The default Vue project screen will appear on your localhost:8080

In this exercise, we saw how to create a Vue.js webpack project using the Vue CLI commands using Command Prompt. Next, we will look at how to prototype a Vue.js component without creating a webpack project.

VUE PROTOTYPING

Let's say, one day you wake up with a great idea for a component or are involved in a large project and you want to debug components without the complex interdependencies of the existing project. Vue prototyping can help you create new components or debug existing ones, even for large projects. This is done by running `.vue` files in a separate and isolated compiler directly, without the need for any local dependencies. Running `.vue` files in this way may save time because you do not need to install a full Vue project as described in *Exercise 3.01*. Instead, all you need to do is install the **Vue CLI service** globally by running either of the following commands: `npm install -g @vue/cli-service-global` or `yarn global add @vue/cli-service-global`.

Once this has been installed, you will have access to the following two commands:

- `vue serve` – This command compiles Vue.js code and runs in a localhost environment in your browser.

- `vue build` – This command compiles Vue.js code into a distributable package.

GETTING STARTED WITH PROTOTYPING

To get started, you will first need to install the global package by opening your command terminal and running the following **install** command:

```
npm install -g @vue/cli-service-global
# or
yarn global add @vue/cli-service-global
```

This will generate the following screenshot:

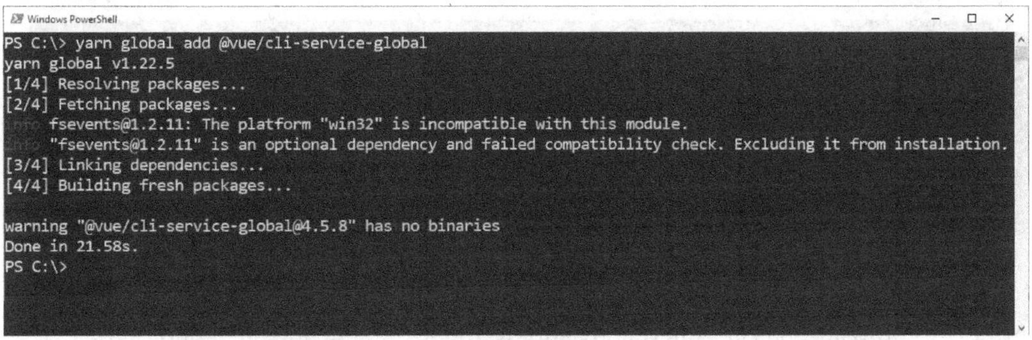

Figure 3.5: Installing global dependencies required for Vue prototyping

The install can take a couple of minutes depending on your internet connection. You will know when it is complete as you will be able to write other commands in the terminal. If the install fails for whatever reason, simply reopen the terminal and run the same command.

To start using prototyping, create an example component called **helloWorld.vue**:

```
// helloWorld.vue
<template>
    <h1>Hello World!</h1>
</template>
```

In your terminal window (in the same directory as your new **.vue** file), use the following command:

```
vue serve helloWorld.vue
```

The preceding command will display as follows:

Figure 3.6: The vue serve command is running on a file in the D:\ directory

After running the **serve** command, there will be a brief period where the component will compile in the terminal window before being accessible in your browser as follows:

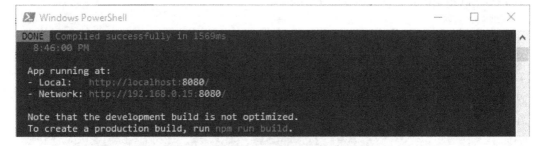

Figure 3.7: The vue serve command will serve your Vue files in the localhost environment

After the compilation is complete, navigate to the localhost URL specified in the command window using the browser. Here, it is **http://localhost:8080/**. In your browser, you should see the text **Hello World!**:

```
Hello World!
```

We have now learned how to prototype a Vue component on the fly without needing to create a full webpack project. Let's see how we can import fonts or libraries for use in a prototype.

DEFINING YOUR OWN ENTRY POINT

In your prototype, you may require the use of external libraries such as fonts or scripts to complete your prototype component. The **index.html** file is the entry point for a Vue.js HTML template. If you do not define an **index.html** file, a global default file is used.

To define a custom entry point, create an **index.html** file in the same directory. Using the following code derived from the default index page, you will see that a Google font has been added to the **\<head\>** tag:

```
// index.html
<!DOCTYPE html>
<html lang="en">
  <head>
    <meta name="viewport" content="width=device-width,
      initial-scale=1.0">
    <title>Hello World</title>
    <link ref="https://fonts.googleapis.com/css2?family=Roboto&
      display=swap" rel="stylesheet">
  </head>
  <body>
    <div id="app"></div>
  </body>
</html>
```

To use this font in your prototyped component, create a **helloWorld.vue** component in the same directory as the **index.html** file and then apply some **css** styling to the component:

```
// helloWorld.vue
<template>
    <h1>Hello World!</h1>
</template>
<style>
h1 {
  font-family: 'Roboto';
}
</style>
```

To view the changes made to these files, run the following command in your terminal:

```
vue serve helloWorld.vue
```

This will generate the following screenshot:

Figure 3.8: Run the vue serve command on the file you want to prototype

After running the **serve** command, there will be a brief period where the component will compile in the terminal window before being accessible in your browser, as follows:

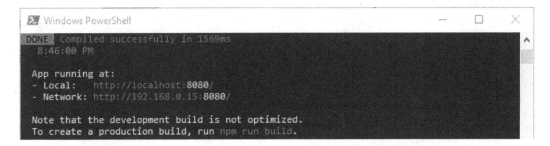

Figure 3.9: The vue serve command will serve your Vue files in the localhost environment

Open the localhost URL in your browser. You should see the formatted text using a new font in your preview. The output will be as follows:

```
Hello World!
```

We have now learned how to include external libraries in a Vue component prototype without needing to create a full webpack project. Next, we will see how to build a prototype ready to be hosted on a website or previewed by your team externally.

BUILDING A PROTOTYPE FOR PRODUCTION

When you have finished making a prototype and want to share it with others on your team or submit it for review by a tech lead, you can export your code as distributable files.

This means that your code can run on other machines or be hosted on an external server without requiring Vue CLI to run it (aka the **vue serve** command).

Using the previous example file to do this, open your command terminal, navigate to the folder that contains your Vue prototype, and run the **vue build helloWorld.vue** command. This will generate an output as follows:

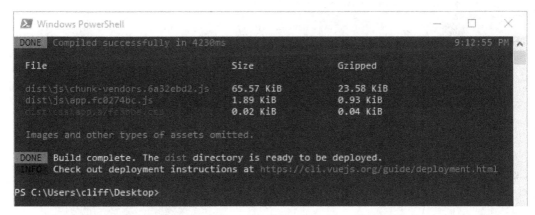

Figure 3.10: Output in the terminal after running the build command

A **dist** folder will be created that contains a compiled version of your prototype that you can upload to a web host. Inside of the **dist** folder, you can expect to see the following files:

- An **index.html** file

- The **/css** folder

- The **/js** folder

All these files will be necessary to properly run your compiled prototype. If you double-click on the **index.html** file, it does not load your app. To view or serve the distributable files on your local machine, you will need the help of a library that can serve a static site or single-page application. An **npm** package called **serve** is built for this purpose.

To serve your **dist** folder, globally install the **serve** package by opening your command terminal and using the following command:

```
npm install -g serve
# or
yarn global add serve
```

The **serve** command works by allowing you to specify a directory or file to serve:

```
serve [path/to/serve]
```

In your command terminal, make sure you are in the root directory where your Vue prototype **dist** folder is located. To serve your **dist** folder located in this folder directory, run the following command:

```
serve dist
```

The preceding command will display output as follows:

```
$ serve dist
INFO: Accepting connections at http://localhost:5000
```

Figure 3.11: Output in the terminal after running the serve command

Navigate to **http://localhost:5000** and you will see your prototyped project as displayed in the following output:

```
Hello World!
```

We have now learned how to build a Vue component prototype that can be hosted on a website, and how to preview the built files locally. Now, we will see these Vue prototyping concepts used in the next exercise.

EXERCISE 3.02: INSTANT PROTOTYPING USING VUE CLI

In this exercise, you will be creating a Vue component that uses Vue's two-way data binding on the fly. Using instant prototyping makes it possible to utilize Vue syntax quickly, with the added benefits of hot reloading.

To access the code files for this exercise, refer to https://packt.live/35kZrd3.

1. In the **Exercise 3.02** folder, create a file called **prototype.vue**.

2. Open a command-line terminal inside of this folder and use the **vue serve prototype.vue** command.

3. Using **Vetur** in VS Code, write **vue**, and hit the *Tab* button to instantly create the Vue component structure:

```
<template>

</template>

<script>
export default {

}
```

```
</script>

<style>

</style>
```

4. Create a data prop called **heading** with the string value **Prototype Vue Component**, then wrap it around **h1** tags in the template. View the result in **localhost:8080** in your browser:

```
<template>
    <h1>{{ heading }}</h1>
</template>

<script>
export default {
    data() {
        return {
            heading: "Prototype Vue Component"
        }
    }
}
</script>

<style>
    h1 {
        font-family: Arial, Helvetica, sans-serif;
    }
</style>
```

The preceding code will display as shown in the following output:

```
Prototype Vue Component
```

To build this component for production, run the **vue build prototype.vue** command. After running this command, you will have a generated **dist** folder in the same directory as your prototyped component, as shown in *Figure 3.12*:

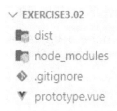

Figure 3.12: The final output for this exercise contains a /dist folder

5. After building your distributable file, run **serve dist** in your command terminal. Then, in your browser, navigate to the localhost URL specified in the terminal. You will be able to view your built prototype as follows:

```
Prototype Vue Component
```

In this exercise, you saw how to run a prototyped Vue component via the command line without installing a full brand-new project. You also saw how to build the new prototype into a distributable file and then serve it. Next, we will look at how you can use the Vue-UI to start and run Vue applications.

THE VUE-UI

The Vue-UI is a graphical interface that allows you to control Vue properties without requiring too much of an understanding of how the command line works or how individual files such as the **package.json** or webpack files are configured. The Vue-UI provides easy access to information such as **module analysis**, which shows the impact of package dependencies on your project that can bloat the file size. You can also review the compiled file size of your project and compare how long your project will take to load across various devices and internet speeds. To get started using the Vue-UI, you can instantiate it anywhere by opening a terminal window and running the **vue ui** command. At the time of writing, the Vue-UI is still in beta. If you run into any issues using this tool, stop the command, and run **vue ui** again.

The Vue-UI can be used on new and existing projects. Generally, you would opt for presets using Vue CLI at the start of the project, such as which **SCSS** compiler, testing framework, or **lint** method to use. Using the Vue-UI, even new Vue developers can easily configure Vue presets at any time, including obscure webpack settings such as the output directory or turning on **sourcemaps**. The following screenshot displays the **General settings** page:

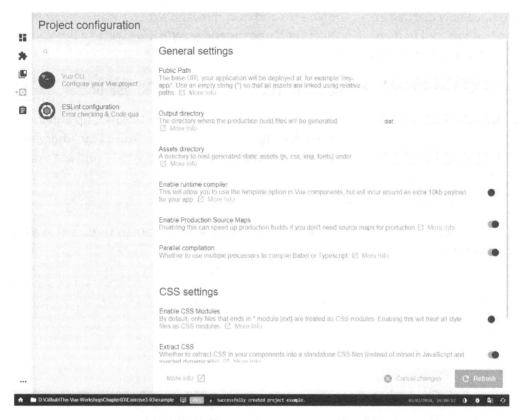

Figure 3.13: Easily configured project settings within the Vue-UI

The **npm** package system is massive. However, it is quite easy for experienced users to navigate. Generally, an experienced developer will install a package via the command line, which will then automatically update the **package.json** file and lock the file with the new package. The locked file is a generated record keeper of interdependencies required for your **npm** packages that you commit with your project. Vue has specific packages called plugins that are special **npm** packages for Vue that not only install a dependency but will usually augment your project for you in helpful ways. For example, if you install the **vue router cli** plugin, it will automatically generate a **route.js** file in your project to get you off the ground faster.

Vuetify is a useful framework when trying to quickly scaffold a more complex component or project, it contains a lot of common UI elements and components such as buttons and input fields so you can focus on the interface rather than building out individual components themselves. If you install **Vuetify** using a Vue CLI plugin package, it will automatically set up Vuetify for you.

We have now learned about the Vue-UI, and how new and experienced developers can use this tool to manage projects and dependencies. Next, we will use the Vue-UI to create and run Vue.js projects.

EXERCISE 3.03: CREATING AND BUILDING A NEW PROJECT FROM THE VUE-UI

In this exercise, you will learn step by step how to use the Vue-UI to set up and install a Vue.js project. You will also be required to install and use the **Vuetify** library as a dependency. Once installed, you will run this project using the Vue-UI and see Vuetify elements running on a page.

To access the code files for this exercise, refer to https://packt.live/35jOsAH.

1. Open a command-line terminal and run the **vue ui** command. You will see the following screen:

Figure 3.14: The Vue-UI without any projects in it

2. Click **Create** to start a new project. Navigate to the folder in which you wish to install the project:

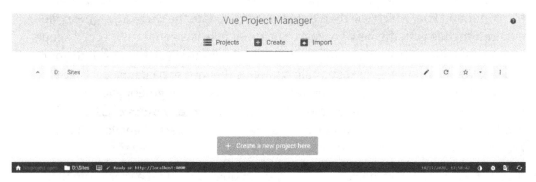

Figure 3.15: Installing the project

3. In the **Project folder** field, write **demo-ui**, choose **yarn** as your package manager and click **Next**, as shown in the following screenshot:

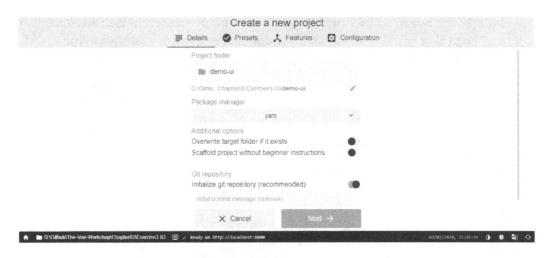

Figure 3.16: Vue-UI's project creation interface

4. Choose **Manual** and you will be taken to the **Features** screen. On this
    screen, select **Babel**, **CSS Preprocessors**, **Linter/Formatter**, and **Use
    config files**. *Figure 3.22* displays a screenshot with these options selected:

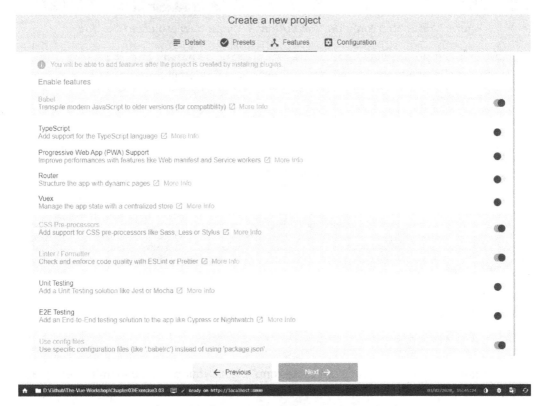

Figure 3.17: Enable features for your new project in the Vue-UI

5. Choose the **Sass/SCSS (with dart-sass)** preprocessor and **ESLint + Prettier** config, and enable the additional lint features shown in the following screenshot:

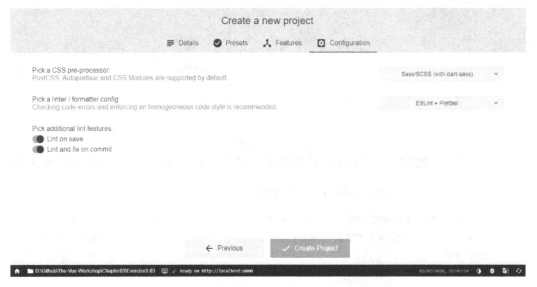

Figure 3.18: Enable configuration options for your new project in the Vue-UI

6. When prompted, select **Continue without saving the preset**, and wait for the project to install. You should see a screen like *Figure 3.19*:

Figure 3.19: Be patient as Vue creates and installs your project dependencies

7. Navigate to the plugins page, click on **Install dependency**, search for **vuetify**, and install **vue-cli-plugin-vuetify**. You can observe on the **Dependencies** page that **vuetify** has been added automatically to the project dependencies list, as follows:

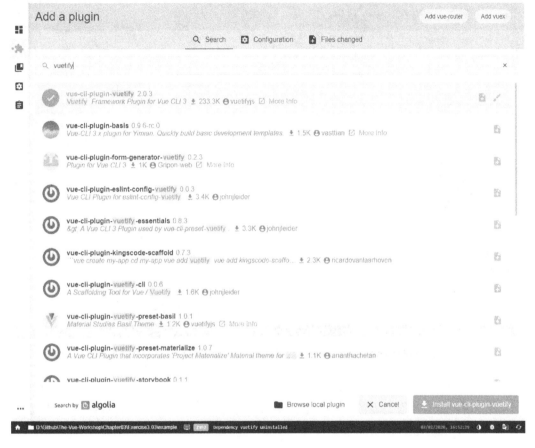

Figure 3.20: Clean interface for dependency search and installation

8. Navigate to the **Project tasks** page and click on the **serve** task. Then, click the **Run task** icon as shown in the following screenshot:

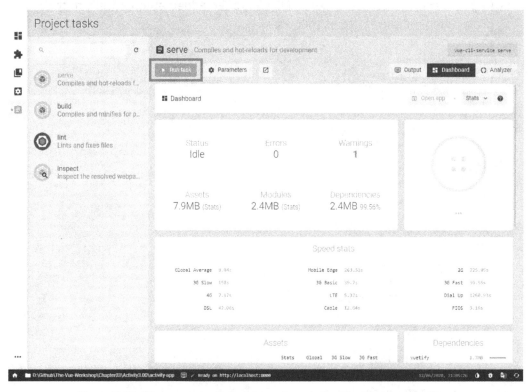

Figure 3.21: The serve task dashboard contains the Run task button

9. Wait for Vue to compile the app. Click on the **Open app** button as shown in *Figure 3.22* when it is ready:

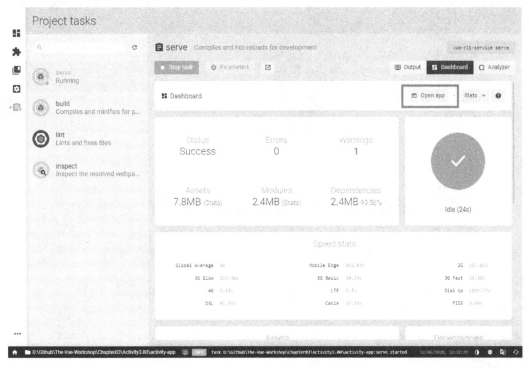

Figure 3.22: The Open app button will take you straight to your app in the browser

You should see your app in the browser as shown in the following screenshot:

Welcome to Vuetify

For help and collaboration with other Vuetify developers,
please join our online Discord Community

What's next?

Explore components   Select a layout   Frequently Asked Questions

Important Links

Documentation   Chat   Made with Vuetify   Twitter   Articles

Ecosystem

vuetify-loader   github   awesome-vuetify

Figure 3.23: On http://localhost:8080, you should see a Vuetify styled page

10. To prepare this project for production, go back into the Vue-UI browser tab and click on the **build** tab in **Project tasks**. Click on the **Parameters** button next to the **Start Task** button. Turn on **Modern mode** and make sure **Output directory** is set to **dist**. **Modern mode** transpiles your code into two versions, one that is lightweight and targeted to modern browsers, and another that is verbose and used to support older browsers. This will be where you find your files after compilation. Your screen should display something like the following screenshot:

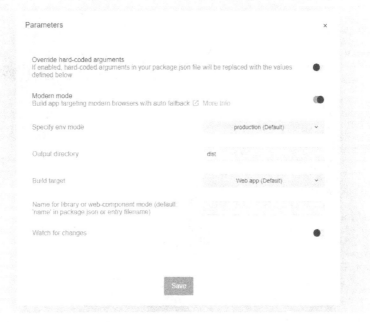

Figure 3.24: Vue-UI build parameters

11. To build this project for production, click on the **Start Task** button and let it run.

> **NOTE**
>
> You do not need to stop the **serve** task to complete this.

When the task is complete, your screen will display as follows:

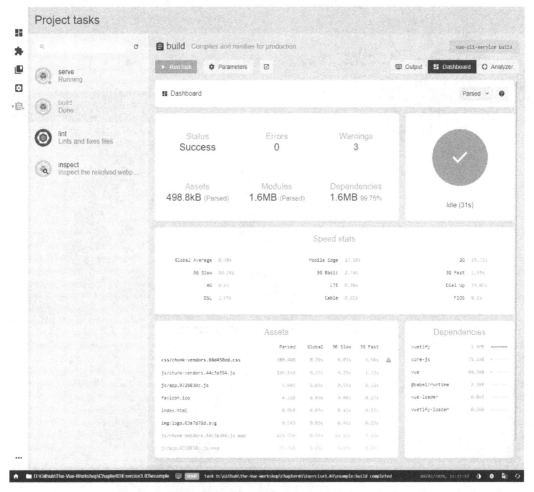

Figure 3.25: When a build is complete, you have a dashboard of useful analytics

In this exercise, you saw how to create a brand-new project, configure presets, use the **serve** task to run an application, and how to build a project for production through the Vue-UI. You should feel comfortable enough to add new Vue CLI plugins and manage npm package dependencies.

VUE.JS DEVTOOLS

Vue.js DevTools is a browser extension for Chrome and Firefox, and an Electron desktop app that can be run from your computer to help you debug locally run Vue.js projects. These tools do not work in production or remotely run projects (for example, if you serve a production-built project or view a website online). You can download the Vue.js DevTools extension from the Chrome extension page, as seen in the following screenshot:

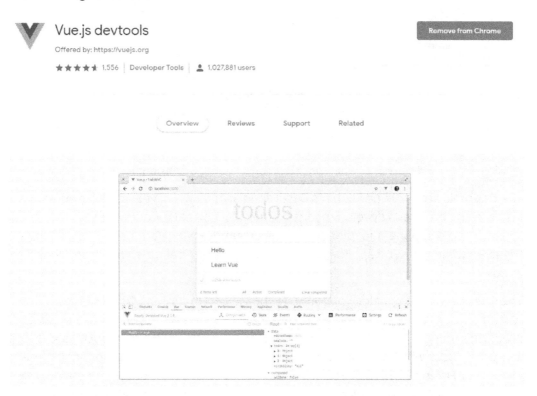

Figure 3.26: The Vue.js DevTools Chrome extension page

You can also download the Vue.js DevTools extension from Firefox (https://addons. mozilla.org/en-US/firefox/addon/vue-js-devtools/):

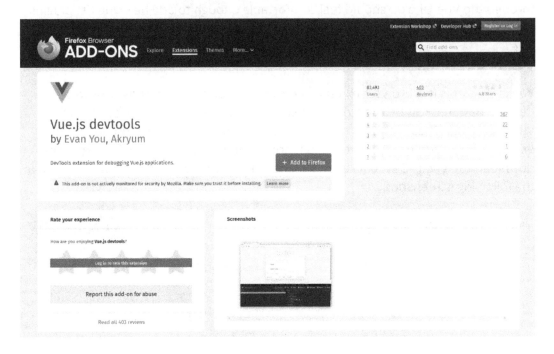

Figure 3.27: The Vue.js DevTools Firefox extension page

The DevTools are a Vue developer's best friend as they will reveal useful information inside of the browser's developer console that you normally would not see. This includes Vue component loading performance and tracking various events that are triggered while your Vue application runs. There are several tabs, which we'll look at now.

The **Components** tab helps you navigate the virtual **Document Object Model (DOM)** of your Vue components on the left panel. On the right, you will see the data properties that are loaded per component. There are small shortcuts such as **< > Inspect DOM**, which will take you directly to the location of this component in the Chrome or Firefox DOM tree. Select the Vue element directly from within the browser UI using the **Select** target icon, highlighted in the following *Figure 3.28* (the top-right corner of the left panel).

Your screen should look as follows:

Figure 3.28: The Components tab in Vue.js DevTools

Vuex - Using this tab, you can navigate the Vuex global state. You will see a transcript of mutations that occur within your Vuex store, as follows:

Figure 3.29: The Vuex tab in Vue.js DevTools

There will be more on this in future chapters.

Events – Using this tab, you can navigate custom events that are emitted from your components. More on this in future chapters. By default, events will be recorded as seen in the following screenshot:

Figure 3.30: The Events tab in Vue.js DevTools

Routing – Using this tab, you can observe routing history and events within this pane. There will be more on this in future chapters. When routing events occur, they will be recorded as shown in the following screenshot:

Figure 3.31: The Routing tab in Vue.js DevTools

Performance – Using this tab, you can navigate to the performance area that records the frame rate and render time of your components as your app is running to optimize your end user experience. When you click the **Start** button to collect performance metrics, they will be shown as blue bars, as seen in the following screenshot:

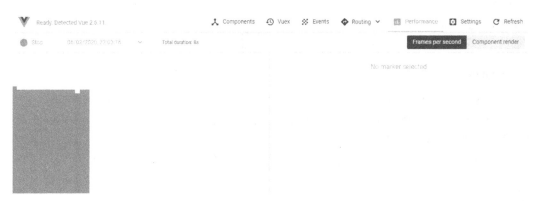

Figure 3.32: The Performance tab in Vue.js DevTools

The blue bar chart in *Figure 3.32* represents the load time in milliseconds.

Settings – Using this tab, you can customize your Vue.js DevTools experience as shown in the following screenshot. For new developers, the default settings do not need to be changed:

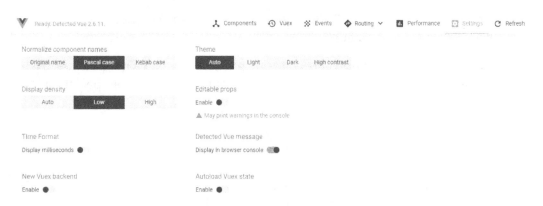

Figure 3.33: The Settings tab in Vue.js DevTools

Refresh – Clicking this button will refresh your Vue.js DevTools instance in the browser.

We have now learned about the Vue.js DevTools, which will help you when developing components in your next Vue application. Next, we will build a Vue component and use the Vue.js DevTools to inspect the code and manipulate the local state of data inside the component.

EXERCISE 3.04: DEBUGGING A VUE APPLICATION USING DEVTOOLS

In this exercise, you will build a basic component that uses several Vue.js patterns you have explored in previous chapters, and you will explore these patterns using DevTools. Ensure you are using either Chrome or Firefox and have DevTools installed. You will use Vue.js DevTools to inspect the code and manipulate the local state of data inside the component.

To access the code files for this exercise, refer to https://packt.live/3eLIcVe.

1. Navigate to the **Exercise3.04** project folder and open it up in VS Code. In your command prompt, install the required scripts by running the **yarn** command.

2. In the same command prompt that **yarn** used, run the project using **yarn serve**.

3. Navigate to **localhost:8080** in your browser so you can view the changes made in the following steps.

4. Create reactive data in **App.vue** by adding a data prop, **frameworkList**, filled with an array of strings, and an **input** prop with a value of an empty string:

```
<script>
export default {
  data() {
    return {
      frameworkList: [
        'Vue',
        'React',
        'Backbone',
        'Ember',
        'Knockout',
        'jQuery',
        'Angular',
      ],

      input: '',
    }
  },
}
</script>
```

5. Next, create a computed property called **computedList** to filter the **frameworkList** prop using the **input** prop value:

```
  ...
  computed: {
    computedList() {
      return this.frameworkList.filter(item => {
        return item.toLowerCase().includes(this.input.
          toLowerCase())
      })
    },
  },
  ...
```

6. In the Vue **template** block, add an **input** field that is bound using v-model to the **input** data prop and loop out **computedList** in a list. Add some styling (optional):

```
<template>
  <div id="app" class="container">
    <h1>Vue devtools debugging</h1>

    <input type="text" placeholder="Filter list" v-model=
      "input" />

    <ul>
      <li v-for="(item, i) in computedList" :key="i">{{ item }}
      </li>
    </ul>
  </div>
</template>
<style lang="scss" scoped>
#app {
  font-family: Avenir, Helvetica, Arial, sans-serif;
  -webkit-font-smoothing: antialiased;
  -moz-osx-font-smoothing: grayscale;
  text-align: center;
  color: #2c3e50;
  margin-top: 60px;
}
ul {
  max-width: 200px;
  margin: 0 auto;
  list-style: none;
  padding: 0;

  > li {
    background: #42b983;
    color: white;
    padding: 6px;
    border-radius: 6px;
    margin-bottom: 2px;
    max-width: 200px;
  }
}
```

```
input {
  padding: 10px 6px;
  margin: 20px 10px 10px 10px;
}
</style>
```

The preceding code will generate the following screenshot:

Figure 3.34: Checkpoint – your list is filterable

7. In your browser, where you can view your app, *right-click* and choose `Inspect` to open the developer console or use the shortcut *Ctrl + Shift + J* (Mac users: *Cmd + Shift + J*) and navigate to the **Vue** tab. This should generate a screenshot as follows:

Figure 3.35: Chrome extension for Vue.js DevTools

8. By default, you will be in the **Components** tab. Select **Anonymous Component** to inspect the data associated with that component. Click into the **Filter list** input field and type **V**. You will observe two things occurring: in the right-hand panel, the data prop **input** now has the value of **V** and the computed list. **computedList** now only contains the string **Vue**. In the browser, this data will be reflected in the UI, as seen in *Figure 3.36*:

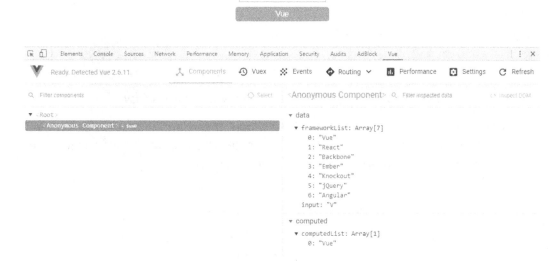

Figure 3.36: Chrome extension for Vue.js DevTools

9. Edit the data directly in the right-hand panel by clicking on the **Pencil** icon next to the **input** prop, and type **R**. The DOM will reactively update for the direct change made to the input prop from the DevTools as shown in the following screenshot:

Figure 3.37: Editing live values in your Vue project is easy

After changing the value in the Vue.js DevTools, the value will reactively change in the UI, where the input value in this example is now **R**, which then triggers the reactive **computedList** array to only show values containing the letter **r**, as displayed in *Figure 3.38*:

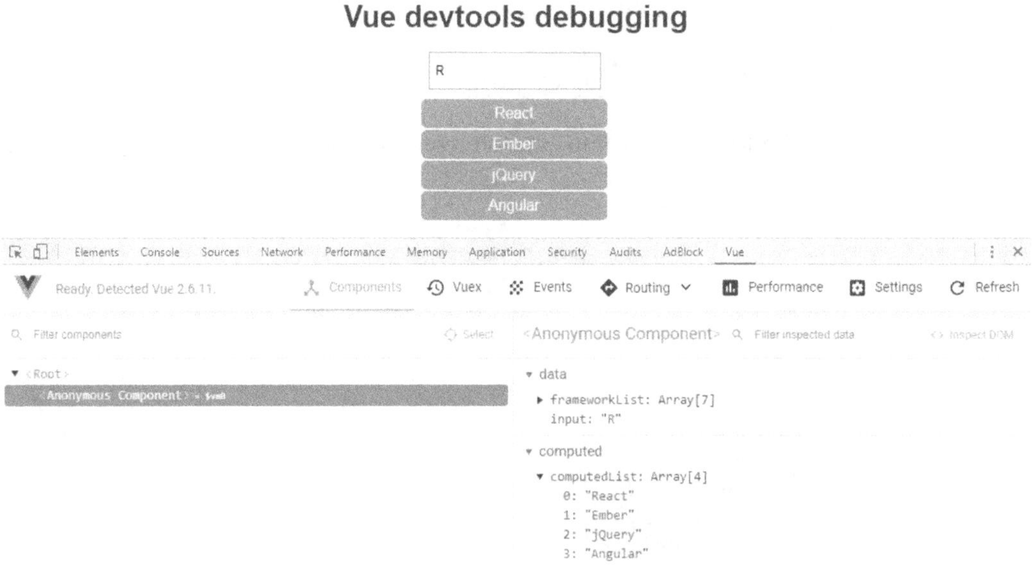

Vue devtools debugging

Figure 3.38: Computed list update to the value written inside of DevTools

10. Go to the **Performance** tab, click on the **Component render** toggle, and click the **Start** button. While this is running, search for several items by writing in the input box **A**, then **B**, then **V**. As you type text into the input box, you will see the performance metrics as blue bars, as seen in the following screenshot:

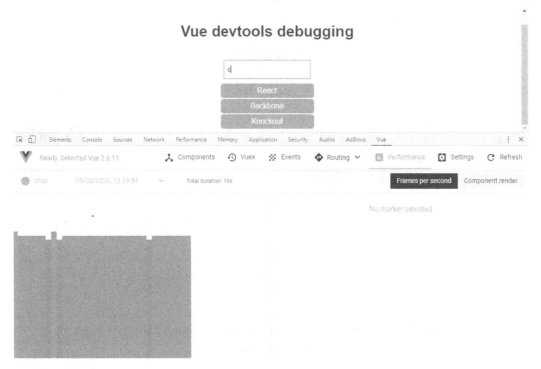

Figure 3.39: Computed list update to the value written inside of DevTools

11. Click **Stop** and observe the **millisecond** timing in the **Component render** tab, which reflects how long it took your component to load, as shown in the following screenshot:

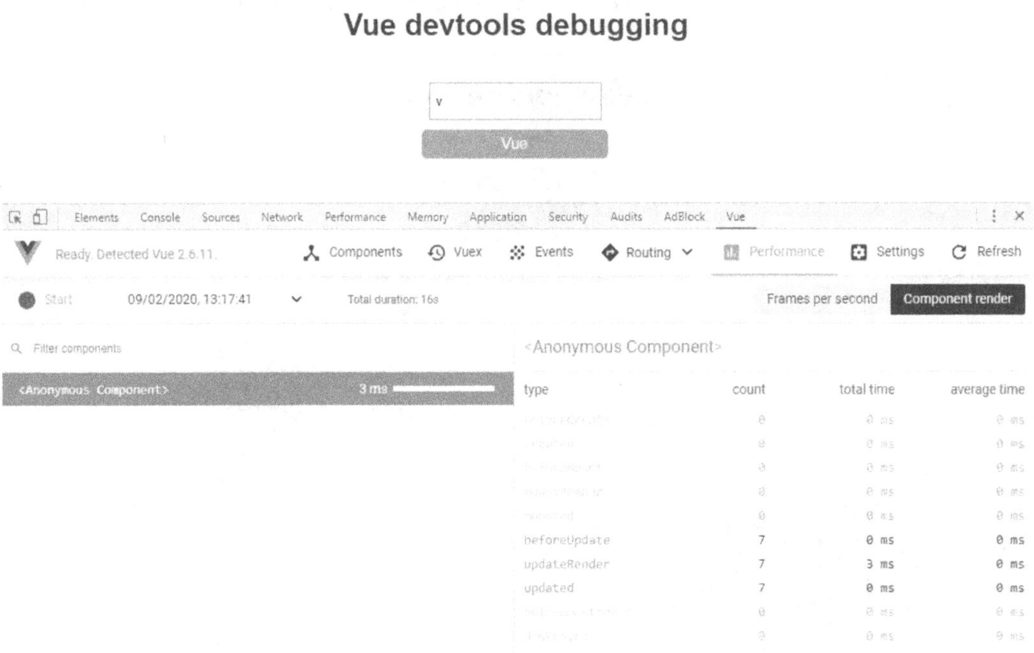

Vue devtools debugging

Figure 3.40: Selecting the component in the right-hand panel will open the lifecycle hooks on the left

> **NOTE**
>
> Repeating the test will allow you to compare benchmarks, however, if you refresh the page you will lose them.

At the end of this exercise, you have seen how to use Vue.js DevTools to navigate a basic component in a Vue application through the **Components** tab. You know how to observe and edit data in DevTools, having seen that computed properties will react to your data prop changes. You know where the **Performance** tab is and how to use it when creating a Vue application.

ACTIVITY 3.01: BUILDING A VUE APPLICATION USING THE VUE-UI AND THE VUETIFY COMPONENT LIBRARY

In this activity, you will build a Vue project using the command line, then import it into the Vue-UI and compare the build size before and after Vuetify installation. This will test your ability to control the various Vue tools at your disposal and highlight the real-world scenarios where you would use these tools.

The following steps will help you complete the activity:

1. Use Vue CLI to create a new project using the Babel presets.

2. Use the Vue-UI to import your newly created project.

3. Use the VueUI to install the `Vuetify` plugin and use Vuetify's Vue components in the project.

4. Copy a premade layout from the Vuetify website or build your own using their components: https://vuetifyjs.com/en/getting-started/pre-made-layouts.

The expected outcome is as follows:

Figure 3.41: The final outcome

This activity also has a toggleable menu, as displayed in *Figure 3.42*:

Figure 3.42: Output displaying a toggleable menu

NOTE

The solution for this activity can be found on page 652.

After the activity has been completed, you should be able to use Vue CLI and the Vue-UI to manage your future Vue projects. You will find that there are situations where both tools can be used interchangeably or in conjunction with each other, depending on what you are more comfortable with.

SUMMARY

In this chapter, you were introduced to the multiple Vue.js tools available to help you maintain and manage your Vue applications. You created Vue.js projects from both the command line and the new Vue-UI, installed new dependencies, and served and built your projects from both those interfaces. You can use these tools together or separately – whichever you feel more comfortable with. Vue.js DevTools has a lot of quality-of-life features that will assist you on your journey through the more advanced portions of this book and as you begin to pass props between your components and route pages together.

In the next chapter, you will learn about more advanced Vue component concepts such as passing and validating information between different components by using data props and template slots.

NESTING COMPONENTS (MODULARITY)

OVERVIEW

In this chapter, you will discover how to modularize a Vue.js application using component hierarchies and nesting. This chapter introduces concepts such as props, events, prop validation, and slots. You will learn how to contrast them and identify which concept should be applied based on the situation. You will then practice implementing a component that encapsulates direct DOM manipulation using refs. You will also learn how to identify component composition scenarios where slots, named slots, and scoped slots can be used. You will then identify when to abstract functionality into filters.

By the end of this chapter, you will be able to define communication interfaces between components using props, events, and validators. You will be exposed to refs to wrap JavaScript libraries as Vue.js components and identify the pitfalls of the Vue.js context when using components.

INTRODUCTION

In the previous chapter, we learned how to initialize, build, and debug a simple Vue.js application. In this chapter, we will have a closer look at how to leverage component composition to enable code re-usability.

Reusable and extensible components are core to building products around a component library. A component library allows a team to build a project with high velocity and high consistency.

If a component library in Vue.js does not expose the right extension points, what often happens is that the component from the library is copied over into the application's code base. This leads to duplicated code and reduced cohesion from a design point of view.

In *Chapter 3*, *Vue CLI*, we learned how to create simple components in Vue. Components are Vue instances that can be instantiated and rendered multiple times. Since there can only be one root component, most components in an application are rendered by another component. For parent components to communicate with their children, we use props and prop passing.

PASSING PROPS

Props in the context of Vue.js are fields, defined in a child component, that are accessible on that component's instance (**this**) and in the component's **template**.

The value of a prop depends on what the parent passes in its **template** to the child component at render time.

DEFINING A SIMPLE COMPONENT THAT TAKES PROPS

Let's look at a simple **Hello** single-file component. This can be found in a **./src/components/Hello.vue** file (in a *Vue CLI-generated* project). Note how the **who** value is set in the **props** array and that it is interpolated as a value using **{{ who }}**. The **props** property of a Vue.js component can be an array of strings or an object literal.

When a value is defined in **props**, it is then accessible as an instance variable in the **template** section of the Vue.js component:

```
<template>
  <div>
    <h1>Hello {{ who }}</h1>
  </div>
```

```
</template>
<script>
export default {
  props: ['who']
}
</script>
```

We will now learn how to render a component using props.

RENDERING A COMPONENT WITH PROPS

What follows is a demonstration of how to use the **Hello** component in our Vue.js application.

First, we need to import and then set it in the **components** property of the Vue.js component that wants to render this imported component.

Then, in the **template** section, we need to render **<Hello>** with the **who** attribute set to **"Vue.js"**, as follows:

```
<template>
  <div id="app">
    <Hello who="Vue.js"/>
  </div>
</template>


<script>
import Hello from './components/Hello.vue'

export default {
  components: {
    Hello
  }
}
</script>
```

This will render the following on the page:

```
Hello Vue.js
```

We have now seen how to use a component and pass it with props in a Vue.js application. This is useful for code reuse and for abstracting application behavior into component-sized chunks.

Next, we will learn how to work with registered components.

COMPONENT REGISTRATION TRICKS

There are a few things to note with regard to the **components** property.

Registered components are available both as **CamelCaseName** and as **kebab-case-name**, so if we changed the template section shown in the previous example to use **<hello />** instead of **<Hello />**, it would work without any issues:

```
<template>
  <div id="app">
    <hello who="Vue.js"/>
  </div>
</template>
```

The updated template renders the same in the browser, as shown in the following output:

```
Hello Vue.js
```

The **components** property tends to leverage ES6 shorthand property syntax. Shorthand property syntax means that instead of writing **{ Hello: Hello }**, we can write **{ Hello }**. We can see it in action in the following example, which registers the **Hello** component:

```
import Hello from './components/Hello.vue'
export default {
  components: {
    Hello
  }
}
```

Vue's **components** declaration is not aware of the component name. It uses the key in the **components** object to register it against both the camelCase and kebab-case names:

```
<template>
  <div id="app">
    <Hey who="Vue.js"/>
  </div>
</template>

<script>
import Hello from './components/Hello.vue'

export default {
  components: {
  Hey: Hello
  }
}
</script>
```

The preceding code will generate the following output:

```
Hello Vue.js
```

We have now learned how to register components in Vue.js using the **components** property and ES6 shorthand object property syntax.

Next, we will look at a practical example of a **Greeting** component.

EXERCISE 4.01: IMPLEMENTING A GREETING COMPONENT

Using our knowledge of how props can be passed from a parent component to a child component, we will create a component that lets you customize both the greeting (for example, **Hello**, **Hey**, or **Hola**) and who is addressed (for example, **World**, **Vue. js**, or **JavaScript developers**).

To access the code files for this exercise, refer to https://packt.live/35jGd7B.

Follow these steps to complete this exercise:

1. Create a new file named **Greeting.vue** in the **./src/components** directory. This will be our single-file component.

2. Start by scaffolding the component with empty **template** and **script** tags:

```
<template>
  <div>Empty</div>
</template>
<script>
export default {}
</script>
```

3. Next, we need to tell Vue.js that our component expects props. For this, we will add a **props** property to our component definition (the object that's set to **export default** in the **script** section) and add a **greeting** and **who** prop to it:

```
export default {
  props: ['greeting', 'who']
}
```

4. Now, we want to render **greeting** and **who**. As we have seen, when values are defined in **props**, they are available at the top level of **template**:

```
<template>
  <div>{{ greeting }} {{ who }}</div>
</template>
```

We can now render the **Greeting** component from **App.vue**.

5. Open the **src/App.vue** file and import the **Greeting** component from **./src/components/Greeting.vue** into the **script** section:

```
<script>
import Greeting from './components/Greeting.vue'
</script>
```

6. Next, register the **Greeting** component in **components**:

```
<script>
export default {
  components: {
    Greeting
  }
}
</script>
```

7. Now that the component has been registered, we can render it in **template**:

```
<template>
  <div id="app">
    <Greeting greeting="Hey" who="JavaScript"/>
  </div>
</template>
```

You will see the following in your browser (make sure you have run **npm install** and **npm run serve** in the **Exercise4.01** directory):

```
Hey JavaScript
```

8. Modify the **greeting** and **who** prop using the attribute values in **template**:

```
<template>
  <div id="app">
    <Greeting greeting="Hi" who="Everyone"/>
  </div>
</template>
```

Upon running the preceding code, you should see an output similar to the following in your browser (make sure you have run **npm install**, followed by **npm run serve**, in the **Exercise4.01** directory):

> **NOTE**
>
> Yarn includes an equivalent of **npm run** command under **yarn**. For example, instead of **npm install** and **npm run serve**, we could use **yarn install** and **yarn serve** commands respectively.

```
Hi Everyone
```

In this exercise, we have learned how props and prop passing can be used to increase reuse scenarios of a component by generalizing it. Instead of the component rendering static data, its parent passes it the data to render.

In the next section, we will learn how to set prop values dynamically.

DYNAMIC PROPS WITH DATA BINDING

The examples we have seen up to now have used hard-coded attribute values as props. But what if we want to pass parent instance data from the parent to child?

This is where **binding** comes in. The prop/attribute binding syntax in Vue.js is **v-bind:**, but you can use **:** for shorthand; they are equivalent.

The **who** prop of **Greeting** is bound to the **appWho** app component's instance property:

```
<template>
  <div id="app">
    <Hello v-bind:who="appWho"/>
  </div>
</template>

<script>
import Hello from './components/Hello.vue'

export default {
  components: {
    Hello
  },
```

```
    data() {
      return {
        appWho: 'Vue.js'
      }
    }
  }
</script>
```

In shorthand, **template** would look as follows:

```
<template>
  <div id="app">
    <Hello :who="appWho"/>
  </div>
</template>
```

Both versions will output the following view to the browser:

```
Hello Vue.js
```

> **NOTE**
>
> **v-bind:prop-name** and **:prop-name** have a striking similarity since
> the delimiter between **v-bind** and **prop-name** is **:** (a semicolon). In
> Vue.js single-file components, since templates are compiled at build time,
> they are functionally equivalent.

An example to showcase that the values have been **synced** (propagated) from the
parent component (**App**) to the child (**Hello**) is as follows, with two buttons that
change the audience of the **Hello** message.

The buttons call a component method called **setWho** with **JavaScript** or
Everyone, depending on the button. This **setWho** function updates the **appWho**
instance property:

```
<template>
  <div id="app">
    <Hello :who="appWho"/>
    <button @click="setWho('JavaScript')">JavaScript</button>
    <button @click="setWho('Everyone')">Everyone</button>
  </div>
</template>
```

```
<script>
import Hello from './components/Hello.vue'

export default {
  components: {
    Hello
  },
  data() {
    return {
      appWho: 'Vue.js'
    }
  },
  methods: {
    setWho(newWho) {
      this.appWho = newWho
    }
  }
}
</script>
```

The initial output to the browser displays `Hello Vue.js`, as shown in the following screenshot:

Hello Vue.js

JavaScript   Everyone

Figure 4.1: Initial Hello Vue.js output in the browser

When clicking the `JavaScript` button, the `appWho` variable updates, as does the bound `Hello` component's `who` prop. Thus, `Hello JavaScript` is displayed, as follows:

Hello JavaScript

JavaScript   Everyone

Figure 4.2: Hello JavaScript after clicking the JavaScript button

When clicking the **Everyone** button, the **appWho** variable updates, as does the bound **Hello** component's **who** prop. Thus, **Hello Everyone** is displayed, as follows:

Hello Everyone

JavaScript Everyone

Figure 4.3: Hello Everyone after clicking the Everyone button

We have now seen how to bind props to values so that they are kept in sync.

The majority of Vue.js applications leverage components beyond modularizing the rendered components (as we did with the **Greeting** and **Hello** components).

As we have seen, we are able to bind props so that any update that's made to a value in the parent will cause an update in the child component.

EXERCISE 4.02: PASSING PROPS THAT CHANGE OVER TIME

To know which greeting to use, we will implement a **greeter** app that has multiple greetings and cycles through them.

To access the code files for this exercise, refer to https://packt.live/3kovKfo.

Follow these steps to complete this exercise:

1. Create a **./src/components/Greeting.vue** component and initialize it with our previously implemented **Greeting** component. This is how we'll display the greetings:

```
<template>
  <div>{{ greeting }} {{ who }}</div>
</template>
<script>
export default {
  props: ['greeting', 'who']
}
</script>
```

2. In the `./src/App.vue` component, import `./src/components/Greeting.vue` as a **Greeting** and register it as a component so that you can render it:

```
<script>
import Greeting from './components/Greeting.vue'

export default {
  components: {
    Greeting
  }
}
</script>
```

3. In the **script** section, create a **data** top-level method that returns an initial **greeting** and **who**:

```
export default {
  data() {
    return {
      greeting: 'Hello',
      who: 'Vue.js'
    }
  }
}
```

4. Render the current **greeting** and **who** using the **Greeting** component:

```
<template>
  <div id="app">
    <Greeting :greeting="greeting" :who="who"/>
  </div>
</template>
```

Your browser will display a message, as follows (make sure you have run **npm install** and **npm run serve** in the **Exercise4.02** directory):

> **NOTE**
>
> The following code requires that you have knowledge of computed properties, which we covered in *Chapter 2, Working with Data*. Please go back to that chapter now if you need a refresher.

5. We will now add some **greeting/who** pairings as an array to the
   script section:

```
<script>
// imports
const possibleGreetings = [
    { greeting: 'Hello', who: 'Vue.js' },
    { greeting: 'Hey', who: 'Everyone' },
    { greeting: 'Hi', who: 'JavaScript' }
]
// components export
</script>
```

6. Let's refactor the **data** method so that it only stores the default index and
   creates computed properties that look up the index to generate a **greeting**
   and **who** based on the current index (with an intermediary **currentGreeting**
   computed property):

```
<script>
// imports and greetings
export default {
  // components definition
  data() {
    return {
      currentIndex: 0
    }
  },
  computed: {
    currentGreeting() {
      return possibleGreetings[this.currentIndex]
    },
    greeting() {
      return this.currentGreeting.greeting
    },
    who() {
      return this.currentGreeting.who
    }
  }
}
</script>
```

At this point, the application should still display the same greeting in the browser, as shown in the following output:

```
Hello Vue.js
```

> **NOTE**
>
> As computed properties clean the code up, we did not need to update our template. Instead, we have replaced the **greeting** and **who** instance properties with computed properties of the same name.

7. Let's add a way to cycle through these **greetings**. This will involve a button that, upon being clicked, will call a **newGreeting** function in our **template**:

```
<template>
  <div id="app">
    <Greeting :greeting="greeting" :who="who"/>
    <button @click="newGreeting()">New Greeting</button>
  </div>
</template>
```

8. Next, we need to implement **newGreeting** in **script**. **newGreeting** should move to the next greeting (by incrementing **currentIndex**). Alternatively, if we have already reached the end of the **possibleGreetings** array, it should reset **currentIndex**:

```
<script>
  // imports and greetings
export default {
    // other component properties
  methods: {
    newGreeting() {
      this.currentIndex = this.currentIndex ===
        possibleGreetings.length - 1
        ? 0
        : this.currentIndex + 1
    }
  }
}
</script>
```

On initial load and after **3n** clicks of the **New Greeting** button, the application displays **Hello Vue.js**, as shown in the following screenshot:

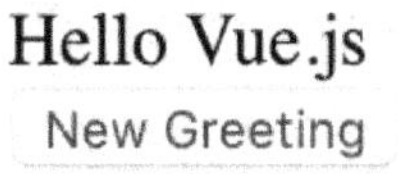

Hello Vue.js

New Greeting

Figure 4.4: Hello Vue.js after 3n button clicks

After the first click and after **3n + 1** clicks of the **New Greeting** button, the application displays **Hey Everyone**, as follows:

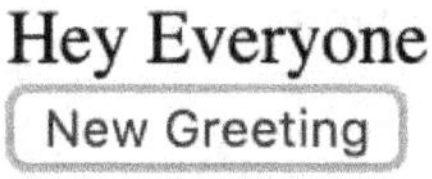

Hey Everyone

New Greeting

Figure 4.5: Hey Everyone after 3n + 1 button clicks

After the second click and after **3n + 2** clicks of the **New Greeting** button, the application displays **Hi JavaScript**, as follows:

Hi JavaScript

New Greeting

Figure 4.6: Hi JavaScript after 3n + 2 button clicks

> **NOTE**
>
> This code can be improved further; for example, **possibleGreetings. length - 1** is constant since we never add or remove greetings. Instead of computing on every **newGreeting** call, we could compute it once, outside of the **newGreeting** method. Reading the length of an array and simple arithmetic (**-1**) is not too costly but this is a good refresher on thinking in terms of mutable versus constant values.

With that, we have seen how props and prop binding can be used to communicate about changing data from parent components to child components they render. To scale a code base or share code widely, it is helpful to give hints to the consumer of the code when they are using it incorrectly.

Next, we will learn how to add type hints to our component's props to ensure they are used correctly.

PROP TYPING AND VALIDATION

Props define the interface of Vue.js components. As JavaScript is a dynamically typed language, Vue.js provides a tool we can use to validate the shape and types of props.

To validate prop types, the **props** component property in its object literal form should be used (as opposed to the simpler array form).

PRIMITIVE PROP VALIDATION

Say we want a **Repeat.vue** component that takes a **times** prop, as well as a **content** prop. We can define the following:

```
<template>
  <div>
    <span v-for="r in repetitions" :key="r">
      {{ content }}
    </span>
  </div>
</template>
<script>
export default {
  props: ['times', 'content'],
  computed: {
    repetitions() {
      return Array.from({ length: this.times });
    }
  }
}
</script>
```

Our **Repeat** component would be consumed as follows:

```
<template>
  <div id="app">
    <Repeat :times="count" content="Repeat." />
    <button @click="increment()">Repeat</button>
  </div>
</template>

<script>
import Repeat from './components/Repeat.vue'
```

```
export default {
  components: {
    Repeat
  },
  data() {
    return { count: 1 }
  },
  methods: {
    increment() {
      this.count += 1
    }
  }
}
</script>
```

The preceding code will lead to the following output in the browser:

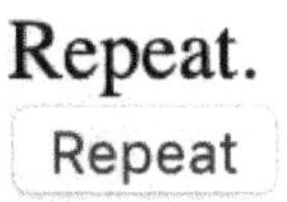

Repeat.

Repeat

Figure 4.7: Output of the repeat example in action (no clicks)

After clicking the **Repeat** button a few times, the **Repeat** component will repeat an additional time for every click generating an output, as follows:

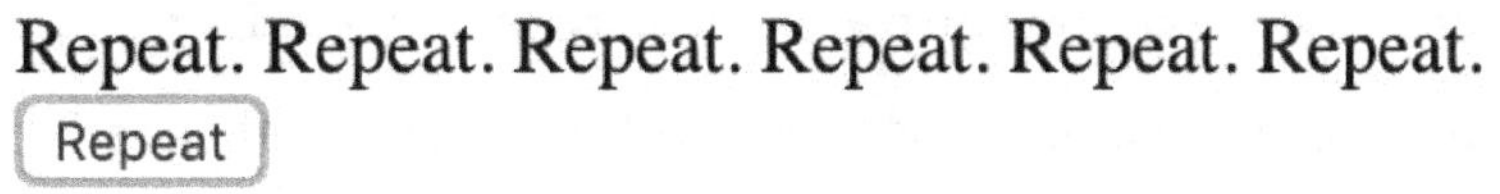

Repeat. Repeat. Repeat. Repeat. Repeat. Repeat.

Repeat

Figure 4.8: Output of the repeat example after five clicks

For this component to work properly, we need **times** to be a **Number**, and ideally **content** to be a **String**.

> **NOTE**
>
> Now is a good time to remind students of the JavaScript primitive types: **String**, **Number**, **Boolean**, **Array**, **Object**, **Date**, **Function**, and **Symbol**.

Vue.js supports all the JavaScript primitive type constructors as type hints in the **props** field.

In this instance, we are defining the **times** prop as a **Number** and the **content** props as a **String**:

```
<script>
export default {
  props: {
    times: {
      type: Number
    },
    content: {
      type: String
    }
  },
  // rest of component definition
}
</script>
```

To consume this component, we can update the **script** section as follows:

```
<script>
import Repeat from './components/RepeatTyped.vue'
// no other changes
</script>
```

The component still behaves the same in the **happy path** case, where the props being passed for **times** and **content** are a **Number** and a **String**, respectively.

If we update **App** so that it wilfully passes props of the wrong type. In this case, **times** is a **String** and **content** is a **Number**.

```
<template>
  <div id="app">
    <Repeat :times="count" :content="55" />
  </div>
</template>

<script>
// no changes to imports
export default {
  data() {
    return { count: 'no-number-here' }
  },
```

```
    // other properties
  }
</script>
```

Here, the **Repeat** component will fail to render, and the following errors will be logged to the console:

```
⊗ ▶ [Vue warn]: Invalid prop: type check failed for prop "times". Expected
    Number with value NaN, got String with value "no-number-here".

    found in

    ---> <Repeat> at src/components/RepeatTyped.vue
           <App> at src/App.vue
             <Root>
⊗ ▶ [Vue warn]: Invalid prop: type check failed for prop "content". Expected
    String with value "55", got Number with value 55.

    found in

    ---> <Repeat> at src/components/RepeatTyped.vue
           <App> at src/App.vue
             <Root>
```

Figure 4.9: Mistyping Vue.js prop errors

The **times** prop check fails with a message that explains that we passed a **String** as a prop that was supposed to be a **Number**:

```
Invalid prop: type check failed for prop "times". Expected Number with
value NaN, got String with value "no-number-here"
```

The **content** prop check fails with a message that explains that we passed a **Number** as a prop that was supposed to be a **String**:

```
Invalid prop: type check failed for prop "content". Expected String with
value "55", got Number with value 55
```

> **NOTE**
>
> As per the Vue.js documentation, *null and undefined values will pass any type validation*, which means that the type validations are not foolproof and that it can make sense to add custom validation to a component.

UNION AND CUSTOM PROP TYPES

In the previous example, we were just rendering the content, so it didn't matter what type it was.

Vue.js supports union types. A union type is a type that can be one of many other types. For example, **String** or **Number** is a **union** type.

Union types in Vue.js are represented using an array for the prop's **type** property, for example, to support numbers and strings as **content**:

```
<script>
export default {
  props: {
    // other prop definitions
    content: {
      type: [String, Number]
    }
  }
  // rest of component definition
}
</script>
```

In this case, we can consume the **RepeatTyped** component as follows without errors:

```
<template>
  <div id="app">
    <Repeat :times="3" :content="55" />
  </div>
</template>
```

This displays **55** three times. Here, **55** was passed as a **Number**, which our component now supports. This can be seen in the following output:

```
55 55 55
```

Any valid constructor can be used as the prop type. For example, **Promise** or a **custom User** constructor can be used. In the following example, we are defining a **TodoList** component prop interface:

```
<script>
import User from './user.js'
export default {
  props: {
```

```
      todoListPromise: {
        type: Promise
      },
      currentUser: {
        type: User
      }
    }
  }
}
</script>
```

The prop interface that's exposed by this component can be used as follows:

```
<template>
  <div>
    <template v-if="todosPromise && !error">
      <TodoList
        :todoListPromise="todosPromise"
        :currentUser="currentUser"
      />
    </template>
    {{ error }}
  </div>
</template>
<script>
import TodoList from './components/TodoList.vue'
import User from './components/user.js'

const currentUser = new User()

export default {
  components: {
    TodoList
  },
  mounted() {
    this.todosPromise = fetch('/api/todos').then(res => {
      if (res.ok) {
        return res.json()
      }
      throw new Error('Could not fetch todos')
    }).catch(error => {
      this.error = error
```

```
    })
  },
  data() {
    return { currentUser, error: null }
  }
}
</script>
```

We have now seen how to use the **union** and **custom** types to validate Vue.js props.

> **NOTE**
>
> Vue.js uses **instanceof** internally, so make sure any custom types are instantiated using the relevant constructor.
>
> Passing **null** or **undefined** will fail the **instanceof** check for **Array** and **Object**.
>
> Passing an array will pass the **instanceof** check for **Object** since, in JavaScript, **Array** instances are also **Object** instances.

CUSTOM VALIDATION OF ARRAYS, OBJECT SHAPES, AND MORE WITH VALIDATORS

Vue.js allows custom validators to be used as props using the **validator** property. This allows us to implement deep checks regarding object and array shape as custom logic for primitive types.

To illustrate this, let's look at a **CustomSelect** component. On a basic level, the prop interface for a **select** comprises an array of **options** and a **selected** option. Each option should have a **label** that represents what is displayed in the select and a **value** that corresponds to the value passed to an API. For example, the **selected** option can be empty or should correspond to the **value** field for one of our **options**.

Our **CustomSelect** can be implemented as follows in a naive way (no validation of the inputs):

```
<template>
  <select>
    <option
      :selected="selected === o.value"
      v-for="o in options"
      :key="o.value"
```

```
      >
        {{ o.label }}
      </option>
    </select>
</template>
<script>
export default {
  props: {
    selected: {
      type: String
    },
    options: {
      type: Array
    }
  }
}
</script>
```

CustomSelect can then be used to display a list of **British Crisp flavors** (in `src/App.vue`):

```
<template>
  <div id="app">
    <CustomSelect :selected="selected" :options="options" />
  </div>
</template>

<script>
import CustomSelect from './components/CustomSelect.vue'

export default {
  components: {
    CustomSelect
  },
  data() {
    return {
      selected: 'salt-vinegar',
      options: [
        {
          value: 'ready-salted',
          label: 'Ready Salted'
```

```
      },
      {
        value: 'cheese-onion',
        label: 'Cheese & Onion'
      },
      {
        value: 'salt-vinegar',
        label: 'Salt & Vinegar'
      },
    ]
  }
 }
}
</script>
```

The preceding application outputs a select where **Salt & Vinegar** is the default selected option, as shown in the following screenshot:

Figure 4.10: Collapsed CustomSelect with Salt & Vinegar selected

The following screenshot displays three flavor options, out of which one is selected:

Figure 4.11: Open CustomSelect with flavor options and Salt & Vinegar selected

To further validate our business logic around what shape options are, we can implement the following prop validator:

```
<script>
export default {
  // other component properties
  props: {
    // other prop definitions
    options: {
      type: Array,
      validator(options) {
        return options.every(o => Boolean(o.value && o.label))
```

```
      }
    }
  }
}
</script>
```

If we pass an option with a missing **value** or **label**, we will get the following message in the console:

```
⊗ ▸ [Vue warn]: Invalid prop: custom validator check failed for prop "options".

  found in

  ---> <CustomSelect> at src/components/CustomSelect.vue
         <App> at src/App.vue
           <Root>
```

Figure 4.12: Vue.js warning when a custom validator fails

With that, we have learned how to use a custom Vue.js validator to do in-depth checks of complex props. Next, we will learn how the **required** prop type property works.

REQUIRED PROPS

To mark a Vue.js prop as required, we can use the **required** prop type property.

In the **CustomSelect** example, we can make **selected** a required prop.

To do this, we need to amend the prop definition so that it includes **required: true**, as follows:

```
<script>
export default {
  // other component properties
  props: {
    selected: {
      type: String,
      required: true
    }
    // other prop definitions
  }
}
</script>
```

Now, if we amend the consumer of **CustomSelect** so that it does *not* pass a **selected** prop, we will see the following error:

```
⊗ ▶ [Vue warn]: Missing required prop: "selected"

    found in

    ---> <CustomSelect> at src/components/CustomSelect.vue
           <App> at src/App.vue
             <Root>
```

Figure 4.13: Vue.js warning when the selected required prop is missing

With that, we have learned how to mark Vue.js props as required and what happens when a required prop is not passed. Next, we will learn how defaulting a prop can be the best choice.

DEFAULTING PROPS

There are situations where defaulting a prop is the best interface for a component.

An example of this is a **PaginatedList** component that takes a list and displays a subset of this list based on the **limit** and **offset** parameters. In this scenario, instead of making **limit** and **offset**, it might be better to default **limit** to something such as **25** and **offset** to **0** (by default, we show the first page, which contains **25** results).

This is how we would implement such a **PaginatedList** component without defaults:

```
<template>
  <ul>
    <li
      v-for="el in currentWindow"
      :key="el.id"
    >
      {{ el.content }}
    </li>
  </ul>
</template>
<script>
export default {
  props: {
    items: {
```

```
        type: Array
    },
    limit: {
      type: Number
    },
    offset: {
      type: Number
    }
  },
  computed: {
    currentWindow() {
      return this.items.slice(this.offset, this.limit)
    }
  }
}
</script>
```

We can consume this using the following code:

```
<template>
  <div id="app">
    <PaginatedList :items="snacks" :offset="offset" :
      limit="limit"/>

    <button @click="offset++">
      Increment Offset (current: {{ offset }})
    </button>
    <button @click="limit++">
      Increment Limit (current: {{ limit }})
    </button>
  </div>
</template>

<script>
import PaginatedList from './components/PaginatedList.vue'

export default {
  components: {
    PaginatedList
  },
  data() {
    return {
```

```
      offset: 0,
      limit: 0,
      snacks: [
        {
          id: 'ready-salted',
          content: 'Ready Salted'
        },
        {
          id: 'cheese-onion',
          content: 'Cheese & Onion'
        },
        {
          id: 'salt-vinegar',
          content: 'Salt & Vinegar'
        },
      ]
    }
  }
}
</script>
```

By incrementing the limit to 3, we can display the whole list, as follows:

```
Hello Vue.js
```

Then, by incrementing the offset, we can skip the first *X* elements in the list. The following screenshot shows **PaginatedList**:

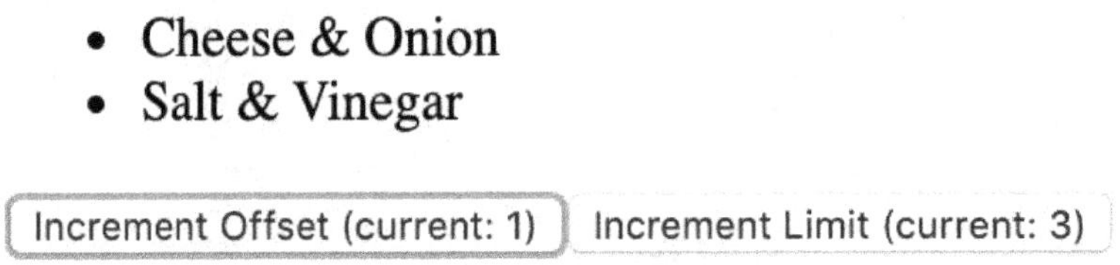

- **Cheese & Onion**
- **Salt & Vinegar**

Increment Offset (current: 1)   Increment Limit (current: 3)

Figure 4.14: PaginatedList with limit 3 and offset 1

Now, to make our **PaginatedList** is resilient, we will default **limit** to **25** and **offset** to **0**. To do so, we can set the **default** property for the relevant props:

```
<script>
export default {
  props: {
    // other props
```

```
      limit: {
        type: Number,
        default: 25,
      },
      offset: {
        type: Number,
        default: 0,
      }
    },
    // other component properties
  }
</script>
```

With these defaults, we will show **25** items from the start of the list by default.

There is a gotcha with **default** in the case of arrays and objects (for example, if we wanted to default **items**), as per the Vue.js documentation; that is, *"Object or array defaults must be returned from a factory function"*.

factory function is a function—in this case, called **default**—that returns the default value we want.

In the case of **items**, we can write the following:

```
<script>
export default {
  props: {
    items: {
      type: Array,
      default() {
        return []
      }
    }
    // other props
  },
  // other component properties
}
</script>
```

With that, we have learned how to default Vue.js component props. This can be helpful when we wish to provide values for optional parameters so that the Vue.js component implementation does not need to handle defaulting prop values.

EXERCISE 4.03: VALIDATING AN OBJECT PROPERTY

In this exercise, we will rewrite the **Repeat** component so that it supports a single **config** prop for passing **times**, which is a **Number**, and **content**, which is a **String**.

We will have to write a custom validator to make sure **times** and **content** exist and are of the correct type.

To access the code files for this exercise, refer to https://packt.live/2Ui1hVU.

Follow these steps to complete this exercise:

1. We will want our **src/components/Repeat.vue** component to support a **config** prop. This will be an **Object** that yields the following **<script>**:

```
<script>
export default {
  props: {
    config: {
      type: Object
    }
  }
}
</script>
```

2. Next, we want something to render when **config** is passed. To do this, we will create an array to **v-for** over a computer property. The array length will be based on the value of **config.times**:

```
<script>
export default {
  // other component properties
  computed: {
    repetitions() {
      return Array.from({ length: this.config.times })
    }
  }
}
</script>
```

3. The next step is to set up **\<template\>** so that it renders **config.content** for each of the **repetitions** items:

```
<template>
  <div>
    <span v-for="r in repetitions" :key="r">
      {{ config.content }}
    </span>
  </div>
</template>
```

4. Currently, we are ensuring that **content** and **times** have been set and are of the correct type. To do so, we will implement **typeof** checks in the config prop's **validator**:

```
<script>
export default {
  props: {
    config: {
      type: Object,
      validator(value) {
        return typeof value.times === 'number' &&
          typeof value.content === 'string'
      }
    }
  },
  // other component properties
}
</script>
```

5. Finally, we can consume **Repeat** from **src/App.vue**. We need to import it, register it (in **script**), and render it in **template**:

```
<template>
  <div id="app">
    <Repeat :config="{}" />
  </div>
</template>

<script>
import Repeat from './components/Repeat.vue'
```

```
export default {
  components: {
    Repeat
  }
}
</script>
```

This will unfortunately not render anything since **config** is an empty object. You will observe a warning, as follows:

```
❌  ▶ [Vue warn]: Invalid prop: custom validator check failed for prop "config".

   found in

   ---> <Repeat> at src/components/Repeat.vue
          <App> at src/App.vue
            <Root>
```

Figure 4.15: Vue.js warning due to the config prop's custom validator check failing

We will see this same error in the following cases:

a) We only add a **times** property; that is, **<Repeat :config="{ times: 3 }" />**.

b) We only add a **content** property; that is, **<Repeat :config="{ content: 'Repeat me.' }" />**.

c) **times** is of the wrong type; that is, **<Repeat :config="{ times: '3', content: 'Repeat me.' }" />**.

d) **content** is of the wrong type property; that is, **<Repeat :config="{ times: 3, content: 42 }" />**.

6. For **Repeat** to work correctly, we can amend the line consuming it in **template** to the following:

```
<Repeat :config="{ times: 3, content: 'Repeat me.' }" />
```

This shows no errors in the console and renders **Repeat me.** three times, as follows:

```
Repeat me. Repeat me. Repeat me.
```

With that, we've shown how we might go about validating props to better define the interface of a Vue.js component.

What follows is a deep dive into slots, a mechanism we can use to compose our components by deferring template logic.

SLOTS, NAMED SLOTS, AND SCOPED SLOTS

Another component composition pattern that enables reusability in Vue.js is **slots**.

Slots are sections of a component where the template/rendering is delegated back to the consumer of the component.

Here, props can be thought of as data that is passed from a parent to a child for said child to run some logic or to render it.

Slots can be thought of as templates or markup that's passed from a parent to a child for said child to render.

PASSING MARKUP TO BE RENDERED IN A CHILD COMPONENT

The simplest type of slot is the default **child** slot.

We can define a **Box** component with a slot as follows. Note that this **Box** component does very little:

```
<template>
  <div>
    <slot />
  </div>
</template>
```

The following markup is for the parent component (**src/App.vue**):

```
<template>
  <div>
    <Box>
      <h3>This whole h3 is rendered in the slot</h3>
    </Box>
  </div>
</template>
<script>
import Box from './components/Box.vue'
export default {
  components: {
    Box
  }
}
</script>
```

The preceding code will look as follows in the browser:

```
This whole h3 is rendered in the slot
```

The **template** section in the Vue Single File Component for the scope is compiled with the parent component's scope.

Consider the following example:

```
<template>
  <div>
    <Box>
      <h3>This whole h3 is rendered in the slot with parent count {{
        count }}</h3>
    </Box>
    <button @click="count++">Increment</button>
  </div>
</template>
<script>
import Box from './components/Box.vue'
export default {
  components: {
    Box
  },
  data() {
    return { count: 0 }
  }
}
</script>
```

The preceding code will render **count** as per its value in the parent component. It does not have access to the **Box** instance data or props and will generate the following output:

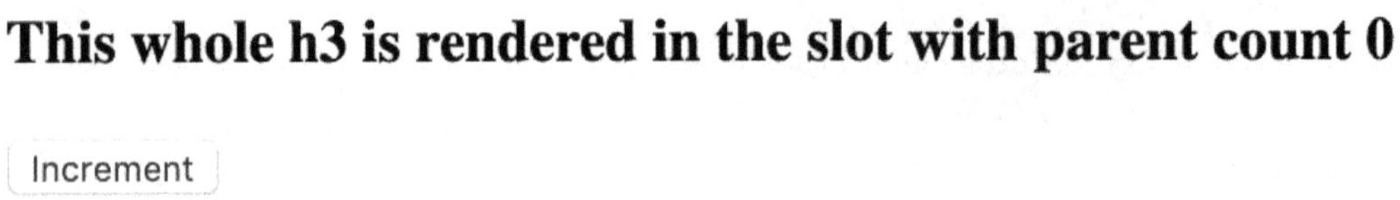

This whole h3 is rendered in the slot with parent count 0

Increment

Figure 4.16: Initial h3 with a count of 0, as per the initial data in the parent component

Incrementing the count does indeed update the template, as we would expect if the variable in the template was bound to data on the parent. This will generate the following output:

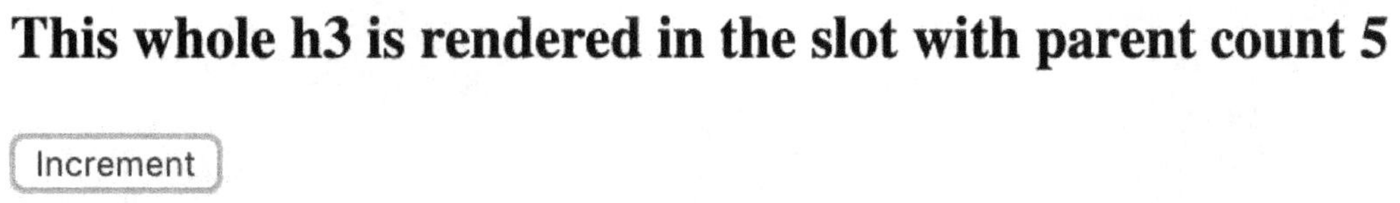

This whole h3 is rendered in the slot with parent count 5

Increment

Figure 4.17: h3 with a count of 5 after five increments of the count in the parent component's scope

Slots are a way to delegate rendering a section of a child component to the parent component. Any references to instance properties, data, or methods will use the parent component instance. This type of slot does not have access to the child component's properties, props, or data.

In the next section, we will look at how to use named slots to render multiple sections.

USING NAMED SLOTS TO DELEGATE RENDERING OF MULTIPLE SECTIONS

Named slots are used when the child component needs to be able to delegate the template of multiple sections to the parent.

For example, an **Article** component might delegate rendering of **header** and **excerpt** to its parent.

In this case, this would look as follows in the **Article.vue** file. Named slots are **slot** entries with **name** attributes that denote the slot's name:

```
<template>
  <article>
    <div>Title: <slot name="title" /></div>
    <div>Excerpt: <slot name="excerpt" /></div>
  </article>
</template>
```

By doing this, you can consume this component in another component.

For passing the slot's contents, we use the **v-slot:name** directive (where **name** should be replaced with the slot's name).

For example, for the slot named **title**, we will use **v-slot:title**, while for the **excerpt** slot, we will use **v-slot:excerpt**:

```
<template>
  <div>
    <Article>
      <template v-slot:title>
        <h3>My Article Title</h3>
      </template>
      <template v-slot:excerpt>
        <p>First paragraph of content</p>
        <p>Second paragraph of content</p>
      </template>
    </Article>
  </div>
</template>
<script>
import Article from './components/Article.vue'
export default {
  components: {
    Article
  }
}
</script>
```

When the preceding application is seen in the browser, it will look as follows:

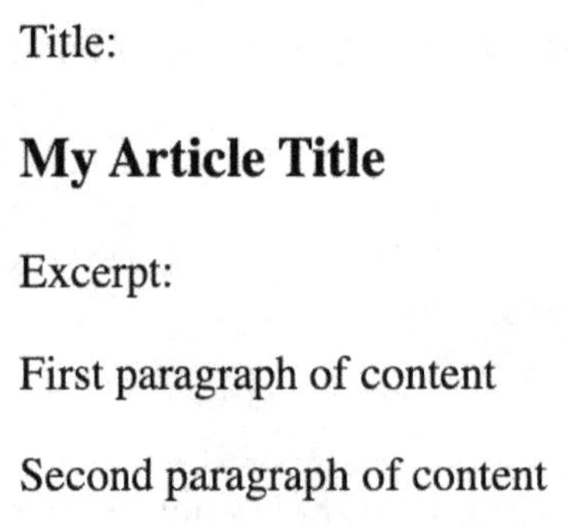

Title:

My Article Title

Excerpt:

First paragraph of content

Second paragraph of content

Figure 4.18: Article using named slots rendering templates defined by the parent

As you can see, the named slots do indeed render the expected content.

The shorthand syntax for **v-slot:slot-name** is **#slot-name**. We could refactor our template that consumes **Article** as follows:

```
<template>
  <div>
    <Article>
      <template #title>
        <h3>My Article Title</h3>
      </template>
      <template #excerpt>
        <p>First paragraph of content</p>
        <p>Second paragraph of content</p>
      </template>
    </Article>
  </div>
</template>
```

v-slot cannot be used with native elements. It can only use **template** and components. For example, the following **<template>** section attempts to set a **v-slot** on a **h3** element:

```
<template>
  <div>
    <Article>
      <h3 v-slot:title>My Article Title</h3>
    </Article>
  </div>
</template>
```

This template will fail with a compilation error of **v-slot can only be used on components or <template>**, as shown in the following screenshot:

```
 error  in ./src/App.vue?vue&type=template&id=7ba5bd90&

Module Error (from ../node_modules/vue-loader/lib/loaders/templateLoader.js):
(Emitted value instead of an instance of Error)

  Errors compiling template:

  v-slot can only be used on components or <template>.

  2 |   <div>
  3 |     <Article>
  4 |       <h3 v-slot:title>My Article Title</h3>
    |           ^^^^^^^^^^^^
  5 |     </Article>
  6 |   </div>
```

Figure 4.19: v-slot on a native element – compilation error

Earlier versions of Vue.js allowed an alternative syntax to be used for denoting named slot contents (this was deprecated in Vue 2.6.0+). Instead of the **v-slot:slot-name** directive style, **slot="slot-name"** was used. The **slot** syntax was allowed on native elements, as well as on templates and components.

> **NOTE**
>
> Everything that applies to the default slot applies to named slots. In fact, the default slot is a named slot called **default**. This means that named slots also have access to the parent instance but not the child instance.

The default slot is just a slot named **default** and gets special treatment by Vue.js as it is used by default in a **slot** with no **name**.

The **default** slot is implicitly inferred as follows:

```
<template>
  <MyComponent>
    <template>Default template</template>
  </MyComponent>
</template>
```

The default slot can be denoted with shorthand slot notation.

```
<template>
  <MyComponent>
    <template #default>Default template</template>
  </MyComponent>
</template>
The default slot can be denoted with longhand slot notation.
<template>
  <MyComponent>
    <template v-slot:default>Default template</template>
  </MyComponent>
</template>
```

We have now seen how named slots allow components to delegate templating of certain sections to a consumer, as well as how these named slots can have a default template to cater for cases where a named slot is optional.

In the next section, we will learn how scoped slots are used to wrap prop passing logic.

USING SCOPED SLOTS TO WRAP PROP PASSING LOGIC

The types of slots we have explored so far only have access to the component instance in which they are declared.

Sometimes, it is useful to let the parent component dictate the rendering while letting the child component transform the data in some way. This is what scoped slots are used for.

A **scoped slot** starts with the child component's slots, where the **slot** element has some attributes bound to it via the use of **v-bind** or the shorthand, :.

In this case, **item** is bound to **el**. **el** is an element of the **items** prop that has been passed to this **PaginatedList** component:

```
<template>
  <ul>
    <li
      v-for="el in currentWindow"
      :key="el.id"
    >
      <slot :item="el" />
    </li>
```

```
    </ul>
</template>
<script>
export default {
  props: ['items', 'limit', 'offset'],
  computed: {
    currentWindow() {
      return this.items.slice(this.offset, this.limit)
    }
  }
}
</script>
```

On the consumer side (the parent component), we can think of the slot template as being called with an object containing all the data bound to the slot in the child component. Hence, these slots are referred to as **scoped**; they are passed through a **scope** object, as defined by the child component.

In this case, we can consume **PaginatedList** as follows:

```
<template>
  <div>
    <PaginatedList :items="snacks">
      <template #default="{ item }">
        {{ item.content }}
      </template>
    </PaginatedList>
  </div>
</template>
```

#default="{ item }" is the shorthand notation for the default scoped slot and allows us to destructure the slot's scope into **item**.

The longhand version of the slot's template definition is as follows:

```
<template v-slot="slotProps">
  {{ slotProps.item.content }}
</template>
```

item is then used to render **{{ item.content }}**. The **script** section (with snacks to render) will be as follows:

```
<script>
import PaginatedList from './components/PaginatedList.vue'
export default {
  components: {
    PaginatedList
  },
  data() {
    return {
      snacks: [
        {
          id: 'ready-salted',
          content: 'Ready Salted'
        },
        {
          id: 'cheese-onion',
          content: 'Cheese & Onion'
        },
        {
          id: 'salt-vinegar',
          content: 'Salt & Vinegar'
        },
      ]
    }
  }
}
</script>
```

We get the following output in the browser:

- Ready Salted
- Cheese & Onion
- Salt & Vinegar

Figure 4.20: Snacks displayed using a scoped slot, meaning the rendering logic is in the parent component

With that, we have learned how scoped slots give components increased flexibility to delegate templating logic to consumers.

> **NOTE**
>
> Scoped slots also have a deprecated (as of Vue.js 2.6.0+) **slot-scope** syntax. The deprecated equivalent of **v-slot:name="slotProps"** would be **slot="name" slot-scope="slotProps"**. For more information, see the Vue.js documentation: https://vuejs.org/v2/guide/components-slots.html#Scoped-Slots-with-the-slot-scope-Attribute.

Now, let's learn how to implement a card component with the help of these named slots.

EXERCISE 4.04: IMPLEMENTING A CARD COMPONENT USING NAMED SLOTS

In this exercise, we will implement a card component using named slots. The card will have a title, image, and description sections. We will use slots to allow **title**, **image**, and **description** to be defined by a parent component.

To access the code files for this exercise, refer to https://packt.live/2UhLxlK.

Follow these steps to complete this exercise:

1. We will start by creating a new **src/components/Card.vue** component that has a template that supports three slots – **title**, **image**, and **description**:

```
<template>
  <div>
    <slot name="image" />
    <slot name="title" />
    <slot name="description" />
  </div>
</template>
```

2. We will then import our **Card.vue** component into the **script** section of a new **src/App.vue** file:

```
<script>
import Card from './components/Card.vue'
export default {
  components: {
    Card
  }
}
</script>
```

3. We can now use **Card** in our **template**:

```
<template>
  <div id="app">
    <Card>
      <template #image>
        <img src="https://picsum.photos/id/1015/300" />
      </template>
      <template #title>
        <h2>My Holiday picture</h2>
      </template>
      <template #description>
        <p>Here I can describe the contents of the picture.</p>
        <p>For example what we can see in the photo is a nice
          landscape.</p>
      </template>
    </Card>
  </div>
</template>
```

Now, we can fire up the **vue-cli dev** server using **npm run serve** and see the **Card** component in action. The output will be as follows:

My Holiday picture

Here I can describe the contents of the picture.

For example what we can see in the photo is a nice landscape.

Figure 4.21: Card component with image, title, and description

With that, we have learned how different types of slots can help to create more generic components. Slots allow child components to defer the rendering of certain parts of themselves to their parent component (**consumer**).

To reuse functionality within a single template, we can use filters. We'll learn how to use them in the next section.

TEMPLATE LOGIC SHARING WITH FILTERS

To share template logic, Vue.js has **filters**.

Filters can be used in mustache interpolations (`{{ interpolatingSomething }}`) or in expressions (for example, when binding a value). `filter` is a function that takes a value and outputs something that can be rendered (usually a **String** or a **Number**).

So, an example filter called **truncate** would be used in a template as follows (here, we have put some long placeholder text):

```
<template>
  <div id="app">
    {{ message | truncate }}
  </div>
</template>
<script>
export default {
  data() {
    return {
      message: 'Lorem ipsum dolor sit amet, consectetur adipiscing
        elit, sed do eiusmod tempor incididunt ut labore et dolore
        magna aliqua. Ut enim ad minim veniam, quis nostrud
        exercitation llamco laboris nisi ut aliquip ex ea commodo
        consequat. Duis aute irure dolor in reprehenderit in
        voluptate velit esse cillum dolore eu fugiat nulla
        pariatur. Excepteur sint occaecat cupidatat non proident,
        sunt in culpa qui officia deserunt mollit anim id
        est laborum.'
    }
  }
}
</script>
```

truncate could also be used in a Vue.js bind expression. For example, **<MessageComponent :msg="message | truncate">** would bind the truncated output of **message** to **msg**.

To define the **truncate** filter, we can define it in a component's **filters** property in the **script** section.

truncate filter will truncate the text down to **120** characters:

```
<script>
export default {
  filters: {
    truncate(value) {
      return value.slice(0, 120)
    }
  },
  // other component properties
}
</script>
```

Without the truncation filter, we get **446** characters of *lorem ipsum*, as follows:

Lorem ipsum dolor sit amet, consectetur adipiscing elit, sed do eiusmod tempor incididunt ut labore et dolore magna aliqua. Ut enim ad minim veniam, quis nostrud exercitation ullamco laboris nisi ut aliquip ex ea commodo consequat. Duis aute irure dolor in reprehenderit in voluptate velit esse cillum dolore eu fugiat nulla pariatur. Excepteur sint occaecat cupidatat non proident, sunt in culpa qui officia deserunt mollit anim id est laborum.

Figure 4.22: Lorem ipsum without truncation

With the **truncate** filter, we are down to **120** characters, as shown in the following screenshot:

Lorem ipsum dolor sit amet, consectetur adipiscing elit, sed do eiusmod tempor incididunt ut labore et dolore magna aliq

Figure 4.23: Lorem ipsum with the truncate filter

The more defensive way to write this **truncate** filter would be to do an early return if **val** is false, then **toString** it (this will convert numbers into strings, for example) before doing the output of **.slice**:

```
<script>
export default {
  filters: {
    truncate(value) {
      if (!value) return
      const val = value.toString()
      return val.slice(0, 120)
    }
  },
```

```
  // other component properties
}
</script>
```

With that, we have learned how to register and implement Vue.js filters for a component. We have also learned how to use filters in the component's template with the interpolation expression's pipe syntax.

In the following exercise, we will learn how to implement an ellipsis filter.

EXERCISE 4.05: IMPLEMENTING AN ELLIPSIS FILTER

Filters are excellent for repeated text processing tasks. In this exercise, we will implement an **ellipsis** filter that works as follows.

If the passed text is more than **14** characters, it should be truncated down to **11** characters and an ellipsis (...) should be added to the end of the text.

When the passed text is empty or not a **String**, we should be quite permissive and either return nothing or convert it into a **String** before doing our processing.

To access the code files for this exercise, refer to https://packt.live/2IsZyuv.

Follow these steps to complete this exercise:

1. First, we need to set up the template so that it will pipe *a string less than 14 characters*, *a string with 14 characters*, and *a string with more than 14 characters* through **ellipsis** to check if it works as expected under all possible conditions (we'll do this in **src/App.vue**, as per the standard Vue CLI setup). We should also pipe a number and an empty value (**null**) through **ellipsis**:

```
<template>
  <div id="app">
    <p>{{ '7 char' | ellipsis }}</p>
    <p>{{ '14 characters' | ellipsis }}</p>
    <p>{{ 'More than 14 characters' | ellipsis }}</p>
    <p>{{ null | ellipsis }}</p>
    <p>{{ 55 | ellipsis }}</p>
  </div>
</template>
```

At this stage, the application should just display the text in the console. There should be some warnings that the **ellipsis** filter has not defined, as shown in the following screenshot:

7 char

14 characters

More than 14 characters

55

Figure 4.24: Application displaying unchanged text

The following screenshot shows the warning:

```
⊗ ▸ [Vue warn]: Failed to resolve filter: ellipsis

    (found in <App> at src/App.vue)
⊗ ▸ [Vue warn]: Failed to resolve filter: ellipsis

    (found in <App> at src/App.vue)
⊗ ▸ [Vue warn]: Failed to resolve filter: ellipsis

    (found in <App> at src/App.vue)
⊗ ▸ [Vue warn]: Failed to resolve filter: ellipsis

    (found in <App> at src/App.vue)
⊗ ▸ [Vue warn]: Failed to resolve filter: ellipsis

    (found in <App> at src/App.vue)
```

Figure 4.25: Vue.js warning that the ellipsis filter is missing

2. Next, we will implement an initial version of the filter in the **script** section of the component. This will check the length of the passed value, truncate it to **11**, and add ... if it is longer than **14** characters:

```
<script>
export default {
  filters: {
    ellipsis(value) {
      return value.length > 14 ? `${value.slice(0, 11)}...` :
        value
    }
  }
}
</script>
```

At this stage, the component fails to render and Vue.js logs an error since **Cannot read property 'length' of null**, as shown in the following screenshot:

```
⊗ ▸ [Vue warn]: Error in render: "TypeError: Cannot read property 'length' of
   null"

   found in

   ----> <App> at src/App.vue
           <Root>
```

Figure 4.26: null piped into the application

3. Next, we need to amend the **ellipsis** implementation so that it short-circuits when the passed value is **false** (to avoid the issue with **null**):

```
ellipsis(value) {
    if (!value) return
    // rest of the function
}
```

We now have the **ellipsis** filter working; it works for all the test cases we have included. The output will be as follows:

7 char

14 characters

More than 1…

55

Figure 4.27: Ellipsis filter working for given inputs

Filters are useful for sharing simple text processing logic in components. A filter is a Vue.js primitive that keeps templating and formatting concerns in the template, such as truncating content and adding an ellipsis.

Vue.js provides an abstraction over the DOM Web API. However, when it becomes necessary to access the DOM directly, such as to integrate a DOM library, Vue.js provides a first-class way to do so with refs. We will learn about Vue.js references in the next section.

VUE.JS REFS

In Vue.js, **refs** are references to DOM elements or other components. This occurs programmatically.

A large use case for refs is direct DOM manipulation and integration with DOM-based libraries (that usually take a DOM node they should mount to).

Refs are defined using **ref="name"** on a native element or child component in the template. In the following instance, the input will be stored in a **theInput** ref:

```
<template>
  <div id="app">
    <input ref="theInput" />
  </div>
</template>
```

Refs can be accessed from the Vue.js component instance through **this.$refs[name]**. So, in the previous example, where we had a ref defined as **ref="theInput"**, we can access it through **this.$refs.theInput**.

To focus the input when a button is clicked, we could write the following:

```
<template>
  <div id="app">
    <input ref="theInput" />
    <button @click="focus()">Focus Input</button>
  </div>
</template>
<script>
export default {
  methods: {
    focus() {
      this.$refs.theInput.focus()
    }
  }
}
</script>
```

When clicking the **Focus Input** button, the input will be focused, as shown in the following screenshot:

Figure 4.28: Input focused on a button click

With that, we have learned how to use **$refs** to abstract DOM manipulation logic in a Vue.js component. Where it makes sense to select a DOM node directly in Vue.js, it is recommended to use a **ref** instead of using the DOM selection API (**querySelector**/**querySelectorAll**).

In the following exercise, we will learn how the **Countable** library helps increase the interactivity in a project.

EXERCISE 4.06: WRAPPING COUNTABLE.JS WITH VUE.JS

Countable is a library that, given an element (usually an HTML **textarea** or input), will add live counts of paragraphs, words, and characters. Live metrics on the text being captured can be quite useful to increase interactivity in a project where editing text is a core concern.

One of the large use cases for using refs in Vue.js is to be able to integrate with libraries that act directly on the DOM.

In this exercise, we will create a component with paragraph/word/character counting for content in a **textarea** by using **Countable.js** and Vue.js refs.

To access the code files for this exercise, refer to https://packt.live/36oOuGz.

Follow these steps to complete this exercise:

1. Install **countable** from **npm**. We will run **npm install --save countable** here, which will add it to our dependencies

2. Next, we will create a new **src/components/TextEditorWithCount.vue** component with a **textarea** that we will have a **ref** to:

```
<template>
  <div>
    <textarea
      ref="textArea"
      cols="50"
      rows="7"
    >
```

```
      </textarea>
    </div>
  </template>
```

3. Next, we will import and render the component in **src/App.vue**:

```
<template>
  <div id="app">
    <TextEditorWithCount />
  </div>
</template>
<script>
import TextEditorWithCount from './components/
  TextEditorWithCount.vue'

export default {
  components: {
    TextEditorWithCount
  }
}
</script>
```

The application renders a **textarea**, as follows:

Figure 4.29: A bare textarea, as rendered by the application

4. We now need to integrate **Countable**. We will import it and initialize it with **this.$refs.textArea**. We will also store the counts on the instance as **this.count**:

```
<script>
import * as Countable from 'countable'
export default {
  mounted() {
    Countable.on(this.$refs.textArea, (count) => {
```

```
          this.count = count
      })
    },
    data() {
      return {
        count: null
      }
    }
  }
</script>
```

5. With a small update to the **template**, we can display the counts we care about:

```
<template>
  <div id="app">
    <!-- textarea -->
    <ul v-if="count">
      <li>Paragraphs: {{ count.paragraphs }}</li>
      <li>Sentences: {{ count.sentences }}</li>
      <li>Words: {{ count.words }}</li>
    </ul>
  </div>
</template>
```

Now, we can see the counts set to **0** when **textarea** is empty, as follows:

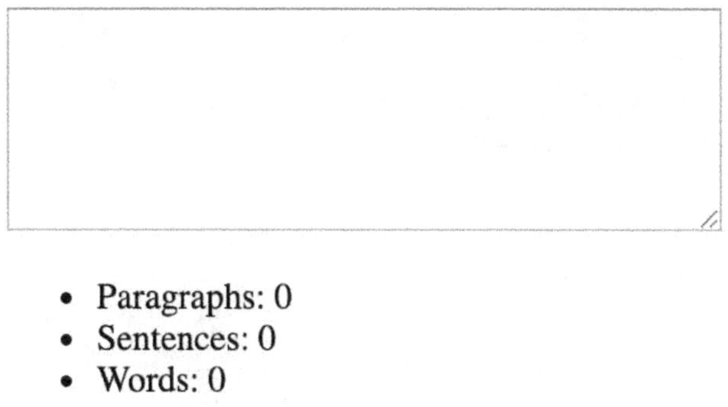

- Paragraphs: 0
- Sentences: 0
- Words: 0

Figure 4.30: Textarea with counts set to 0 when empty

If we drop some *Lorem ipsum* into our **textarea**, the counts will update accordingly, as follows:

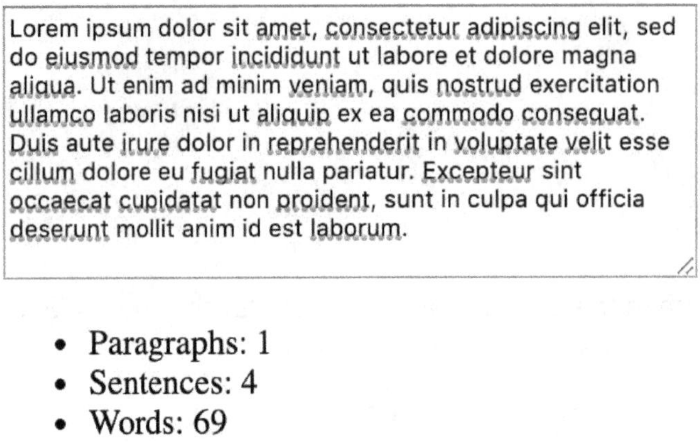

Lorem ipsum dolor sit amet, consectetur adipiscing elit, sed do eiusmod tempor incididunt ut labore et dolore magna aliqua. Ut enim ad minim veniam, quis nostrud exercitation ullamco laboris nisi ut aliquip ex ea commodo consequat. Duis aute irure dolor in reprehenderit in voluptate velit esse cillum dolore eu fugiat nulla pariatur. Excepteur sint occaecat cupidatat non proident, sunt in culpa qui officia deserunt mollit anim id est laborum.

- Paragraphs: 1
- Sentences: 4
- Words: 69

Figure 4.31: Textarea with counts updated when filled

6. One last thing we need to do is remove the **Countable** event listener when the component is destroyed:

```
<script>
// imports
export default {
  mounted() {
    Countable.on(this.$refs.textArea, (count) => {
      this.count = count
    })
    this.$once('hook:beforeDestroy', function () {
      Countable.off(this.$refs.textArea)
    })
  },
  // other component properties
}
</script>
```

> **NOTE**
>
> We have achieved this with programmatic listeners, though we could have achieved the same with the **beforeDestroy** life cycle method.

This integration of a JavaScript/DOM library inside of Vue.js is a key application of Vue.js refs. Refs allow us to pick from the existing ecosystem of libraries and wrap or integrate them into a component.

Vue.js refs are useful for integrating DOM libraries or for accessing DOM APIs directly.

To round off our learning of component composition, we need to know how to pass data from child components to parent components.

VUE.JS EVENTS FOR CHILD-PARENT COMMUNICATION

We have already seen that props are used to pass data from a parent component to a child component.

To pass data from a child component back to a parent component, Vue.js has custom events.

In a component, an event can be emitted using the **$emit** instance method. It can be used from within the **script** section using **this.$emit('eventName', /* payload */)**, but it is also exposed within the **template** section as **$emit**.

Assuming we have got a reactive instance property, **this.message**, we could emit a **send** event with the **message** value in the **script** section using **this.$emit**. This could be the basis for a **MessageEditor** component:

```
<script>
export default {
  data () {
        return {
            message: null
        }
    },
  methods: {
    send() {
      this.$emit('send', this.message);
    }
  }
}
</script>
```

In the same scenario, we could trigger a **send** event from the **template** section:

```
<template>
  <div>
    <input v-model="message" />
    <button @click="$emit('send', message)">Emit inline</button>
  </div>
</template>
```

From a parent component, we can use **v-on:event-name** or the shorthand **@ event-name**. **event-name** must match the name passed to **$emit**; **eventName** and **event-name** are not equivalent.

For example, a parent component would be how we listen to the **send** event using **@send** and save the event payload contained in the **$event** magic value. To use the event payload in a method call, we can use **@ eventName="methodToCall($event)"**:

```
<template>
  <div id="app">
    <p>Message: {{ message }}</p>
    <MessageEditor @send="message = $event" />
    <button @click="message = null">Reset</button>
  </div>
</template>
<script>
import MessageEditor from './components/MessageEditor.vue'

export default {
  components: {
    MessageEditor
  },
  data() {
    return {
      message: null
    }
  }
}
</script>
```

Using the inline and method versions of **$emit** yields the same result. The full **MessageEditor** app should look as follows:

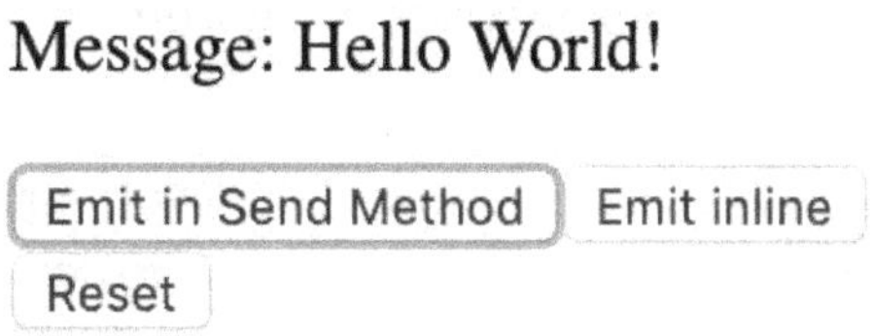

Message: Hello World!

[Emit in Send Method] Emit inline

[Reset]

Figure 4.32: Hello World! message being emitted from child-parent

Vue.js custom events support passing any JavaScript type as the payload. The event name, however, must be a **String**.

> **NOTE**
>
> Binding a listener to Vue.js custom events is very similar to binding to native events such as **click**.

Now, let's complete an activity based on what we've learned about so far.

ACTIVITY 4.01: A LOCAL MESSAGE VIEW WITH REUSABLE COMPONENTS

This activity aims to leverage components, props, events, and refs to render a **chat** interface where the user can add messages and they are displayed.

Follow these steps to complete this activity:

1. Create a **MessageEditor** component (in **src/components/ MessageEditor.vue**) that displays a **textarea** to the user.

2. Add a **message** reactive instance variable to **MessageEditor**, defaulted to **''**.

3. Listen to **change** events for **textarea** and set the value of **message** to the value of the content of **textarea** (it is exposed as the value of the event).

4. Add a **Send** button that, on **click**, emits a **send** event with **message** as the payload.

5. Add a **main App** component to **src/App.vue** that renders **MessageEditor**.

6. In **App**, listen to **send** events from **MessageEditor** and store each message in a **messages** reactive instance variable (**messages** is an array).

7. Create a **MessageFeed** (in **src/components/MessageFeed.vue**) that has a required **messages** prop, which is an **Array**.

8. In **MessageFeed**, render each passed message from the **messages** prop in a paragraph (the **p** element).

9. Import and render **MessageFeed** into **App**, binding the **messages** app instance variable as the **messages** prop of **MessageFeed**.

10. Improve **MessageEditor** so that the message is reset when it is sent. To do this, we will need to set **textarea.value** using a Vue.js ref and reset the **message** instance variable.

> **NOTE**
>
> The easier way to reset **textarea** would have been to use **v-model="message"** in the first place instead of binding @**change** and manually syncing **textarea.value** to **message**.

The expected output is as follows:

Figure 4.33: Message app with Hello World! and Hello JavaScript sent

> **NOTE**
>
> The solution for this activity can be found on page 660.

SUMMARY

Throughout this chapter, we have looked at Vue.js primitives that allow us to build components in such a way that they can be composed efficiently.

Props and slots are used to defer behavior within a component to whichever parent component is rendering them. Props, with their ability to be validated, are great for passing data into nested components. Slots are geared toward yielding control of rendering back to the parent component. Events enable child components to send data back to their parent, thus completing the parent-child communication cycle (props down, events up).

Global templating helpers can be encapsulated in filters to reduce boilerplate and increase code reuse. Refs unlock integration opportunities with third-party JavaScript or DOM libraries by allowing us to access DOM elements directly.

We're now able to compose and create components that clearly define their interfaces with inputs (props and slots) and outputs (rendered templates and events), while also visiting commonly faced use cases (wrapping a DOM library, abstracting templating concerns in a filter, and so on).

In the next chapter, we'll look at advanced component composition patterns and techniques that enable better code reuse.

5

GLOBAL COMPONENT COMPOSITION

OVERVIEW

In this chapter, you will learn how to reduce duplication in your Vue.js application code using global abstractions, new composition models, and new types of components. You will experiment with Vue.js **mixins**, **plugins**, and new types of components and ways of composing them.

By the end of this chapter, you will be able to identify situations where **mixins** and **plugins** can be used to achieve global composition and keep code **DRY** (**don't repeat yourself**) in a Vue.js application, as well as how to define global components, functional components, and components in non-Vue files. You will also be able to contrast the advantages and drawbacks of global composition and select the right abstraction to maximize component flexibility.

INTRODUCTION

Component nesting is an approach to composition where the application is built up from smaller units (components). The application can be thought of as components fitting within each other. In this scenario, any shared functionality will be provided through components. Vue.js provides other methods of composition.

Component-based composition can be very verbose and will mean we repeat imports wherever a certain piece of functionality is needed. This does not follow the DRY principle. To avoid this duplication and verbosity, we can globally register **mixins**, **plugins**, and **components** to inject the globally available resources to be used throughout the application. This can reduce friction and frustration at having to type out `import MyComponent from` ... in every consumer of `MyComponent`.

Much in the same way, applications can be built from different types of primitives (mixins, plugins, and components). For maximum flexibility, components can be defined in different ways beyond Vue.js single-file component files (`.vue` files). In this category, we have the case of functional components, as well as components defined with **JSX**, string templates, and **render** functions. Each of these types of components has some advantages and drawbacks.

To keep code DRY, a component should be easy to use and extend. This chapter will look at a few tips that we can follow to make a component more reusable, thereby making the application more DRY.

MIXINS

Mixins can add methods, properties, and default life cycle methods to components that consume them. In the following example, we are defining a mixin that adds a **greet** method and a **greeting** field to the component's **data** function:

```
export default {
  methods: {
    greet(name) {
      return `${this.greeting} ${name}`
    }
  },
  data() {
    return {
      greeting: 'Hello'
    }
  }
}
```

Mixins allow multiple components' shared functionality to be defined independently. They are used through a **mixins** component property, which accepts an array.

In the **App.vue** file, we can consume the mixin by setting the component's **mixins** property.

The properties and methods of the mixin are then available in the component (just as they would be if they were defined in the component itself):

```
<template>
  <div>{{ greet('World') }}</div>
</template>
<script>
import greeter from './mixins/greeter.js'
export default {
  mixins: [greeter]
}
</script>
```

This displays the following message in the browser:

Figure 5.1: Hello World using a greeter mixin

When there is a conflict, in terms of instance properties or methods that are named the same, between the component and the mixin, the component wins. This can be thought of as the component adopting mixin behavior by default unless said component declares the same instance property or method. In this case, instance access that is defined in the mixin would access the component's instance.

For example, let's add a **data()** initializer to our **App** component that has **greeting** set to **Hi**:

```
<script>
// other imports
export default {
  // other component properties
  data() {
    return {
      greeting: 'Hi'
    }
```

```
    }
  }
</script>
```

The mixin defines a **data** method, but so does the component. In this case, the component *wins*, hence why the greeting displayed is **Hi** (as defined in the component) instead of **Hello** (as defined in the mixin), as displayed in the following screenshot:

Hi World

Figure 5.2: Hi World using a greeter mixin with overridden data

Note that when the component does not define a **data** method, the mixin's implementation is used but the component "wins" if both the mixin and the component define it.

Vue.js life cycle hooks are prime candidates to be extracted into mixins. The life cycle hooks we can use are (in order of execution) **beforeCreated, created, beforeMount, mounted, beforeUpdate, updated, beforeDestroy,** and **destroyed**.

Life cycle hooks are an exception to the mixin/component conflict resolution rule mentioned previously. In the case of Vue.js life cycle hooks functions, for each mixin, component, and hook, the hook functions are all executed in the order of mixins first (in order of addition to the component), component last.

We can see this in action in the following example. Let's create two mixins that implement the **mounted** life cycle hook and implement that hook in the component. This illustrates the case of life cycle hooks for mixin/component conflict resolution:

```
<template>
  <div ref="zone" />
</template>
<script>
const firstMixin = {
  mounted() {
    console.log('First mixin mounted hook')
  }
}
const secondMixin = {
  mounted() {
```

```
      console.log('Second mixin mounted hook')
  }
}
export default {
  mixins: [firstMixin, secondMixin],
  mounted() {
    console.log('Component mounted hook')
  }
}
</script>
```

The browser console output for this component will be (in order) **First mixin mounted hook**, **Second mixin mounted hook**, and **Component mounted hook**, as shown in the following screenshot:

```
First mixin mounted hook
Second mixin mounted hook
Component mounted hook
```

Figure 5.3: Browser console output showing the hooks defined in the mixins that were executed before the component hooks

All the examples we have seen have used mixins directly to inject functionality into components. Mixins can also be created globally by using a **Vue.mixin** function call.

We can, for example, make our greeting function a global instance method:

```
Vue.mixin({
  methods: {
    $greet(greeting, name) {
      return `${greeting} ${name}`
    }
  }
})
```

this.$greet will now be available on all Vue instances declared after the **Vue.mixin** call. This use case, however, is better served by a plugin.

> **NOTE**
>
> The **$methodName** convention is used in Vue.js for methods that are provided by the Vue.js application instance (as opposed to the current component instance).

EXERCISE 5.01: CREATING YOUR OWN MIXIN

In this exercise, we will create a mixin called **debug** that will return the JSON-stringified representation of the input it has been passed. **JavaScript Object Notation** or **JSON** is a subset of JavaScript that allows the annotations of objects and arrays to be put in a compact human and machine-readable format. This can be useful for printing data to the console or even onto the page. We will make **debug** do what is called pretty-printing so that we can read it more easily.

This can also be useful for printing data inside HTML when debugging a Vue.js application in a situation where Vue.js DevTools are not available or reliable. To access the code files for this exercise, refer to https://packt.live/38ivgFq.

We will start with a clean Vue CLI project (this can be created with the **vue new exercise5.01** command). The application in the Vue CLI project can be started with **npm run serve**.

Follow these steps to complete this exercise:

1. Create a new **src/mixins** folder and a **src/mixins/debug.js** file where we will define the skeleton of our mixin:

```
export default {}
```

2. The mixin will add a **debug** method, which we should define under **methods**. The **debug** method will take an **obj** parameter and return the output of **JSON.stringify** for that data. We will use **JSON.stringify(obj, null, 2)** to output two-space pretty-printed JSON:

```
export default {
  methods: {
    debug(obj) {
      return JSON.stringify(obj, null, 2)
    }
  }
}
```

3. We are now able to import the **debug** mixin from **src/App.vue** and register it under the **mixins** property:

```
<script>
import debug from './mixins/debug.js'
export default {
  mixins: [debug],

}
</script>
```

4. To see the **debug** method in action, we will add a **data** method and a **created** hook (from which we can print the output of **debug**) in the **src/App.vue** file:

```
<script>
// imports
export default {
  // other component properties
  data() {
    return {
      myObj: {
        some: 'data',
        other: 'values'
      }
    }
  },
  created() {
    console.log(this.debug(this.myObj))
  }
}
</script>
```

You should get the following output:

```
{
  "some": "data",
  "other": "values"
}
```

Figure 5.4: Browser console output due to the created hook

5. **debug** is also available in the template; we can interpolate its output in a **pre** tag so that whitespace is respected:

```
<template>
  <div id="app">
    <pre>{{ debug(myObj) }}</pre>
  </div>
</template>
```

The application, as well as this template, will look as follows:

```
{
  "some": "data",
  "other": "values"
}
```

Figure 5.5: Browser printing myObj using the debug method from the mixin

With that, we have learned how mixins can be used to inject shared functionality into multiple components in a manner that is quite explicit (a **mixins** property). We also got a chance to see what happens when a component's implementation overwrites properties and methods provided by the mixin (the component usually wins).

We will now look at how to inject instance and global functionality and distribute it through plugins.

PLUGINS

Vue.js plugins are a way to add custom functionality to Vue.js globally. Good candidates for plugins are core to the application and used widely. Classic examples of plugin candidates are translation/internationalization libraries (such as **i18n-next**) and HTTP clients (such as the **axios**, **fetch**, and **GraphQL** clients). The plugin initializer has access to the **Vue** instance, so it can be a good way to wrap global directive, mixin, component, and filter definitions.

Plugins can inject functionality by registering directives and filters. They can also add **global** and **instance** Vue.js methods, as well as defining global component mixins.

A Vue.js plugin is an object that exposes an **install** method. The **install** function is called with **Vue** and **options**:

```
const plugin = {
  install(Vue, options) {}
}
```

Within the **install** method, we can register directives, filters, and mixins and add global and instance properties and methods:

```
const plugin = {
  install(Vue, options) {
    Vue.directive('fade', { bind() {} })
    Vue.filter('truncate', str => str.slice(0, 140))
    Vue.mixin({
      data() { return { empty: true } }
    })
    Vue.globalProperty = 'very-global-value'
    Vue.prototype.$myInstanceMethod = function() {}

  }
}
```

Plugins are registered using the **Vue.use** method:

```
import plugin from './plugin'
Vue.use(plugin)
```

Vue.use can also be passed options as the second argument. These options are passed to the plugin:

```
Vue.use(plugin, { optionProperty: true })
```

One of the features of **Vue.use** is that it does not allow you to register the same plugin twice. This is a nice feature that avoids edge case behavior when attempting to instantiate or install the same plugin multiple times.

A popular HTTP client to use in combination with Vue.js is **axios**. It is common to configure **axios** with interceptors or **axios** options to achieve things such as retries, passing cookies, or following redirects.

axios can be installed using: **npm install –save axios**.

EXERCISE 5.02: CREATING A CUSTOM AXIOS PLUGIN

In order to avoid having to add **import axios from 'axios'** or having to wrap our custom **axios** instance under an **http** or **transport** internal module, we'll inject our custom **axios** instance into the Vue object and Vue component instances under **Vue.axios** and **this.axios**. This will make it easier and more ergonomic to use in our application, which needs to call out to an API using **axios** as the HTTP client. To access the code files for this exercise, refer to https://packt.live/36po08b.

We will start with a clean Vue CLI project (this can be created with the **vue new exercise5.02** command). The application in the Vue CLI project can be started with **npm run serve**.

Follow these steps to complete this exercise:

1. To organize our code properly, we will create a new folder in **src/plugins** and a new file for our **axios** plugin at **src/plugins/axios.js**. In the new file, we will scaffold the **axios** plugin:

```
import axios from 'axios'
export default {
    install(Vue, options) {}
}
```

2. We will now register our **axios** plugin on the Vue.js instance in **src/main.js**:

```
// other imports
import axiosPlugin from './plugins/axios.js'

// other code
Vue.use(axiosPlugin)
// Vue instantiation code
```

3. We will now install **axios** through **npm** using the following command. This will allow us to import **axios** and expose it on Vue through a plugin:

```
npm install --save axios
```

4. We will now add **axios** to Vue as a global property in **src/plugins/axios. js**:

```
import axios from 'axios'
export default {
  install(Vue) {
    Vue.axios = axios
  }
}
```

5. **axios** is now available on **Vue**. In **src/App.vue**, we can make a request to an API that will populate a list of **todos**:

```
<template>
  <div id="app">
    <div v-for="todo in todos" :key="todo.id">
      <ul>
        <li>Title: {{ todo.title }}</li>
        <li>Status: {{ todo.completed ? "Completed" :
          "Not Completed" }}</li>
      </ul>
    </div>
  </div>
</template>
<script>
import Vue from 'vue'
export default {
  async mounted() {
    const { data: todos } = await
      Vue.axios('https://jsonplaceholder.typicode.com/todos')
    this.todos = todos
  },
  data() {
    return { todos: [] }
  }
}
</script>
```

The following is the expected output:

- Title: delectus aut autem
- Status: Not Completed

- Title: quis ut nam facilis et officia qui
- Status: Not Completed

- Title: fugiat veniam minus
- Status: Not Completed

- Title: et porro tempora
- Status: Completed

Figure 5.6: Global Vue.axios todo display sample

6. Having to add **import Vue from 'vue'** is a bit odd in our case. The whole point of injecting **axios** through a plugin was to get rid of the **import** boilerplate. The better way to expose **axios** is through the component instance; that is, **this.axios**. To do so, we need to update the install step in the **src/plugins/axios.js** file and add **axios** to the **Vue.prototype** so that any **new Vue()** component will have it as a property:

```
// imports
export default {
  install(Vue, options) {
    // other plugin code
    Vue.prototype.axios = axios

  }
}
```

7. We can now remove the **import Vue from 'vue'** line and access **axios** through **this.axios** in **src/App.vue**:

```
<script>
export default {
  async mounted() {
    const { data: todos } = await
      this.axios('https://jsonplaceholder.typicode.com/todos')
    this.todos = todos
  },
  data() {
    return { todos: [] }
  }
```

```
  }
</script>
```

The following is the output:

- Title: delectus aut autem
- Status: Not Completed

- Title: quis ut nam facilis et officia qui
- Status: Not Completed

- Title: fugiat veniam minus
- Status: Not Completed

- Title: et porro tempora
- Status: Completed

Figure 5.7: Vue instance axios todo display sample

With that, we have used a plugin to inject both global and instance-level properties and methods, as well as having learned how they can be used to create directives and other Vue constructs in a format that is easy to distribute.

We will now look at how globally registering components can help reduce boilerplate for high usage components in a code base.

GLOBALLY REGISTERING COMPONENTS

A reason for using plugins is to reduce boilerplate in all Vue application files by removing **imports** and replacing them with access to **this** and/or **Vue**.

Vue.js components are usually defined in a single-file component and imported explicitly. Much for the same reasons as we define global methods and properties, we might want to register components globally. This will allow us to use these components in all our other component templates without having to import them and register them under the **components** property.

A situation where this can be very useful is when using a design system or when a component is used across the code base.

Globally registering a component helps with some types of updates, such as if the filename is not exposed to the consumer so that when changing the filename, there is only one path to update as opposed to one per user.

Let's assume we have a **CustomButton** component in the **CustomButton.vue** file that looks as follows:

```
<template>
  <button @click="$emit('click', $event)">
    <slot />
  </button>
</template>
```

We can register **CustomButton** globally as follows (this is usually done in the **main.js** file):

```
// other imports
import CustomButton from './components/CustomButton.vue'

Vue.component('CustomButton', CustomButton)

// other global instance setup
```

We can now use it in the **App.vue** file without locally registering it or importing it:

```
<template>
  <div>
    <CustomButton>Click Me</CustomButton>
  </div>
</template>
```

This renders as expected, with a button called **Click Me**:

Figure 5.8: CustomButton rendering with a Click Me button

With that, we have explored how globally registering components can cut down on boilerplate when components are used often across a code base.

Next, we will look at some tips on how to increase component flexibility in Vue.js.

MAXIMIZING COMPONENT FLEXIBILITY

Vue.js components take props and slots as input; their output is rendered as HTML and emitted events.

To maximize component flexibility, it always makes sense to leverage slots and props.

Leveraging props and default values judiciously means a component can be reused and extended. For example, instead of hardcoding a value in the component, we could set it as a default prop. In this case, **date** defaults to the current date, **new Date()**. We then extract the epoch using a computed property:

```
<template>
  <div>Date as epoch: {{ epoch }}</div>
</template>
<script>
export default {
  props: {
    date: {
      type: Date,
      default() {
        return new Date()
      }
    }
  },
  computed: {
    epoch() {
      return Number(this.date)
    }
  }
}
</script>
```

When registered and used, this renders as follows:

```
Date as epoch: 1574289255348
```

Slots can be thought of as a way for a component to delegate rendering back to its consumers. Delegating parts of the template to the parent component helps with reusability.

A specific example of slots used to maximize reusability is the **renderless component** pattern. For example, in the epoch display example, we could leverage scoped slots and remove any rendering logic from the component:

```
<template>
  <div>
    <slot :epoch="epoch" />
  </div>
</template>
```

In the parent component, the rendering can be defined using a scoped slot:

```
<template>
  <div>
    <Epoch>
      <template v-slot:default="{ epoch }">
        Epoch as rendered with parent template {{ epoch }}
      </template>
    </Epoch>
  </div>
</template>
```

This means that the delegation of the component is delegated to the parent and displays the following:

```
Epoch as rendered with parent template 1574289270190
```

The next set of practices maximize the reuse of components by making their API predictable. In many ways, forwarding attributes, leveraging the **style** and **class** attributes being merged, and implementing a **v-model** interface is another way of making Vue.js custom components behave more like HTML elements.

Forwarding attributes can be interesting. For example, a **CustomInput** component (in the **CustomInput.vue** file) might need to pass the **type** attribute, as well as a **required** attribute:

```
<template>
  <input v-bind="$attrs">
</template>
```

The **CustomInput** component can be used to render any type of component (**src/App.vue**):

```
<template>
  <div id="app">
    <fieldset>
      <label for="textinput">
        Text Input
      </label>
      <CustomInput
      type="text"
      name="textinput"
      id="textinput"
      />
    </fieldset>
    <fieldset>
      <label for="dateinput">
        Date Input
      </label>
      <CustomInput
        type="date"
        name="dateinput"
        id="dateinput"
      />
    </fieldset>
  </div>
</template>
<script>
import CustomInput from './components/CustomInput.vue'

export default {
  components: {
    CustomInput
  }
}
</script>
```

This renders the text and date inputs correctly:

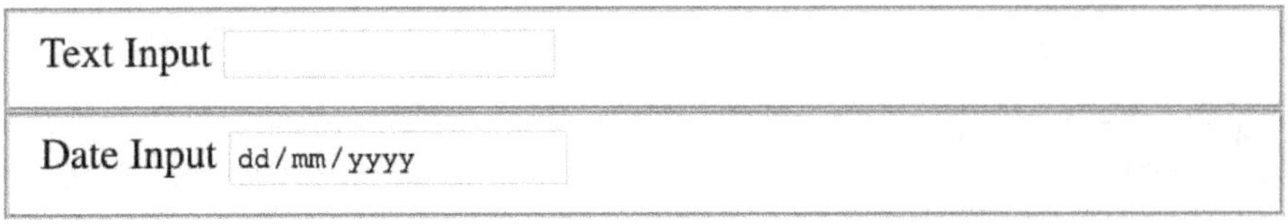

Text Input	
Date Input	dd / mm / yyyy

Figure 5.9: CustomInput with text and date as types

Vue.js does a lot of the heavy lifting around classes/inline styles since it merges the **style** and **class** objects defined on a component with the **style** and **class** objects of the root element in said component. As per the documentation, "*the class and style attributes are a little smarter, so both values are merged*" (*Vue.js Component Props guide*: https://vuejs.org/v2/guide/components-props.html#Replacing-Merging-with-Existing-Attributes).

In Vue.js, the tendency is for input elements and components to be controlled through **v-model**, a two-way reactive Vue.js binding. **v-model** is shorthand for using **v-bind:value** and **v-on:input** to provide a value and keep it in sync with the output from the child component or element.

The **controlled** denomination is the opposite of **uncontrolled**. In an uncontrolled scenario, the **value** that is passed is only used as the starting value; **input** events are emitted when the input is done being captured (for example, typing is done).

If a component implements the **v-model** shape, it works as a direct replacement for form elements.

For example, a **TextInput** that implements the **v-model** interface can be used interchangeably with **input** and **textarea**:

```
<template>
  <div>
    <textarea
      v-if="type === 'long'"
      :value="value"
      @input="$emit('input', $event.target.value)"
    >
    </textarea>
    <input
      v-else
```

```
      :value="value"
      @input="$emit('input', $event.target.value)"
      type="text"
    />
  </div>
</template>
<script>
export default {
  props: ['value', 'type']
}
</script>
```

This can then be used as follows in **src/App.vue**:

```
<template>
  <div id="app">
    <label>Short Text: {{ shortText }}</label>
    <TextInput v-model="shortText" type="short" />
    <label>Long Text: {{ longText }}</label>
    <TextInput v-model="longText" type="long" />
  </div>
</template>
<script>
import TextInput from './components/TextInput.vue'

export default {
  components: {
    TextInput
  },
  data() {
    return {
      shortText: '',
      longText: ''
    }
  }
}
</script>
```

The application renders as follows:

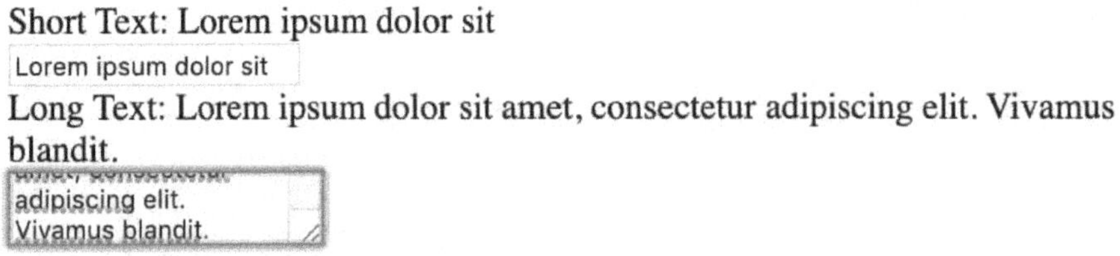

Short Text: Lorem ipsum dolor sit

Lorem ipsum dolor sit

Long Text: Lorem ipsum dolor sit amet, consectetur adipiscing elit. Vivamus blandit.

adipiscing elit.
Vivamus blandit.

Figure 5.10: Custom component implementing v-model

With that, we have looked at how to leverage props and slots, inherit attributes, and implement well-known Vue.js interfaces to help maximize component flexibility.

The next section is dedicated to deepening our understanding of Vue.js components by learning how to use them without **.vue** files.

USING VUE.JS COMPONENTS WITHOUT A .VUE SINGLE-FILE COMPONENT

Most of the examples we have seen of Vue.js components have leveraged **.vue** single-file components.

This is not the only way to define a Vue.js component. In this section, we will look at four different ways to define Vue.js components without using a **.vue** file.

Evaluating these options will help us understand what a Vue.js component is at its core.

RUNTIME DEFINITION WITH A STRING TEMPLATE

A component can use a **template** property that accepts a string value. This is commonly called a **string template**. This template is evaluated at runtime (in the browser).

We can define a component in the **StringTemplate.js** file by defining an object with a **template** property:

```
export default {
  template: `<div>String Template Component</div>`
}
```

This can then be consumed from the **App.vue** file, as follows:

```
<template>
  <div id="app">
    <StringTemplate />
  </div>
</template>
<script>
import StringTemplate from './components/StringTemplate.js'

export default {
  components: {
    StringTemplate
  }
}
</script>
```

Unfortunately, this crashes on load and displays the following Vue warning in the console:

```
⊗ ▶ [Vue warn]: You are using the runtime-only build of Vue vue.runtime.esm.js?e832:619
  where the template compiler is not available. Either pre-compile the templates into
  render functions, or use the compiler-included build.

  found in

  ---> <StringTemplate>
         <App> at src/App.vue
           <Root>
```

Figure 5.11: Vue runtime compiler missing warning

As per the Vue warning, for this component to work when imported, we need to include the Vue.js compiler in the runtime build. To do so, in a Vue CLI project, we can set the **runtimeCompiler** option to **true** in **vue.config.js** (the Vue CLI configuration file).

Your **vue.config.js** should look like the following:

```
module.exports = {
  runtimeCompiler: true
};
```

After setting this option and restarting the development server, a message from the **StringTemplate** component appears in the browser:

```
String Template Component
```

Props and other component instance properties can be defined with **.vue** component objects.

THE RENDER FUNCTION

A Vue.js single-file component **template** section gets compiled into a **render** function at build time.

A **render** function tends to be used in the **main.js** file of a Vue CLI project – specifically, the **new Vue()** call:

```
new Vue({
    render: h => h(App),
}).$mount('#app')
```

A **render** function takes a **createElement** parameter and returns a virtual DOM node. This is done by calling the **createElement** function (in the preceding example, this is **h**).

h is often used as shorthand for **createElement** due to its compactness.

We can define a component in a JavaScript file (**RenderFunction.js**) with a **render** property like so:

```
export default {
    render(createElement) {
        return createElement(
            'h2',
            'Render Function Component'
        )
    }
}
```

This can be rendered in the **App.vue** file as follows:

```
<template>
    <div id="app">
        <RenderFunction />
    </div>
</template>
```

```
<script>
import RenderFunction from './components/RenderFunction.js'

export default {
  components: {
    RenderFunction
  }
}
</script>
```

This component displays a **h2** with **Render Function Component** as its content in the browser:

```
Render Function Component
```

Beyond writing components in non `.vue` files, **render** functions can be useful for highly dynamic components.

JSX

JSX has been popularized by React. As per the React documentation, *JSX is a syntax extension to JavaScript. We recommend using it with React to describe what the UI should look like* (https://reactjs.org/docs/introducing-jsx.html). JSX is a superset of JavaScript that allows **HTML-style** tags and interpolation using braces.

React, like Vue.js, does not render JSX to the DOM. Like Vue.js templates, React application build tools compile JSX to **render** functions that are used at runtime so that they can be rendered to the Virtual DOM. The Virtual DOM is then *reconciled* (synced) with the real DOM.

JSX compiles to **render** functions and Vue.js supports component definitions with **render** functions. Moreover, **Vue CLI 3+** compiles JSX out of the box.

This means we can write the following, which is the equivalent of the **RenderFunction** component, **JSXRender.js** file:

```
export default {
  render() {
    return <h2>JSX Render Function Component</h2>
  }
}
```

The equivalent **render** function without JSX looks as follows (based on the example from the previous section):

```
export default {
  render(createElement) {
    return createElement(
      'h2',
      'JSX Render Function Component'
    )
  }
}
```

The following **App.vue** file renders **JSXRender** to the browser:

```
<template>
  <div id="app">
    <JSXRender />
  </div>
</template>
<script>
import JSXRender from './components/JSXRender.js'

export default {
  components: {
    JSXRender
  }
}
</script>
```

Now, we can see the **h2** from **JSXRender** on the screen with the expected content:

```
JSX Render Function Component
```

With that, we have learned that Vue.js components are just objects with a **render** or **template** function. **.vue** component **template** sections are compiled to **render** functions at build time, which means that to use string templates, we need to include the Vue.js compiler in the application runtime. We have also learned how to use **render** functions, as well as JSX, to define components and pointed out some things React and Vue.js have in common from an implementation point of view. When choosing to use JSX or **render** functions, JSX can be easier to read with the full flexibility of **render** functions (which regular templates do not always have).

We will now look at how components can be rendered dynamically from runtime data using the Vue.js **component** tag.

THE VUE COMPONENT TAG

JSX and **render** functions are great for situations where the component being rendered needs to be very dynamic.

The way to achieve this within regular Vue.js templates is by using the **component** tag.

The **component** tag uses the **is** prop to dynamically select which component will be rendered.

To render a dynamic component, we use a **component** tag with a bound **is** property (here, we are using the shorthand **:is**, which is equivalent to **v-bind:is**):

```
<component :is="componentName" />
```

We will now learn how to render dynamic components using a name or component reference.

RENDERING DYNAMIC COMPONENTS BY NAME OR COMPONENT REFERENCE

Let's say we have a grid that contains items whose display can be toggled between a card display (a design element with an image and text) or an image-only view.

First, we need to import the relevant components and register them as components. We will also set some fixture data to loop through for the grid:

```
<template>
  <div id="app">
    <div class="grid">
      <component
        class="grid-item"
        v-for="item in items"
        :key="item.id"
      />
    </div>
  </div>
</template>
<script>
import Card from './components/Card.vue';
import ImageEntry from './components/ImageEntry.vue';
```

```
export default {
  components: {
    Card,
    ImageEntry
  },
  data() {
    return {
      items: [
        {
          id: '10',
          title: 'Forest Shot',
          url: 'https://picsum.photos/id/10/1000/750.jpg',
        },
        {
          id: '1000',
          title: 'Cold cross',
          url: 'https://picsum.photos/id/1000/1000/750.jpg',
        },
        {
          id: '1002',
          title: 'NASA shot',
          url: 'https://picsum.photos/id/1002/1000/750.jpg',
        },
        {
          id: '866',
          title: 'Peak',
          url: 'https://picsum.photos/id/866/1000/750.jpg'
        },
      ]
    }
  }
}
</script>
```

We can then reference the components by name – that is, **card** and **image-entry** – and set **itemComponent** as the value for **is**:

```
<template>
    <!-- rest of template -->
    <component
```

```
      :is="itemComponent"

      class="grid-item"
      v-for="item in items"
      :key="item.id"
    />
    <!-- rest of template -->
</template>
<script>
// rest of script
export default {
  // other component properties
  data() {
    return {
      itemComponent: 'card',
      // other data properties eg. `items`
    }
  }
}
</script>
```

In this case, the **Card** component will render since we are passing its lowercased name (**card**) to the **component** tag.

If we turned **itemComponent** into **image-entry**, the **ImageEntry** component would render. This switch can be made as follows using **v-model**:

```
<template>
  <!-- rest of template -->
  Display mode:
  <input
    type="radio"
    name="style"
    value="card"
    v-model="itemComponent"
    id="card-radio"
  />
  <label for="card-radio">Card</label>

  <input
    type="radio"
    name="style"
```

```
    value="image-entry"
    v-model="itemComponent"
    id="image-radio"
  />
  <label for="image-radio">Image</label>

  <!-- rest of template -->
</template>
```

We can also pass components to **is** using the component reference itself (instead of the name). For example, we could set **itemComponent** to **Card**:

```
<script>
// rest of script
export default {
  // other component properties
  data() {
    return {
      itemComponent: Card,
      // other data properties eg. `items`
    }
  }
}
</script>
```

In this case, switching between card and image views would be more difficult since we would need to use component references instead of using names.

We can pass props to components that have been dynamically rendered with **component** as we would pass regular props either with **v-bind:prop-name** or the **:prop-name** shorthand:

```
<template>
    <!-- rest of template -->
    <component
      class="grid-item"
      v-for="item in items"
      :key="item.id"
      :is="itemComponent"
```

```
      :url="item.url"
      :title="item.title"
    />
    <!-- rest of template -->
</template>
```

Given the following **Card** and **ImageEntry** components, we get an application that has toggleable views for grid items.

Card.vue renders the image and the title and has a **150px** maximum width:

```
<template>
  <div class="card">
    <img :src="url" width="100%" />
    <h3>{{ title }}</h3>
  </div>
</template>

<script>
export default {
  props: {
    url: String,
    title: String
  }
}
</script>

<style scoped>
.card {
  margin: 10px;
  max-width: 150px;
}
h3 {
  font-weight: normal;
}
</style>
```

Your output will display the entries in card view, as follows:

Figure 5.12: Grid rendering entries in card view

Use **ImageEntry.vue** to render only the image at double the width of the card view:

```
<template>
  <img class="image" :src="url" />
</template>

<script>
export default {
  props: {
    url: String
  }
}
</script>

<style scoped>
.image {
  margin: 20px;
  max-width: 300px;
}
</style>
```

You will now see the entries in an image view, as shown in the following screenshot:

Figure 5.13: Grid rendering entries in an image view

A caveat of the **component** tag is that the rendered dynamic component gets completely torn down when it is not displayed anymore. In this example, the dynamic components being rendered do not have any state, so this teardown does not create any issues.

We will now learn how a dynamic component state is cached.

CACHING A DYNAMIC COMPONENT STATE WITH KEEP-ALIVE

Components that are dynamically rendered through the **component** tag can have state, such as in a multipart form, with a **name** field and an **address** field on the next page.

Let's implement this with a **component** tag, as follows:

```
<template>
  <div id="app">
    <component
      :is="activeStep"
      @next="activeStep = 'second-step'"
      @back="activeStep = 'first-step'"
    />
  </div>
</template>
<script>
import FirstStep from './components/FirstStep.vue'
import SecondStep from './components/SecondStep.vue'

export default {
  components: {
    FirstStep,
    SecondStep
  },
  data() {
    return {
      activeStep: 'first-step',
    }
  }
}
</script>
```

By doing this, we can enter data in the **Name** field:

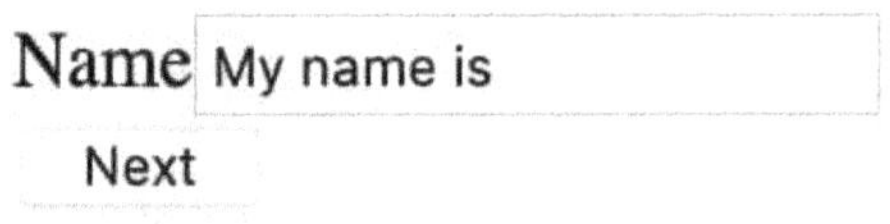

Name My name is

Next

Figure 5.14: My name is entered in the name field

If we navigate, using **Next**, (to the address part of the form) and then **Back**, the name will disappear, as shown in the following screenshot:

Name

Next

Figure 5.15: Empty name field upon clicking Next and then Back in the address step

This is due to the component being torn down (destroyed) when it is not the currently rendered dynamic component.

To fix this, we can use the **keep-alive** element around the **component** tag:

```
<template>
  <!-- rest of template -->
  <keep-alive>
    <component
      :is="activeStep"
      @next="activeStep = 'second-step'"
      @back="activeStep = 'first-step'"
    />
  </keep-alive>
  <!-- rest of template -->
</template>
```

In this manner, filling out the name and going **Back** from the address section of the form shows the following:

Name My name is

Next

Figure 5.16: My name is is still the value in the Name field after navigation

With that, we have learned how to use the **component** tag to denote an area within which we can dynamically display a component based on a string or the component itself (as imported). We have also explored how to work around the main gotcha of **component**; namely, how to use **keep-alive** to maintain component state when it is not the component being actively used in the **component** tag.

EXERCISE 5.03: CREATING A DYNAMIC CARD LAYOUT WITH THE COMPONENT TAG

A modern application layout is a grid with cards. **Card** layouts have the benefit of being well-suited to mobile, desktop, and tablet displays. In this exercise, we will create a dynamic **card** layout with three different modes and a way to select between the three of them. This layout will allow the user to select how much information is displayed on the screen to suit their preference.

The **Rich** view will display all the details for an item, including the image, the title, and the description.

The **Compressed** view will display all the details but not the image preview.

The **List** view will only display the title and should be a vertical layout.

Each of the **card** views will be implemented as a separate component that will then be dynamically rendered using the **component** tag. To access the code files for this exercise, refer to https://packt.live/3mYYvkq.

Follow these steps to complete this exercise:

1. Create the rich layout at **src/components/Rich.vue**. It contains three props called **url** (the image URL), **title**, and **description** and renders the image, the title, and the description, respectively:

```
<template>
  <div class="card">
    <img :src="url" width="100%" />
    <h3>{{ title }}</h3>
    <p>{{ description }}</p>
  </div>
</template>

<script>
export default {
  props: ['url', 'title', 'description']
}
</script>

<style scoped>
.card {
  display: flex;
  flex-direction: column;
  max-width: 200px;
```

```
    }
    h3 {
      font-weight: normal;
      margin-bottom: 0;
      padding-bottom: 0;
    }
    </style>
```

2. Set up **src/App.vue** with some fixture data:

```
<template>
  <div id="app">
  </div>
</template>
<script>
export default {
  data() {
    return {
      items: [
        {
          id: '10',
          title: 'Forest Shot',
          description: 'Recent shot of a forest overlooking a
            lake',
          url: 'https://picsum.photos/id/10/1000/750.jpg',
        },
        {
          id: '1000',
          title: 'Cold cross',
          description: 'Mountaintop cross with snowfall from
            Jan 2018',
          url: 'https://picsum.photos/id/1000/1000/750.jpg',
        },
      ]
    }
  }
}
</script>
```

3. Import the **Rich** view component into **src/App.vue** and register it locally:

```
<script>
import Rich from './components/Rich.vue'

export default {
  components: {
    Rich
  },
  // other component properties, eg. "data"
}
</script>
```

4. Once we have got the **Rich** view component, wire it into the application in **src/App.vue**, render it with **component**, and pass the relevant props through:

```
<template>
  <!-- rest of template -->
    <component
      v-for="item in items"
      :key="item.id"
      :is="layout"
      :title="item.title"
      :description="item.description"
      :url="item.url"
    />
  <!-- rest of template>
</template>
<script>
export default {
 // other component properties
  data() {
    return {
      layout: 'rich',
      // other data definitions eg. `items`
    }
  }
}
</script>
```

5. This is a good point to add a bit of styling to make the grid look like a grid:

```
<template>
  <!-- rest of template -->
    <div class="grid">
      <component
        v-for="item in items"
        :key="item.id"
        :is="layout"
        :title="item.title"
        :description="item.description"
        :url="item.url"
      />
    </div>
  <!-- rest of template -->
</template>

<style scoped>
.grid {
  display: flex;
}
</style>
```

This displays the following output:

Forest Shot

Recent shot of a forest
overlooking a lake

Cold cross

Mountaintop cross with
snowfall from Jan 2018

Figure 5.17: Rich component rendering dynamically

6. Now, implement the **Compressed** view, which is just the **Rich** view without the image in the **Compressed.vue** file:

```
<template>
  <div class="card">
    <h3>{{ title }}</h3>
    <p>{{ description }}</p>
  </div>
</template>

<script>
export default {
  props: ['title', 'description']
}
</script>

<style scoped>
.card {
  display: flex;
  flex-direction: column;
  max-width: 200px;
}
h3 {
  font-weight: normal;
  padding-bottom: 0;
}
p {
 margin: 0;
}
</style>
```

7. Import and register the **Compressed** component in **src/App.vue**:

```
<script>
// other imports
import Compressed from './components/Compressed.vue'

export default {
  components: {
    Rich,
```

```
    Compressed,
  },
  // other component properties
}
```

8. Add a **select** to switch between views. It will have two options with values for **rich** and **compressed** and will be bound to **layout** using **v-model**:

```
<template>
  <!-- rest of template -->
  Layout: <select v-model="layout">
      <option value="rich">Rich</option>
      <option value="compressed">Compressed</option>
    </select>
  <!-- rest of template -->
</template>
```

Using this **select**, we can switch to the **compressed** layout, which looks as follows:

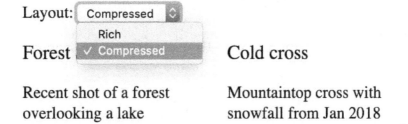

Figure 5.18: Compressed layout with select open

9. Add the **List** layout to **src/components/List.vue**. The **list** view is the compressed view but without the description:

```
<template>
  <h3>{{ title }}</h3>
</template>

<script>
export default {
  props: ['title']
}
</script>
```

```
<style scoped>
h3 {
  width: 100%;
  font-weight: normal;
}
</style>
```

10. Import the **List** component into **src/App.vue** and register it locally:

```
<script>
// other imports
import List from './components/List.vue'

export default {
  components: {
    Rich,
    Compressed,
    List
  },
  // other component properties
}
```

11. Add an extra option with **value="list"** to switch to the **List** layout:

```
<template>
  <!-- rest of template -->
    Layout: <select v-model="layout">
      <option value="rich">Rich</option>
      <option value="compressed">Compressed</option>
      <option value="list">List</option>
    </select>
  <!-- rest of template -->
</template>
```

When switching to the **list** layout, the items are displayed in a horizontal row, as follows:

Layout: List

Forest Shot   **Cold cross**

Figure 5.19: List view with incorrect horizontal stacking

12. To fix this horizontal stacking, create a new **grid-column** class that sets **flex-direction: column** (as opposed to **row**, which is the default) and conditionally applies it when the layout is **list**:

```
<template>
  <!-- rest of template -->
    <div class="grid" :class="{ 'grid-column': layout ===
      'list' }">
      <!-- grid using component tag -->
    </div>
  <!-- rest of template -->
</template>

<style scoped>
/* existing rules */
.grid-column {
  flex-direction: column;
}
</style>
```

Our **List** layout now looks as follows:

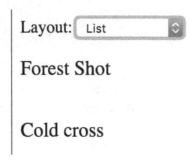

Figure 5.20: List view with vertical stacking

With that, we have learned how to use the **component** tag to dynamically render different components both by name and by using the component object itself. We have also explored the pitfalls of stateful dynamic components, namely the teardown of components when they are not displayed anymore and how to circumvent them using the **keep-alive** element.

We will now look at how simple components can be implemented using only a **render** function or **template** tag using functional components.

FUNCTIONAL COMPONENTS

Functional components are a subset of regular Vue.js components. They do not have state or a component instance. They can be thought of as **render** functions (as shown earlier in this chapter) to which props are passed.

> **NOTE**
>
> We can mark components as functional, which means that they are stateless (no reactive data) and instance-less (no **this** context).

See the Vue.js documentation for more (https://vuejs.org/v2/guide/render-function. html#Functional-Components).

Functional components can only access props, children, slots, and scoped slots, as passed from their parent component. They also receive references to **parents** and **listeners**.

The following is a **Greet** component (in the **Greet.vue** file). Note the **functional** annotation in **template**:

```
<template functional>
  <div>Functional Component: {{ props.greeting }} {{
    props.audience }}</div>
</template>
```

Functional components must access props through **props.propName**. Functional components can also be denoted by the **functional: true** Boolean and be used with a **render** function:

```
export default {
  functional: true,
  render(h, context) {
    return h(
      'h2',
      `Functional Render: ${context.props.greeting}
        ${context.props.audience}`
    )
  }
}
```

We can use both these functional components in the **App.vue** file:

```
<template>
  <div id="app">
    <Greet greeting="Hello" audience="World" />
    <GreetRender greeting="Hello" audience="World" />
  </div>
</template>
<script>
import Greet from './components/Greet.vue'
import GreetRender from './components/GreetRender.js'

export default {
  components: {
    Greet,
    GreetRender
  }
}
</script>
```

This renders the following to the browser:

Functional Component: Hello World

Functional Render: Hello World

Figure 5.21: Functional component rendering

Functional components are a great way to encapsulate functionality that is render-only; that is, they derive their templates from props. They have a slightly better performance profile than regular components since they do not have any associated reactive state or a component instance.

A common use case we have covered for non-functional components is emitting events, which can be done as follows:

```
<template>
  <input
    type="submit"
    @click="$emit('click', $event)"
  />
</template>
```

To emit an event with a functional component, we can bind elements to properties in the **listeners** object.

To delegate all events to a child, we can use **v-on="listeners"**:

```
<template functional>
  <input
    v-on="listeners"
    v-bind="data.attrs"
  />
</template>
```

To bind a specific listener, we can use **v-on:eventName="listeners. listenerName"**, where **listenerName** is the listener that the parent of the functional component is bound to:

```
<template functional>
  <input
    type="submit"
    v-on:click="listeners.click"
    v-bind="data.attrs"
  />
</template>
```

> **NOTE**
>
> Binding to a listener property that does not exist will result in an error. To avoid this, we can use the **listeners.listenerName || (() => {})** expression.

With that, we have learned how to implement common Vue.js component patterns using functional components with both the **.vue** component **template** variant and **render** functions.

We will now build a to-do application that uses all the patterns we have looked at throughout this chapter.

ACTIVITY 5.01: BUILDING A VUE.JS APPLICATION WITH PLUGINS AND REUSABLE COMPONENTS

In this activity, we will build a **to-do** app that integrates **jsonplaceholder** as a data source.

Our to-do app will load todos and display them as a list. It will display a checkbox based on whether the to-do has been completed, as well as the name of the to-do.

When checking off a to-do, the application will sync it to the API.

We will inject **axios** as a plugin to query against https://jsonplaceholder.typicode.com.

Follow these steps to complete this activity:

1. Install **axios** into the project.

2. To inject **axios** as a property into **this** component instances, create a **src/plugins/axios.js** plugin file that, on **install**, will mean component instances have an **axios** property.

3. For the plugin to work, import and register it in **src/main.js**.

4. We also want to inject our API's **baseUrl** into all our components. We will create a plugin inline of the **src/main.js** file to do this.

5. We now want to fetch all the to-dos from our **src/App.vue**. A good place to do this is in the **mounted** life cycle method.

6. To display the to-do list, we will create a **TodoList** functional component in **src/components/TodoList.vue** that takes a **todos** prop, loops through the items, and defers rendering of the to-do under a **todo** scoped slot that binds the to-do.

7. We can now use the **TodoList** component to render out the todos we have already fetched in **src/App.vue**.

8. We now need to create a **TodoEntry** component where we will implement most of the to-do-specific logic. A good practice for components is to have the props be very specific to the component's role. In this case, the properties of the **todo** object we will tackle are **id**, **title**, and **completed**, so those should be the props that our **TodoEntry** component receives. We will not make **TodoEntry** a functional component since we will need a component instance to create HTTP requests.

9. We will then update **src/App.vue** so that it consumes **TodoEntry** (making sure to bind **id**, **title**, and **completed**).

10. Add the ability to toggle the **Complete** status of a **todo**. We will implement the majority of this in **src/components/TodoEntry.vue**. We will listen to the **input** change event. On change, we will want to read the new value and send a **PATCH** request to **/todos/{todoId}** with an object containing **completed** set to the new value. We will also want to emit a **completedChange** event in Vue.js so that the **App** component can update the data that's in-memory.

11. In **App.vue**, we will want to update the relevant **todo** when **completeChange** is triggered. Since **completeChange** does not include the ID of the **todo**, we will need to read that from the context when setting the **handleCompleteChange** function to listen to **completeChange**.

The expected output is as follows:

- delectus aut autem ☐
- quis ut nam facilis et officia qui ☐
- fugiat veniam minus ☐
- et porro tempora ☑
- laboriosam mollitia et enim quasi adipisci quia provident illum ☐
- qui ullam ratione quibusdam voluptatem quia omnis ☐
- illo expedita consequatur quia in ☐
- quo adipisci enim quam ut ab ☑
- molestiae perspiciatis ipsa ☐
- illo est ratione doloremque quia maiores aut ☑
- vero rerum temporibus dolor ☑
- ipsa repellendus fugit nisi ☑
- et doloremque nulla ☐
- repellendus sunt dolores architecto voluptatum ☑
- ab voluptatum amet voluptas ☑
- accusamus eos facilis sint et aut voluptatem ☑
- quo laboriosam deleniti aut qui ☑
- dolorum est consequatur ea mollitia in culpa ☐
- molestiae ipsa aut voluptatibus pariatur dolor nihil ☑
- ullam nobis libero sapiente ad optio sint ☑
- suscipit repellat esse quibusdam voluptatem incidunt ☐
- distinctio vitae autem nihil ut molestias quo ☑
- et itaque necessitatibus maxime molestiae qui quas velit ☐
- adipisci non ad dicta qui amet quaerat doloribus ea ☐
- voluptas quo tenetur perspiciatis explicabo natus ☑
- aliquam aut quasi ☑
- veritatis pariatur delectus ☑
- nesciunt totam sit blanditiis sit ☐
- laborum aut in quam ☐
- nemo perspiciatis repellat ut dolor libero commodi blanditiis omnis ☑
- repudiandae totam in est sint facere fuga ☐
- earum doloribus ea doloremque quis ☐
- sint sit aut vero ☐

Figure 5.22: Our to-do app using jsonplaceholder data

> **NOTE**
>
> The solution for this activity can be found on page 665.

SUMMARY

Throughout this chapter, we have looked at global composition patterns and advanced component setups that can be used to reduce duplication throughout a Vue.js application.

First, we learned about mixins, which explicitly share functionality while letting components have the last say and saw the exceptions to this rule. We then saw how plugins are a great hook into multiple Vue.js primitives.

Next, we looked at how prescriptive patterns maximize component reusability in Vue.js. Ideas such as leveraging props to delegate data, slots to delegate templates, and implementing interfaces that allow components to be used with Vue-idiomatic shorthand such as **v-model** were shown.

We also took an in-depth look at what Vue.js components are beyond **.vue** files. We delved into what a Vue.js component is by introducing string templates, **render** functions, and JSX, as well as the requirements for each of these approaches to work. The **component** tag and **keep-alive** showed another approach to dynamically rendering components in Vue.js applications based on reactive data. Finally, we saw how functional components cement how we can define components with **.vue** files.

So far, we have learned how to build applications in terms of components, mixins, and plugins. To build applications that span multiple pages, we need to implement routing. This is what we will tackle in the next chapter.

6

ROUTING

OVERVIEW

In this chapter, we will understand how routing and Vue Router work. We will also set up, implement, and manage the routing system in our app with Vue Router. Then we will look at dynamic routing for passing parameter values and nested routes for better reusability in complex applications. In addition, we will look at JavaScript Hooks, which can be used for features such as authentication and error handling. By the end of this chapter, you will be ready to handle static and dynamic routing in any Vue application.

INTRODUCTION

Routing is one of the most essential and primary parts of building dynamic web applications. You may be familiar with the word in its everyday context. For example, when we use Google Maps, we find the best route to get to a location. Routing in Vue and other frameworks is much the same. It is the process of getting a user to their desired location. When a user enters **website.com/about** into their URL bar, they are routed to the about page.

With **Single-Page Applications** (**SPAs**), routing allows navigation within the application to be done smoothly and without the need for page refreshing. In web development, routing is the matching mechanism by which we decide how to connect HTTP requests to the code that handles them. We use routing whenever there is a need for URL navigation in our application. Most modern web applications contain a lot of different URLs, even single-page ones. Thus, routing plays a significant role in creating a navigation system and helps users move around our application and the web quickly.

In short, routing is a way for an application to interpret what resource users want based on the URL provided. It is a system for web-based resource navigation with URLs, such as paths to assets (images and videos), scripts, and stylesheets.

VUE ROUTER

Vue Router, as stated in the Vue.js documentation, is officially recommended as a router service for any Vue.js application. It provides a single entry point for communication between components with routes, hence controlling the flow of the application effectively, regardless of the user's behavior.

With a wide range of features, it eases the process of switching pages without the need to refresh the page.

SETTING UP VUE ROUTER

Vue Router is not installed by default; however, it can easily be enabled when creating an application with Vue CLI. Create an application by running the following command:

```
vue create <your-project-name>
```

Select the **Manually select features** option as shown in *Figure 6.1*:

```
? Please pick a preset:


  default (babel, eslint)
> Manually select features


(Move up and down to reveal more choices)
```

Figure 6.1: Select the manual preset to create a new Vue.js project

After choosing the option to manually select features, you will be shown a list of features as presented in *Figure 6.2*. At the time of writing, by default **Babel** and **Linter / Formatter** are selected. Using the *down arrow* key, navigate to the **Router** option. With the option highlighted, press the *spacebar* to enable it, and then press *Enter* to continue.

```
? Please pick a preset: Manually select features
? Check the features needed for your project:
 ⦿ Babel
 ○ TypeScript
 ○ Progressive Web App (PWA) Support
 ⦿ Router
 ○ Vuex
 ○ CSS Pre-processors
 ○ Linter / Formatter
>⦿ Unit Testing
 ○ E2E Testing
```

Figure 6.2: Add Vue Router to the project

Next, you will be shown a prompt asking if you want to use **history mode** for router configuration, as shown in *Figure 6.3*. Enable history mode by entering **Y**. History mode allows navigating between pages without the reload required by the default hash mode. We'll compare the two modes more closely later in the chapter:

```
? Please pick a preset: Manually select features
? Check the features needed for your project: Babel, Router, Unit
? Use history mode for router? (Requires proper server setup for index fallback
in production) (Y/n) Y
```

Figure 6.3: Configure Vue Router with history mode

Finally, continue with the rest of the process and we will have a Vue.js application with Vue Router ready to use.

> **NOTE**
>
> If you would like to add Vue Router to an existing Vue.js application, you can install it as an application's dependency with the following command:
>
> `npm install vue-router`

The next step is to understand the basics of how **vue-router** performs synchronization between the browser URL and the application's view.

First, let's look at the **router-view** element.

THE ROUTER-VIEW ELEMENT

The **router-view** element is a **functional** component in which the app routing system loads the matched and up-to-date view content of any given URL path received from the user.

In short, **router-view** is a Vue component whose job is to do the following:

- Render different child components

- Mount and unmount itself automatically at any nesting level, depending on the route's given path

Without **router-view**, it is almost impossible to have dynamic content rendered correctly for users at runtime. For example, when a user navigates to the **Home** page, **router-view** knows and renders the content related to that page only.

In the next section, we will see how we can set the entry point (default route) of an application by passing it a prop.

USING PROPS TO DEFINE THE ENTRY POINT OF AN APPLICATION

Since **router-view** is a component, it can also receive props. The only prop it receives is **name**, which is the same name registered in the corresponding route's record defined in the **router** object at the initialization phase.

Any other additional attributes are passed directly to the child component of **router-view** during rendering. Here is an example with a class attribute:

```
<router-view class="main-app-view"/>
```

If **router-view** renders as a child component, we can create an associated template where the layout is defined. A very simple example of a template is as follows:

```
<template>
  <div>Hello World</div>
</template>
```

The child component receives the passed attribute class, and the actual output after rendering becomes the following:

```
<div class="main-app-view">Hello World</div>
```

Of course, for our template to be useful, it should also contain the **<router-view/>** element so that content we want to route has somewhere to be rendered. One common setup is to have a navigation menu within the template and **router-view** underneath. That way the content changes between pages but the menu stays the same.

Navigate to **App.vue** and ensure your template has the following code:

```
<template>
  <div id="app">
    <div id="nav">
      <router-link to="/">Home</router-link> |
      <router-link to="/about">About</router-link>
    </div>
    <router-view/>
  </div>
</template>
```

Let's remove all the code within **<div id="app">** and leave only one single **<router-view/>** component:

```
<div id="app">
    <router-view/>
  </div>
```

We will now comment out all the code for **routes** as follows:

```
const routes = [
  // {
  //   path: '/',
  //   name: 'Home',
  //   component: Home
```

```
// },
// {
//    path: '/about',
//    name: 'About',
//    // route level code-splitting
//    // this generates a separate chunk (about.[hash].js) for
  this route
//    // which is lazy-loaded when the route is visited.
//    component: () => import(/* webpackChunkName: "about" */
  '../views/About.vue')
// }
]
```

Now our app output will be rendered as a blank page running on **localhost:8080**, as shown in *Figure 6.4*:

Figure 6.4: Hello Vue Router application in the browser

The output is an empty page because we have not set up any router configurations in our file, including mapping the paths with the related view. Without this step, the routing system will not be able to pick the right view and render it into our **router-view** element dynamically.

In the next section, we will see how to set up Vue Router.

SETTING UP VUE ROUTER FOR VUE TO USE

When we add Vue Router to our project, Vue CLI creates and adds a **router** folder to the code directory, containing a single auto-generated **index.js** file. This file contains the necessary configurations for our router.

We will navigate to the file and go through the basic predefined configuration for Vue Router.

First, you will notice that we need to import both **Vue** and **VueRouter** from the **vue** and **vue-router** packages, respectively. Then we call **Vue.use (VueRouter)** to install it as a plugin for use within our application:

```
import Vue from 'vue'
import VueRouter from 'vue-router'

Vue.use(VueRouter)
```

Vue.use is a global method, as discussed in *Chapter 5, Global Component Composition*. It triggers the internal **install** method of **VueRouter** together with the Vue constructor as soon as Vue is available as a global variable of the application. This method has a built-in mechanism to prevent installing a plugin more than once.

After executing **Vue.use (VueRouter)**, the following objects are available for access in any component:

- **this.$router** – The global router object

- **this.$route** – The current route object

this points to the component in context.

Now that we have registered the use of Vue Router in our application, let's move on to the next step – defining the routes for the configuration object of the router instance.

DEFINING THE ROUTES

In a web application, a **route** is a URL path pattern and is mapped to a specific handler. The **handler**, in modern web development, is a component, defined and located in a physical file. For example, when the user enters the route **localhost:8080//home**, if **Home** is mapped to this specific route, the routing system knows to trigger the handler **Home** to render the content accordingly.

As seen in the preceding example, it is crucial to set up the routes (or paths) for navigation within the application.

Each route is an object literal whose properties are declared by the
RouteConfig interface:

```
interface RouteConfig = {
  path: string,
  component?: Component,
  name?: string, // for named routes
  components?: { [name: string]: Component }, // for named views
  redirect?: string | Location | Function,
  props?: boolean | Object | Function,
  alias?: string | Array<string>,
  children?: Array<RouteConfig>, // for nested routes
  beforeEnter?: (to: Route, from: Route, next: Function) => void,
  meta?: any,

  // 2.6.0+
  caseSensitive?: boolean, // use case sensitive match? (
    default: false)
  pathToRegexpOptions?: Object // path-to-regexp options for
    compiling regex
}
```

All the routes needed for an application are located within the **Array** instance
of **routes**:

```
const routes = [
  //Route1,
  //Route2,
  //...
]
```

Now, let's come back to the previous file, and uncomment the code inside **routes**.
There will be two predefined routes, **home** and **about**, each as an object and located
in the **routes** array, for our convenience.

Let's take a closer look at the first route as an example:

```
{
  path: '/',
  name: 'home',
  component: Home
}
```

The **path** property is a **required** string that indicates the path of the targeted route and is resolved to an absolute URL path for the browser's navigation. For instance, the **/about** path will be translated into **<app domain>/about** (**localhost:8080/about** or **example.com/about**).

In this case, Vue Router understands **/** – the empty path – as the default path for loading the application when there is no other indicator after the forward slash **/**, for example when the user navigates to **<app-domain>** or **<app-domain>/**.

The next property is **name**, which is a string, indicating the name given to the targeted route. Even though it is **optional**, it's strongly recommended to have every route defined with a name, for better code maintenance and route tracking purposes, which we will discuss further later in this chapter, in the *Passing route parameters* section.

The last property is **component**, which is a Vue component instance. **router-view** uses this property as a reference to the view component to render the page content when the path is active.

Here we have the route defined as the **home** route, mapped as the default path to the application and tied to the **Home** component for content.

Vue CLI also auto-generates two simple components for these two sample routes – **Home** and **About**.

In the next section, we'll go over some tips that can be helpful when loading components to be used with routes.

TIPS ON LOADING COMPONENTS FOR ROUTE CONFIGURATION

Certainly, we need to import the component to tie it to the targeted route in the same **index.js** file. The classic and most popular way is to import it at the top of the file, as follows:

```
import Home from '../views/Home.vue'
```

Often this will be added under the main imports as shown in *Figure 6.5*:

```
1   import Vue from 'vue'
2   import VueRouter from 'vue-router'
3   import Home from '../views/Home.vue'
```

Figure 6.5: Import Home component on line 3 – src/router/index.js

However, a more efficient way is to lazy-load the component.

Lazy loading, also known as on-demand loading is a technique that aims to optimize the content of a website or web application at runtime. It helps to reduce the time consumption and amount of resources required to download for an application on the first load. This optimization is critical to ensure the best user experience possible, where every millisecond of waiting matters. Besides this, lazy loading also allows better code-splitting at the route level, along with performance optimization in large or complex applications.

We can lazy-load the component with the benefit of using **webpack**. Instead of importing the **About** component at the top of the file, as we did with **Home** (see *Figure 6.5*), we can instead dynamically add the following right after defining the name for the **about** route:

```
component: () => import(/* webpackChunkName: "about" */
  '../views/About.vue')
```

Here we dynamically lazy-load the **About** view component for the **about** route. During compilation, **webpack** generates a separate chunk with the designated name (**"about"**) for the **about** route, and only loads it when the user visits this route.

In most cases, since the user will likely land on the default path on the first go, it is better to not lazy-load the default component (**Home** in our app) but to import it in the normal way. Hence, the tip here is to determine which components should be lazy-loaded when designing your routing and combine the two methods for the most benefit.

We will now see how to set up the router instance.

SETTING UP THE ROUTER INSTANCE

After defining the routes, the final step is to create the **router** instance based on the given configuration options:

```
const router = new VueRouter({
  mode: 'history',
  base: process.env.BASE_URL,
  routes
})
```

A configuration is an object consisting of different properties that help to form the app's router. We will now examine these properties in the following subsections.

ROUTES

routes is a must-have option to pass to the constructor. Without this, the router won't be able to recognize the paths and direct users to the suitable view content accordingly.

MODE

mode determines the router's mode. There are two modes in **VueRouter** for URLs:

- **history** mode: This leverages the default **history.pushState()** API by means of the **HTML5 History** API. It allows us to achieve URL navigation without a page reload and makes the URL path human-readable, such as **yourapplication.com/about**.

- **hash** mode: This uses a hash symbol (**#**) to simulate a URL, for example, **yourapplication.com/#about** for an **about** page or **youapplication/#/** for the **home** URL of your application.

BASE

base determines the base URL for the app. It will be set as **process.env.BASE_URL** to allow developers to control this from outside of the application code (from a **.env** file, for example). Hence developers can set the directory from which the code should be served upon running.

With **base** finally out of the way now, we have the **router** instance created. All that is left is to export it:

```
export default router
```

Then import it in **main.js**, right before the creation of the main app instance's **new Vue** object. We still need to specify **router** in the instance configuration, as shown in the following:

```
import router from './router'

Vue.config.productionTip = false

new Vue({
  router, //specify the router configuration for use
  render: h => h(App)
}).$mount('#app')
```

With this updated code, our application will now render as follows:

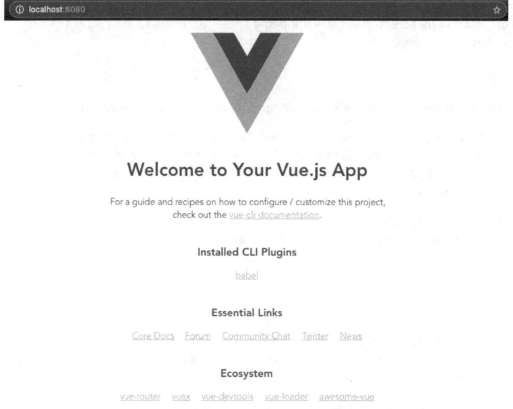

Figure 6.6: Home page of the Hello Vue Router application in the browser

If we navigate to **localhost:8080/about**, we will see the rendered content of the **about** component from the auto-generated code:

```
<template>
  <div class="about">
    <h1>This is an about page</h1>
  </div>
</template>
```

The website should look similar to that shown in *Figure 6.7*:

This is an about page

Figure 6.7: About page of the "Hello Vue Router" application in the browser

In this section, we looked at how lazily loading components can be used to speed up large and complex SPAs. We also looked at some of the options that can be set when setting up your router, such as routes, mode, and base. In the next section, we will learn how to implement and add a message feed page with the help of Vue Router.

EXERCISE 6.01: IMPLEMENTING AND ADDING A MESSAGE FEED PAGE USING VUE ROUTER

We are going to create a new page that displays a list of messages to the user. Users will be able to visit this page whenever they enter the **localhost:8080/ messages** path in the browser.

To access the code files for this exercise, refer to https://packt.live/35alpze.

1. Use the application generated with **vue create** as a starting point or create a new one with **vue-cli**. Ensure you had the router enabled when generating your project as described earlier in the chapter:

```
vue create Exercise6.01
```

2. Let's create a new view component called **MessageFeed** by adding a **MessageFeed.vue** file to the **./src/views/** folder:

Figure 6.8: The views directory hierarchy

The component will render a list of messages. Our message list is defined as an array of strings called **messages** in the component's **data** property as follows:

```
<template>
  <div>
    <h2> Message Feed </h2>
    <p v-for="(m, i) in messages" :key="i">
    {{ m }}
    </p>
  </div>
</template>
<script>
export default {
  data() {
```

```
      return {
        messages: [
          'Hello, how are you?',
          'The weather is nice',
          'This is message feed',
          'And I am the fourth message'
        ]
      }
    }
  }
}
</script>
```

3. Create a router file at **src/router/index.js**. It should import **VueRouter** and tell Vue to use the router as follows:

```
import Vue from 'vue'
import VueRouter from 'vue-router'
import Home from '../views/Home.vue'


Vue.use(VueRouter)
```

4. Next, in **./src/router/index.js**, we declare a route designated for **MessageFeed**, named **messageFeed** and with its path set to **/messages**. We will also lazy-load the component. This step will be completed by appending an object with the required information to the **routes** array:

```
export const routes = [
  {
    path: '/',
    name: 'home',
    component: Home
  },
  {
    path: '/about',
    name: 'about',
    // route level code-splitting
    // this generates a separate chunk (about.[hash].js) for
      this route
    // which is lazy-loaded when the route is visited.
    component: () => import(/* webpackChunkName: "about" */ '../
      views/About.vue')
  }, {
    path: '/messages',
```

```
    name: 'messageFeed',
    component: () => import(/* webpackChunkName: "messages" */ '../
      views/MessageFeed.vue')
  }
]
```

5. Finally, in the same file, create a **router** instance using the **routes** we defined:

```
const router = new VueRouter({
  mode: 'history',
  base: process.env.BASE_URL,
  routes
})


export default router
```

6. Run the application using the following command:

```
yarn serve
```

7. Upon visiting **localhost:8080/messages** in the browser, the page should appear with the correct content – the **Message Feed** page as shown in the following screenshot:

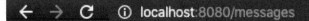

Message Feed

Hello, how are you?

The weather is nice

This is message feed

And I am the fourth message

Figure 6.9: Message feed page rendered by the application

This demonstrates how simple it is to add a new page route to a Vue.js application using Vue Router, while keeping your code organized and easy to read. Now that we have our routes ready to use, we can provide users with the ability to navigate between pages, without typing the full path.

SETTING UP NAVIGATION LINKS

If **router-view** is in charge of rendering the correct active view content relative to the URL path, **router-link** is a Vue component that helps users to navigate within an app that has routing enabled. By default, it renders an anchor tag **<a>** with a correct **href** link generated by its **to** prop.

In our example app generated by Vue CLI, since there are two routes pre-populated, there are also two **router-link** instances added to the **<template>** section of **App.vue** right before **<router-view/>**:

```
<div id="nav">
  <router-link to="/">Home</router-link> |
  <router-link to="/about">About</router-link>
</div>
```

Since we are using the **base** option with the **history** mode, the **to** prop of each **router-link** should receive an identical value with the **path** property declared in the targeted **route** object.

In addition, because our routes are named, another alternative to the **to** prop is to have the same value as the name, instead of the path. Using the name is highly recommended to avoid complex link refactoring in case we have to adjust the paths given to some routes in our app. Hence, we can rewrite our links as follows:

```
<div id="nav">
    <router-link to="home">Home</router-link> |
    <router-link to="about">About</router-link> |
  </div>
```

We can also choose to bind a location descriptor object to the **to** prop, in a similar format as a **route** object. Consider the following example:

```
<router-link :to="{path: '/'}">Home</router-link>
```

In addition, an extra **CSS** class **router-link-active** will be added to the **<a>** tag, when the related route is **active**. This class can be customized through the **active-class** prop of the **router-link** component.

In **DevTools**, we can see the **router-link** component rendered as follows:

```
▼<div id="nav">
    <a href="/" class="router-link-exact-active router-link-active">Home</a>
    " | "
    <a href="/about" class>About</a>
  </div>
```

Figure 6.10: router-link in the browser's DevTools

The view in the browser will be as follows:

Figure 6.11: Home page of Hello Vue Router app with navigation links

Note that since we have access to **this.$router** within a component, we can trigger a navigation route programmatically by using **this.$router.push()** and pass a path or a router object in a similar way to using **to**:

```
this.$router.push('/home')
```

In this section, we created an example page that rendered a list of messages at the **/messages** route location. We also looked at how you can use the **<router-link/>** element to navigate between our views in a way similar to traditional HTML **<a>** tags.

Next, we will see how you can programmatically send a user to their last viewed route in a manner similar to the web browser's *back* button.

TIP TO IMPLEMENT THE BACK BUTTON

Sometimes we would like to navigate back to the previous page. Using `this.$router.push()` can achieve this, but this adds more routes in the history stack, instead of going back. The correct technique is to use `this.$router.go(steps)`, in which `steps` is an integer indicating the number of steps to go back/forward in the history stack. This functionality works similarly to `window.history.go(steps)`.

Consider the following example:

```
this.$router.go(-1) // similar to window.history.back()  -
   go back one page
```

Besides this, you can also navigate forward to a page that was loaded before and still exists in the history stack by using the same method, as follows:

```
this.$router.go(1) // similar to window.history.forward() -
   go forward one page
```

In this section, we looked at how you can manually access the router's history in order to send a user to the page they were previously on.

In the next section, we'll make use of navigation links to add our new message feed page to our application's **nav** menu.

EXERCISE 6.02: ADDING THE NAVIGATION LINK TO THE MESSAGEFEED ROUTE

We will add a quick link to the **MessageFeed** route we created in *Exercise 6.01, Implementing and Adding a Message Feed Page Using Vue Router*, using the **to** prop and **router-link** as explained in the preceding topic.

To access the code files for this exercise, refer to https://packt.live/3lr8cYR.

1. Use the starter application generated by Vue as a starting point or create a new one with **Vue cli**. Ensure you have the router enabled when generating your project as described earlier in the chapter:

```
vue create Exercise6.02
```

2. In the `./src/App.vue` file, besides the auto-generated **router-link** components for **home** and **about**, add another **router-link** component that points to the **/messages** path under the **Message Feed** title:

```
<template>
  <div id="app">
    <div id="nav">
      <router-link to="/">Home</router-link> |
      <router-link to="/about">About</router-link> |
      <router-link to="/messages">Message Feed</router-link>
    </div>
    <router-view/>
  </div>
</template>
```

We will see the navigation links available in any view and they will not disappear when users navigate away since they are not a part of the **router-view** component. Our screen should look as follows:

Figure 6.12. Home page of the Hello Vue Router app with updated navigation links

3. Let's change the **to** value to point to the object named **messageFeed**, which is the same as the **name** given for this route in **./src/App.vue**:

```
<router-link :to="{ name: `messageFeed` }">Message Feed
  </router-link>
```

4. The navigation should work as before; clicking on the **Message Feed** link should direct you to **/messages**, as shown in the following screenshot:

Home I About I Message Feed

Message Feed

Hello, how are you?

The weather is nice

This is message feed

And I am the forth message

Figure 6.13: Message Feed page of Hello Vue Router after clicking on the Message Feed link

5. Now, open the **index.js** file located in the **./src/router/** folder and change the path defined for the **messageFeed** route from **/messages/** to **/ messagesFeed**:

```
export const routes = [
  {
    path: '/',
    name: 'home',
    component: Home
  },
  {
    path: '/about',
    name: 'about',
    // route level code-splitting
    // this generates a separate chunk (about.[hash].js) for
      this route
    // which is lazy-loaded when the route is visited.
```

```
    component: () => import(/* webpackChunkName: "about" */ '../
views/About.vue')
  }, {
    path: '/messagesFeed',
    name: 'messageFeed',
    component: () => import(/* webpackChunkName: "messageFeed" */
      '../views/MessageFeed.vue')
  }
]
```

6. Run the application using the following command:

```
yarn serve
```

Navigate to the app's **Home** page and click on **Message Feed** again. It should display the same **messages feed** page as before but note that the URL path changed to **/messagesFeed**:

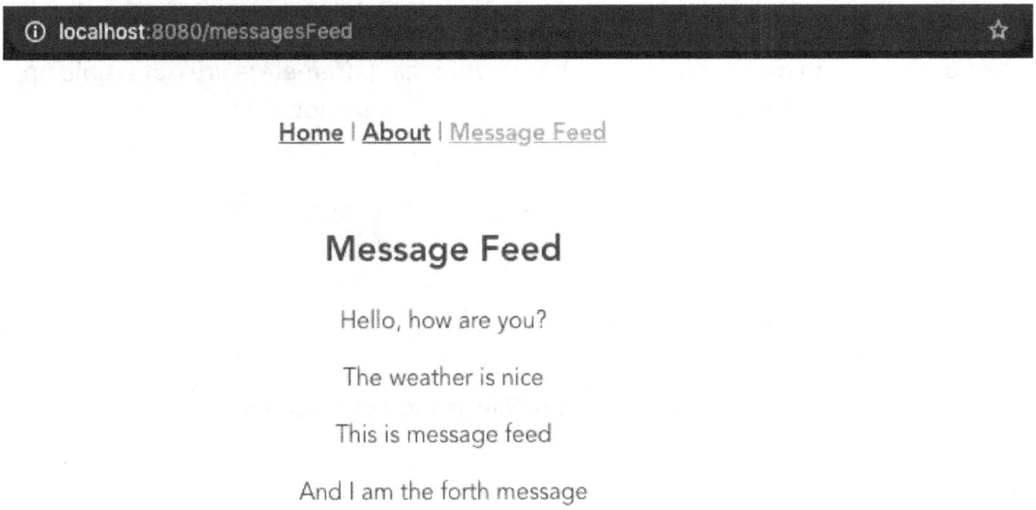

localhost:8080/messagesFeed ☆

Home | About | Message Feed

Message Feed

Hello, how are you?

The weather is nice

This is message feed

And I am the forth message

Figure 6.14: Message Feed page rendered with the updated URL path

Note how easy it is to set up the link to the **/messages** path with just one line of code, as well as updating the related path without refactoring. So far, we have just defined some simple routes without any additional parameters for the targeted route. This will be our next challenge.

PASSING ROUTE PARAMETERS

In the previous sections of this chapter, each route was a standalone view and did not need to pass or connect any data to the other routes. But the power of routing is not limited only to this. With **named** routes, we can also easily enable data communication between routes.

In our example app, we want our **about** page to be able to receive a data string called **user** as the user's name from the link trigger. This can be achieved by changing the **to** prop from a string literal to an object literal of **:to="{ name: 'about' }"**, and then adding a new **params: { user: 'Adam' }** property to that object:

```
<router-link :to="{ name: 'about', params: { user: 'Adam' }}">
  About
</router-link>
```

This change informs the router to pass the desired parameters to the **About** page when users click on the targeted link. These additional parameters are not visible on the rendered **href** link, as shown in the following screenshot:

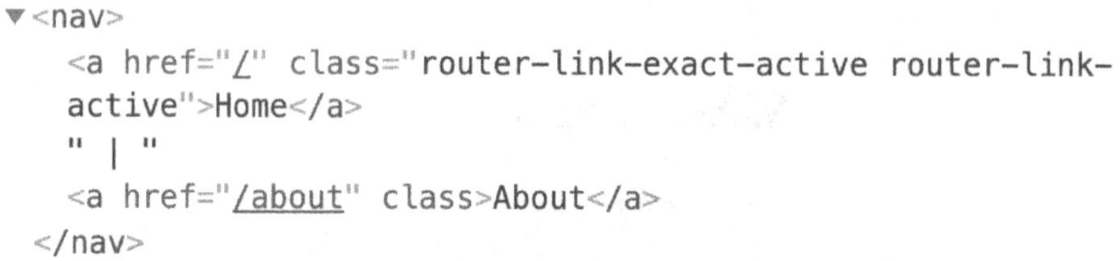

```
▼ <nav>
    <a href="/" class="router-link-exact-active router-link-
    active">Home</a>
    " | "
    <a href="/about" class>About</a>
  </nav>
```

Figure 6.15: Generated href link is without parameters

However, the Vue system is tracking these additional parameters. Using the Vue DevTools, we can view the parameters by expanding the **to** prop as shown in *Figure 6.16*:

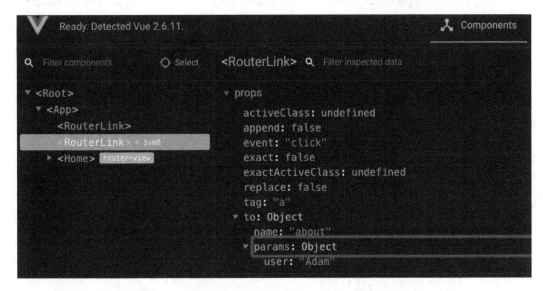

Figure 6.16: The params of the to object in Vue DevTools

In the **About.vue** file, since we have access to the currently active **$route** (see the *Vue Router* section earlier in this chapter), we can retrieve the data passed with the link as **$route.params.user** and print out the value:

```
<template>
  <div class="about">
    <h1>About {{$route.params.user}}</h1>
  </div>
</template>
```

The output will be as follows:

About Adam

Figure 6.17: The About page renders the user passed through route params

Any prop user of **params** will not be visible on the URL path, thus keeping the path clean and securing the data transferred between views from the user.

But using **$route.params.user** is not convenient or readable and doesn't keep the component reusable in the long run. We can improve this by decoupling the passed **params** with the **props** within the component.

We will now see how to decouple the **params** with the help of **props**.

DECOUPLING PARAMS WITH PROPS

In the **index.js** file, let's adjust the configuration of the **about** route with an additional property called **props**. By setting this property's value to **true**, the router will automatically understand and map **$route.params** into the **props** component accordingly:

```
{
    path: '/about',
    name: 'about',
    component: () => import(/* webpackChunkName: "about" */
        '../views/About.vue'),
    props: true
}
```

In the **About.vue** file, we will declare the **props** type as follows:

```
props: {
    user: String
}
```

And in the **<template>** section, we will replace **$route.params.user** with **user**:

```
<template>
  <div class="about">
    <h1>About {{user}}</h1>
  </div>
</template>
```

The output will still be the same, as shown in the following screenshot:

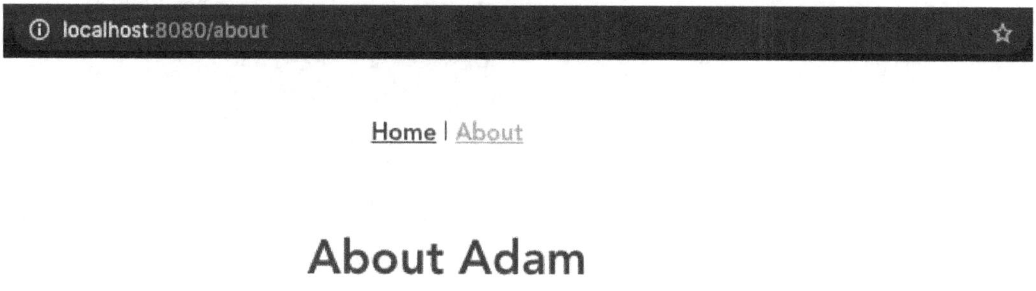

① localhost:8080/about ☆

Home | About

About Adam

Figure 6.18: The About page renders the user passed through route params and mapped to props

In addition to this, you can also define the data that you want to pass within the **props** property of the **route** configuration. Instead of a Boolean value, **props** can now be declared as an object with the required data, as in the following example:

```
{
    path: '/about',
    name: 'about',
    component: () => import(/* webpackChunkName: "about" */
        '../views/About.vue'),
    props: { age: 32 }
}
```

With a similar step, we will declare **age** as a **props** component in **About.vue**, and print it out to the screen as text:

```
<template>
  <div class="about">
    <h1>About {{user}}</h1>
    <h2>Age: {{age}}</h2>
  </div>
</template>
<script>
export default {
  props: {
    user: String,
    age: Number
  }
}
</script>
```

Now when the **About** page is clicked, the page will render as follows:

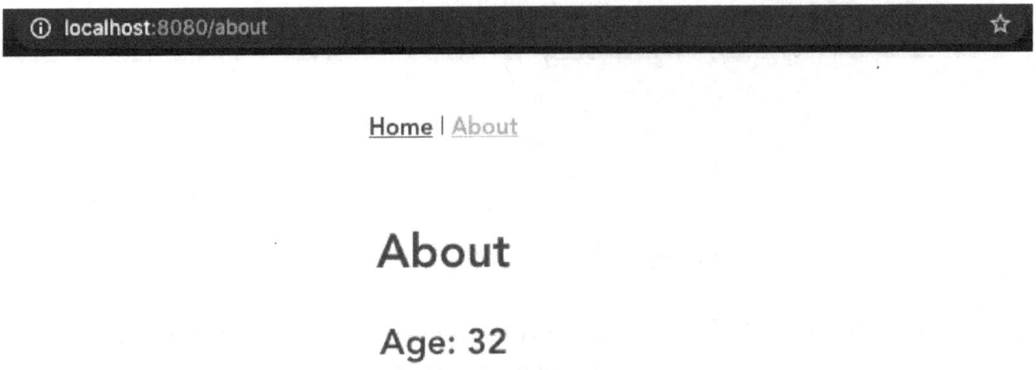

Home | About

About

Age: 32

Figure 6.19: About page rendered with the props preset in the router configuration

Our previous user data is not visible anymore! This is because, now, **props** is declared with static data in the configuration of the **About** route and can't be overridden from outside. Its value is and will remain the same throughout the process of navigating around the app, regardless of what values we pass in **params** of the **to** prop in the targeted **router-link** component.

We will now learn how to pass the content of the selected message to a new message page and print it.

EXERCISE 6.03: PASSING THE CONTENT OF THE SELECTED MESSAGE TO A NEW MESSAGE PAGE AND HAVING IT PRINTED OUT

We shall continue from *Exercise 6.02, Adding the Navigation Link to the MessageFeed Route*, where we defined the **MessageFeed** route with a URL path to **messages**. This view will render a list of predefined messages in the **data** property of the **view** component's options.

In this exercise, we will create a new **message** page, designated to render the content of a message selected by the user. It should be reusable.

To access the code files for this exercise, refer to https://packt.live/36mTwTY.

1. In the `./src/views/` folder, we create a new single-file component called **Message.vue**. This component receives a **content** prop of type **string** and renders it under a **<p>** tag:

```
<template>
    <div>
        <p>{{content}}</p>
    </div>
</template>
<script>
export default {
    props: {
        content: {
            default: '',
            type: String
        }
    }
}
</script>
```

2. Let's register the created view component to the existing **routes** in `./src/router/index.js`. We will define the new route as a **message** with the path to **/message**. It will also accept **props: true** in order to map all parameters passed to the route to the related prop accordingly. The full list of routes to be used is as follows:

```
export const routes = [
    {
        path: '/',
        name: 'home',
        component: Home
    },
    {
        path: '/about',
        name: 'about',
        component: () => import(/* webpackChunkName: "about" */
            '../views/About.vue')
    },
    {
        path: '/messages',
```

```
      name: 'messageFeed',
      component: () => import(/* webpackChunkName: "messages" */ '../
views/MessageFeed.vue')
    },
    {
      path: '/message',
      name: 'message',
      component: () => import(/* webpackChunkName: "message" */ '../
views/Message.vue'),
      props: true
    }
]
```

3. Since the route is registered and ready to be used, we need to make changes to the **<template>** section of **./src/views/MessageFeed.vue** to ensure each message line is now clickable and will redirect the user to the new route when clicked. Let's replace the **<p>** tag with **router-click**. And because we have named our new route as **message**, we will set **to** to bind to **{ name: 'message' }**:

```
<template>
  <div>
  <h2> Message Feed </h2>
  <div v-for="(m, i) in messages" :key="i" >
    <router-link :to="{ name: 'message'}">
      {{ m }}
    </router-link>
  </div>
</div>
</template>
```

4. Under **template**, we'll add a **script** tag containing some sample data for our **messages**:

```
<script>
export default {
  data() {
    return {
      messages: [
        'Hello, how are you?',
        'The weather is nice',
        'This is message feed',
```

```
            'And I am the fourth message'
        ]
      }
    }
  }
</script>
```

5. When you open the **./messages** page, all the messages are now clickable as shown in the following screenshot:

Home | About | Message Feed

Message Feed

Hello, how are you?
The weather is nice
This is message feed
And I am the fourth message

Figure 6.20: Message Feed page after changing messages to be clickable

6. Now when the user clicks on a message, it will open a new page. However, the page content will be empty, as we have not passed any content parameter to the **<route-click>** component, as shown in the following screenshot:

Home | About | Message Feed

Figure 6.21: Message page with no content generated

7. Let's go back to `./src/views/MessageFeed.vue` and add **params: { content: m }**:

```
<template>
  <div>
  <h2> Message Feed </h2>
  <div v-for="(m, i) in messages" :key="i" >
    <router-link :to="{ name: 'message', params: { content: m
      }}">
      {{ m }}
    </router-link>
  </div>
  </div>
</template>
```

8. Now when you click on the first message, **Hello, how are you?**, the output will be the following:

Home | About | Message Feed

Hello, how are you?

Figure 6.22: Message page with the clicked message's content rendered

Simple, isn't it? We have completed the flow from a feed of messages to a detailed page of a single selected message dynamically with **router-link** and the combination of **params** and **props** of the component. However, there is one significant downside to this approach.

Let's refresh the page while you are still on the `./message` path of the first message. The output will be the same as in *Step 5* – an empty content page. Upon refresh, the route is triggered without any **content params** passed, unlike when the user clicked on a specific link, and the **params** passed previously were not saved or cached. Hence there is no content.

In the following section, we will learn how to intercept the navigation flow and solve this problem with **Router Hooks**.

ROUTER HOOKS

The general flow of route navigation is described in the following diagram:

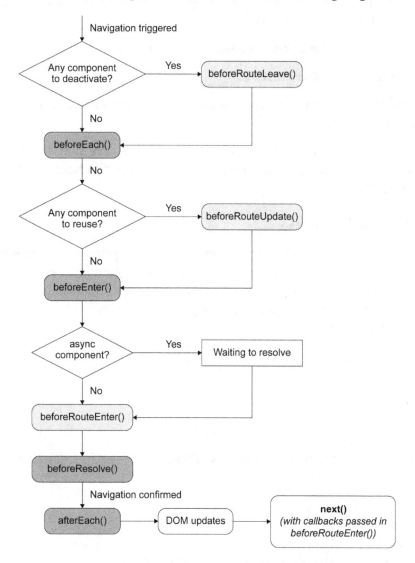

Figure 6.23: Navigation resolution flow diagram

Once navigation is triggered on a certain route, Vue Router provides several primary navigation guards, or Hooks, for developers to guard or intercept that navigation process. These guards can be hooked either globally or in the component, depending on the type. Some examples are as follows:

- Globally: **beforeEach**, **beforeResolve**, and **afterEach**

- Per component: **beforeEnter**

- In-component: **beforeRouteUpdate**, **beforeRouteEnter**, and **beforeRouterLeave**

As seen in *Figure 6.23*, navigation is considered completed only after all the Hooks or guards have been resolved, including any asynchronous guard. Now, let's see how to set up **beforeEach** Hooks.

SETTING UP BEFOREEACH HOOKS

beforeEach is a global Hook and is called at the very beginning of navigation, **before** the other global and in-component Hooks are triggered (**except** for **beforeRouteLeave** of the previous view component). It should be defined as a global method of the **router** instance during initialization in the **index.js** file and takes the following syntax:

```
const router = new VueRouter({
  //...
})


router.beforeEach(beforeEachCallback)
```

In the preceding snippet, **beforeEachCallback** is a **hook** function that receives three arguments:

```
const beforeEachCallback = (
  to, // The destination route
  from, //The source route
  next //The function to trigger to resolve the hook
) => { … })
```

Or we could write this directly as follows:

```
router.beforeEach((to, from, next) => { … })
```

For example, if we want to display a different page to display a generic message whenever a user navigates to **About** without a param value for the user, we can hook **beforeEach** as follows:

```
router.beforeEach((
  to, // The destination route
  from, //The source route
  next //The function to trigger to resolve the hook
) => {
  if (to.name === 'about' && (!to.params || !to.params.user)) {
    next({ name: 'error' })
  }
  else {
    next();
  }
})
```

Here, we check if the destination route is **about** and if it doesn't have any additional params passed, nor any value for the **user** param passed, we will navigate to an **error** route instead. Otherwise, just proceed as normal with **next()**.

> **NOTE**
>
> **next()** is required to be called **exactly once in any given non-overlapped flow logic** (once for **if** and once for **else**), or else there will be errors.

We still need to create an **error** page with an **Error.vue** view component that displays a simple message:

```
<template>
    <div>
        <h2>No param passed.</h2>
    </div>
</template>
```

Also, make sure to register the path accordingly:

```
{
    path: '/error',
    name: 'error',
    component: () => import(/* webpackChunkName: "error" */
      '../views/Error.vue'),
}
```

Now, in the **Home** view, after clicking on the **About** link, the app will render the **Error** page instead of the **About** page as seen in the following screenshot:

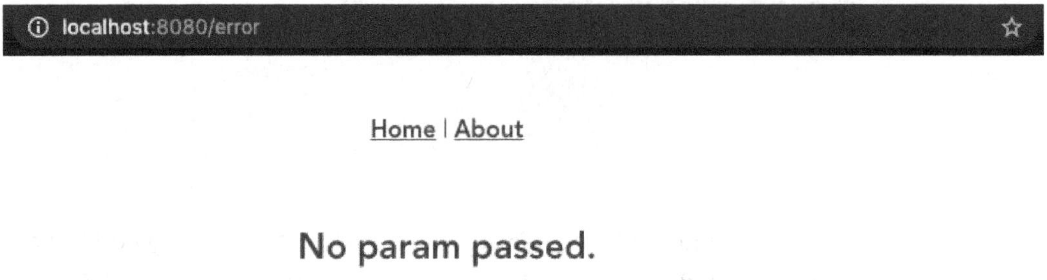

Figure 6.24: Error page displayed when About is clicked without any param passed

Now let's go to the **App.vue** file and assign the **to** prop to bind to an **{ name: 'about', params: { user: 'Adam' }}** object instead:

```
<router-link :to="{ name: 'about', params: { user: 'Adam'
  }}">About</router-link>
```

Let's navigate back to our app's **Home** page and click on the **About** link. Since we have a proper **params** passed, the output will be as follows:

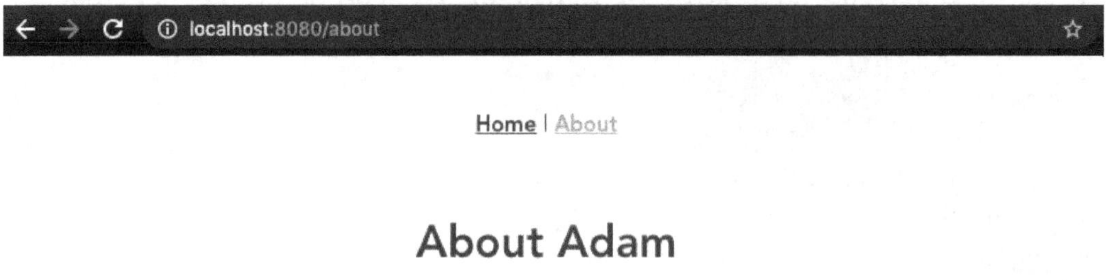

Figure 6.25: About page displayed when there is a user passed in the params

Moreover, from now on, every time we refresh the **About** page, we will get redirected to the **Error** page instead since there is no **user** param passed on refreshing.

We shall now look at a few key distinguishing points between the **beforeEach** and **beforeResolve** Hooks.

DIFFERENTIATING BETWEEN THE BEFOREEACH AND BEFORERESOLVE HOOKS

We can also register the global Hook with **beforeResolve** with the same syntax. However, unlike **beforeEach**, which is triggered at the creation phase of navigation, **beforeResolve** will be triggered just before the navigation is carried out and confirmed, **after all the Hooks (both global and in-component) are resolved**:

```
router.beforeResolve((
  to, // The destination route
  from, //The source route
  next //The function to trigger to resolve the hook
) => {
  if (to.name === 'about' && (!to.params || !to.params.user)) {
    next({ name: 'error' })
  }
  else {
    next();
  }
})
```

The output results will remain the same as in *Figure 6.25*:

Figure 6.26: About page displayed when there is a user passed in the params

Let's now look at the **afterEach** Hook in detail.

THE AFTEREACH HOOK

The **afterEach()** Hook is the last global navigation guard to be triggered after the navigation is confirmed (which means after **beforeResolve()**). Unlike the other global guards, the Hook function to pass to **afterEach()** does not receive a **next** function, hence it won't affect the navigation.

In addition, the **to** and **from** parameters are read-only **Route** objects. Hence the best use case for **afterEach** is to save data such as the last visited **Route** object for a **Back** button, the passed **params** of the **route** destination, or page view tracking. For example, we can have a default value of **user**, assign it, and save it whenever needed:

```
let user = 'Adam';

router.beforeEach((to, from, next) => {
  if (to.name === 'about' && (!to.params || !to.params.user)) {
    next({ name: 'about', params: { user }})
  }
  else {
    user = to.params.user;
    next()
  }
});

router.afterEach((to, from) => {
  if (to.name === 'about' && to.params && to.params.user) {
    user = to.params.user;
  }
})
```

Now in the **App.js** file, instead of **Adam**, add the following:

```
<router-link
  :to="{ name: 'about', params: { user: 'Adam' }}"
>
  About
</router-link>
```

Let's change it to **Alex**:

```
<router-link
  :to="{ name: 'about', params: { user: 'Alex' }}"
>
  About
</router-link>
```

The output now when clicking on the **About** link is as follows:

Home | About

About Alex

Figure 6.27: About page displaying the new user's name – Alex

But on reload, the **About** page renders with the default user – **Adam** – instead since there is a user passed to the **params**, as follows:

Home | About

About Adam

Figure 6.28: About page displaying the default user value on reload – Adam

In this section, we looked at the **afterEach** Hook. We used the **afterEach** Hook to pass data through to the **about** page without having to have that data contained in the URL. This same technique can be used for updating other behavior such as the desired target page when pressing the **back** button.

PERSONALIZING HOOKS PER ROUTE

Instead of defining a global Hook, which can cause unseen bugs and requires a route check, we can define a **beforeEnter** guard directly in the targeted route's configuration object, for example, our **About** route:

```
beforeEnter: (to, from, next) => {
    if (!to.params || !to.params.user) {
      to.params.user = 'Adam'
    }
    next()
}
```

With this approach, both on reload and on clicking a link to navigate to the **About** page, the output is now consistent, as shown in the following screenshot:

Home | About

About Adam

Figure 6.29: About page rendered with the user value Adam

> **NOTE**
>
> With **beforeEnter()**, **to** is write-able and you will have access to
> **this** (which points to the specific route – **About**). It will only be triggered
> when users trigger navigation to the **About** page.

In this section, we looked at the different router Hooks available in Vue, including **beforeEach**, **beforeResolve**, and **afterEach**. We saw how each of these Hooks is called at a different point in the routing process. As a practical example, we looked at a route that, if not provided a parameter, instead directs the user to an error page. These Hooks can be very useful especially when setting up an authenticated route. In the next section, we'll look at setting up in-component Hooks.

SETTING UP IN-COMPONENT HOOKS

Finally, we can also use in-component Hooks as component life cycle Hooks where we want to scope those Hooks to component-level for better code maintenance or enhance the workflow where the same component needs to behave differently in a certain use case.

We can have the **About** component now with the **beforeRouteEnter()** Hook defined as follows:

```
<script>
export default {
  data() {
    return {
      user: ''
    }
  },
  beforeRouteEnter(to, from, next) {
    if (!to.params || !to.params.user) {
      next(comp => {
        comp.user = 'Alex'
      })
    }
    else {
      next();
    }
  }
}
</script>
```

As you can see, we don't have access to the **this** scope of the component during **beforeRouteEnter**, because the view component is still being created at the moment of triggering. Luckily, we can access the instance through a callback passed to **next()**. Whenever the navigation is confirmed, which means the component is created, the callback will be triggered, and the component instance will be available as the sole argument (**comp**) of the callback.

> **NOTE**
>
> For **beforeRouteUpdate** and **beforeRouteLeave**, the component has been created, hence this instance is available and there won't be a need for a callback for **next()**. In fact, a callback function is only supported in **next()** within the use of **beforeRouteEnter()**.

beforeRouteUpdate is called when the same component is reused for a different route. This applies when we use dynamic routing, which will be discussed in the next section.

beforeRouteLeave is triggered when the component is going to be deactivated or before the user navigates away from the current view. This is called right before the **beforeEach** guard of the new navigation and is usually used in editor components to prevent users from navigating away without saving.

In this guard, we can cancel the new navigation by passing **false** to the **next()** function.

For example, imagine that we add the following Hook to the component's option in the **About.vue** file:

```
//...
  beforeRouteLeave(to, from, next) {
    const ans = window.confirm('You are about to leave the About
      page. Are you sure?');
    next(!!ans);
  }
```

When we navigate away from the **About** page, a pop-up dialog will appear asking for confirmation as shown in the following screenshot and then continue navigating accordingly:

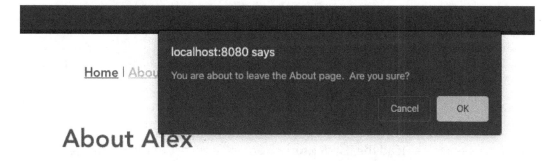

Figure 6.30: Dialog asking to confirm before navigating away from the About page

In this section, we looked at setting up in-component Hooks, that is, Hooks that are scoped to specific components. We set up an in-component Hook for our **About** component that asks a user to confirm before leaving the page. In the next section, we will move our message list into an external file to be loaded only when **MessageFeed** is in view.

EXERCISE 6.04: EXTRACTING A MESSAGES LIST TO AN EXTERNAL FILE AND LOADING IT ONLY WHEN MESSAGEFEED IS IN VIEW

Going back to *Exercise 6.03, Passing the Content of the Selected Message to a New Message Page and Having It Printed Out*, now we will do a bit of code enhancement using the **beforeEnter** and **beforeRouteEnter** router hooks. This exercise is meant to make you more familiar with using router hooks.

To access the code files for this exercise, refer to https://packt.live/3lg1F2R.

1. Let's extract the **messages** static data from **./src/views/MessageFeed. vue** and save it in **./src/assets/messages.js**:

```
const messages = [
  'Hello, how are you?',
  'The weather is nice',
  'This is message feed',
  'And I am the fourth message'
];


export default messages;
```

2. In `./src/views/MessageFeed.vue`, we will replace the local data property with **props: { messages: { type: String, default: [] }}**:

```
export default {
  props: {
    messages: {
      type: Array,
      default: () => []
    }
  }
}
```

3. Now we need to load the list of **messages** and assign it to the **messages params** upon navigation to the **messages** route. We will do this by using the **beforeEnter** Hook in the route's configuration object. Don't forget to add **props: true** to normalize the **params** into related **props** for rendering. You can do that by modifying your **route** defined in **src/router/index.js** as follows:

```
{
    path: '/messages',
    name: 'messageFeed',
    component: () => import(/* webpackChunkName: "messages" */
      '../views/MessageFeed.vue'),
    props: true,
    async beforeEnter(to, from, next) {
      next()
    }
},
```

4. We will lazy-load the list of messages with **import**:

```
const module = await import (/* webpackChunkName: "messagesFeed"
  */ '../assets/messages.js');
```

5. Then, retrieve the needed information as follows:

```
const messages = module.default;
if (messages && messages.length > 0) {
  to.params.messages = messages;
}
```

6. The full code for the route in **src/router/index.js** should be the following:

```
{
    path: '/messages',
    name: 'messageFeed',
    component: () => import(/* webpackChunkName: "messages" */
      '../views/MessageFeed.vue'),
    props: true,
    async beforeEnter(to, from, next) {
      if (!to.params || !to.params.messages) {
        const module = await import (/* webpackChunkName:
          "messagesFeed" */ '../assets/messages.js');
        const messages = module.default;
        if (messages && messages.length > 0) {
          to.params.messages = messages;
        }
      }

      next()
    }
},
```

When viewing the website, we should see a message feed similar to that of the last exercise. This is shown in the following screenshot:

Home | About | Message Feed

Message Feed

Hello, how are you?
The weather is nice
This is message feed
And I am the fourth message

Figure 6.31: Message Feed page after refactoring

At this point, we have learned and practiced how to configure routers, pass parameters, and intercept navigation between pages in the application using different routing Hooks. In the next section, we are going to look at a more advanced topic – **dynamic routing**.

DYNAMIC ROUTING

If there is a lot of data that follows the same format, such as a list of users, or a list of messages, and it's required to create a page for each of them, we need to use a routing pattern. With a routing pattern, we can create a new route dynamically from the same component based on some additional information. For example, we want to render the **User** view component for every user but with different **id** values. Vue Router provides us with the ability to use dynamic segments denoted by a colon (:) to achieve dynamic routing.

Instead of using **params**, which doesn't persist its value on refresh or appear in the URL, we define the required **params** directly in the path as follows:

```
{
    path: '/user/:id',
    name: 'user',
    component: () => import(/* webpackChunkName: "user" */
      '../views/User.vue')
}
```

In the preceding code, **:id** means the **params** here are not static. When the route matches the given pattern, Vue Router will render the corresponding component with the appropriate content, while keeping the URL as it should be. And the value of **:id** will be exposed as this **$route.params.id** in that view component's instance:

```
<template>
  <div>
    <h1>About a user: {{$route.params.id}}</h1>
  </div>
</template>
```

When users select URLs such as **/user/1** and **/user/2** (**./src/App.vue**), Vue will automatically generate sub-pages using our template.

Navigation paths will be mapped to the same route pattern and component, but with different information, as shown in the following screenshot:

Home | About | User 1 | User 2

About a user: 2

Figure 6.32: Navigate to /user/2

When you click on **User 1**, you will see the following:

Home | About | User 1 | User 2

About a user: 1

Figure 6.33: Navigate to /user/1

We can also normalize **id** to the **props** of the **User** component with **props: true** and combine it with **beforeRouteEnter()** to load data of the selected user before the instance is created and rendered:

```
<script>
import users from '../assets/users.js';
export default {
  props: {
    id: Number
  },
  data() {
    return {
      name: '',
      age: 0
    }
  },
  beforeRouteEnter(to, from, next) {
```

```
    next(vm => {
      const user = users[vm.id];
      vm.name = user.name;
      vm.age = user.age;
    })
  }
}
</script>
```

Now we can adjust **<template>** to print out the details of the user:

```
<template>
  <div>
    <h1>About a user: {{$route.params.id}}</h1>
    <h2>Name: {{name}}</h2>
    <p>Age: {{age}}</p>
  </div>
</template>
```

The output when selecting **/user/1** will now be as follows:

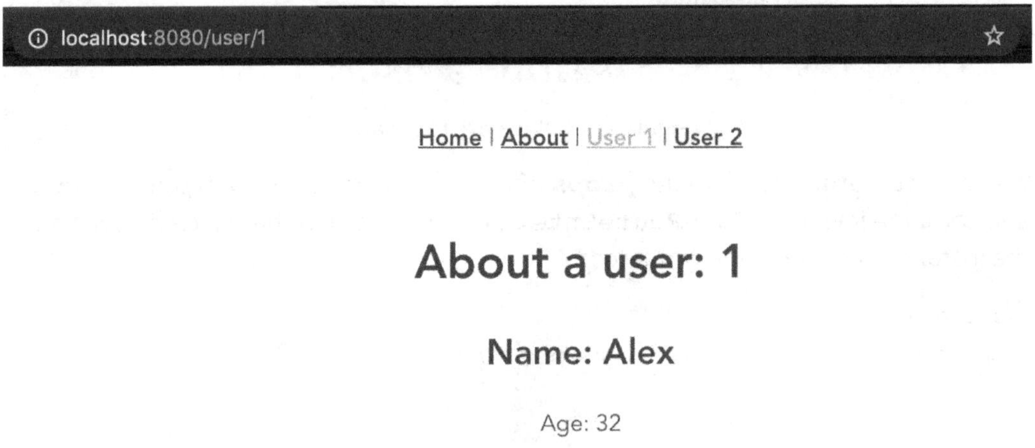

localhost:8080/user/1   ☆

Home | About | User 1 | **User 2**

About a user: 1

Name: Alex

Age: 32

Figure 6.34: Navigate to /user/1 with updated UI

And if we are in the **user/:id** route and change the **:id** to another user, we need to update the local data accordingly since **beforeRouteEnter** will not be triggered again in this case. In fact, all the lifecycle Hooks of the components will not be called, as the component instance is not re-created:

```
beforeRouteUpdate(to, from, next) {
    const user = users[to.params.id - 1];
    this.name = user.name;
```

```
    this.age = user.age;
    next();
  }
```

In this section, we looked at dynamic routing by setting up a route that extracts a parameter from the given URL. This technique allows you to create user-friendly URLs and pass information to routes dynamically. In the next section, we will look at catching error paths.

CATCHING ERROR PATHS

Other important routes that we always need to remember to handle besides the **Home** page ('/') include **error** routes, such as **404 Not found** when the URL path doesn't match any registered path, among others.

For **404 Not found**, we can use the **regex** asterisk *****, which stands for *matching everything* to collect all the cases that don't match the routes. This router's configuration should be located at the end of the array routes to avoid matching the wrong path:

```
{
  path: '*',
  name: '404',
  component: () => import(/* webpackChunkName: "404" */
    '../views/404.vue'),
}
```

When we type a wrong path for **/users**, the output will be as follows:

Home | About | User 1 | User 2

Not found. Please try again

Figure 6.35: Redirect to 404 when the '/users' path is not found

In this section, we looked at how the ***** regex wildcard can be used to create a catch-all **404** page displayed to anyone that navigates to a non-existent route. Next, we will be implementing a message route that passes relevant data in the URL itself using a dynamic routing pattern.

EXERCISE 6.05: IMPLEMENTING A MESSAGE ROUTE FOR EACH MESSAGE WITH A DYNAMIC ROUTING PATTERN

Going back to our message feed in *Exercise 6.04, Extracting a Messages List to an External File and Loading Only When MessageFeed Is in View*, we will refactor our **Message** path to use routing patterns to dynamically navigate to a specific message path upon the user's selection. This will get you familiar with creating and maintaining dynamic routes in combination with other navigation Hooks.

To access the code files for this exercise, refer to https://packt.live/32sWogX.

1. Let's open **./src/router/index.js** and have the path configuration of the message route change to **/message/:id**, where **id** will be the index of that **message** in the list of messages:

```
{
    path: '/message/:id',
    name: 'message',
    component: () => import(/* webpackChunkName: "message" */
      '../views/Message.vue'),
    props: true,
}
```

2. Now navigate to **./src/views/MessageFeed.vue** and change the **to** prop of **router-link** for each message to the following:

```
<router-link :to="`/message/${i}`">
```

3. Let's go back to **./src/router/index.js** and define **beforeEnter** as an asynchronous Hook for lazy-loading the content of the message into the content prop of our **Message** component:

```
async beforeEnter(to, from, next) {
    if (to.params && to.params.id) {
      const id = to.params.id;
      const { module } = await import (/* webpackChunkName:
        "messagesFeed" */ '../assets/messages.js');
      const messages = module.default;
      if (messages && messages.length > 0 && id <
        messages.length) {
        to.params.content = messages[id];
      }
    }
}
```

```
      next()
   },
```

4. Run the application using the following command:

```
yarn serve
```

When clicking on the first message in the **Message Feed**, the next page will be as follows:

Home | About | Message Feed

Hello, how are you?

Figure 6.36: The page displayed when visiting the /message/0 path

Now that you have learned how to use dynamic routing, you can play around even further with more layers of routing patterns, such as **message/:id/ author/:aid**. However, for such a case, we normally use a better approach, **nested routes**.

NESTED ROUTES

In reality, many applications are composed of components that consist of several multiple-level nested components. For example, **/user/settings/general** indicates that a general view is nested in the **settings** view and this **settings** view is nested within the **user** view. It represents the **General information** section of a user's settings page.

Most of the time, we want the URL to correspond to such a structure, as demonstrated in the following screenshot:

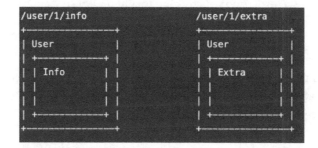

Figure 6.37: User with two nested views – Info and Extra

Vue Router makes it easy to achieve this structure using **nested** route configurations and the **router-view** component.

Let's go back to the **User.vue** view in our previous example (located in **./src/views/**) and add a nested **router-view** component in the **<template>** section:

```
<div>
  <h1>About a user: {{$route.params.id}}</h1>
  <router-link :to="{ name: 'userinfo', params: { id: id }}">Info
    </router-link> |
  <router-link :to="/user/${id}/extra">Extra</router-link>

  <router-view/>
</div>
```

In order to start rendering components to this **router-view**, we will configure the **user** route to have the children option, which accepts an array of route configurations for the child routes. For our example, we'll be adding an **info** and **extra** page for each user. These child routes will be accessed as **/user/:id/info** and **/user/:id/extra** giving each user a unique **info** and **extra** page:

```
{
    path: '/user/:id',
    name: 'user',
    component: () => import(/* webpackChunkName: "user" */
      '../views/User.vue'),
    props: true,
    children: [{
      path: 'info',
      name: 'userinfo',
      component: () => import(/* webpackChunkName: "info" */
        '../views/UserInfo.vue')
    }, {
      path: 'extra',
      component: () => import(/* webpackChunkName: "extra" */
        '../views/UserExtra.vue')
    }]
}
```

Not all the nested paths need to start with **/** as their parent path, which will avoid them being treated as a root path and make things easier for Vue Router to compute the matching route.

Of course, we will have to create two new views in the folder that will render all the information about a user based on the **id** received:

```
<template>
  <div>
    <h2>Name: {{name}}</h2>
    <p>Age: {{age}}</p>
  </div>
</template>
<script>
import users from '../assets/users.js';

export default {
  data() {
    return {
      name: '',
      age: 0
    }
  },
  beforeRouteEnter(to, from, next) {
    next(vm => {
      const user = users[to.params.id - 1];
      vm.name = user.name;
      vm.age = user.age;
    })
  },
  beforeRouteUpdate(to, from, next) {
    const user = users[to.params.id - 1];
    this.name = user.name;
    this.age = user.age;
    next();
  }
}
</script>
```

We also create **UserExtra.vue**, which will render extra information (if there is any). In this example, it will render only simple text:

```
<template>
  <div>
    <h2>I'm an extra section</h2>
  </div>
</template>
```

The nested views are ready! Whenever the user clicks on the **Info** link, it will load the **UserInfo** view into it and update the URL as follows:

Figure 6.38: User page with nested UserInfo view

When the user clicks on **Extra**, they will see the same as is shown in the following screenshot:

Figure 6.39: User page with nested UserExtra view

In this section we looked at nested routes, that is, routes that have multiple children. In our example, the child routes were user info and user extra. This pattern allows us to create pages that extend their parent pages. In the preceding example, we can now make edits to the **About a user** header and have it take effect on all child routes. As projects grow, making use of this pattern will allow you to avoid having duplicate code across multiple views.

In the next section, we will use what we've learned so far to create navigation tabs for our message view component.

EXERCISE 6.06: BUILDING NAVIGATION TABS WITHIN THE MESSAGE VIEW

We will adapt the knowledge learned from the *Nested Routes* section to build a **Navigation** tab section within the **Message** view from *Exercise 6.05, Implementing a Message Route for Each Message with a Dynamic Routing Pattern*.

To access the code files for this exercise, refer to https://packt.live/2U9Bn6I.

1. Firstly, let's make some changes to our **messages** database in **src/assets/messages.js** by adding the following **author** and **sent** fields:

```
const messages = [
  {
    content: 'Hello, how are you?',
    author: 'John',
    sent: '12 May 2019'
  }, {
    content: 'The weather is nice',
    author: 'Lily',
    sent: '12 Jun 2019'
  },
  {
    content: 'This is message feed',
    author: 'Smith',
    sent: '10 Jan 2020'
  },
  {
    content: 'And I am the fourth message',
    author: 'Chuck',
    sent: '1 Apr 2021'
  },
];
```

2. Next, we will create a **MessageAuthor.vue** view that renders only the name of the creator of the message:

```
<template>
  <div>
    <h3>Author:</h3>
    <p>{{message.author}}</p>
  </div>
</template>
<script>
export default {
  props: {
    message: {
      type: Object,
      default: () => {}
    }
  }
}
</script>
```

3. Then we will create a **MessageInfo.vue** view that renders the **message.sent** value:

```
<template>
  <div>
    <h3>Message info: </h3>
    <p>{{message.sent}}</p>
  </div>
</template>
<script>
export default {
  props: {
    message: {
      type: Object,
      default: () => {}
    }
  }
}
</script>
```

4. Once we are done with the components, we need to register the new nested route under the children of the **message** route, inside our router at **src/router/index.js**:

```
{
    path: '/message/:id',
    name: 'message',
    component: () => import(/* webpackChunkName: "message" */
    '../views/Message.vue'),
    async beforeEnter(to, from, next) { ... },
    props: true,
    children: [{
      path: 'author',
      name: 'messageAuthor',
      props: true,
      component: () => import(/* webpackChunkName:
        "messageAuthor" */ '../views/MessageAuthor.vue'),
    }, {
      path: 'info',
      props: true,
      name: 'messageInfo',
      component: () => import(/* webpackChunkName: "messageInfo"
        */ '../views/MessageInfo.vue'),
    }]
}
```

5. Finally, in **Message.vue**, we will refactor the code to the following:

```
<template>
  <div>
    <p>Message content: {{message.content}}</p>
    <router-link :to="{ name: 'messageAuthor', params: { message
}}">Author</router-link> |
    <router-link :to="{ name: 'messageInfo', params: { message
}}">Info</router-link>
    <router-view/>
  </div>
</template>
<script>
export default {
  props: {
    id: {
      type: String
    },
```

```
    message: {
      default: () => {},
      type: Object,
    }
  }
}
</script>
```

And now we can navigate between the **Author** and **Info** tabs within a **Message** as follows:

Figure 6.40: Message page with Info selected

6. Run the application using the following command:

```
yarn serve
```

You will see the following when you select the **Author** option:

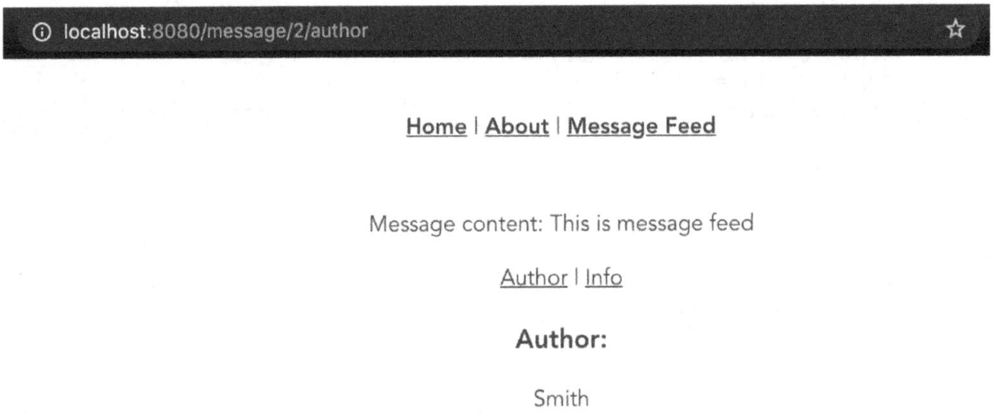

Figure 6.41: Message page with Author selected

With this exercise, we have covered almost all the basic functionalities of Vue Router, especially on handling dynamic and nested routing. In the final section, we will go through how to create a reusable layout for view- templating our application.

USING LAYOUTS

There are many ways to implement layouts in a Vue.js application. One of them is using **slot** and creating a static wrapper layout component on top of **router-view**. Despite its flexibility, this approach results in a heavy performance cost, both in the unnecessary re-creation of the component and in the extra data-fetching required on every route change.

In this section, we will discuss a better approach, which is to take advantage of the power of the dynamic component. The components are as follows:

```
<component :is="layout"/>
```

In the **App.vue** file, we will change the default view generated by Vue CLI to only **<router-view>** and a wrapper around it. This wrapper is a dynamic component that will render whatever component is defined in the **layout** variable:

```
<template>
  <div id="app">
    <component :is="layout">
      <router-view/>
    </component>
  </div>
</template>
<script>
```

By default, we will define **layout** in **data** to be the **default.vue** layout:

```
<script>
export default {
  data() {
    return {
      layout: () => import(/* webpackChunkName: "defaultlayout" */
        './layouts/default.vue')
    }
  }
}
</script>
```

And in the **layouts** folder, we will create the **default** layout component with a simple header navigation, a **main** slot to render the actual content (which is whatever **<router-view>** renders), and a footer:

```
<template>
  <div class="default">
    <nav>
      <router-link to="/">Home</router-link> |
      <router-link to="/about">About</router-link>
    </nav>
    <main class="main">
      <slot/>
    </main>
    <footer>
      <div>Vue Workshop Chapter 06</div>
    </footer>
  </div>
</template>
```

Going back to our **App.vue** file, in order to make the layout **component** render in response to corresponding route changes, **router-view** should control which layout to render. In other words, **layout** should be updatable and decided by the view component rendered inside **router-view**. To achieve this, we will define the **currentLayout** property as synchronous with **layout** using **sync** on **<router-view>**:

```
<component :is="layout">
  <router-view :currentLayout="layout"/>
</component>
```

And upon creating an instance of the **Home.vue** component, we will emit an **update:currentLayout** event with the desired layout to be updated and rendered accordingly:

```
import DefaultLayout from '../layouts/default.vue';

export default {
  name: 'home',
  components: {
    HelloWorld,
  },
  created() {
```

```
    this.$emit('update:currentLayout', DefaultLayout)
  }
}
```

The output will be as follows:

Vue Workshop Chapter 06

Figure 6.42: Home page rendered with a layout

Since the `layout` component is not part of the `router-view` component, it will only re-render whenever the layout changes from within the view. This will maintain the performance of the app during user navigation.

In this section, we looked at how the dynamic `component` component can be used to provide different layouts for different routes. This gives us the ability to have different common layouts, for example, one global menu for user-facing pages and another for admin pages, rendered based on the routes used. In the next section, we'll build on what we learned here by creating a message application with dynamic nested routing and layouts.

ACTIVITY 6.01: CREATING A MESSAGE SPA WITH DYNAMIC, NESTED ROUTING, AND LAYOUTS

This activity aims to leverage your knowledge about Vue Router regarding registering routes and handling dynamic routes, nested routes, and route Hooks to create a **Message SPA**. This application will allow users to compose new messages, view a message feed, and navigate between messages to see their details:

1. Create a **MessageEditor** view (at **src/views/MessageEditor.vue**) that will render a view with **textarea** to the user and a **submit** button to save the message.

2. Register the **editor** route with **MessageEditor** as its view in **src/router/index.js**.

3. Create a **MessageList** view (at **src/views/MessageList.vue**) that will render a list of **message id** values wrapped by an **a** tag, which will direct to the single message page with the given **id** upon selection.

4. Register the **list** route with **MessageList** as its view in **src/router/index.js**.

5. Add the **Messages** view (at **src/views/Messages.vue**), which will render links to either **editor** or **list** as its nested routes and render the nested view accordingly.

6. When the user navigates away from **editor**, should some content not yet have been submitted, display a message asking if they want to save before navigating away. **Yes** will continue, **No** will abort the navigation.

7. Add a **Message** view (at **src/views/Message.vue**), which will render message content from **props** and have a **back** button to go back to the previous view. By default, it should go to **messages**.

8. Register the **Message** view with the dynamic route of **message/:id** in **src/router/index.js**.

9. Improve the UI by creating two different simple layouts, one for **messages** (with the title only) and one for **message** (with both the **title** and the **back** button).

The expected output is as follows:

- The **/list** view that displays a feed of messages should look as follows:

Messages section

List | Editor

Message Feed

0
1
2

Figure 6.43: The /list view in the Messages app

- The **/editor** view that allows the user to compose and send a new message looks as follows:

Messages section

List | Editor

Figure 6.44: The /editor view in the Messages app

- The **/message/:id** dynamic route (here, **/message/0** for a message with the **id** of **0**) in the **Message** app looks as follows:

Message content:

asfd

Back

Figure 6.45: The /message/0 view in the Message app

An alert will be displayed when the user tries to navigate away with an unsaved message as shown in the following screenshot:

Figure 6.46: The /editor view when the user tries to navigate away with an unsaved message

> **NOTE**
>
> The solution to this activity can be found on page 674.

SUMMARY

Throughout this chapter, we have learned about the most basic and useful functionalities offered by Vue Router for building routing for any Vue.js application in an effective and organized manner.

router-view and **router-link** allow app developers to easily set up the navigation paths to their related views and maintain the SPA concept. The fact that they are Vue components themselves provides us as developers with the benefits of the Vue architecture, giving us flexibility in implementing nested views or layouts.

Defining the route as an object with different properties simplifies the architecture process, including refactoring existing paths and adding a new route to the system. Using router parameters and patterns provides dynamic routing with reusable views and allows communication and data preservation between pages.

And finally, with Hooks, we saw how we can intercept the navigation flow, setting up authentication where needed, redirecting to the desired path, or even loading and keeping some important data before the users land on the targeted page. There is an unlimited number of use cases where these Hooks can be extremely useful, such as when implementing a back button for instance.

With these, we are now capable of composing a Vue.js application with a proper navigation system for users to explore, while maintaining the data flow in every navigation use case (dynamic routes and nested views) and the application design layout.

In the next chapter, you are going to explore how to apply transitions to the routing and different animations for beautiful loading effects for your Vue components and application.

7

ANIMATIONS AND TRANSITIONS

OVERVIEW

This chapter deals with creating transition and animation effects in a Vue application. Throughout this chapter, you will explore the basics of Vue transitions. We will cover single-element transitions, using transition groups to animate a list of elements, and creating full-page animations with transition routes. You will also learn how to create your transitions and learn how to combine with external libraries to do various animations.

By the end of the chapter, you will be ready to implement and handle the fundamental transition and animation effects for any Vue application.

INTRODUCTION

In *Chapter 6, Routing*, you learned about routes and how to set up an essential routing navigation system using Vue Router. Empowering the transition between different routes with smoothness or providing your application with proper animation effects when users interact with the application is the next level to achieve. While the smooth transition between pages provides a better user experience, animation effects such as loading or the way we render content can keep users engaged with the application. Hence, our next focus is transitions and animations in Vue and what we can do to apply these concepts to our Vue application.

VUE TRANSITIONS

Unlike other frameworks, Vue.js provides developers with built-in support for animating Vue.js applications, including transitions and animations. Transitioning is implemented in such a simple and straightforward manner that developers can easily configure and add it to their application. The Vue.js transition mechanism supports CSS transitions, programmatic manipulation with JavaScript, and even integration with third-party animation libraries such as GSAP or Animate.css.

First, we will discuss the difference between transitions and animations. A transition happens when a component (or element) moves from one state to another, such as hovering on a button, navigating from one page to another, displaying a pop-up modal, and so on. Meanwhile, animations are like transitions but are not limited to just two states. Understanding the basics of transitions allows you to get started with animations.

TRANSITION ELEMENTS

In this example, to enable transitions for a single component or element, Vue.js provides the built-in **transition** component that will wrap around the targeted element, as seen in **./src/components/HelloWorld.vue**:

```
<transition name="fade-in">
  <h1>{{ msg }}</h1>
</transition>
```

The **transition** component adds two transition states—**enter** and **leave**—for any targeted element or component, including components with conditional rendering (**v-if**) and conditional display (**v-show**).

This component receives a prop called **name** that represents the name of the transition—in this case, it's **fade-in**—and is also the prefix for the transition class names, which will be discussed next.

TRANSITION CLASSES

Vue.js implements a CSS-based and class-based transition effect for **leave**/**enter**, hence the transition will be applied to the target component through a set of class selectors.

Each of these class selectors has the **v-** prefix in case there is no **name** prop given on the **transition** component. And there are some standard classes that are grouped into two main groups.

The first group of transition classes is for the **enter** transition, when the component is first displayed. Here is a list of **enter** transition classes:

v-enter (or **<name>-enter**): This is the starting state and is added to the component before the component is added or updated. This class will be removed once the transition finishes it at the ending state. In the **<style>** section of **src/components/HelloWorld.vue**, we will set the **.fade-in-enter** starting state as completely hidden with **opacity: 0**:

```
<style>
.fade-in-enter {
  opacity: 0;
}
</style>
```

v-enter-active (or **<name>-enter-active**): This class defines the delay, duration, and the easing curve when the component is actively entering the transition. It will be added to the component before the component is inserted, applied to the component during the entire entering phase, and removed once the effect completes.

Let's add **.fade-in-enter-active**, which will do a transition to the opacity state within **3** seconds:

```
.fade-in-enter-active {
  transition: opacity 3s easein;
}
```

v-enter-to (or **<name>-enter-to**): This is the last sub-state of entering, where the effect frame is added after the component is inserted and removed when the effect finishes. In our example, we do not need to define anything since the **opacity** value for this state should be **1**.

The second group of classes consists of **leave** transitions, which trigger when the component is disabled or removed from view:

- **v-leave** (or **<name>-leave**): This is the starting state for the leaving transition. Similar to **v-enter-to**, we don't need to define styling effects for this state.

- **v-leave-active** (or **<name>-leave-active**): This is applied during the leaving phase and acts similarly to **v-enter-active**. And since we want to have a fade-out effect, we will use the same styling as with **fade-in-enter-active**:

```
.fade-in-enter-active, .fade-in-leave-active {
    transition: opacity 3s ease-in;
}
```

- **v-leave-to** (or **<name>-leave-to**): This is the ending state with similar behavior to **v-enter-to**. Since the component is going to disappear from view, we will reuse the styling defined for the starting phase of **enter fade-in-enter**:

```
.fade-in-enter, .fade-in-leave-to {
    opacity: 0;
}
```

The following screenshot is a recap of all the states of **transition** described so far:

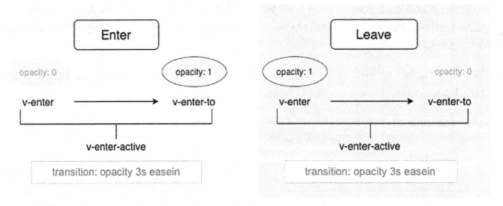

Figure 7.1: Diagram of transition phases

In this section, we looked at three different transition states for entering and three transition states for leaving. We also walked through using a transition state to slowly fade in some text when the user presses a button.

ANIMATION FOR A COMPONENT

Since animation is basically an extended form of a transition (with more than two states), it is applied in the same way as transitions, with the exception that **v-enter** will only be removed on an **animationend** event triggered by Vue.js.

> **NOTE**
>
> **animationend** is a DOM event that is fired once the CSS animation finishes execution, with the condition that the target element still exists within the DOM and the animation is still attached to that element.

For the next example, in the **<template>** section, we can define a new transition called **slide** using an animation CSS effect as a wrapper for the **h1** element that displays msg. This transition provides the animation effect of sliding from the left to the center on entering and vice versa on leaving.

To get started, generate a **vue** starter project using the CLI with the following command:

```
vue create hello-world
```

Next, open up the project and go into **src/components/HelloWorld.vue**, and then modify the existing **<h1>{{msg}}</h1>** code:

```
<transition name="slide">
  <h1 v-if="show">{{ msg }}</h1>
</transition>
```

In **<style>**, we need to define keyframes for the **slide** animation effect:

```
@keyframes slide {
  0% { transform: translateX(-100px) }
  100% { transform: translateX(0px) }
}
```

The related transition classes will be assigned the following stylings:

```
.slide-enter, .slide-leave-to {
  transform: translateX(-100px);
}

.slide-enter-active {
  animation: slide 5s;
}

.slide-leave-active {
  animation: slide 5s reverse;
}
```

This means at the starting phase of entering and at the ending phase of leaving, the text position will be **-100px** from the designated position on the page. The browser will animate the element using the slide keyframe for a duration of 5 seconds, and in the active state of leaving, the animation will be exactly the opposite of the one in the active stage of entering.

You'll also want to add a show data variable. You can do this by modifying the existing export, as shown:

```
<script>
export default {
  name: 'HelloWorld',
  data: {
    showHello: true,
  },
  props: {
    msg: String
  }
}
</script>
```

And with that, we have implemented our animation. Now comes the next challenge: what if we want to combine different animation or transition effects to leave and enter states, or use an external CSS library for these states? Let's take a look at custom transition classes.

CUSTOM TRANSITION CLASSES

In this section, we'll again be starting from the default starter project created with vue create hello-world. Instead of setting the transition name and letting the Vue.js mechanism populate the required class names, there is an option to provide custom classes through the following attributes and replace the conventional defaults.

For entering a state, use the following:

- **enter-class**

- **enter-active-class**

- **enter-to-leave**

For leaving a state, use the following:

- **leave-class**

- **leave-active-class**

- **leave-to-class**

We will start by creating a file based on the previous example, but now we will use a **swing** animation effect on the active phase of the entering state, and the **tada** effect for the active phase of the leaving state. We will define the **enter-active-class** and **leave-active-class** attributes in our **transition** component as follows:

```
<transition
    name="slide"
    enter-active-class="swing"
    leave-active-class="tada"
>
    <h1 v-if="show">{{ msg }}</h1>
</transition>
```

And in the **<style>** section, we just need to define **.tada** and **.swing**, without any suffix pattern:

```
.tada {
  animation-fill-mode: both;
  animation-name: tada;
  animation-duration: 3s;
}
```

```
.swing {
  animation-fill-mode: both;
  transform-origin: top center;
  animation-duration: 2s;
  animation-name: swing;
}
```

Then add the dedicated keyframes to set up the animation:

```
@keyframes tada {
  0% {
    transform: scale3d(1, 1, 1);
  }

  10%, 20% {
    transform: scale3d(.8, .9, .8) rotate3d(0, 0, 1, -5deg);
  }

  30%, 50%, 70%, 90% {
    transform: scale3d(1.1, 1.1, 1.1) rotate3d(0, 0, 1, 5deg);
  }

  40%, 60%, 80% {
    transform: scale3d(1.1, 1.1, 1.1) rotate3d(0, 0, 1, -5deg);
  }

  100% {
    transform: scale3d(1, 1, 1);
  }

@keyframes swing {
  20% { transform: rotate(5deg); }
  40% { transform: rotate(-10deg); }
  60% { transform: rotate(5deg); }
  80% { transform: rotate(-10deg); }
  100% { transform: rotate(0deg); }
}
```

You'll also want to add a show data variable. You can do this by modifying the existing **export**, as shown:

```
<script>
export default {
  name: 'HelloWorld',
  data: {
    showHello: true,
  },
  props: {
    msg: String
  }
}
</script>
```

When we run the application using the **yarn serve** command, we will have our animations set separately for entering and leaving. The following screenshot displays how the screen will now appear:

Figure 7.2: Swing animation effect on action

You should see the welcome text shrink while rotating, transitioning from what was shown in *Figure 7.2* to the following:

Toggle Hello World msg

Welcome to Your Vue.js App

Figure 7.3: tada animation effect on action

In this section, we looked at creating custom transition effects. As examples, we made `swing` and `tada`. We did this by defining the transition classes in our stylesheet and then adding keyframes for each of the effects. This technique can be used to create all kinds of custom transition effects. In the next section, we'll look at JavaScript hooks and how they can be used for more complex animations.

JAVASCRIPT HOOKS

As we learned in the previous section, we can use custom transition classes to integrate external third-party CSS animation libraries for styling effects. However, there are external libraries that are not CSS-based, but JavaScript-based, such as **Velocity.js** or **GreenSock Animation API** (**GSAP**), which require hooks to be set using JavaScript events and external animation handlers.

In order to use the Velocity.js or GSAP libraries in the Vue app, you need to install them separately by using the **npm install** or **yarn add** command, as follows:

- To install Velocity.js, use these commands:

```
npm install velocity-animate
#Or
yarn add velocity-animate
```

- To install GSAP, use these commands:

```
npm install gsap
#or
yarn add gsap
```

Being a Vue.js component means the **transition** component supports binding custom handlers to a list of events as props. Consider the following example:

```
<transition
  @before-enter="beforeEnter"
  @enter="enter"
  @leave="leave"
>
  <h1 v-if="show">{{ msg }}</h1>
</transition>
```

We bind the animation methods programmatically to the respective events on the transition element:

- **beforeEnter** is the animation state before the component is inserted—similar to the v-enter phase.

- **enter** for the animation during the entire entering phase—similar to the v-enter-active phase.

- **leave** for the animation during the entire leaving phase. This is similar to the v-leave-active phase.

We need to define these event handlers in the **methods** section of the **HelloWorld.vue** component's configuration:

```
<script>
export default {
  name: 'HelloWorld',
  props: {
    msg: String
  },
  data() {
    return {
      show: false
```

```
      }
    },
  methods: {
    beforeEnter() {
      //...
    },
    enter() {
      //...
    },
    leave() {
      //...
    }
  }
}
</script>
```

In this example, we will create our animation events using the **TweenMax** and **TimelineMax** functionalities provided by the GSAP library, as follows:

```
    beforeEnter(el) {
      el.style.opacity = 0;
    },
    enter(el, done) {
      TweenMax.to(el, 2, {
        opacity: 1,
        fontSize: '20px',
        onComplete: done
      })
    },
    leave(el, done) {
      const tl = new TimelineMax({
        onComplete: done
      });

      tl.to(el, {rotation: -270,duration: 1, ease: "elastic"})
        .to(el, {rotation: -360})
```

```
      .to(el, {
        rotation: -180,
        opacity: 0
      });
  }
```

For both **TweenMax** and **TimelineMax**, the syntax of the **to()** animation trigger method is pretty simple:

```
TimelineMax.to(<element>, <effect properties>, <time position>)
TweenMax.to(<element>, <effect properties>, <time position>)
```

Most of the effect properties have a similar syntax to CSS so they're not difficult to learn and use. In addition, we must pass a **done** callback received from the event emitter for events such as **enter** and **leave** to **onComplete** to make sure it is triggered, and the hooks will not be called synchronously. Also, note that all the event emitters also pass **el**, which is a pointer to the current element in transition for use.

Other than these three events, there are other events we can bind, depending on the complexity of the animations and transitions, such as **afterEnter**, **enterCancelled**, **beforeLeave**, **afterLeave**, and **leaveCancelled**.

Please note, it's highly recommended to add **v-bind:css="false"** (or **:css="false"**) if you are using transitions with JavaScript only. This is to prevent Vue.js from detecting and applying any related CSS, therefore avoiding transition interference by accident:

```
<transition
    @before-enter="beforeEnter"
    @enter="enter"
    @leave="leave"
    :css="false"
  >
    <h1 v-if="show">{{ msg }}</h1>
```

In this section, we looked at how external JavaScript libraries can be used for animations. We implemented a simple tween using the GSAP library, making use of its **TweenMax** and **TimelineMax** functions.

Let's now learn how to add a new message using an animation effect.

EXERCISE 7.01: ADDING A NEW MESSAGE WITH AN ANIMATION EFFECT

We are going to create a message editor where the user will compose and submit a new message. The new message will be displayed instantly with a sliding-from-right animation effect.

To access the code files for this exercise, refer to https://packt.live/338ZXJv:

> **NOTE**
>
> Before you begin this exercise, run the **vue create** command to generate a Vue starter project.

1. First create a new component called **MessageEditor.vue** located in the **/src/components/** folder. In this component, **<template>** will contain two sections, **textarea**, for composing a new message with a button to submit it, and **section**, where the newly composed message will be displayed:

```
<template>
  <div>
    <div class="editor--wrapper">
      <textarea ref="textArea" class="editor">
      </textarea>
      <button @click="onSendClick()" class="editor--submit">
      Submit</button>
    </div>
    <section v-if="message" class="message--display">
      <h4>Your saved message: </h4>
      <span>{{message}}</span>
    </section>
  </div>
</template>
```

2. Next, wrap the whole message section with the **transition** element, to prepare for our animation.

```
<transition name="slide-right">
    <section v-if="message" class="message--display">
      <h4>Your saved message: </h4>
      <span>{{message}}</span>
    </section>
  </transition>
```

3. We'll need our **export** component with a method for changing the message text. Add that with the following code:

```
<script>
export default {
  data() {
    return {
      message: ''
    }
  },
  methods: {
    onSendClick() {
      const message = this.$refs.textArea.value;
      this.message = message;
      this.$refs.textArea.value = '';
    }
  }
}
</script>
```

4. Next, we will define the **slide-right** animation effect using @**keyframes** in our **style** section by using the following command:

```
<style scoped>
@keyframes slide-right {
  100% {
    transform: translateX(0)
  }
}
</style>
```

This means it will re-position the element that has this effect horizontally (on the *X* axis) to the original starting point, (0,0).

5. Now we will define the two classes, one for sliding in from left to right (**slide-right**), and one for the opposition direction (**slide-left**):

```
.slide-right {
  animation: 1s slide-right 1s forwards;
  transform:translateX(-100%);
  transition: border-top 2s ease;
}
```

```
.slide-left {
    animation: 1s slide-right 1s reverse;
    transform:translateX(-100%);
}
```

6. Add **border-top:0** as the starting point for our **slide-right** transition to do a bit of an effect on the **border-top** of this section:

```
.slide-right-enter {
    border-top: 0;
}
```

7. Next, using what we learned about custom transition classes, let's bind **enter-active** to the **slide-right** class, and similarly bind **leave-active** to **slide-left**. These three properties are added to the **transition** element that was created in *Step 2*:

```
<transition
        name="slide-right"
        enter-active-class="slide-right"
        leave-active-class="slide-left"
    >
Add CSS stylings using CSS Flexbox to make the editor look nice:
.editor--wrapper {
    display: flex;
    flex-direction: column;
}


.editor {
    align-self: center;
    width: 200px;
}


.editor--submit {
    margin: 0.5rem auto;
    width: 50px;
    align-self: center;
}
```

```
.message--display {
  margin-top: 1rem;
  border-top: 1px solid lightgray;
}
```

8. Run the application using the **`yarn serve`** command.

   This will generate a component that will display the typed message with a sliding animation effect, as shown in *Figure 7.4*:

Hello, enjoy the lesson?
Submit

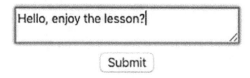

Figure 7.4: Message Editor text area

The following screenshot shows how the message component appears with a slide-from-left-to-right animation effect:

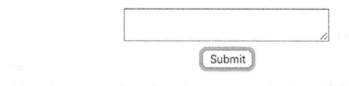

Submit
ur saved message:
lo, enjoy the lesson?

Figure 7.5: Message in transition for display

After animating in from the left, the component should stop in the centered position, as shown in *Figure 7.6*:

Figure 7.6: Message after the animation

This exercise helped you to get used to some of the transform effects in CSS, such as **translateX** and **transition**. It also demonstrates how easy it is to add animation to an element in the Vue application. What about transitioning for multiple elements in the same group, such as a list? We will find out in the next topic.

TRANSITION GROUPS

So far, we have gone through the fundamentals of Vue transition elements for simple components and elements, with both custom CSS-only and JavaScript-only support for animations. Next, we will explore how to apply a transition on a group of components, for instance, a list of items that will be rendered simultaneously, by using **v-for**.

Vue.js provides another component for this specific purpose, the **transition-group** component.

We will now assume that we have a list of messages displayed on a feed, and we would like to add a transition to this list to have some effect when each item appears on the screen. In the **./src/components/Messages.vue** file, let's wrap the main container with a **transition-group** component, and pass the same props we used previously for our **transition** component. They share the same prop types:

```
<transition-group name="fade">
  <p v-for="message in messages" :key="message" v-show="show">
    {{message}}
  </p>
</transition-group>
```

And we need to set the CSS styling effect for the transition effect passed as **fade**, following the same syntax rules for transition classes:

```css
.fade-enter-active, .fade-leave-active {
  transition: all 2s;
}
.fade-enter, .fade-leave-active {
  opacity: 0;
  transform: translateX(30px);
}
```

Upon running the application using the **yarn serve** command, your list's item will have a fading effect when it appears. The following screenshot displays how your screen should appear:

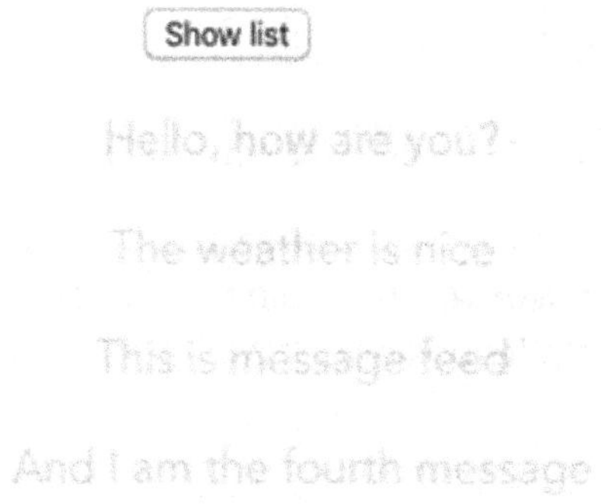

Figure 7.7: Fading of the list item

Note that unlike the **transition** component, which does not render any wrapper container element, **transition-group** will render an actual element and you can change the element tag name by using a **tag** prop. By default, the element used is **span**:

```html
<transition-group
  name="fade"
  tag="div"
>
  <p v-for="message in messages" :key="message" v-show="show">
      {{message}}
  </p>
</transition-group>
```

In the browser, the actual HTML output will look as follows:

```
▼<div>
    <p style="display: none;">Hello, how are you?</p>
    <p style="display: none;">The weather is nice</p>
    <p style="display: none;">This is message feed</p>
    <p style="display: none;">And I am the forth message</p>
  </div>
```

Figure 7.8: Transition container element rendered according to the tag attribute

Furthermore, all the transition classes will only be applied to the list item elements that have the **v-for** attribute and not to the wrapper.

Finally, you *must* have the **:key** attribute for every list item, in order for Vue.js to index and know which item to apply the transition to.

We will now create a moving effect on the list.

CREATING A MOVING EFFECT WHILE TRANSITIONING A LIST

Besides all the classes provided in the **transition** component, **transition-group** has another class, **v-move**, which allows us to add additional effects while each item is being moved into its position. It can be manually assigned through the **move-class** attribute:

```
.fade-move {
  transition: transform 2s ease-in;
}
```

Next, we will look at making animations on the initial rendering of a page or component.

MAKING AN ANIMATION ON INITIAL RENDER

Usually, the list of items will be displayed on the first initial page load, and our animation won't work because the element is already in the view. In order to trigger the animation, we need to use a different transition attribute, **appear**, to force the animation on the initial page render, right after the page has been loaded:

```
<transition-group
    appear="true"
    tag="div"
>
```

```
    <p v-for="message in messages" :key="message">{{message}}</p>
</transition-group>
```

We can also set hooks with **v-on:after-appear**, **v-on:appear**, **v-on:after-appear**, and **v-on:appear-cancelled**, or we can create custom classes by using the following format:

```
<transition-group
    appear="true"
    appear-class="fade-enter"
    appear-active-class="fade-enter-active"
    tag="div"
>
    <p v-for="message in messages" :key="message">{{message}}</p>
</transition-group>
```

Animating on render is a commonly used feature that can be used in many situations, such as fading in components as we did here. In the next section, we will look at sorting a list of messages with an animation.

EXERCISE 7.02: SORTING A LIST OF MESSAGES WITH AN ANIMATION

In this short exercise, we will add additional functionality to the message list: **sorting**. Upon sorting (A-Z or Z-A), there will be a flipping animation effect on the list.

To access the code files for this exercise, refer to https://packt.live/35TFs5l:

> **NOTE**
>
> Before you begin this exercise, run the **vue create** command to generate a Vue starter project.

1. We will use the same component code as previously for rendering messages in the **Messages.vue** component. The list will be wrapped with a **transition-group** component, ready for animation. And do not forget to set **appear="true"**, or simply **appear** for short, in order for the element to be animated only after the page has finished loading:

```
<transition-group
    appear
    name="flip"
    tag="div"
    >
```

```
            <p v-for="message in messages" :key="message"
        class="message--item"
            >{{message}}</p>
        </transition-group>
```

2. Run the application using the **yarn serve** command. This will generate the following output:

Figure 7.9: Message list before animation

3. There's no animation because we haven't defined the CSS animation styling for **flip** yet. Let's do it. In the **<style>** section of **src/components/Messages.vue**, we will add **opacity: 0** and then reposition each element in the list vertically (on the *Y* axis) by **20px** from the original position. This should be the initial stage when the element enters **flip-enter** or is about to leave the transition with **flip-leave-to**:

```
<style scoped>
  .flip-enter, .flip-leave-to {
    opacity: 0;
    transform: translateY(20px);
  }
</style>
```

4. In the same **<style>** section, add custom CSS styling to each message element (the **message—item** class) with **transition: all 2s**. This is to make sure the transition effect for the element will be done with all CSS properties within **2** seconds:

```
.message--item {
  transition: all 2s;
}
```

5. Once the **flip-move** is in action, we need to add the transition effect only for **transform** (which was defined previously as vertically **20px** away). We can see the moving up and down effect for each message flawlessly. In addition, we also need to add **position: absolute** for when the transition is in the middle of the leaving stage:

```
.flip-leave-active {
  position: absolute;
}
.flip-move {
  transition: transform 1s;
}
```

6. We will next add three buttons—allowing sorting from A to Z, sorting from Z to A, and to shuffle randomly:

```
<button @click="sorting()">Sort A-Z</button>
<button @click="sorting(true)">Sort Z-A</button>
<button @click="shuffle()">Shuffle</button>
```

7. We'll also need to add our basic component export code as well as our message feed data. Feel free to use any content you like for your messages:

```
export default {
  data() {
    return {
      messages: [
        'Hello, how are you?',
        'The weather is nice',
        'This is message feed',
        'And I am the fourth message',
        'Chapter 7 is fun',
        'Animation is super awesome',
        'Sorry, I didn't know you called',
```

```
                'Be patient, animation comes right up'
        ],
          show: false
      }
    },
  }
```

8. Next, we'll add the logic for sorting and shuffling. The **methods** section should be inside the component **export** created in the last step:

```
methods: {
    sorting(isDescending) {
        this.messages.sort();

        if (isDescending) { this.messages.reverse(); }
    },
    shuffle() {
        this.messages.sort(() => Math.random() - 0.5);
    }
  }
```

The output after clicking on one of the buttons will be similar to the following:

Animations super awesome
Chapter 7 is fun

Be patient, animation comes right up
And I am the forth message
This is message feed
The weather is nice?
Hello, how are you?

Sorry, I didn't know you called

Figure 7.10: Message list during sorting with animation

In this exercise, we learned how to add a flip animation effect with **transition-group** to a list of components dynamically based on a change of the order of its element. Next, let's explore how to apply transition effects when navigating between pages.

TRANSITION ROUTES

With the combination of the **router-element** component from Vue Router and the **transition** component, we can easily set up the transition effects when a user navigates from one URL (route) to another.

To give you a more fundamental understanding, we demonstrate in the following section an underlying case where a user redirects from the **home** page to the **about** page on a website.

Let's wrap **router-element** with **transition** and add the **name="zoom"** attribute:

```
<transition
  name="zoom"
  mode="out-in"
>
  <router-view/>
</transition>
```

Here we will use the **mode** attribute to indicate the transition mode. There are currently two modes to set:

- **in-out**: The new element comes in first, and only after that will the current element go out of view.

- **out-in**: The current element goes out first, and only then will the new element come in. We will use this for our example, and it's more common than the previous one.

Then, we just need to set up the transition CSS effect with the transition classes as usual and it's done. Simple as that:

```css
/**Zoom animation **/
.zoom-enter-active,
.zoom-leave-active {
  animation-duration: 0.3s;
  animation-fill-mode: both;
  animation-name: zoom;
}

.zoom-leave-active {
```

```
  animation-direction: reverse;
}


@keyframes zoom {
  from {
    opacity: 0;
    transform: scale3d(0.4, 0.4, 0.4);
  }


  100% {
    opacity: 1;
  }
}
```

In this section, we looked at transition routes. Transition effects are animations that occur between the rendering of routes, such as navigating from one page to another. In the next section, we will look at creating a transition effect for each route navigated in our application.

EXERCISE 7.03: CREATING A TRANSITION EFFECT FOR EACH ROUTE NAVIGATED

In this exercise, we will adapt what we have learned about transitions with the router element from the *Transition Routes* section to create different transition effects for different routes. The default effect will be **fade**.

To access the code files for this exercise, visit https://packt.live/376DoXo:

> **NOTE**
>
> Before you begin this exercise, run the **vue create** command to generate a Vue starter project.

1. Create a simple application with Vue Router, and add a route for **messages** using the **Messages.vue** view, located in the **src/views/** folder. Use the code from the previous exercise and add a link to this newly created route in **App.vue**.

2. Next, we wrap the **router-view** element with the **transition** component, in **App.vue**:

    ```
    <transition :name="transition" :mode="mode">
      <router-view/>
    </transition>
    ```

3. Inside the **export** section of **App.vue**, make sure the **data** function includes values for **transition** and **mode**, as shown here:

    ```
    data() {
      return {
        transition: 'fade',
        mode: 'out-in',
      };
    },
    ```

4. Add the CSS style for fading in and out using the following CSS in **App.vue**:

    ```
    <style>
      .fade-enter, .fade-leave-to {
        opacity: 0;
      }

      .fade-enter-active, .fade-leave-active {
        transition: opacity 1s ease-in;
      }
    </style>
    ```

5. At this point, all the pages are loaded with the **fade** effect, even **/messages**. But we want to make the messages page load with a different effect—the **zoom** effect. Next, add the relevant CSS code for the **zoom** animation inside the same **style** tag:

    ```
    /**Zoom animation */
    .zoom-enter-active,
    .zoom-leave-active {
      animation-duration: 0.5s;
      animation-fill-mode: both;
      animation-name: zoom;
    }
    ```

```
.zoom-leave-active {
  animation-direction: reverse;
}


@keyframes zoom {
 from {
    opacity: 0;
    transform: scale3d(0.4, 0.4, 0.4);
 }


  100% {
    opacity: 1;
  }
}
```

6. We will now add some standard CSS stylings for the app's default layout with the help of the following code:

```
#app {
  font-family: 'Avenir', Helvetica, Arial, sans-serif;
  -webkit-font-smoothing: antialiased;
  -moz-osx-font-smoothing: grayscale;
  text-align: center;
  color: #2c3e50;
}

#nav {
  padding: 30px;
}

#nav a {
  font-weight: bold;
  color: #2c3e50;
}

#nav a.router-link-exact-active {
  color: #42b983;
}
```

7. Now we need to map the **/messages** route with this specific transition effect and without affecting other routes. In order to do that, we need to add a field called **transition** to the **meta** property of this route configuration, in **src/router/index.js**:

```
{
    path: '/messages',
    name: 'messages',
    meta: {
        transition: 'zoom',
    },
    component: () => import(/* webpackChunkName: "about" */
        '../views/Messages.vue')
}
```

8. Check the code for your **routes** object to confirm it's the same as the following code. Here, we are matching each URL for our application with a view file:

```
const routes = [
    {
        path: '/',
        name: 'home',
        component: Home
    },
    {
        path: '/about',
        name: 'about',
        component: () => import(/* webpackChunkName: "about" */
            '../views/About.vue')
    },
    {
        path: '/messages',
        name: 'messages',
        meta: {
            transition: 'zoom',
        },
        component: () => import(/* webpackChunkName: "messages" */
            '../views/Messages.vue')
    }
]
```

9. This won't show in the browser, since this transition declaration is not yet tied to the **data** field of the **App.vue** component, and it needs to be tied before the view starts loading. For that, we will take advantage of the **created** life cycle hook and the **beforeEach** route hook of the **$router** global mentioned in *Chapter 6, Routing*.

10. Let's add a hook for before each route change in **App.vue**. We will check whether the destination route (**to**) has a custom **transition** effect. If it does, we will map the value of **transition** in the **App** instance to it; otherwise, we'll use the fallback default value before continuing the navigation, as follows:

```
created() {
    this.$router.beforeEach((
        to, // The destination route
        from, //The source route
        next //The function to trigger to resolve the hook
    ) => {
        let transition = 'fade';

        if (to.meta && to.meta.transition) {
            transition = to.meta.transition;
        }

        this.transition = transition;
        next();
    })
}
```

11. Run the application using the following command:

```
yarn serve
```

12. Now if you open **localhost:8080** in your browser and navigate to **/messages**, you should see something similar to *Figure 7.11*:

<u>Home</u> | **About** | Messages

Sort A-Z   Sort Z-A   Shuffle

Hello, how are you?

The weather is nice

This is message feed

And I am the fourth message

Chapter 7 is fun

Animation is super awesome

Sorry, I didn't know you called

Be patient, animation comes right up

Figure 7.11: Navigating to /messages with a zoom effect in progress

While navigating to other routes, we should see the default transition shown in *Figure 7.12*:

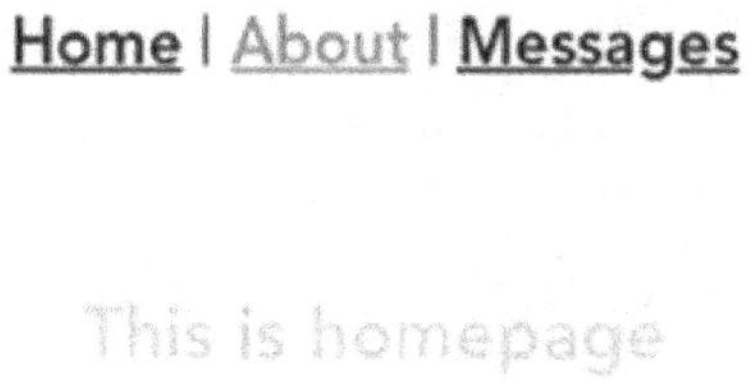

<u>Home</u> | About | **<u>Messages</u>**

This is homepage

Figure 7.12: Navigating to /home with a fade effect in progress

This exercise demonstrates how we can easily set up different transitions on different pages with minimum effort, by combining the right hooks and methods. You can experiment a bit further with an external library to make your app animation smoother and livelier.

USING THE GSAP LIBRARY FOR ANIMATION

GSAP is an open source scripted library that focuses solely on fast animation using JavaScript and provides cross-platform consistency support. It supports animation on a wide range of element types, such as Scalar Vector Graphics (SVG), React components, canvas, and so on.

GSAP is flexible, easy to install, and will adjust to any configuration given, from CSS properties or SVG attributes to a numeric value for rendering an object into a canvas.

The core library is a suite of different tools, divided into core and others, such as plugins, easing tools, and utilities.

INSTALLING GSAP

Installing GSAP is straightforward using **npm install** or **yarn add**:

```
yarn add gsap
#or
npm install gsap
```

After installation, you should see a success output similar to that shown in the following screenshot:

```
philip@philip-Aspire-ES1-522:/tmp/test$ yarn add gsap
yarn add v1.22.4
info No lockfile found.
[1/4] Resolving packages...
[2/4] Fetching packages...
[3/4] Linking dependencies...
[4/4] Building fresh packages...

success Saved lockfile.
success Saved 1 new dependency.
info Direct dependencies
└─ gsap@3.5.1
info All dependencies
└─ gsap@3.5.1
Done in 1.73s.
philip@philip-Aspire-ES1-522:/tmp/test$ 
```

Figure 7.13: Results after successful installation

Now that we have GSAP installed, we'll look at basic tweens in GSAP.

BASIC TWEENS

Tween is a concept defined by the GSAP library creator as a high-performance setter for performing all desired animation work based on the user's configuration inputs. The inputs can be the targeted objects to animate, a period, or any specific CSS properties to animate. Upon performing the animation, the tween figures out what the values of CSS properties should be according to the given duration and applies them accordingly.

The following are the fundamental methods to create basic tweens.

gsap.to()

The most commonly used tween is **gsap.to()**, which is called to create an animation, based on the two main parameters:

- **Targets**: These are the elements that we want to apply the animation to. Targets can be an array of elements, a raw object, a DOM element, or an element selector text such as **#myId**.

- **Vars**: An object containing all the animation configuration properties, for example CSS-like properties such as **opacity: 0**, **rotation: 90**, or **fontSize: '20px'**, animation properties such as **duration: 1**, **stagger: 0.2**, or **ease: "elastic"**, and event handler properties such as **onComplete** or **onUpdate**.

For example, if we want to animation the logo of Vue in **HelloWorld.vue**, we run the following:

```
gsap.to(el, {duration: 3, opacity: 1, onComplete: done});
```

Or use the following to move an object with **x** properties (same as **transform: translateX()**):

```
gsap.to(".green", {duration: 3, x: 500, rotation: 360});
```

gsap.from() and gsap.fromTo

We don't always want to define the expected animation effect for the element in view. Instead, we define the default values where the animation should start from for the targeted element. And that's when we use **gsap.from()**.

For example, assuming the current **opacity** value of a box is **1**, the **scale** value is **1**, and the **x** position is **0**, we want to set up an animation to these current values *from* a position **x** of **300**, with an **opacity** value of **0** and a **scale** value of **0.5**. In other words, the animation will be done from **{x: 300, opacity: 0, scale: 0.5}** to whatever values the element has currently:

```
gsap.from(".red", {duration: 3, x: 300, scale: 0.5, opacity: 0});
```

But in many cases, we need to set up the starting and ending values for an animation since one side is not good enough. For that purpose, GSAP provides **gasp.fromTo()** with the following syntax:

```
gsap.fromTo(target, fromValues, toValues)
```

Let's define an animation for a gray box with original values of **{ opacity: 0, scale: 0.5, x: 300 }** to values of **{ opacity: 1, scale: 1, x: 100, rotation: 360}**:

```
gsap.fromTo(".grey",
    { duration: 3, opacity: 0, scale: 0.5, x: 600 },
    { duration: 3, opacity: 1, scale: 1, x: 200, rotation: 360}
  )
```

In order to translate all the CSS-like values to the corresponding CSS values, one of the core plugins for GSAP is **CSSPlugin**. This plugin will detect whether the target is a DOM element automatically, intercept the passed values, translate them into proper CSS values, and then apply them to the element as inline styles accordingly.

In the next section, we'll walk through an exercise of creating a simple tween using GSAP.

EXERCISE 7.04: TWEENS WITH GSAP

The goal of this exercise is to get you comfortable with working with external libraries such as GSAP. We'll make a simple animation, but you can apply this same pattern anywhere in your Vue code. We'll be applying the animation during mount, but JavaScript animations can be triggered dynamically based on things such as timers, random integers, or inputs such as buttons.

To access the code files for this exercise, visit https://packt.live/3kVO4gm:

> **NOTE**
>
> Before you begin this exercise, run the **vue create** command to generate a Vue starter project.

1. Create a Vue project by running the following command:

```
vue create Exercise7.04
```

2. Install GSAP with **yarn** or **npm** using one of the following commands:

```
yarn add gsap
# OR
npm install gsap
```

3. In **src/App.vue**, import GSAP:

```
import gsap from 'gsap'
```

4. Find the existing **img** tag in **src/App.vue** and add **ref="logo"** to it as follows:

```
<img ref="logo" alt="Vue logo" src="./assets/logo.png">
```

5. Add a function called **mounted** to the exported object in **src/App.vue** that defines the logo as a variable and adds an animation, which is **10** rotations over **30** seconds:

```
mounted() {
    const { logo } = this.$refs;
    gsap.to(logo, {duration: 30, rotation: 3600});
}
```

6. Next, start the application by running **yarn serve** in the terminal.

7. Open your browser to **localhost:8080** and you should see the default Vue starter page but with the logo spinning, as shown in the following screenshot:

Welcome to Your Vue.js App

For a guide and recipes on how to configure / customize this project,
check out the vue-cli documentation.

Installed CLI Plugins

babel   eslint

Essential Links

Core Docs   Forum   Community Chat   Twitter   News

Figure 7.14:Simple animation with GSAP

In this exercise, we implemented a simple spinning animation using GSAP in Vue. Next, we will see how we can modify the look and feel of an animation with easing.

MODIFYING THE LOOK AND FEEL WITH EASING

Easing is important because it determines the movement style between the original starting point and the destination point of an animation. It controls the rate of change during a tween; hence a user has the time to see the effect, whether it be smooth, sudden, bouncing, or some other transition effect:

```
gsap.from(".bubble", 2, {
    scale: 0.2,
    rotation: 16,
    ease: "bounce",
})
```

In addition, there are additional built-in plugins in GSAP providing extra capabilities for configuring the easing effect, such as power, back, elastic, and so on. Take a bubble effect, for instance; to make the movement smooth within a certain degree, we use **Back.easeOut.config()** and **Elastic.easOut.config()** and pass the related settings:

```
gsap.to(".bubble", 2, {
    scale: 0.2,
    rotation: 16,
    ease: Back.easeOut.config(1.7),
})
    gsap.to(".bubble", 4, {
    scale: 1.2,
    rotation: '-=16',
    ease: Elastic.easeOut.config(2.5, 0.5),
})
```

With **ease**, we can make the same animation look completely different based on the style set. Next, we'll look at **stagger**, another option that affects the look and feel of an animation.

MODIFYING THE LOOK AND FEEL WITH STAGGER

We have gone through how to animate a list of items using Vue transitions in the previous sections. Staggering is one of the animations we should take into consideration for a list of objects since it makes animation for this type of target easy and with an appropriate delay between each of the item's animations.

For example, by assigning a value to the **stagger** property, we can create and apply some configuration options besides just the delay duration number (in milliseconds):

```
gsap.to('.stagger-box', 2, {
    scale: 0.1,
    y: 60,
    yoyo: true,
    repeat: 1,
    ease: Power1.inOut,
    delay:1,
    stagger: {
      amount: 1.5,
      grid: "auto",
```

```
        from: "center"
    }
  })
```

You can use **repeat** to define how many times it should repeat the animation. A negative number will make it repeat infinitely.

USING TIMELINE

Timeline is a schedule of tweens under your total control to define overlap or gaps between the tweens. It's useful when you need to control a group of animations according to an order, build a sequence of animations, chain the animations for a final callback, or modularize your animation code for reusability.

In order to use Timeline, you can choose to create a timeline instance by using the built-in **gsap.timeline()** method, or import **TimelineMax** or **TimelineLite** from the core library and set up the instance with a set of configurations, as follows:

```
import { TimelineMax } from 'gsap';
const tl = new TimelineMax({
  onComplete: done
})
//OR
const tl = gsap.timeline();
```

We will look briefly into the two main use cases of Timeline, **sequencing** and **chaining**.

Sequencing

With similar core functionalities to GSAP, Timeline also provides **to()**, **from()**, and **fromTo()** methods. All animations by default can be sequenced as one after another, with the option to force timing to control where or when things go using the **position** attribute, which is an optional argument:

```
var tl = gsap.timeline({ repeat: -1});
    tl.to("#box-green", {duration: 2, x: 550})
    //1 second after end of timeline (gap)
    tl.to("#box-red", {duration: 2, x: 550, scale: 0.5}, "+=1")
    //0.5 seconds before end of timeline (overlap)
    tl.to("#box-purple", {duration: 2, rotation: 360, x:550,
      scale: 1.2, ease: "bounce"}, "-=1")
```

In this section, we looked at using the GSAP Timeline feature to schedule a series of animations all running one after the other, some with a gap and others with an overlap. In the next section, we'll look further at sequencing animations with the concept of chaining.

Chaining

As with sequencing, chaining arranges animation into an order. Instead of calling each animation with the instance method each time separately, it will be placed in a chain. All the special values that are used between the child tweens can be defined, or in the instance created as defaults, or alternatively in the first call, get other timelines (list of animations) in the chain to inherit these values:

```
var tl = gsap.timeline({ defaults: { duration: 2 }, repeat: -1});

tl.to("#box-green", { x: 550 })
  .to("#box-red", { scale: 0.5, x: 450 })
  .to("#box-purple", { scale: 1.2, ease: "bounce", x: 500 })
```

We can also intercept the timing position of each chained timeline using **position**, as described earlier:

```
tl.to("#box-green", { x: 550 })
  .to("#box-red", { scale: 0.5, x: 450 }, "+=1")
  .to("#box-purple", { scale: 1.2, ease: "bounce", x: 500 }, "-=1")
```

GSAP has very detailed documentation, so just visit https://greensock.com/get-started and start animating.

In the next section we'll build on what we've learned about GSAP to make a message-viewing app with animated transitions.

ACTIVITY 7.01: BUILDING A MESSAGES APP WITH TRANSITION AND GSAP

In this activity, you will use CSS to write custom transitions, use transition groups and routes to do more complex transitions, and use a third-party transition library such as GSAP to do animations and transitions in the app. You will be creating a simple messages app that makes use of transition effects:

> **NOTE**
>
> Before you begin this exercise, run the **vue create** command to generate a Vue starter project.

1. Create a **Messages** route (at **src/views/Messages.vue**) that renders two nested views: **Messages (src/views/MessageList.vue)** displaying list of messages and **MessageEditor (src/views/MessageEditor.vue)** with one **textarea** and a submit button for creating a new message.

2. Create a **Message** route (at **src/views/Message.vue**) that renders a view of a single message with a given ID.

3. Register all the routes.

4. Add a transition to the main **router-view** in the **src/App.vue** file with a simple transition name, **fade**, and **out-in** mode.

5. Add the transition to the nested **router-view** in **src/views/Messages. vue** by using custom transition classes

6. Write an animation effect for zooming in on entering the route and zooming out on leaving the route.

7. Write another animation effect for fading in on a leaving event.

8. Add a transition to the list of messages in **MessageList.vue** with a bounce-in effect.

9. Use GSAP to animate the bounce-in effect.

10. Add a moving effect for an item when it appears.

11. When navigating from the list page to the editor page, you should see the feed slide away to the left as the editor appears, as shown in *Figure 7.15*:

Figure 7.15: Fade out when navigating from message list view to editor view

When navigating from the message view to the editor view, you should see the text input slide out to the left, as shown in *Figure 7.16*:

Messages section

List | Editor

Message Feed

Figure 7.16: Fade out when navigating from editor view to message list view

Next, the message list will appear with the numbers spinning with a bounce effect, as shown in *Figure 7.17*:

Messages section

List | Editor

Message Feed

Figure 7.17: Bounce effect when displaying the message feed in message list view

When clicking on a specific message, **0** or **1** in our example, our list will slide out to the left and you should see the message content, as shown in *Figure 7.18*:

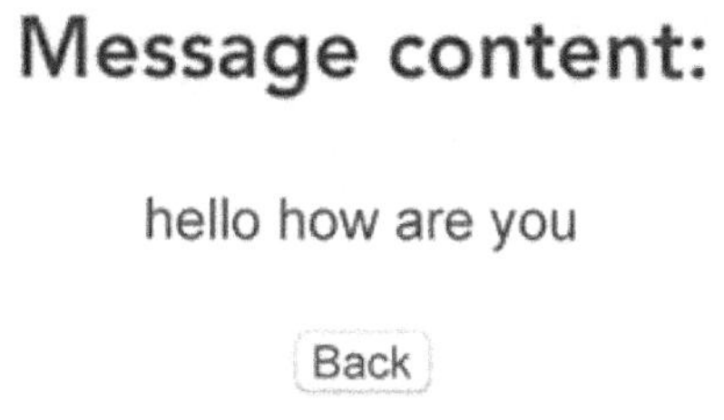

Message content:

hello how are you

Back

Figure 7.18: Single message view

> **NOTE**
>
> The solution for this activity can be found on page 685.

SUMMARY

In this chapter, we explored the built-in support Vue.js has for transitions and animations, both on single and multiple components, and we saw how easy it is to set it up. At this point, you have created your transition and animation effects for routes and components and witnessed all the basic features of Vue.js transitions: the custom transition class, group transition, and transition modes. Moreover, you also learned about other leading animation third-party libraries such as GSAP and saw how to integrate them with your Vue application, in order to get better animation effects on the web.

The next chapter focuses on another crucial topic for building a production-ready Vue application, state management, and how components within an application communicate with one another using Vuex, a state management library.

8

THE STATE OF VUE.JS STATE MANAGEMENT

OVERVIEW

By the end of this chapter, you will be able to use and contrast approaches for sharing state and holding global state in a Vue.js application. To this end, you will use a shared ancestor to hold state required by components that do not have a parent-child relationship (sibling components). You will also gain familiarity with an event bus in the context of a Vue.js application. As we proceed, you will understand how and when to leverage Vuex for state management, and its strengths and weaknesses when compared to other solutions such as event buses or Redux. Towards the end of the chapter, you will become comfortable with selecting which parts of state should be stored globally and locally and how to combine them to build a scalable and performant Vue.js application.

In this chapter, we will look at the state of Vue.js state management, from local state to component-based state sharing patterns to more advanced concepts such as leveraging event buses or global state management solutions like Vuex.

INTRODUCTION

In this chapter, we'll explore the concept of state management in Vue.

In previous chapters, we have seen how to use local state and **props** to hold state and share it in a **parent-child** component hierarchy.

We will begin by showing how to leverage **state**, **props**, and **events** to share state between components that are not in a **parent-child** configuration. These types of components are called **siblings**.

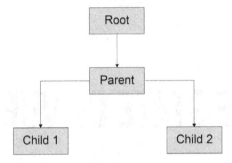

Figure 8.1: Child 1 and Child 2 are "sibling" components

Throughout the chapter, we will be building a **profile card generator** app that demonstrates how state flows down the component tree as props in an application, and how updates are propagated back up using events, event buses, and store updates.

Given that we want to build a **profile card generator**, we can break the application down into three sections: a **Header**, where we will have global controls and display the title of the page; a **ProfileForm**, where we will capture data; and finally, a **ProfileDisplay**, where we will display the profile card.

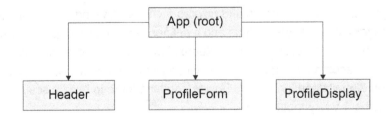

Figure 8.2: Representation of a profile card application component tree

We have now seen how to reason about a component tree and how our application can be structured in a component tree.

HOLDING STATE IN A COMMON ANCESTOR COMPONENT

To hold state only with component state and props and update it with events, we will store it in the nearest common ancestor component.

State is propagated only through **props** and is updated only through **events**. In this case, all the **state** will live in a shared ancestor of the components that require state. The App component, since it is the root component, is a good default for holding shared state.

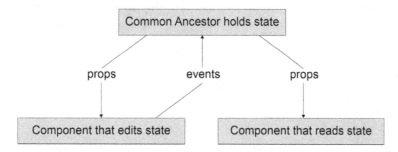

Figure 8.3: Common ancestor component holds state with props and event propagation

To change the **state**, a component needs to emit an **event** up to the component holding state (the shared ancestor). The shared ancestor needs to update **state** according to the event data and type. This in turn causes a re-render, during which the ancestor component passes updated **props** to the component reading the **state**.

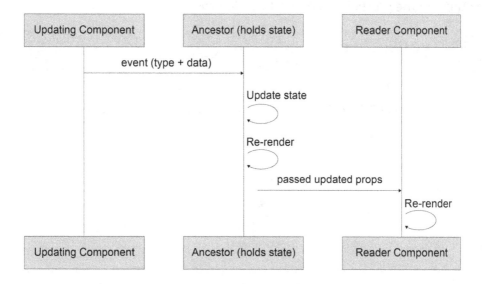

Figure 8.4: Updating a sibling component when the ancestor holds state

To build a header, we need to create an **AppHeader** component in the **AppHeader.vue** file, which will contain a template and an **h2** heading with TailwindCSS classes:

```
<template>
  <header class="w-full block p-4 border-b bg-blue-300
    border-gray-700">
    <h2 class="text-xl text-gray-800">Profile Card Generator</h2>
  </header>
</template>
```

We will then import it, register it, and render it in the **App.vue** file:

```
<template>
  <div id="app">
    <AppHeader />
  </div>
</template>
<script>
import AppHeader from './components/AppHeader.vue'
export default {
  components: {
    AppHeader
  }
}
</script>
```

The output of the preceding code will be as follows:

Profile Card Generator

Figure 8.5: AppHeader displayed in the profile card generator

We will similarly create an **AppProfileForm** file:

```
<template>
  <section class="md:w-2/3 h-64 bg-red-200 flex">
  <!-- Inputs -->
  </section>
</template>
```

We will create an **AppProfileDisplay** file with the following initial content:

```
<template>
  <section class="md:w-1/3 h-64 bg-blue-200 flex">
  <!-- Profile Card -->
  </section>
</template>
```

Both of our containers (**AppProfileForm** and **AppProfileDisplay**) can now be imported and rendered in **App**:

```
<template>
    <!-- rest of template, including AppHeader -->
    <div class="flex flex-col md:flex-row">
      <AppProfileForm />
      <AppProfileDisplay />
    </div>
    <!-- rest of template -->
</template>
<script>
// other imports
import AppProfileForm from './components/AppProfileForm.vue'
import AppProfileDisplay from './components/AppProfileDisplay.vue'

export default {
  components: {
    // other component definitions
    AppProfileForm,
    AppProfileDisplay,
  }
}
</script>
```

The output of the preceding code will be as follows:

Profile Card Generator

Figure 8.6: App skeleton with AppHeader, AppProfileForm, and AppProfileDisplay

To add a form field, in this case **name**, we will start by adding an input to
AppProfileForm:

```
<template>
  <section class="md:w-2/3 h-64 bg-red-200 flex flex-col p-12
    items-center">
    <!-- Inputs -->
    <div class="flex flex-col">
      <label class="flex text-gray-800 mb-2" for="name">Name
      </label>
      <input
        id="name"
        type="text"
        name="name"
        class="border-2 border-solid border-blue-200 rounded
          px-2 py-1"
      />
    </div>
  </section>
</template>
```

The preceding code will display as follows:

Figure 8.7: AppProfileForm with a name field and label

To keep track of the name input data, we will add a two-way binding to it using **v-model** and set a **name** property in the component's **data** initializer:

```
<template>
    <!-- rest of the template -->
    <input
      id="name"
      type="text"
      name="name"
      class="border-2 border-solid border-blue-200 rounded
        px-2 py-1"
      v-model="name"
    />
    <!-- rest of the template -->
</template>
<script>
export default {
  data() {
    return {
      name: '',
    }
  }
}
</script>
```

We will also need a **submit** button that, on click, sends the form data to the parent by emitting a **submit** event with the form's contents:

```
<template>
    <!-- rest of template -->
    <div class="flex flex-row mt-12">
      <button type="submit" @click="submitForm()">Submit</button>
    </div>
    <!-- rest of template -->
</template>
<script>
export default {
  // rest of component
  methods: {
    submitForm() {
      this.$emit('submit', {
        name: this.name
      })
    }
  }
}
</script>
```

This will display as follows:

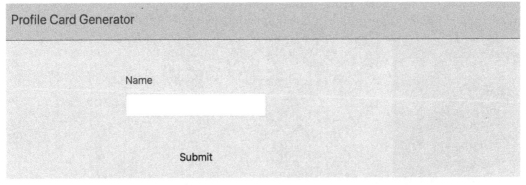

Figure 8.8: AppProfileForm with a wired-up submit button

The next step is to store the form's state in the **App** component. It is a good candidate for storing form state since it is a common ancestor to **AppProfileForm** and **AppProfileDisplay**.

To begin with, we will need a **formData** attribute returned from **data()**. We will also need a way to update **formData**. Hence, we will add an **update(formData)** method:

```
<script>
export default {
  // rest of component
  data() {
    return {
      formData: {}
    }
  },
  methods: {
    update(formData) {
      this.formData = formData
    }
  }
  // rest of component
}
</script>
```

Next, we need to bind **update()** to the **submit** event emitted by **AppProfileForm**. We will do this using the @**submit** shorthand and with the magic event object notation as **update($event)**:

```
<template>
    <!-- rest of template -->
      <AppProfileForm @submit="update($event)" />
    <!-- rest of template -->
</template>
```

To display the name inside of **AppProfileDisplay**, we will need to add **formData** as a prop:

```
<script>
export default {
  props: {
    formData: {
      type: Object,
      default() {
        return {}
      }
```

```
    }
  }
}
</script>
```

We will also need to display the name using **formData.name**. We will add a **p-12** class to the container to improve the appearance of the component:

```
<template>
  <section class="md:w-1/3 h-64 bg-blue-200 flex p-12">
    <!-- Profile Card -->
    <h3 class="font-bold font-lg">{{ formData.name }}</h3>
  </section>
</template>
```

Finally, **App** needs to pass **formData** to **AppProfileDisplay** as a prop:

```
<template>
    <!-- rest of template -->
      <AppProfileDisplay :form-data="formData" />
    <!-- rest of template -->
</template>
```

We are now able to update the name on the form. When you click on the **Submit** button, it will show the name in the profile card display as follows:

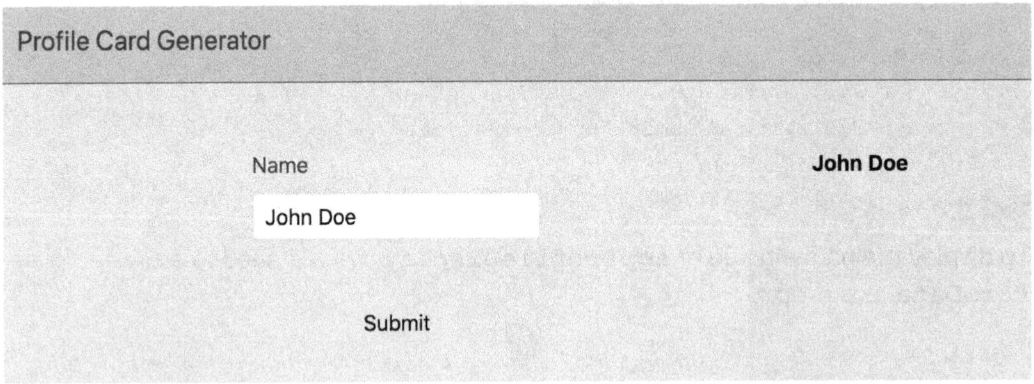

Figure 8.9: App storing state, passing as props to AppProfileDisplay

We have now seen how to store shared state on the **App** component and how to update it from the **AppProfileForm** and display it in **AppProfileDisplay**.

In the next topic, we will see how to add an additional field to the profile card generator.

EXERCISE 8.01: ADDING AN OCCUPATION FIELD TO THE PROFILE CARD GENERATOR

Following on from the example of storing the **name** shared state, another field that would be interesting to capture in a **profile card** is the occupation of the individual. To this end, we will add an **occupation** field to **AppProfileForm** to capture this extra piece of state, and we'll display it in **AppProfileDisplay**.

To access the code files for this exercise, refer to https://packt.live/32VUbuH.

1. The first place to start is by adding the new **occupation** field to **src/ components/AppProfileForm**. We'll also take this opportunity to get rid of the **h-64** and **bg-red-200** classes from the **section** element (if they're present), which will mean the form displays without a background and without a set height:

```
<template>
  <section class="md:w-2/3 flex flex-col p-12 items-center">
    <!-- rest of template -->
    <div class="flex flex-col mt-2">
      <label class="flex text-gray-800 mb-2"
for="occupation">Occupation</label>
      <input
        id="occupation"
        type="text"
        name="occupation"
        class="border-2 border-solid border-blue-200 rounded
          px-2 py-1"
      />
    </div>
    <!-- rest of template -->
  </section>
</template>
```

The output of the preceding code will be as follows:

Figure 8.10: AppProfileForm with the new Occupation field

2. To track the value of **occupation** with a two-way data binding, we will add a new property to the output of the **data()** property:

```
<script>
export default {
  // rest of component
  data() {
    return {
      // other data properties
      occupation: '',
    }
  },
  // rest of component
}
```

3. We will now apply a two-way data binding from the **occupation** reactive data property to the **occupation** input using **v-model**:

```
<template>
  <!-- rest of template -->
    <input
      id="occupation"
      type="text"
      name="occupation"
      v-model="occupation"
```

```
      class="border-2 border-solid border-blue-200 rounded
        px-2 py-1"
    />
  <!-- rest of template -->
</template>
```

4. For the **occupation** value to be transmitted when **submit** is clicked, we will need to add it to the **submitForm** method as a property of the **submit** event payload:

```
<script>
export default {
  // rest of component
  methods: {
    submitForm() {
      this.$emit('submit', {
        // rest of event payload
        occupation: this.occupation
      })
    }
  }
}
</script>
```

5. The final step of adding this field is to display it in the **AppProfileDisplay** component. We add a paragraph with a couple of styling classes. We'll also take this opportunity to remove the **h-64** and **bg-blue-200** classes from the container (if they are present):

```
<template>
  <section class="md:w-1/3 flex flex-col p-12">
    <!-- rest of template -->
    <p class="mt-2">{{ formData.occupation }}</p>
  </section>
</template>
```

Our browser should look as follows:

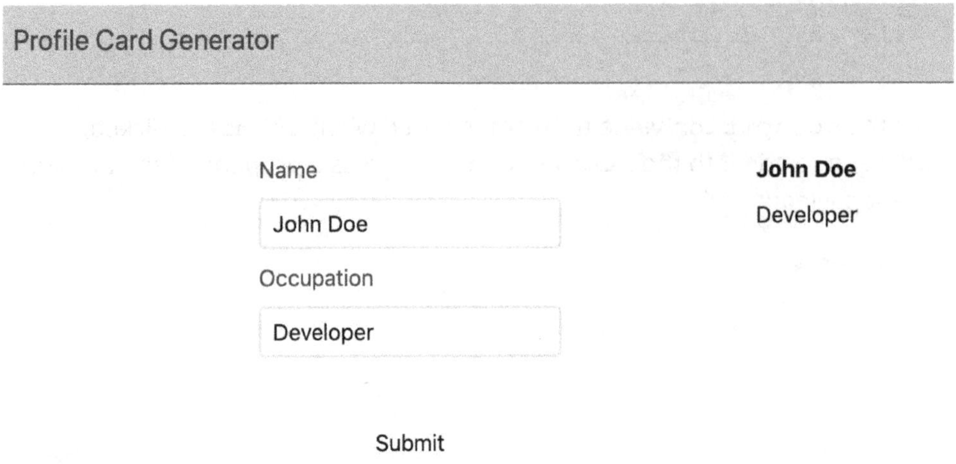

Figure 8.11: AppProfileForm

As we have just seen, adding a new field using the common ancestor to manage state is a case of passing the data up in an event and back down in the props to the reading component.

We will now see how we can reset the form and profile display with a **Clear** button.

EXERCISE 8.02: ADDING A CLEAR BUTTON TO THE PROFILE CARD GENERATOR

When creating a new profile with our application, it is useful to be able to reset the profile. To this end, we will add a **Clear** button.

A **Clear** button should reset the data in the form but also in **AppProfileDisplay**. To access the code files for this exercise, refer to https://packt.live/2INsE7R.

Now let's look at the steps to perform this exercise:

1. We want a **Clear** button to be displayed. We will take this opportunity to improve the styling of both the **Clear** and **Submit** buttons (in **src/ components/AppProfileForm.vue**):

```
<template>
  <!-- rest of template -->
    <div class="w-1/2 flex md:flex-row mt-12">
      <button
        class="flex md:w-1/2 justify-center"
        type="button"
```

```
    >
      Clear
    </button>
    <button
      class="flex md:w-1/2 justify-center"
      type="submit"
      @click="submitForm()"
    >
      Submit
    </button>
  </div>
  <!-- rest of template -->
</template>
```

2. To clear the form, we need to reset the **name** and **occupation** fields. We can create a **clear** method that will do this (in **src/components/ AppProfileForm.vue**):

```
<script>
export default {
  // rest of the component
  methods: {
    // other methods
    clear() {
      this.name = ''
      this.occupation = ''
    }
  }
  // rest of the component
}
```

3. We want to bind the **clear** method to **click** events on the **Clear** button to reset the form (in **src/components/AppProfileForm.vue**):

```
<template>
  <!-- rest of template -->
    <button
      class="flex md:w-1/2 justify-center"
      type="button"
      @click="clear()"
    >
```

```
        Clear
      </button>
  <!-- rest of template -->
</template>
```

Thus, we can now enter data into the form and submit it as per the following screenshot:

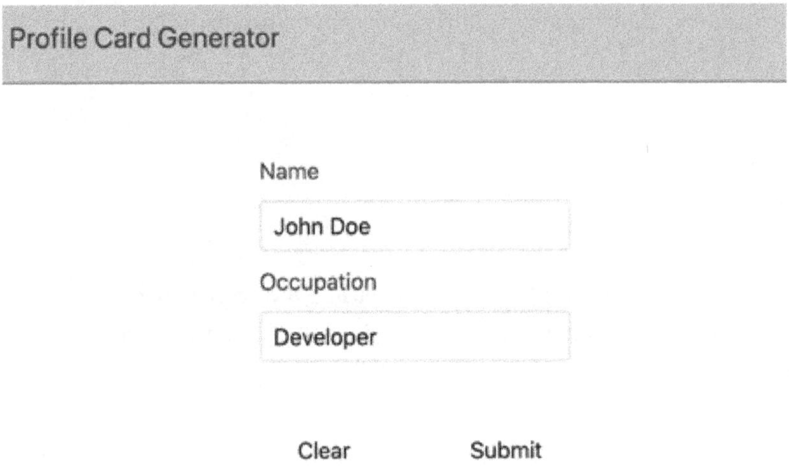

Figure 8.12: AppProfileForm with Name and Occupation fields filled in

On clicking the **Submit** button, it will propagate data to **AppProfileDisplay** as follows:

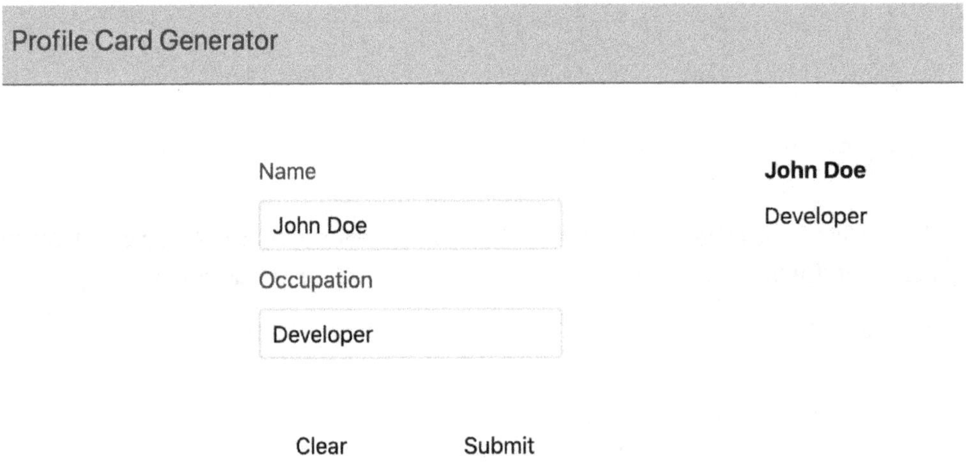

Figure 8.13: AppProfileForm and AppProfileDisplay with data filled in and submitted with a Clear button

Unfortunately, **AppProfileDisplay** still has stale data, as shown in the following screenshot:

Profile Card Generator

Name

John Doe

Developer

Occupation

Clear   Submit

Figure 8.14: AppProfileForm and AppProfileDisplay with only AppProfileForm cleared AppProfileDisplay still has stale data

4. To also clear the contents of **AppProfileDisplay**, we will need to update **formData** in **App.vue** by emitting a **submit** event with an empty payload in **src/components/AppProfileForm.vue**:

```
<script>
export default {
  // rest of component
  methods: {
    // other methods
    clear() {
      // rest of the clear() method
      this.$emit('submit', {})
    }
  }
}
</script>
```

When we fill out the form and submit it, it will look as follows:

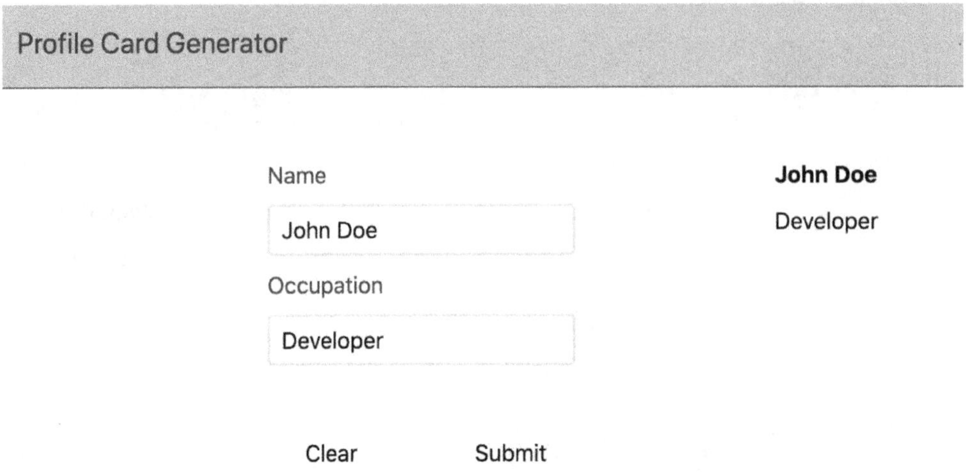

Figure 8.15: AppProfileForm and AppProfileDisplay with data filled out and submitted with a Clear button

We can click **Clear** and reset the data displayed in both **AppProfileDisplay** and **AppProfileForm** as per the following screenshot:

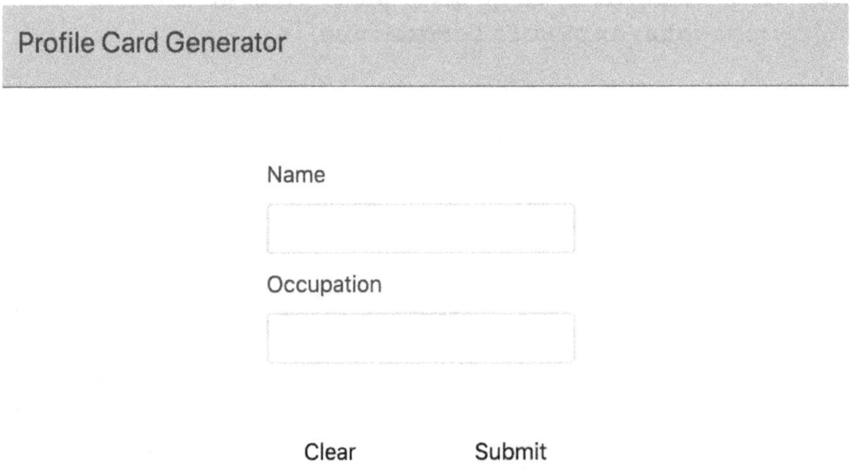

Figure 8.16: AppProfileForm and AppProfileDisplay after data is cleared (using the Clear button)

We have now seen how to set up communication between sibling components through a common ancestor.

> **NOTE**
>
> There is quite a bit of bookkeeping and mental work required to keep track of all the bits of state that need to stay in sync across the application.

In the next section, we will look at what an event bus is and how it can help alleviate some of the issues we have encountered.

THE EVENT BUS

The second scenario we will look at is when there is a global event bus.

The **event bus** is an entity on which we can publish and subscribe to events. This allows all the different parts of the application to hold their own state and keep it in sync without passing events up to or props down from the common ancestors.

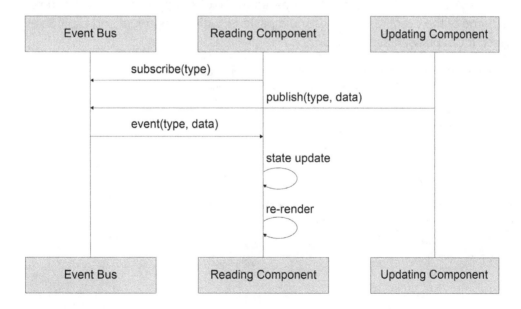

Figure 8.17: Sequence diagram of a reader component and an updating component leveraging an event bus

To provide this, our event bus needs to provide a **subscribe** method and **publish** method. It's also useful to be able to unsubscribe.

The Vue instance is an event bus since it provides three crucial operations: **publish**, **subscribe**, and **unsubscribe**. We can create an event bus as follows in the `main.js` file:

```
import Vue from 'vue'

const eventBus = new Vue()
```

Our event bus has a few methods, namely **$on**, which is the **subscribe** operation, supporting two parameters—the name of the event to subscribe to (as a string) and a callback to which the event will be passed through a **publish** operation. We can add a subscriber using **$on(eventName, callback)**:

```
// rest of main.js file
console.log('Registering subscriber to "fieldChanged"')
eventBus.$on('fieldChanged', (event) => {
  console.log(`Received event: ${JSON.stringify(event)}`)
})
```

We can then use **$emit** to trigger the subscriber callback. **$emit(eventName, payload)** is the event bus' **publish** operation. **$emit** supports two parameters—the name of the event (as a string) and a payload, which is optional and can be any object. It can be used as follows:

```
// rest of main.js file
console.log('Triggering "fieldChanged" for "name"')
eventBus.$emit('fieldChanged', {
  name: 'name',
  value: 'John Doe'
})

console.log('Triggering "fieldChanged" for "occupation"')
eventBus.$emit('fieldChanged', {
  name: 'occupation',
  value: 'Developer'
})
```

Running this file in the browser will yield the following console output, where the subscriber is registered first, and the callback is then triggered on every **$emit**:

```
Registering subscriber to "fieldChanged"                          main.js:6
Triggering "fieldChanged" for "name"                             main.js:11
Received event: {"name":"name","value":"John Doe"}                main.js:8
Triggering "fieldChanged" for "occupation"                       main.js:17
Received event: {"name":"occupation","value":"Developer"}         main.js:8
```

Figure 18.18: Console output from a Vue.js instance being used as an event bus with a subscriber and two event publications

$off, the **unsubscribe** operation, needs to be called with the same parameters with which the **subscribe** operation was called. Namely, two parameters, the event name (as a string) and the callback (which is run with the event as a parameter on every event publication). To use it properly, we need to register a subscriber using a reference to a function (as opposed to an inline anonymous function):

```
// rest of main.js, including other subscriber
const subscriber = (event) => {
  console.log('Subscriber 2 received event: ${JSON.stringify
    (event)}')
}
console.log('Registering subscriber 2')
eventBus.$on('fieldChanged', subscriber)

console.log('Triggering "fieldChanged" for "company"')
eventBus.$emit('fieldChanged', {
  name: 'company',
  value: 'Developer'
})

console.log('Unregistering subscriber 2')
eventBus.$off('fieldChanged', subscriber)

console.log('Triggering "fieldChanged" for "occupation"')
eventBus.$emit('fieldChanged', {
  name: 'occupation',
  value: 'Senior Developer'
})
```

Note that once **$off** is called, the second subscriber does not trigger but the initial one does. Your console output when run in the browser will look as follows:

```
Registering subscriber 2                                                main.js:26
Triggering "fieldChanged" for "company"                                 main.js:29
Received event: {"name":"company","value":"Developer"}                   main.js:8
Subscriber 2 received event: {"name":"company","value":"Developer"}     main.js:24
Unregistering subscriber 2                                              main.js:35
Triggering "fieldChanged" for "occupation"                             main.js:38
Received event: {"name":"occupation","value":"Senior Developer"}          main.js:8
```

Figure 8.19: Console output showing the effect of $off

By setting an event bus in the **event-bus.js** file, we can avoid the confusion of having to send data up to the **App** component (the common ancestor):

```
import Vue from 'vue'


export default new Vue()
```

We can **$emit profileUpdate** events to the event bus from the **AppProfileForm.vue** file on form submission instead of using **this.$emit**:

```
<script>
import eventBus from '../event-bus'

export default {
  // rest of component
  methods: {
    submitForm() {
      eventBus.$emit('profileUpdate', {
        name: this.name,
        occupation: this.occupation
      })
    },
    clear() {
      this.name = ''
      this.occupation = ''
      eventBus.$emit('profileUpdate', {})
    }
  }
}
</script>
```

In the **AppProfileDisplay.vue** file, we can subscribe to **profileUpdate** events using **$on** and update **formData** in state. Note that we have removed the **formData** prop. We use the **mounted()** and **beforeDestroy()** hooks to subscribe to and unsubscribe from the event bus:

```
<script>
import eventBus from '../event-bus'
export default {
  mounted() {
    eventBus.$on('profileUpdate', this.update)
  },
  beforeDestroy() {
    eventBus.$off('profileUpdate', this.update)
  },
  data() {
    return {
      formData: {}
    }
  },
  methods: {
    update(formData) {
      this.formData = formData
    }
  }
}
</script>
```

The application works as expected. The following screenshot displays how your screen will look:

Profile Card Generator

Name

John Doe

Occupation

Developer

John Doe

Developer

Clear   Submit

Figure 8.20: AppProfileForm and AppProfileDisplay communicating with an event bus

Since we have removed the **formData** prop for **AppProfileDisplay**, we can stop passing it in the **App.vue** file. Since we are not relying on **submit** events from **AppProfileForm**, we can also remove that binding:

```
<template>
  <!-- rest of template -->
      <AppProfileForm />
      <AppProfileDisplay />
  <!-- rest of template -->
</template>
```

We can also remove the unused **App update** and **data** methods from the **App. vue** file, which means the whole **App** script section is as follows (only registers **components**, not state or handlers):

```
<script>
import AppHeader from './components/AppHeader.vue'
import AppProfileForm from './components/AppProfileForm.vue'
import AppProfileDisplay from './components/AppProfileDisplay.vue'

export default {
  components: {
    AppHeader,
    AppProfileForm,
```

```
    AppProfileDisplay,
  }
}
</script>
```

We have now simplified the application data flow by using an event bus instead of storing shared state in a common ancestor component. Now, we will see how to move the **Clear** button to the application header in the profile card generator.

EXERCISE 8.03: MOVING THE CLEAR BUTTON TO THE APPLICATION HEADER PROFILE CARD GENERATOR

In our profile card generator application, the **Clear** button clears the state in the whole application. Its presence inside the form makes the **Clear** button's functionality unclear since it looks like it might only affect the form.

To reflect the fact that the **Clear** button is global functionality, we will move it into the header.

To access the code files for this exercise, refer to https://packt.live/2UzFvwZ.

The following steps will help us perform this exercise:

1. We will start by creating a **button** in **src/components/AppHeader.vue**:

```
<template>
  <header class="w-full flex flex-row p-4 border-b
    bg-blue-300 border-gray-700">
    <h2 class="text-xl flex text-gray-800">Profile Card
      Generator</h2>
    <button class="flex ml-auto text-gray-800 items-center">
      Reset
    </button>
  </header>
</template>
```

2. We can import the event bus and create a **clear()** handler in **AppHeader**, in which we'll trigger an update event with an empty payload (in **src/components/AppHeader.vue**):

```
<script>
import eventBus from '../event-bus'

export default {
  methods: {
```

```
     clear() {
       eventBus.$emit('profileUpdate', {})
     }
   }
 }
</script>
```

3. We should bind the **clear()** function to the **button** (in **src/components/ AppHeader.vue**):

```
<template>
  <!-- rest of template -->
    <button
      @click="clear()"
      class="flex ml-auto text-gray-800 items-center"
    >
      Reset
    </button>
  <!-- rest of template -->
</template>
```

At this stage, we should be able to fill out the form and a **Reset** button should appear as follows:

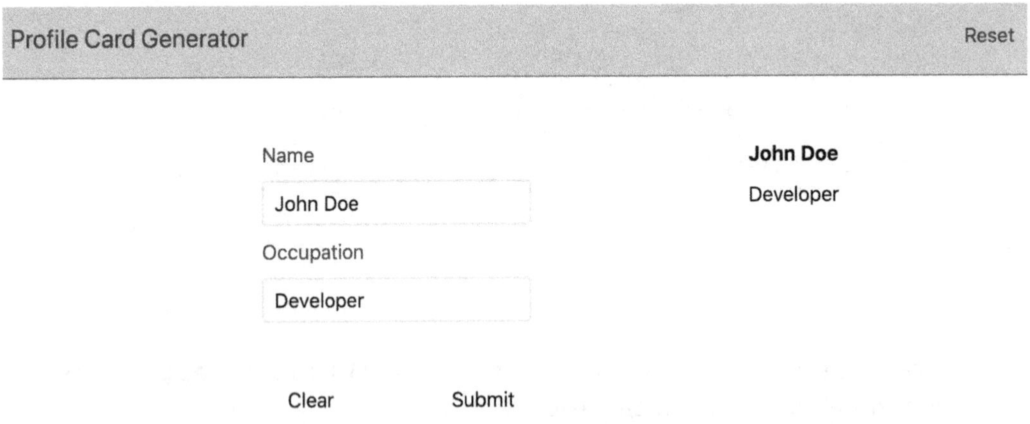

Figure 8.21: Form filled out and the Reset button in the header

The **Reset** button only resets the **AppProfileDisplay** data:

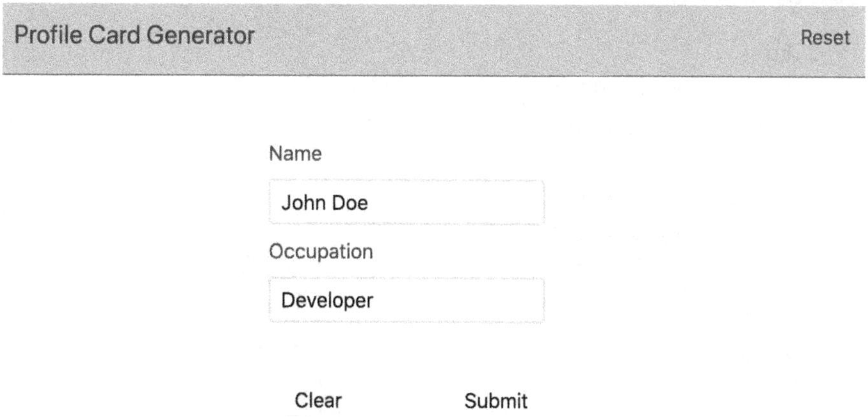

Profile Card Generator	Reset

Name

John Doe

Occupation

Developer

Clear   Submit

Figure 8.22: Form filled out, but the card section has been cleared

4. For **Reset** to clear the form, we need to subscribe to the **profileUpdate** events in the mounted life cycle method of **AppProfileForm** and react to said events by resetting the form (using **handleProfileUpdate**):

```
<script>
import eventBus from '../event-bus'

export default {
  mounted() {
    eventBus.$on('profileUpdate', this.handleProfileUpdate)
  },
  beforeDestroy() {
    eventBus.$off('profileUpdate', this.handleProfileUpdate)
  },
  // rest of component
  methods: {
    // other methods
    handleProfileUpdate(formData) {
      this.name = formData.name || ''
      this.occupation = formData.occupation || ''
    }
  }
}
</script>
```

5. We also take this opportunity to delete the **Clear** button and adjust the **Submit** button:

```
<template>
  <!-- rest of template -->
    <div class="flex align-center mt-12">
      <button
        type="submit"
        @click="submitForm()"
      >
        Submit
      </button>
    </div>
  <!-- rest of template -->
</template>
```

The form looks as follows when it gets filled out and submitted:

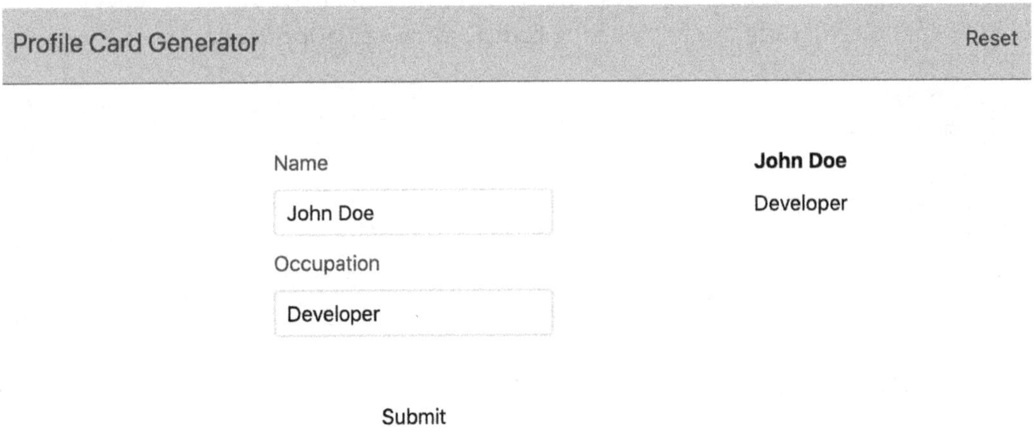

Figure 8.23: Filled-out and submitted form

Resetting the form now clears the form fields as well as **AppProfileDisplay**:

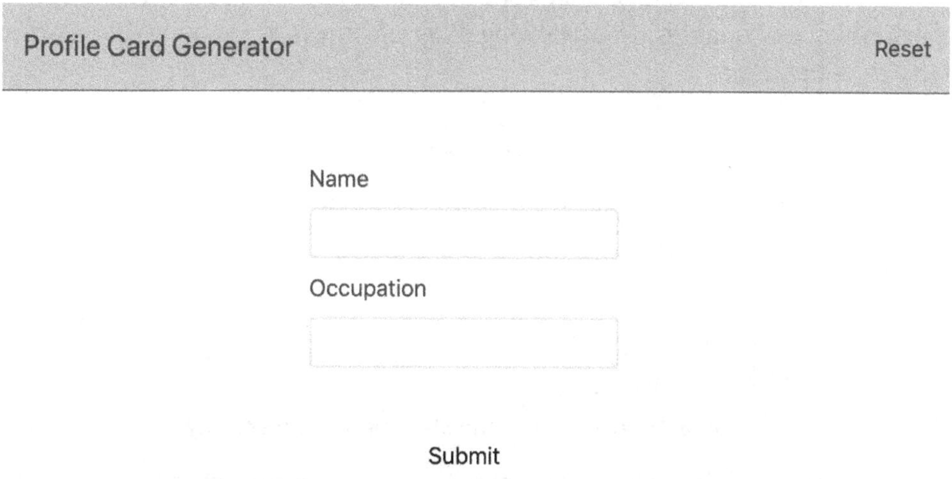

Profile Card Generator	Reset

Name

Occupation

Submit

Figure 8.24: Resetting the form and the display using the Reset button

This final step using the event bus, triggering an event and listening for the same event, is part of the basis of the Vuex pattern where events and state updates are encapsulated.

USING THE VUEX PATTERN IN CONTRAST WITH OTHER PATTERNS SUCH AS REDUX

The final scenario we will look at is using the Vuex pattern. In this case, all state is held in a single store. Any updates to the state are dispatched to this store. Components read shared and/or global state from the store.

Vuex is both a state management pattern and a library implementation from the Vue.js core team. The pattern aims to alleviate issues found when global state is shared by different parts of the application. The state of the store cannot be directly manipulated. **Mutations** are used to update store state and, since store state is reactive, any consumers of the Vuex store will automatically update.

Vuex draws inspiration from previous work in the JavaScript state management space such as the **Flux** architecture, which popularized the concept of unidirectional data flow, and **Redux**, which is a single-store implementation of Flux.

Vuex is not just another Flux implementation. It is a Vue.js-specific state management library. It can therefore leverage Vue.js-specific things such as reactivity to improve the performance of updates. The following diagram shows a hierarchy of the props and the state updates:

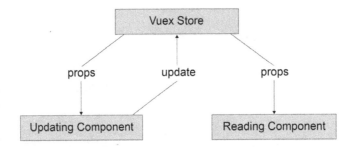

Figure 8.25: Vuex props and state updates hierarchy

To update pieces of global state, components trigger an update called a mutation in the store. The store knows how to handle this update. It updates state and propagates props back down accordingly through Vue.js reactivity:

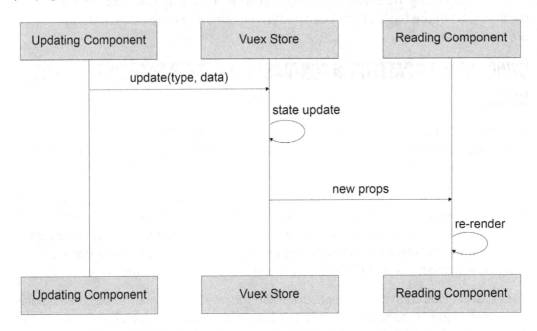

Figure 8.26: Sequence diagram of a global state update with Vuex

We can extend the existing application using Vuex.

First, we need to add the **vuex** module using **yarn add vuex** or **npm install --save vuex**.

Next, we need to register Vuex with Vue using **Vue.use()** in the **store.js** file:

```
import Vue from 'vue'
import Vuex from 'vuex'


Vue.use(Vuex)
```

Finally, we create a Vuex store with a default state. This state includes the same **formData** object we have been using in the **store.js** file. We then export it using **export default**:

```
export default new Vuex.Store({
  state: {
    formData: {
      name: '',
      occupation: ''
    }
  },
})
```

Finally, we need to register our store with our main application instance of Vue.js in the **main.js** file:

```
// other imports
import store from './store'
// other imports and code
new Vue({
  render: h => h(App),
  store
}).$mount('#app')
```

The great thing is that every component has a reference to the store under **this.$store**. For example, to access **formData**, we can use **this.$store. state.formData**. Using this, we can replace the event bus subscription and local state updates in the script section of the **AppProfileDisplay.vue** file with a single computed property:

```
<script>
export default {
  computed: {
    formData() {
      return this.$store.state.formData
    }
```

```
    }
  }
</script>
```

To trigger state updates, we need to define some mutations. In this case, we need **profileUpdate** in the **store.js** file. Mutations receive **state** (the current state) and **payload** (the store **commit** payload) as properties.

```
export default new Vuex.Store({
  // other store properties
  mutations: {
    profileUpdate(state, payload) {
      state.formData = {
        name: payload.name || '',
        occupation: payload.occupation || ''
      }
    }
  }
})
```

Now that we have got a **profileUpdate** mutation, we can update the **Reset** button in the **AppHeader.vue** file to use the Vuex **$store.commit()** function:

```
<script>
export default {
  methods: {
    clear() {
      this.$store.commit('profileUpdate', {})
    }
  }
}
</script>
```

We should also update the **AppProfileForm.vue** file to commit to the **$store** instead of emitting to the event bus:

```
<script>
export default {
  // rest of component
  methods: {
    submitForm() {
      this.$store.commit('profileUpdate', {
        name: this.name,
```

```
        occupation: this.occupation
      })
    },
    // other methods
  }
}
</script>
```

The application will now support updating the name and occupation:

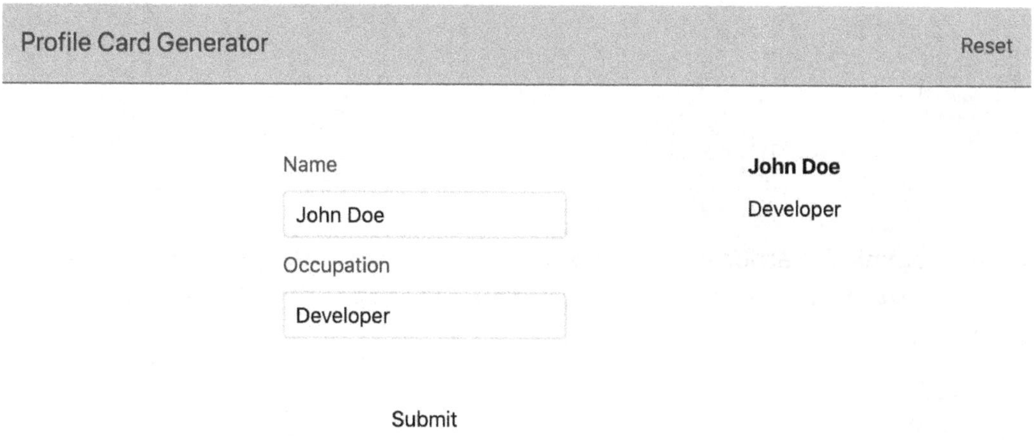

Figure 8.27: Application with AppProfileForm filled out and submitted

Unfortunately, the **Reset** button does not clear the form:

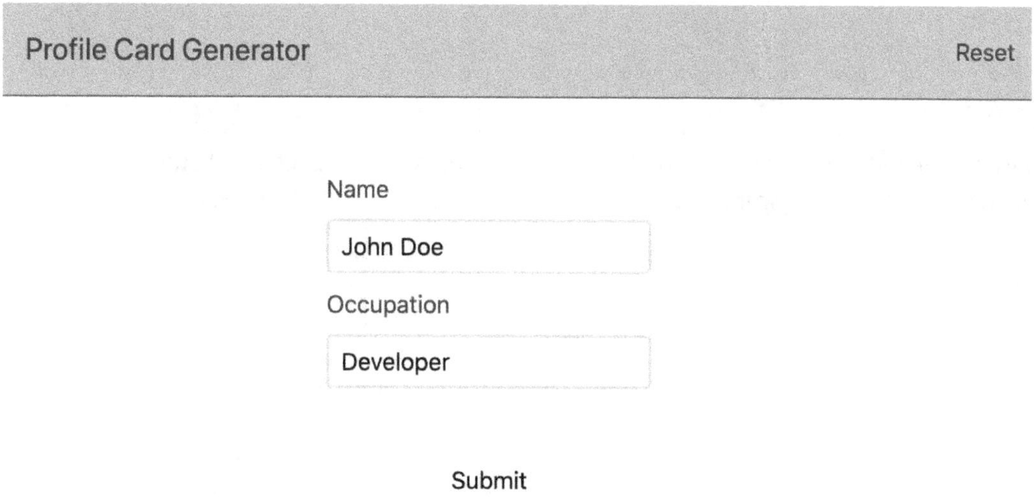

Figure 8.28: Application with AppProfileForm not clearing on Reset button click

To reset more efficiently, we will add a **profileClear** mutation in the **store.js** file:

```
export default new Vuex.Store({
  // other store properties
  mutations: {
    // other mutations
    profileClear(state) {
      state.formData = {
        name: '',
        occupation: ''
      }
    }
  }
})
```

We will commit this action instead of **profileUpdate** in the **AppHeader.vue** file. Using **profileClear** instead of **profileUpdate** with empty data makes our code cleared:

```
<script>
export default {
  methods: {
    clear() {
      this.$store.commit('profileClear')
    }
  }
}
</script>
```

Finally, we will need to subscribe to store changes and reset the local state when **profileClear** is committed to the store in the **AppProfileForm** file:

```
<script>
export default {
  created() {
    this.$store.subscribe((mutation) => {
      if (mutation.type === 'profileClear') {
        this.resetProfileForm()
```

```
      }
    })
  },
  // other component properties
  methods: {
    // other methods
    resetProfileForm() {
      this.name = ''
      this.occupation = ''
    }
  }
}
</script>
```

Now the application's **Reset** button will work correctly with Vuex. Our screen should display as follows:

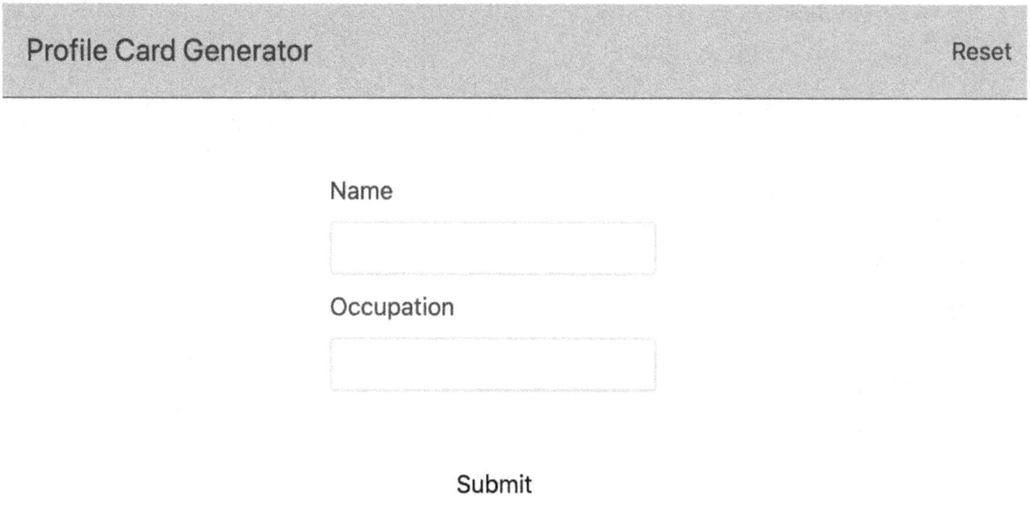

Profile Card Generator	Reset

Name

Occupation

Submit

Figure 8.29: Application Reset button clearing both the form and the display

We have now seen how to use the Vuex store to store global state in our application.

EXERCISE 8.04: ADDING AN ORGANIZATION FIELD TO THE PROFILE GENERATOR

In a **profile card generator**, in addition to the name and occupation of an individual, it's also useful to know where they work, in other words, their organization.

To do this, we will add an **organization** field in **AppProfileForm** and **AppProfileDisplay**. To access the code files for this exercise, refer to https://packt.live/3lIHJGe.

1. We can start by adding a new text input and label to **AppProfileForm**:

```
<template>
  <!-- rest of template -->
    <div class="flex flex-col mt-2">
      <label class="flex text-gray-800 mb-2"
        for="organization">Organization</label>
      <input
        id="occupation"
        type="text"
        name="organization"
        class="border-2 border-solid border-blue-200
          rounded px-2 py-1"
      />
    </div>
  <!-- rest of template -->
</template>
```

The new field looks as follows:

Figure 8.30: Application with a new Organization field

2. We can then add the **organization** field to the initial state and mutations in **src/store.js** so that **organization** gets initialized, set during **profileUpdate**, and reset during **profileClear**:

```
// imports & Vuex setup
export default new Vuex.Store({
  state: {
    formData: {
      // rest of formData fields
      organization: ''
    }
  },
  mutations: {
    profileUpdate(state, payload) {
      state.formData = {
        // rest of formData fields
        organization: payload.organization || '',
      }
    },
    profileClear(state) {
      state.formData = {
        // rest of formData fields
        organization: ''
      }
    }
  }
})
```

3. We need to track **organization** in the local state of the **src/components/ AppProfileForm.vue** component using **v-model** and initializing it in the **data()** function:

```
<template>
  <!-- rest of template -->
    <div class="flex flex-col mt-2">
      <label class="flex text-gray-800 mb-2"
        for="organization">Organization</label>
      <input
        id="occupation"
        type="text"
        name="organization"
        v-model="organization"
```

```
            class="border-2 border-solid border-blue-200 rounded
               px-2 py-1"
        />
      </div>
    <!-- rest of template -->
  </template>
  <script>
  export default {
    // rest of component
    data() {
      return {
        // other data properties
        organization: ''
      }
    }
  }
  </script>
```

4. For the payload of the mutation to contain **organization**, we'll need to add it
    to the **$store.commit('profileUpdate')** payload and also reset it in the
    form when a component triggers a **profileClear** mutation:

```
<script>
export default {
  // rest of component
  methods: {
    submitForm() {
      this.$store.commit('profileUpdate', {
        // rest of payload
        organization: this.organization
      })
    },
    resetProfileForm() {
      // other resets
      this.organization = ''
    }
  }
}
</script>
```

5. For **organization** to display, we need to render it in **src/components/ AppProfileDisplay.vue** using a conditional span (to hide **at** when there is no **organization** set):

```
<template>
  <!-- rest of template -->
    <p class="mt-2">
      {{ formData.occupation }}
      <span v-if="formData.organization">
        at {{ formData.organization }}
      </span>
    </p>
  <!-- rest of template -->
</template>
```

The application will now allow us to capture an **organization** field and display it.

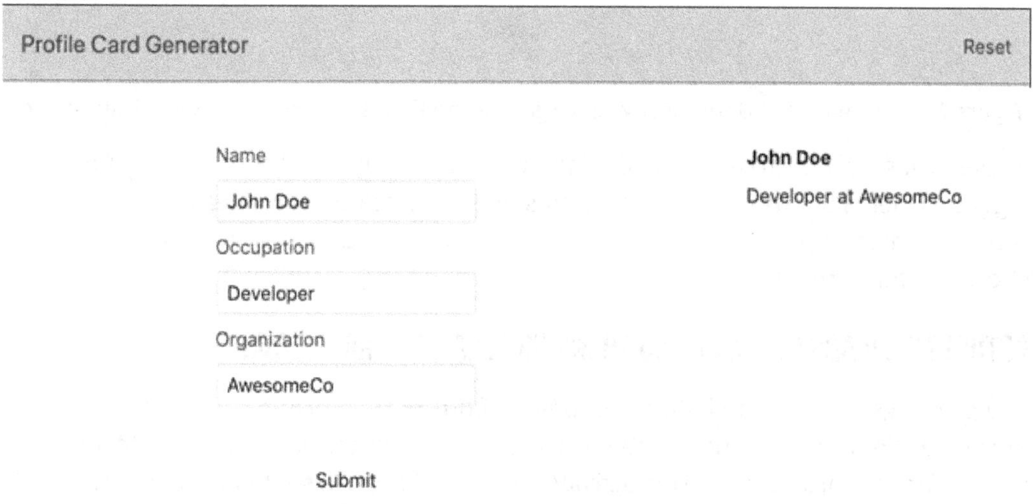

Profile Card Generator   Reset

Name   **John Doe**

John Doe   Developer at AwesomeCo

Occupation

Developer

Organization

AwesomeCo

Submit

Figure 8.31: Profile Card Generator with Organization field support, filled out and submitted

It will allow us to clear the profile without any issues too:

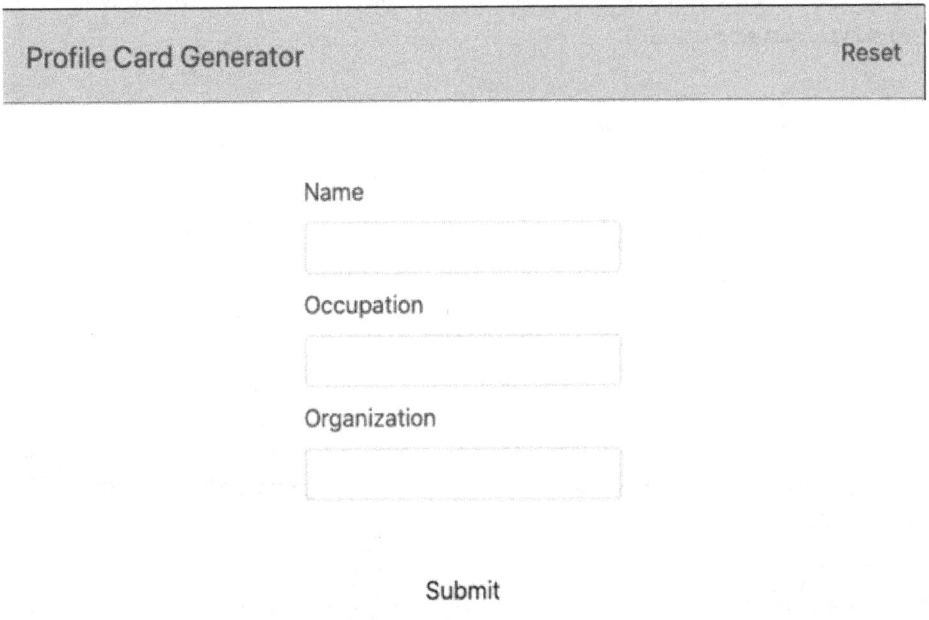

Profile Card Generator   Reset

Name

Occupation

Organization

Submit

Figure 8.32: Profile Card Generator with Organization field support, after Reset button click

We've now seen how to add a field to an application that uses Vuex. One of the biggest benefits of Vuex over an event bus or storing state in an ancestor component is that it scales as you add more data and operations. The following activity will showcase this strength.

ACTIVITY 8.01: ADDING EMAIL AND PHONE NUMBER TO A PROFILE CARD GENERATOR

In a profile generator, you look at a profile to find some information about the individual. Email and phone number are often the most crucial pieces of information looked for on a profile card. This activity is about adding these details to a profile card generator.

To do this, we will add **Email** and **Phone Number** fields in **AppProfileForm** and **AppProfileDisplay**:

1. We can start by adding a new **email** input field and label to **AppProfileForm** for the **Email** field.

2. We can then add a new **phone** input field (of type **tel**) and a label to **AppProfileForm** for the **Phone Number** field:

The new fields look as follows:

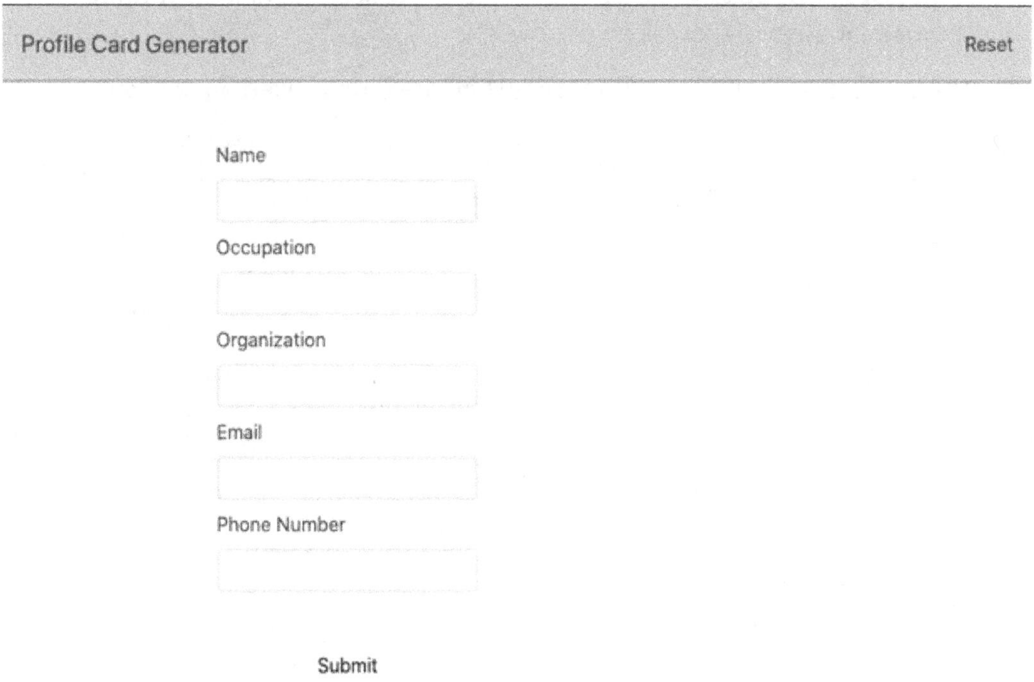

| Profile Card Generator | Reset |

Name

Occupation

Organization

Email

Phone Number

Submit

Figure 8.33: Application with new Email and Phone Number fields

3. We can then add the **email** and **phone** fields to the initial state and mutations in **src/store.js** so that organization gets initialized, set during **profileUpdate**, and reset during **profileClear**.

4. We need to track **email** in the local state of the **src/components/ AppProfileForm.vue** component using **v-model** and initialize it in the **data()** function.

5. We need to track **phone** in the local state of the **src/components/ AppProfileForm.vue** component using **v-model** and initialize it in the **data()** function.

6. For the payload of the mutation to contain **email** and **phone**, we'll need to add it to the **$store.commit('profileUpdate')** payload. We'll also want to reset it in the form when a component triggers a **profileClear** mutation.

7. For **email** to display, we need to render it in **src/components/ AppProfileDisplay.vue** using a conditional paragraph (to hide the **Email** label when there is no email set).

8. For **phone** to display, we need to render it in **src/components/ AppProfileDisplay.vue** using a conditional span (to hide the **Phone Number** label when there is no phone set).

The application should look as follows when the form is filled out and submitted:

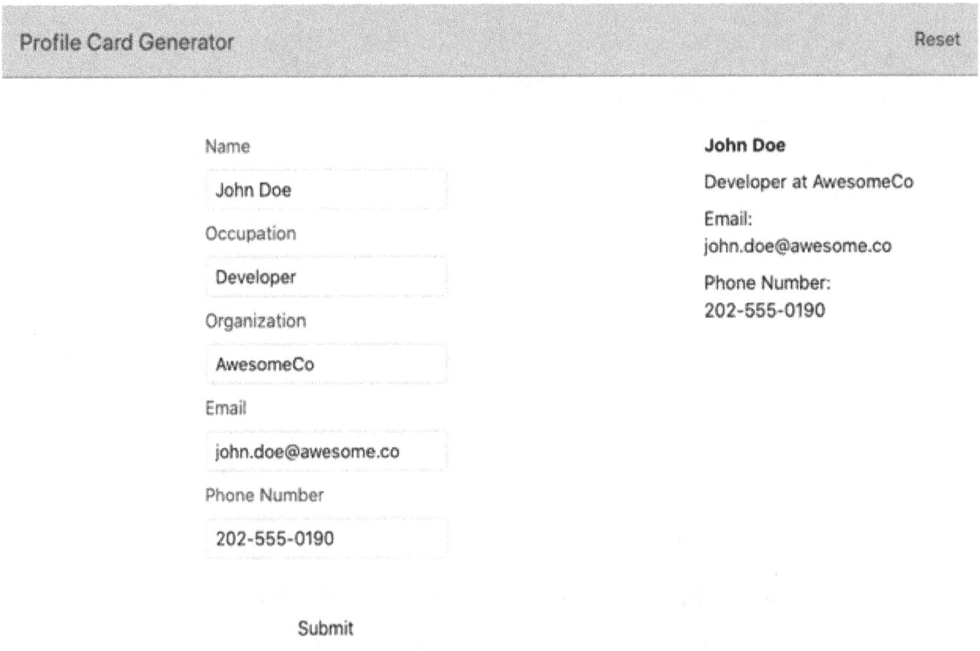

Profile Card Generator		Reset

Name

John Doe

Occupation

Developer

Organization

AwesomeCo

Email

john.doe@awesome.co

Phone Number

202-555-0190

Submit

John Doe

Developer at AwesomeCo

Email:
john.doe@awesome.co

Phone Number:
202-555-0190

Figure 8.34: Application with Email and Phone Number fields

> **NOTE**
>
> The solution for this activity can be found on page 695.

WHEN TO USE LOCAL STATE AND WHEN TO SAVE TO GLOBAL STATE

As we have seen through the common ancestor, event bus, and Vuex examples, the Vue.js ecosystem has solutions for managing shared and global state. What we will look at now is how to decide whether something belongs in local state or global state.

A good rule of thumb is that if a prop is passed through a depth of three components, it is probably best to put that piece of state in global state and access it that way.

The second way to decide whether something is local or global is to ask the question *when the page reloads, does the user expect this information to persist?*. Why does this matter? Well, global state is a lot easier to save and persist than local state. This is due to global state's nature as *just a JavaScript object* as opposed to component state, which is more closely tied to the component tree and Vue.js.

Another key idea to bear in mind is that it is very much possible to mix Vuex and local state in a component. As we have seen with the **AppProfileForm** examples, exercises, and activity, we can selectively sync data from mutations into a component using **$store.subscribe**.

At the end of the day, there is nothing wrong with wrapping a Vue.js data property in a computed property and accessing the computed property to make a potential transition to Vuex easier. In this scenario, since all access is already done through the computed property, it is just a change from **this.privateData** to **this.$store.state.data**.

SUMMARY

Throughout this chapter, we have looked at different approaches to shared and global state management in a Vue.js application.

State in a shared ancestor allows data sharing between sibling components through props and events.

An event bus has three operations—**subscribe**, **publish**, and **unsubscribe**—that can be leveraged to propagate state updates in a **Vue.js** application. We have also seen how a **Vue.js** instance can be used as an event bus.

You know what the Vuex pattern and library entail, how they differ from Redux and Flux, as well as the benefits of using a Vuex store over a shared ancestor or event bus.

Finally, we have had a look at what criteria can be used to decide whether state should live in local component state or a more global or shared state solution such as Vuex. This chapter was an introduction to the state management landscape in **Vue.js**.

The next chapter will be a deep-dive into writing large-scale **Vue.js** applications with Vuex.

9

WORKING WITH VUEX – STATE, GETTERS, ACTIONS, AND MUTATIONS

OVERVIEW

In this chapter, you will learn how to use Vuex to build more complex Vue applications. You'll learn the specifics concerning how to add Vuex to a Vue application, how to define state with the Vuex store, and then use getters, actions, and mutations to read data from, and update it in, the store. By the end of the chapter, you will have seen multiple examples of how Vuex transforms your Vue applications, preparing them to grow much more complex in a much more manageable fashion.

INTRODUCTION

In the previous chapter, you learned how to use the Event Bus pattern to help solve an important problem: communicating events back and forth between complex and highly nested sets of components. The Event Bus pattern provided a simple **pub and sub** system by which any component could emit an event and any component could then listen to that event as well. While writing your own solution to this problem is a great way to keep your coding skills sharp, it would be better, in this case, to use an already developed, well-tested solution already in use in the Vue community—**Vuex** (https://vuex.vuejs.org/):

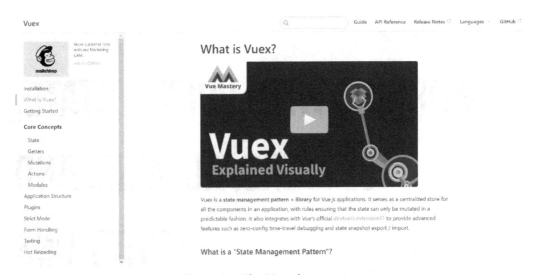

Figure 9.1: The Vuex home page

Vuex is a core part of the Vue ecosystem and provides what we already built in the previous chapter along with much more. Let's take a high-level look at the main features of Vuex.

STORE

At a high level, a Vuex instance, or one use of Vuex, is considered a **store**. The store is the top-level container employing everything described in the following subsections.

STATE

The most important aspect of Vuex is the **state**, or data, that it represents. This is the *single source of truth* that all components can rely on. As the state changes, every component making use of the state can be assured its copy will always be in sync. Imagine a Vue application that lets you edit blog entries. The store could consist of the blog entries themselves as well as values for the current blog entry you're editing. As blog entries are edited in one place, any other place using them gets updated immediately.

GETTERS

While Vue can directly read state data from a Vuex instance, sometimes you may need to provide additional logic or an abstraction to the data itself. Much like how Vue provides a `computed` property for virtual or derived data, **getters** provide an abstraction to the state for cases where you need to manipulate the data before it is returned. Returning to our previous example of working with blog entries, imagine a getter that returns the top blog entries by views. The getter abstracts away the logic of how "popular" blog entries are and lets you easily change that logic in the future.

MUTATIONS

Components making use of state data in Vuex never directly modify that data. Instead, a component can execute a **mutation**. Think of it as an order from the component for Vuex to perform a change to its state. By using mutations to wrap changes to state, Vuex can ensure every component making use of that state is kept up to date on changes.

ACTIONS

Actions are like mutations, except that they must be used to handle asynchronous changes. Asynchronous actions are any logic that takes an indeterminate amount of time to finish. The most common example would be a network call to a remote API. Synchronous calls are those that execute and finish immediately. It will make more sense when you see them being used, but generally, anything asynchronous should be done via actions while synchronous logic can be done via mutations. Actions will typically chain to mutations once they have completed whatever asynchronous work they need to do.

MODULES

The last aspect of Vuex this chapter will cover is modules. **Modules** are simply a way to package more complex sets of data for larger applications. While one simple state may be fine for a typical application, a much larger application can have a much more complex state that needs better organization via modules. In *Chapter 11, Working with Vuex – Organizing Larger Stores*, you will see how modules can be used to better organize the Vuex instance.

INSTALLING VUEX

There are two main methods of using Vuex, depending on the type of Vue application you're building. If you are not using the CLI to scaffold out an application and simply added Vue via a script tag, you can include Vuex the same way. Assuming you've downloaded both Vue and Vuex to a folder named **js**, you would load them both like so:

```
<script src="js/vue.js"></script>
<script src="js/vuex.js"></script>
```

You can also load both Vue and Vuex via **Content Delivery Networks** (**CDNs**):

```
<script src="https://unpkg.com/vue"></script>
<script src="https://unpkg.com/vuex"></script>
```

> **NOTE**
>
> It is important that Vuex is loaded after Vue. Doing so makes Vuex available to your Vue code without any other configuration.

If you created an application using the CLI, remember first that the CLI itself will prompt you during creation if you want to add Vuex:

```
? Please pick a preset: Manually select features
? Check the features needed for your project: (Press <space> to select, <a> to toggle all
? Check the features needed for your project:
 ❋ Babel
 ○ TypeScript
 ○ Progressive Web App (PWA) Support
 ○ Router
>❋ Vuex
 ○ CSS Pre-processors
 ❋ Linter / Formatter
 ○ Unit Testing
 ○ E2E Testing
```

Figure 9.2: Selecting Vuex during application scaffolding

If you didn't do this though, you can still add Vuex later using the CLI: **vue add vuex**. When Vuex is added (or selected during scaffolding), your Vue application is modified in the ways we'll discuss now.

First, a new folder, **store**, is added, containing one file, **index.js**:

```
import Vue from 'vue'
import Vuex from 'vuex'

Vue.use(Vuex)

export default new Vuex.Store({
  state: {
  },
  mutations: {
  },
  actions: {
  },
  modules: {
  }
})
```

This is an empty store with spots prepared for your state, mutations, actions, and modules. Note that there isn't a place for getters defined here, but you can absolutely add them. This is just the default layout for a new store, and you can modify it as you see fit.

Next, **main.js** is modified to load and install this store:

```
import Vue from 'vue'
import App from './App.vue'
import store from './store'

Vue.config.productionTip = false

new Vue({
  store,
  render: h => h(App)
}).$mount('#app')
```

Again, this is how the CLI scaffolds using Vuex, and if you prefer to use another method (perhaps a different folder name than **store**), you are free to do so.

WORKING WITH STATE

At the lowest level in a Vuex store, you will find the actual data (the state) that Vuex manages. All components have access to the state via a special **$store** variable. While there's more within this variable, to read the state, you can use **$store. state.someStateValue**. So, for example: **Hello, my name is {{ $store.state.name }}** would output the name value from your Vuex store in a component. For simple operations reading from the store, that's all you need.

We will now learn how to display state values in the following exercise.

EXERCISE 9.01: DISPLAYING STATE VALUES

In this exercise, you will create an empty Vue application using Vuex. The previous section described how that was done via the CLI, and if you followed along, you've got one ready to go. If not, go ahead and create one now, ensuring you enable Vuex. In this exercise, we'll simply set a few values in the state and display them in a component.

To access the code files for this exercise, refer to https://packt.live/32s4RkN.

1. Once you've scaffolded the application, open **store/index.js** and modify the **state** block to add three new values. The data here is arbitrary and can be anything that JavaScript can handle (strings, numbers, arrays, and so on):

```
import Vue from 'vue'
import Vuex from 'vuex'

Vue.use(Vuex)

export default new Vuex.Store({
  state: {
    name:"Lindy",
    favoriteColor: "blue",
    profession: "librarian"
  },
  mutations: {
  },
  actions: {
  },
  modules: {
  }
})
```

2. Now we need to modify the component to display the values from the state. Open up **App.vue** and modify it like so:

```
<template>
  <div id="app">
    <p>
    My name is {{ $store.state.name }} and
    my favorite color is {{ $store.state.favoriteColor }}.
    My job is a {{ $store.state.profession }}.
    </p>
    <HelloWorld />
  </div>
</template>

<script>
import HelloWorld from '@/components/HelloWorld';
export default {
  name: 'app',
  components:{
    HelloWorld
  }
}
</script>
```

3. Next, edit the **HelloWorld.vue** component to also display a value from the state:

```
<template>
  <div>
    <p>
      Hi, I'm a component, and I also have access to state!
      My name is {{ $store.state.name }}.
    </p>
  </div>
</template>

<script>
export default {
  name: 'HelloWorld'
}
</script>
```

To see your application, type **npm run serve** in your terminal. When the CLI is done, you can then open the URL displayed in your browser to see your application, which should appear as follows:

```
My name is Lindy and my favorite color is blue. My job is a
librarian.

Hi, I am a component, and I also have access to state! My name is
Lindy.
```

As you can see, both the main component and the child component have access to the state and see the same values. This shouldn't be a surprise, but it's always nice to confirm that things are working as expected.

While directly accessing state values makes things easy, let's look at a more complex usage: derived values with getters.

APPLYING GETTERS

In the previous exercise, you saw how simple it was to directly access state, but there are times when you may need more complex views of your state. To make this easier, Vuex supports a feature called **getters**.

Getters have their own block within the store, and you can define as many as necessary. Each getter is passed the state as an argument, which lets you use whatever you need to create your value. Finally, the name of the getter is how it will be exposed. Consider this simple example:

```
state: {
  name: "Raymond",
  gender: "male",
  job: "Developer Evangelist"
},
getters: {
  bio(state) {
    return `My name is ${state.name}. I'm a ${state.job}`;
  }
}
```

This store defines three state values (**name**, **gender**, and **job**), and also provides a "virtual" property named **bio** that returns a description of the data. Note that the getter only uses two of the state values, and that's totally fine.

To reference the getter in your component, you use **$store.getters.name**, where **name** is the name of the getter. So, to access the bio getter defined in the preceding code, you would use the following:

```
{{ $store.getters.bio }}
```

Along with being passed the state, getters are passed *other* getters as their second argument, which allows one getter to call another getter, if necessary.

In the next exercise, we will see an example of putting this to use.

EXERCISE 9.02: ADDING GETTERS TO A VUEX STORE

In this exercise, you will build an example that makes use of the Getters feature. You will add Getters to a Vuex store and add a call to it from the main Vue application.

To access the code files for this exercise, refer to https://packt.live/36ixlyf.

1. Scaffold a new application, remembering to use Vuex in the settings (and if you forget, just use **vue add vuex**). Type **npm run serve** to start the application and open the URL in your browser.

2. Open your store file (**store/index.js**) and then modify it to define two state values and a getter that will return both:

```
import Vue from 'vue'
import Vuex from 'vuex'

Vue.use(Vuex)

export default new Vuex.Store({
  state: {
    firstName: "Lindy",
    lastName: "Roberthon"
  },
  getters: {
    name(state) {
      return `${state.firstName} ${state.lastName}`;
    }
  },
  mutations: {
  },
  actions: {
  },
```

```
    modules: {
    }
})
```

3. Now open **App.vue** and modify it such that you make use of the **name** getter:

```
<template>
  <div id="app">
    <p>
    My name is {{ $store.getters.name }}
    </p>
  </div>
</template>
```

As you can see in the following screenshot, this will show the complete name based on the logic used in the getter:

```
My name is Lindy Roberthon
```

While rather simple, hopefully, you can see the power of what Getters achieves here. Right now, we have a concept of a name that consists of a first and last name. That isn't terribly complex logic, but by placing it within the Vuex store, we defined it as one place that's available to all components within our application. If this name definition changed (perhaps with the last name listed first, separated by a comma), you could modify it once and be done.

Next, we'll consider how to enhance Getters with additional logic.

GETTERS WITH PARAMETERS

While Getters can be accessed directly via **$store.getters** properties, you may run into situations where you need a bit more control over how the getter works. Parameters provide a way to customize how Getters works. Consider the following store:

```
import Vue from 'vue'
import Vuex from 'vuex'

Vue.use(Vuex)

export default new Vuex.Store({
  state: {
    books:[
      {type:'nonfiction', title:'Truth about Cats', pages: 200},
```

```
            {type:'nonfiction', title:'Truth about Dogs', pages: 100},
            {type:'fiction', title:'The Cat Said Meow', pages: 400},
            {type:'fiction', title:'The Last Dog', pages: 600},
        ]
    },
    getters: {
        fiction(state) {
            return state.books.filter(book => book.type === 'fiction');
        },
        nonfiction(state) {
            return state.books.filter(book => book.type ===
                'nonfiction');
        }
    },
    mutations: {
    },
    actions: {
    },
    modules: {
    }
})
```

There's only one state value in this store, and it's an array of books. Each book has a type (nonfiction or fiction), title, and page count. To make it easy to get one book versus another, two getters are used. They filter by either fiction or nonfiction books.

Here's how you could use this in a component. First, we iterate over the **fiction** getter and then the **nonfiction** one:

```
<h2>Fiction Books</h2>
<ul>
  <li v-for="book in $store.getters.fiction" :key="book.title">
  {{ book.title }}
  </li>
</ul>


<h2>Non-Fiction Books</h2>
<ul>
    <li v-for="book in $store.getters.nonfiction" :key=
      "book.title">
    {{ book.title }}
    </li>
</ul>
```

In the preceding template, two unordered lists are used to iterate over each type of book. The result can be seen as shown here:

Fiction Books

- The Cat Said Meow
- The Last Dog

Non-Fiction Books

- Truth about Cats
- Truth about Dogs

Figure 9.3: Rendering fiction and non-fiction books via getters

Okay, so far so good. But what if you want to get books based on their page count? That isn't a simple boolean or string property, but rather a number. But, because getters can accept parameters, we can create a new getter that lets us ask for a maximum number of pages. (We could support more than one parameter, so, if you wanted a getter that asked for books within a range of values, you could support both a min and max number of pages.) In order to create a getter that accepts a parameter, your code itself must return a function.

Here's an example where we define a getter that returns a portion of the full name:

```
shortName(state) {
  return function(length) {
    return ('${state.firstName} ${state.lastName}').
      substring(0, length);
  }
}
```

The resulting getter can then be used with the **length** parameter: **{{ $store. getters.shortName(10) }}**.

In the next exercise, you'll build an application that makes use of the Getter with the parameters feature.

EXERCISE 9.03: EMPLOYING A GETTER WITH PARAMETERS

You will test out this feature in the following exercise. By adding parameters to a getter, you'll be able to build more flexible getters that are more useful across different components. In this exercise, you will create a getter that takes one parameter.

To access the code files for this exercise, refer to https://packt.live/2Ioi2vy.

1. Scaffold yet another application using Vuex and, once open, edit the store to include a set of books and getters for fiction, non-fiction, and page size. This is found in the store directory in **index.js**:

```js
import Vue from 'vue'
import Vuex from 'vuex'

Vue.use(Vuex)

export default new Vuex.Store({
  state: {
    books:[
      {type:'nonfiction', title:'Truth about Cats', pages: 200},
      {type:'nonfiction', title:'Truth about Dogs', pages: 100},
      {type:'fiction', title:'The Cat Said Meow', pages: 400},
      {type:'fiction', title:'The Last Dog', pages: 600},
    ]
  },
  getters: {
    fiction(state) {
      return state.books.filter(book => book.type === 'fiction');
    },
    nonfiction(state) {
      return state.books.filter(book => book.type ===
        'nonfiction');
    },
    booksByMaxPages(state) {
      return function(pages) {
        return state.books.filter(book => book.pages <= pages);
      }
    }
  }
})
```

2. Now edit **App.vue** to use all three getters – first the fiction and nonfiction getters, and then books that have **150** or fewer pages:

```
<template>
  <div id="app">
    <h2>Fiction Books</h2>
    <ul>
      <li v-for="book in $store.getters.fiction" :key=
        "book.title">
        {{ book.title }}
      </li>
    </ul>

    <h2>Non-Fiction Books</h2>
    <ul>
      <li v-for="book in $store.getters.nonfiction" :key=
        "book.title">
        {{ book.title }}
      </li>
    </ul>

    <h2>Short Books</h2>
    <ul>
      <li v-for="book in $store.getters.booksByMaxPages(150)"
        :key="book.title">
        {{ book.title }}
      </li>
    </ul>

  </div>
</template>

<script>
export default {
  name: 'app'
}
</script>
```

Once done, you can see the result by starting your Vue application (type **npm run serve** in your terminal) and opening the URL in your browser. Here is what you should see:

Fiction Books

- The Cat Said Meow
- The Last Dog

Non-Fiction Books

- Truth about Cats
- Truth about Dogs

Short Books

- Truth about Dogs

Figure 9.4: The parameterized getter in action

In this exercise, we learned how to use more powerful getters that use parameters. This makes them flexible and more adaptable to what your components may need. Now that you've seen multiple ways of reading data from a Vuex store, it's time to look at how to modify state.

MODIFYING STATE WITH MUTATIONS

So far, you've seen how to read data from a Vuex store, both with direct access to state and by using getters. But to actually change the state of a store, Vuex supports the idea of mutations. Mutations are methods you define in your store that handle changing state. So, for example, instead of your component simply setting a new value in the state, your component will ask the store to perform a mutation, and the store handles that logic itself.

Here's a simple example:

```
state: {
  totalCats: 5,
  name:'Lindy'
},
mutations: {
  newCat(state) {
    state.totalCats++;
```

```
  },
  setName(state, name) {
   state.name = name;

  }

}
```

In the preceding snippet, the store has two values in its state, **totalCats** and **name**. Two mutations exist to allow you to change these values. All mutations are passed a state object that gives you direct access to read and change values. The first mutation, **newCat**, simply increments the **totalCats** value. The second mutation, **setName**, shows an example of a mutation that takes an argument. In this case, you could use **setName** to change the name value in the store.

In order to execute a mutation, your components will use the **commit** method. See the following, for example:

```
$store.commit('newCat');
$store.commit('setName', 'Raymond');
```

You can also pass multiple values if you pass them as an object instead of a simple value. In the next exercise, you'll get a chance to practice building your own mutations.

EXERCISE 9.04: WORKING WITH MUTATIONS

In this exercise, you will build an application that uses mutations to modify state data in Vuex. Scaffold a new application and, once ready, open up the store file located in **store/index.js**. Your store is going to be somewhat based on the preceding examples.

To access the code files for this exercise, refer to https://packt.live/3kcARiN.

1. Define a **totalCats** state variable and name state value, then three mutations to work with them – one mutation to increase the number of cats, one to reduce it, and one final one to set the name:

```
import Vue from 'vue'
import Vuex from 'vuex'

Vue.use(Vuex)

export default new Vuex.Store({
  state: {
    totalCats:5,
```

```
        name: "Lindy"
      },
    mutations: {
      adoptCat(state) {
        state.totalCats++;
      },
      placeCat(state) {
        if(state.totalCats > 0) state.totalCats--;
      },
      setName(state, name) {
        state.name = name;
      }
    }
})
```

Next, you will build a simple interface to work with this store. The template needs to have a UI to report on the name and the number of cats. You also need a text field and button to handle updating the name.

2. Open **App.vue** and update it to include outputting the current values from the store as well as providing a simple form to allow updates:

```
<template>
  <div id="app">
    <h1>About Me</h1>
    <p>
      My name is {{ $store.state.name }} and
      I have {{ $store.state.totalCats }} cats.
    </p>
    <p>
      <input v-model="newName">
      <button @click="setName" :disabled="!newName">Update Name
        </button>
    </p>
    <Cat/>
  </div>
</template>

<script>
import Cat from './components/Cat.vue'

export default {
```

```
    name: 'app',
    components: {
      Cat
    },
    data() {
      return {
        newName:''
      }
    },
    methods: {
      setName() {
        if(this.newName) {
          this.$store.commit('setName', this.newName);
          this.newName = '';
        }
      }
    }
  }
</script>
```

3. Build the **Cat** component. This component will have simple buttons to execute the mutations we defined to both increase and decrease the number of cats:

```
<template>
  <div>
    <button @click="addCat">More Cats!</button>
    <button @click="removeCat">Less Cats :(</button>
  </div>
</template>

<script>
export default {
  name: 'Cat',
  methods: {
    addCat() {
      this.$store.commit('adoptCat');
    },
    removeCat() {
      this.$store.commit('placeCat');
    }
```

```
    }
  }
</script>
```

Once done, start up your application as you have before with **npm run serve** and open the displayed URL in your browser. Your application should look like so:

About Me

My name is Lindy and I have 5 cats.

| | Update Name |

| More Cats! | Less Cats :(|

Figure 9.5: Vue application with mutation support

While this was a trivial exercise, there are a few important things to note. First, notice how both the root and child components have no problems interacting with the store. Your component hierarchy can be incredibly deep, and it simply just works. Secondly, notice how the Vue application is simpler because the logic of working with the data is in the store. The two components we worked with simply display data and handle passing off mutation calls to the store. If our logic ever needs to update, we can handle it in the store, and everything will be updated properly.

So far, you've seen how to implement changes to your store in an immediate, synchronous way. You'll now learn how to handle asynchronous updates.

USING ACTIONS FOR ASYNCHRONOUS STATE CHANGES

Actions in Vuex are the primary way of handling asynchronous logic for your store. Mutations have to be synchronous, but actions can be asynchronous if they choose. The other difference is that actions get a **context** object that represents the store itself. This lets actions call mutations or work with the state directly. In general, most developers will call mutations from their actions.

This probably seems a bit confusing, but in general, think of actions as your asynchronous support for your store. It will make sense once we see an example or two.

Let's look at a sample action. The following snippet contains one mutation and an asynchronous action that will make use of the mutation:

```
mutations: {
  setBooks(state, books) {
    state.books = books;
  }
},
actions: {
  loadBooks(context) {
    fetch('/data/books.json')
    .then(res => res.json())
    .then(res => {
      context.commit('setBooks', res);
    });
  }
},
```

Looking at **loadBooks**, you can see it makes a network request, and when done, it makes a call to the preceding mutation and lets it store the result data.

Calling an action is slightly different than mutations; instead of a **commit** call, you use **dispatch**:

```
this.$store.dispatch('loadBooks');
```

Like mutations, actions can take arguments that get passed to the action method as the second argument. Next, you'll build an example of this in action.

EXERCISE 9.05: USING ACTIONS FOR ASYNCHRONOUS LOGIC

In this exercise, you will build an example of an action requiring asynchronous logic in order to complete. This closely resembles many real-world scenarios where the data required for the application is found on a remote API. You'll implement the network call and work with the results in your Vuex store.

For this example, you will set up a JSON resource available in your **public** folder under a subdirectory named **data**. When Vue builds your code, it will copy anything in the **public** folder to the application, making it available at runtime. The JSON file contains an array of four books. Each book has a type, title, and number of pages.

To access the code files for this exercise, refer to https://packt.live/3eE6KQd.

1. While not necessary, this is how the JSON data looks. Feel free to build your own:

```json
[
    {
        "type": "nonfiction",
        "title": "Truth about Cats",
        "pages": 200
    },
    {
        "type": "nonfiction",
        "title": "Truth about Dogs",
        "pages": 100
    },
    {
        "type": "fiction",
        "title": "The Cat Said Meow",
        "pages": 400
    },
    {
        "type": "fiction",
        "title": "The Last Dog",
        "pages": 600
    }
]
```

2. In a new store (located in the usual place at **store/index.js**), set up an empty array for books, and then define an action that will use the Fetch API to retrieve the JSON content. (You'll see more examples of using APIs in *Chapter 10, Working with Vuex - Fetching Remote Data*, as well as a more powerful way of doing HTTP, in the form of the **Axios** library.) When the data is retrieved, it should then call a mutation to store the result:

```js
import Vue from 'vue'
import Vuex from 'vuex'

Vue.use(Vuex)

export default new Vuex.Store({
  state: {
    books: []
```

```
    },
    mutations: {
      setBooks(state, books) {
        state.books = books;
      }
    },
    actions: {
      loadBooks(context) {
        fetch('/data/books.json')
        .then(res => res.json())
        .then(res => {
          context.commit('setBooks', res);
        });
      }
    }
})
```

3. In order to call this action, add a **dispatch** call in your component to run the actions and then add code to display the books:

```
<template>
  <div id="app">
    Books
    <ul>
      <li v-for="book in $store.state.books" :key="book.title">
        {{ book.title }}</li>
    </ul>
  </div>
</template>

<script>

export default {
  name: 'app',
  created() {
    this.$store.dispatch('loadBooks');
  }
}
</script>
```

In *Figure 9.6*, you can see the result of the asynchronous action requesting its data:

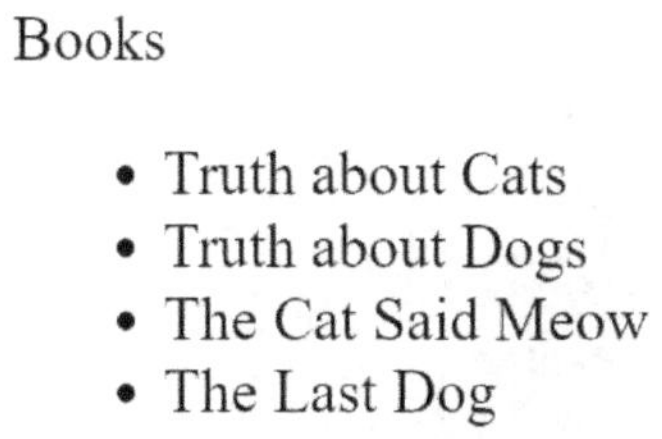

Books

- Truth about Cats
- Truth about Dogs
- The Cat Said Meow
- The Last Dog

Figure 9.6: An example of data loaded asynchronously

Now you've seen an example of working with asynchronous operations in your Vuex store. Note that you can use actions even if your code is synchronous. This may be a good idea in general if you aren't sure whether your data is going to be asynchronous in the future. Now let's look at a nice way to simplify some boilerplate Vuex syntax.

SIMPLIFYING WITH MAPSTATE AND MAPGETTERS

As one of the last features we'll cover with Vuex, let's look at **mapState** and **mapGetters**. These are handy utilities that help map state values and getters into your component's computed property. As a practical matter, it makes your HTML templates simpler. So instead of **{{ $store.state.firstName }}**, you can simply use **{{ firstName }}**. Instead of using **{{ $store.getters.name }}**, you can just use **{{ name }}**.

Both **mapState** and **mapGetters** can either take an array of values to map or an object where each key represents the name you wish to use in your component and the value is the **state value** or **getter** in the Vuex store. They are both used with your Vue application's **computed** block.

In this first example, two state values and three getters are mapped by their name alone:

```
mapState(["age", "rank", "serialNumber"]);
mapGetters(["name", "fiction", "nonfiction"]);
```

But if those names were perhaps too generic, or perhaps conflicted with existing data, you could specify other names for them:

```
mapState({
    howOld:"age",
    level:"rank",
    sn:"serialNumber"
});
mapGetters({
    ourName:"name",
    fictionBooks:"fictionBooks",
    nonfictionBooks: "nonfictionBooks"
});
```

In order to use both **mapState** and **mapGetters**, you will need to import them first:

```
import { mapState, mapGetters } from 'vuex';
```

Usage of both these features will definitely help reduce the amount of code you write to work with Vuex.

You will learn how to add **mapState** and **mapGetters** with the help of the following exercise.

EXERCISE 9.06: ADDING MAPSTATE AND MAPGETTERS

Let's look at a simple example of this. In *Exercise 9.02*, we used getters to create a shortcut for getting a name value. We can simplify that code by applying what we just learned. We can use the map functions to simplify our code.

To access the code files for this exercise, refer to https://packt.live/3ldBxpb.

1. Create a new Vue application with Vuex and then copy over the store (located at **store/index.js**) into this new version. You will need state values for the first and last name, and a getter that returns the complete name:

```
import Vue from 'vue'
import Vuex from 'vuex'

Vue.use(Vuex)

export default new Vuex.Store({
  state: {
```

```
      firstName: "Lindy",
      lastName: "Roberthon"
    },
    getters: {
      name(state) {
        return `${state.firstName} ${state.lastName}`;
      }
    }
  })
```

2. Edit the main component. You will want to edit all three values from the store (both the state values and the getter), but make use of **mapState** and **mapGetters** to simplify it:

```
<template>
  <div id="app">
    <p>
    My name is {{ firstName }} {{ lastName}}, or just {{ name }}.
    </p>
  </div>
</template>

<script>
import { mapGetters } from 'vuex';
import { mapState } from 'vuex';

export default {
  name: 'app',
  computed: {
    ...mapState([ "firstName", "lastName" ]),
    ...mapGetters([
      "name"
    ])
  }
}
</script>
```

As you can see, by using **mapState** and **mapGetters**, we've provided a way for the template portion of the app to make use of the data somewhat simpler:

```
My name is Lindy Roberthon, or just Lindy Roberthon.
```

When done, you should see exactly the same output as you've seen before. The important part is that the amount of code you needed to write was reduced!

In the next section, we'll briefly talk about **mapMutations** and **mapActions**.

SIMPLIFYING WITH MAPMUTATIONS AND MAPACTIONS

The final features we'll cover are very similar to the previous one: **mapMutations** and **mapActions**. As you can probably guess, these two features work very similarly to **mapState** and **mapGetters**, in that they provide a shorthand way to connect your code to Vuex mutations and actions without writing boilerplate code.

They follow the exact same format in that you can specify a list of items to map or specify a list while also providing a different name, as in the following example:

```
mapMutations(["setBooks"]);
mapActions(["loadBooks"]);
```

These can be used in your Vue component's **methods** block:

```
methods:{
    ...mapMutations(["setBooks"]),
    ...mapActions(["loadBooks"])
}
```

This then allows your Vue code to call either **setBooks** or **loadBooks** without specifying the **store** object, or **dispatch** and **commit**.

Now, let's try to create a simple shopping cart and a price calculator on our own.

ACTIVITY 9.01: CREATING A SIMPLE SHOPPING CART AND PRICE CALCULATOR

Imagine a hypothetical corporate hardware site that lets employees select products they need shipping to their office. This cart is much simpler than a typical e-commerce site as it doesn't need to process credit cards or even ask the person where they are (IT knows where you sit!). It still needs to present you with a list of items, let you select how much you want, and then provide you with a total price that will be billed to your department.

In this activity, you need to build a Vuex store that represents the available products and their prices. You will need multiple components to handle the different aspects of the application and properly interact with the store data.

Steps:

1. Build a store and define an array of products and a cart in the state. Every product will have **name** and **price** properties.

2. Define a component that lists out each product and price.

3. Modify the component to have buttons to add, or remove, one of the products from your cart.

4. Define a second component that shows the current cart (every product and quantity).

5. Use a third component that displays the total cart price and has a button to complete the checkout. The total price is the sum of each product in the cart multiplied by the quantity of the product. For this activity, the **checkout** button should simply alert the user that the checkout process is done but take no other steps.

You should get the following output initially, showing an empty cart:

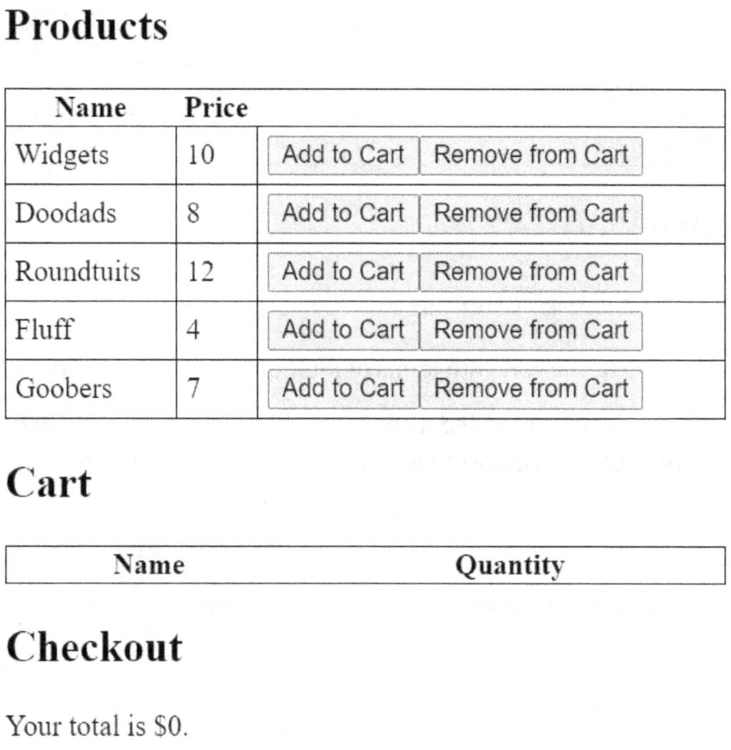

Products

Name	Price		
Widgets	10	Add to Cart	Remove from Cart
Doodads	8	Add to Cart	Remove from Cart
Roundtuits	12	Add to Cart	Remove from Cart
Fluff	4	Add to Cart	Remove from Cart
Goobers	7	Add to Cart	Remove from Cart

Cart

Name	Quantity

Checkout

Your total is $0.

Figure 9.7: Initial display of the cart

As you add and remove items, you'll see the cart and totals update in real time:

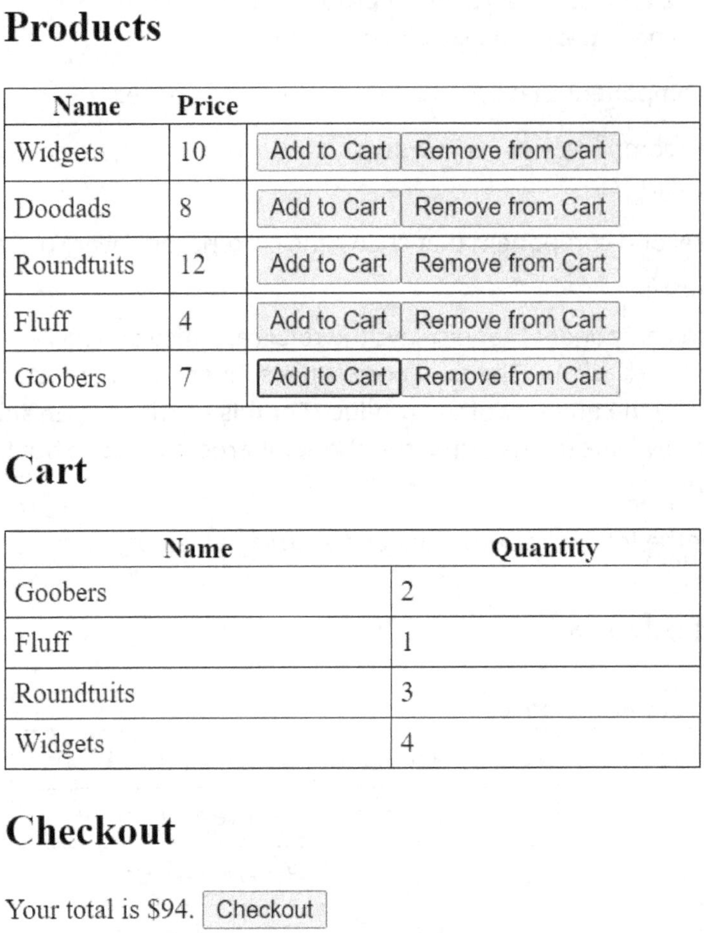

Products

Name	Price		
Widgets	10	Add to Cart	Remove from Cart
Doodads	8	Add to Cart	Remove from Cart
Roundtuits	12	Add to Cart	Remove from Cart
Fluff	4	Add to Cart	Remove from Cart
Goobers	7	Add to Cart	Remove from Cart

Cart

Name	Quantity
Goobers	2
Fluff	1
Roundtuits	3
Widgets	4

Checkout

Your total is $94. Checkout

Figure 9.8: The cart with items of multiple quantities added

As you can see, as products are added, the cart display updates to show quantity values and the total in the **Checkout** section accurately reflects the total price.

> **NOTE**
>
> The solution to this activity can be found on page 701.

SUMMARY

In this chapter, you have seen most of Vuex's features and should now have an idea of how to both read from and write to the store. You employed mutations for synchronous changes and actions for asynchronous modifications. You created getters to provide access to virtual values based on your state. You have also seen how components look when working with the store. They've got less logic and simply hand off that part to the store. In larger Vue applications, this will become even more important. Your components will handle the UI and UX, but let the store handle the data layer. Having the store as a single source of truth, then, relieves you of so much "grunt" work that you will come to greatly appreciate Vuex, even in smaller applications.

In the next chapter, you will learn about using remote data with Vuex stores. Working with remote APIs is a common need in modern web applications. Integrating these APIs in Vuex will make it easier for the rest of your Vue application to use the data provided by remote services.

10

WORKING WITH VUEX – FETCHING REMOTE DATA

OVERVIEW

In this chapter, you will learn how to work with remote APIs using the **Axios** library. You will make network calls and store results using Vuex. You will also see an example of how to store authentication tokens with Vuex and use it for further API calls.

By the end of this chapter, you will have a good idea of how Vuex can help abstract and create a wrapper for remote APIs, and ease their integration into a Vue application. This abstraction makes it easier to migrate to other APIs in the future, ensuring that the rest of your applications continue to work properly.

INTRODUCTION

In *Chapter 9*, *Working with Vuex – State, Getters, Actions, and Mutations*, you were introduced to Vuex and saw multiple examples of how to work with it to both read data from and write data to a store. We saw how multiple components could work with the store and all be kept in sync with little to no work at our end. In this chapter, we are going to expand our Vuex usage by integrating it with remote data by using **Axios**, a popular open source library that makes it easy to use network resources. Let's start off with a deeper look at **Axios**.

Axios (https://github.com/axios/axios) is a JavaScript library with both **Node** and **browser** support. It has a Promise-based API, which means you can use **async** and **await** if you wish. Other features include supporting default parameters (handy for APIs that require a key for every call) and the ability to transform your input and output data. We will not be covering every use case in this chapter, but you will get a good idea of how to work with **Axios** for your future projects.

To be clear, you need not use **Axios** if you do not like it. You can use any other library or no library at all. The Fetch API (https://developer.mozilla.org/en-US/docs/Web/API/Fetch_API) is a modern browser API for working with network requests that, while not as powerful as **Axios**, doesn't require an additional library.

In the next section, we will look at how to install **Axios**.

INSTALLATION OF AXIOS

Much like Vuex, you have multiple ways of including **Axios** in your project. The simplest is pasting in a **<script>** tag pointing to the **Content Delivery Network** (**CDN**) for the library:

```
<script src="https://unpkg.com/axios/dist/axios.min.js"></script>
```

The other option is to use the **Node Package Manager**, **npm**. Within an existing Vue application, you can install **Axios** as follows:

```
npm install axios
```

Once you have done this, your Vue components can then import the library as follows:

```
import axios from 'axios';
```

How you use **Axios** will depend on the API you are interacting with. Here is a simple example of hitting an imaginary API:

```
axios.get('https://www.raymondcamden.com/api/cats')
.then(res => {
  this.cats = res.data.results;
})
.catch(error => {
  console.error(error);
});
```

In the preceding example, we are performing a **GET** request (**GET** is the default) against an imaginary API, *https://www.raymondcamden.com/api/cats*. **Axios** returns promises, which means we can chain results and errors with **then** and **catch**. The resulting JSON (again, this is an imaginary API) is automatically parsed so all that is left is to assign the result to a value, in this case, a value named **cats** used in my Vue application.

Let's now look at a step-by-step process of using **Axios** to load the data from an API.

EXERCISE 10.01: USING AXIOS TO LOAD DATA FROM AN API

Let's look at a complex example using **Axios**. This example will make two different API calls against the Star Wars API and return two lists of information. For now, we will skip using Vuex to make this introduction a bit simpler.

To access the code files for this exercise, refer to https://packt.live/3kbn1x1.

1. Generate a new Vue application and, after the CLI has completed, add **Axios** as an **npm** dependency:

```
npm install axios
```

2. Open the **App.vue** page and add the import for **axios**:

```
import axios from 'axios';
```

3. Open the **App.vue** page and add the data values for the **films** and **ships** arrays:

```
data() {
    return {
      films:[],
```

```
      ships:[]
    }
  },
```

4. Open **App.vue** and use the created method to load in **films** and **starships** from the API:

```
created() {

    axios.get('https://swapi.dev/api/films')
    .then(res => {
      this.films = res.data.results;
    })
    .catch(error => {
      console.error(error);
    });

    axios.get('https://swapi.dev/api/starships')
    .then(res => {
      this.ships = res.data.results;
    })
    .catch(error => {
      console.error(error);
    });

}
```

5. Next, edit the template to iterate over the values and display them:

```
<h2>Films</h2>
<ul>
    <li v-for="film in films" :key="film.url">
        {{ film.title }} was released in {{ film.release_date }}
    </li>
</ul>

<h2>Starships</h2>
<ul>
    <li v-for="ship in ships" :key="ship.url">
        {{ ship.name }} is a {{ ship.starship_class }}
    </li>
</ul>
```

> **NOTE**
>
> Error handling is done using the catch handler but is just sent to the browser console. It would be better to tell the user something if the remote data did not load, but for now, this is acceptable. Another suggestion would be to handle a **loading** state, which you will see an example of later in this chapter.

6. Start the application with the following command:

```
npm run serve
```

Opening the URL in your browser will generate the following output:

Films

- A New Hope was released in 1977-05-25
- Attack of the Clones was released in 2002-05-16
- The Phantom Menace was released in 1999-05-19
- Revenge of the Sith was released in 2005-05-19
- Return of the Jedi was released in 1983-05-25
- The Empire Strikes Back was released in 1980-05-17
- The Force Awakens was released in 2015-12-11

Starships

- Executor is a Star dreadnought
- Sentinel-class landing craft is a landing craft
- Death Star is a Deep Space Mobile Battlestation
- Millennium Falcon is a Light freighter
- Y-wing is a assault starfighter
- X-wing is a Starfighter
- TIE Advanced x1 is a Starfighter
- Slave 1 is a Patrol craft
- Imperial shuttle is a Armed government transport
- EF76 Nebulon-B escort frigate is a Escort ship

Figure 10.1: Results of the API calls rendered in the browser

This simple example shows how easy it is to add **Axios** to a Vue application. Remember that **Axios** is not required for Vue and you're welcome to use any library you want, or simply use the browser's native Fetch API.

Now that you have seen how to get **Axios** into a project, let's look at one of the cooler features of **Axios**: specifying default values.

USING DEFAULTS WITH AXIOS

While the code in *Exercise 10.01, Using Axios to Load Data from an API* works well, let's consider a slightly more advanced example. One of the features of **Axios** is the ability to set up defaults that are used in future calls. If you look at the two calls made in the preceding code, you can see they are similar. You can update the **created** method to make use of this:

```
created() {

  const api = axios.create({
    baseURL:'https://swapi.dev/api/',
    transformResponse(data) {
      data = JSON.parse(data);
      return data.results;
    }
  });

  api.get('films')
  .then(res => this.films = res.data);

  api.get('starships')
  .then(res => this.ships = res.data);

}
```

In this updated version, we switch to an instance of **Axios**. A default **baseURL** value is specified that saves on typing later. Next, the **transformResponse** feature is used to, well, transform the response. This lets us modify data before it is sent to the handler of our calls later. Since all the API calls return a results value and that is the only thing we are concerned with, we simplify things a bit by returning that instead of the rest of the result. Note that **Axios** lets you use an array of functions in **transformResponse** if you want to build a complex set of transformations.

In the next section, we will learn how to use **Axios** with Vuex.

USING AXIOS WITH VUEX

Now that you have seen the basics of working with **Axios**, it is time to consider how you could use it with Vuex. One way to do this simply is to just use Vuex to handle wrapping calls to the API, using **Axios** to perform the HTTP calls.

EXERCISE 10.02: WORKING WITH AXIOS IN VUEX

We are going to take the previous functionality (loading the **films** and **ships** arrays) and rebuild it within the context of a Vuex store instead. As before, you will need to use the CLI to scaffold a new application and ensure you ask for Vuex to be included. When the CLI is done, you can then use the **npm** command to add **Axios** as well.

This exercise will be pretty much like the first application that we built in *Exercise 10.01, Using Axios to Load Data from an API*, but with some slight differences. Let's look at the UI first. On the initial load, both **Films** and **Ships** are empty:

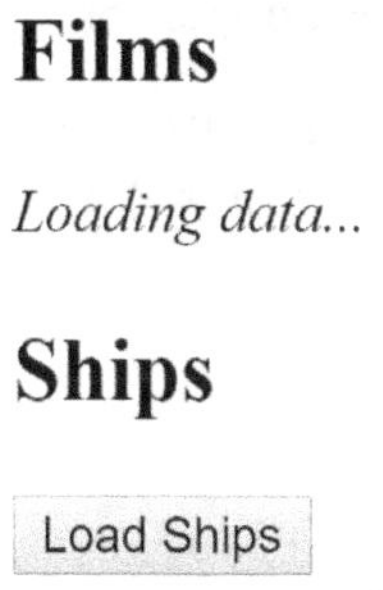

Films

Loading data...

Ships

Load Ships

Figure 10.2: Initial application UI

Notice that the **Films** portion has a loading message. As soon as the application loads, we will fire off a request to get that data. For **Ships**, though, we wait for the user to specifically request they want that data. Here is how it looks after the **films** array loads:

Films

- A New Hope was released in 1977-05-25
- Attack of the Clones was released in 2002-05-16
- The Phantom Menace was released in 1999-05-19
- Revenge of the Sith was released in 2005-05-19
- Return of the Jedi was released in 1983-05-25
- The Empire Strikes Back was released in 1980-05-17
- The Force Awakens was released in 2015-12-11

Ships

Load Ships

Figure 10.3: The application's rendered films

Finally, after clicking the **Load Ships** button, the button will disable (to prevent the user from requesting the data multiple times) and then the entire button is removed after the data is loaded:

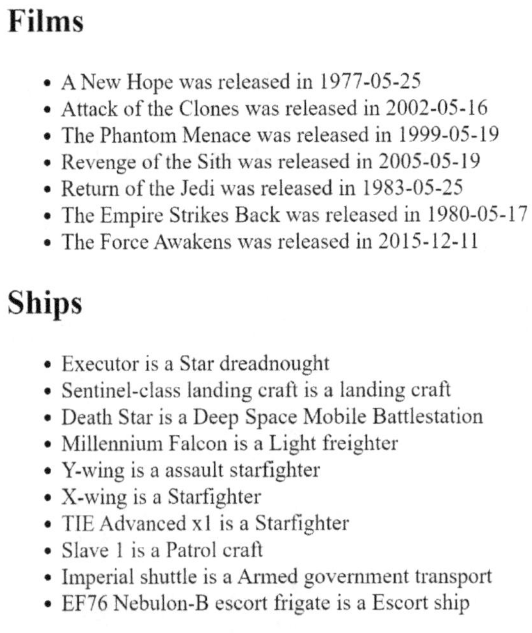

Films

- A New Hope was released in 1977-05-25
- Attack of the Clones was released in 2002-05-16
- The Phantom Menace was released in 1999-05-19
- Revenge of the Sith was released in 2005-05-19
- Return of the Jedi was released in 1983-05-25
- The Empire Strikes Back was released in 1980-05-17
- The Force Awakens was released in 2015-12-11

Ships

- Executor is a Star dreadnought
- Sentinel-class landing craft is a landing craft
- Death Star is a Deep Space Mobile Battlestation
- Millennium Falcon is a Light freighter
- Y-wing is a assault starfighter
- X-wing is a Starfighter
- TIE Advanced x1 is a Starfighter
- Slave 1 is a Patrol craft
- Imperial shuttle is a Armed government transport
- EF76 Nebulon-B escort frigate is a Escort ship

Figure 10.4: The final view after everything is loaded

To access the code files for this exercise, refer to https://packt.live/32pUsWy.

1. Start with the first component, **App.vue**. Write the HTML. Remember that the **films** are displayed in the component, but **ships** will be in their own component. Make use of **v-else** to add a loading message that will be shown while **Axios** makes the HTTP request:

```
<template>
  <div id="app">
    <h2>Films</h2>
    <ul v-if="films.length">
      <li v-for="film in films" :key="film.url">
        {{ film.title }} was released in {{ film.release_date }}
      </li>
    </ul>
    <div v-else>
      <i>Loading data...</i>
    </div>
    <Ships />
  </div>
</template>
```

2. Now add the code necessary to load and register the **Ships** component:

```
import Ships from './components/Ships.vue'

export default {
  name: 'app',
  components: {
    Ships
  },
```

3. Import **mapState** as well:

```
import { mapState } from 'vuex';
```

4. Next, add code to map the **films** array from our store to a local computed value. Remember to import **mapState**:

```
computed: {
    ...mapState(["films"])
  },
```

5. Finally, the **created** method is used to fire off an action in our store:

```
created() {
    this.$store.dispatch('loadFilms');
}
```

6. Next, build the **Ships** component in **components/Ship.vue**. The **Ships** component also contains a list of data but uses a button so that the user can request the data to be loaded. The button should automatically be dismissed when done and be disabled during the loading process:

```
<template>
  <div>
    <h2>Ships</h2>
    <div v-if="ships.length">
      <ul>
        <li v-for="ship in ships" :key="ship.url">
          {{ ship.name }} is a {{ ship.starship_class }}
        </li>
      </ul>
    </div>
    <button v-else @click="loadShips" :disabled="loading">Load
      Ships</button>
  </div>
</template>
```

7. Add the code to handle mapping the **ships** state and fire off the action to Vuex to load the **ships**:

```
<script>
import { mapState } from 'vuex';

export default {
  name: 'Ships',
  data() {
    return {
      loading:false
    }
  },
  computed: {
    ...mapState(["ships"])
  },
  methods:{
```

```
        loadShips() {
          this.loading = true;
          this.$store.dispatch('loadShips');
        }
      }
    }
</script>
```

8. Now, build the store. First, define the **state** to hold both the **films** and **ships** arrays:

```
import Vue from 'vue'
import Vuex from 'vuex'
import axios from 'axios'

Vue.use(Vuex)

export default new Vuex.Store({
  state: {
    films:[],
    ships:[]
  },
```

9. Next, add the actions to load **ships** and **films** data. They should both use **mutations** to assign values to the **state**:

```
  mutations: {
    setFilms(state, films) {
      state.films = films;
    },
    setShips(state, ships) {
      state.ships = ships;
    }
  },
  actions: {
    loadFilms(context) {
      axios.get('https://swapi.dev/api/films')
      .then(res => {
        context.commit('setFilms', res.data.results);
      })
      .catch(error => {
        console.error(error);
```

```
    });
  },
  loadShips(context) {
    axios.get('https://swapi.dev/api/starships')
    .then(res => {
      context.commit('setShips', res.data.results);
    })
    .catch(error => {
      console.error(error);
    });
  }

  }
})
```

10. Run your application using the following command:

```
npm run serve
```

Your output will be as follows:

Films

- A New Hope was released in 1977-05-25
- Attack of the Clones was released in 2002-05-16
- The Phantom Menace was released in 1999-05-19
- Revenge of the Sith was released in 2005-05-19
- Return of the Jedi was released in 1983-05-25
- The Empire Strikes Back was released in 1980-05-17
- The Force Awakens was released in 2015-12-11

Ships

- Executor is a Star dreadnought
- Sentinel-class landing craft is a landing craft
- Death Star is a Deep Space Mobile Battlestation
- Millennium Falcon is a Light freighter
- Y-wing is a assault starfighter
- X-wing is a Starfighter
- TIE Advanced x1 is a Starfighter
- Slave 1 is a Patrol craft
- Imperial shuttle is a Armed government transport
- EF76 Nebulon-B escort frigate is a Escort ship

Figure 10.5: The final output

All in all, this is not a huge change from the initial version without Vuex (if we ignore the UI changes), but now all our API usage is handled by the store. If for some reason we decide to stop using **Axios** and switch to Fetch, it can be done here. Whether we decide to add a caching system or store the data for offline use, it can all be done in the store. Test this version yourself by running **npm run serve** and opening the URL in your browser.

Now it is time to put what you have learned into action with the next activity!

ACTIVITY 10.01: USING AXIOS AND VUEX WITH AUTHENTICATION

One of the more interesting things you can do with Vuex is manage authentication. What do we mean by that? In many APIs, authentication is required before the service can be used. After the user authenticates, they are given a token. On future calls to the API, the token is passed along, typically as a header, which lets the remote service know this is an authorized user. Vuex can handle all of this for you, and **Axios** makes it easy to work with headers, so let's consider an example of this in action.

Building a server with authentication and authorization is way outside the scope of this book, so instead, we are going to *fake* it. We will have two **endpoints** that are simple uses of **JSONBin.io**, a service we used in *Chapter 9, Working with Vuex – State, Getters, Actions, and Mutations*. The first endpoint will return a token:

```
{
  "token": 123456789
}
```

The second endpoint will return an array of **cats**:

```
[
  {
    "name": "Luna",
    "gender": "female"
  },
  {
    "name": "Pig",
    "gender": "female"
  },
  {
    "name": "Cracker",
    "gender": "male"
  },
  {
```

```
    "name": "Sammy",
    "gender": "male"
  },
  {
    "name": "Elise",
    "gender": "female"
  }
]
```

In this activity, we will use Vue Router to handle representing two **views** of the application, the login screen and the cat display screen.

Steps:

1. Present a login screen for the initial view of the application. It should prompt for a username and password.

2. Pass the login credentials to an endpoint and get a token. This part will be faked as we are not building a full, real authentication system.

3. Load the cats from a remote endpoint and pass the token as an authentication header.

You should get the following output initially:

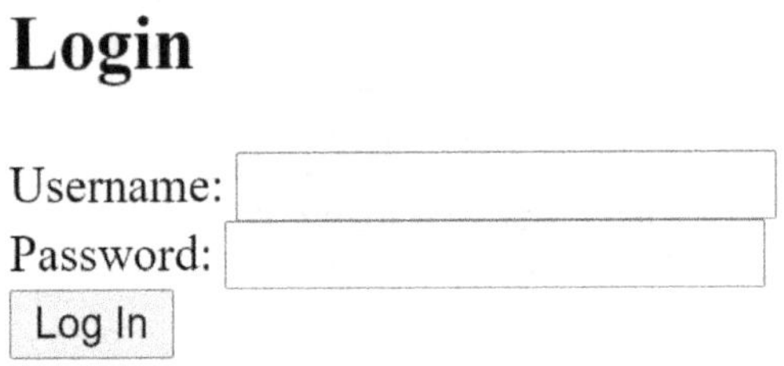

Login

Username: [   ]
Password: [   ]
[Log In]

Figure 10.6: Initial login screen

After logging in, you will then see the data, as follows:

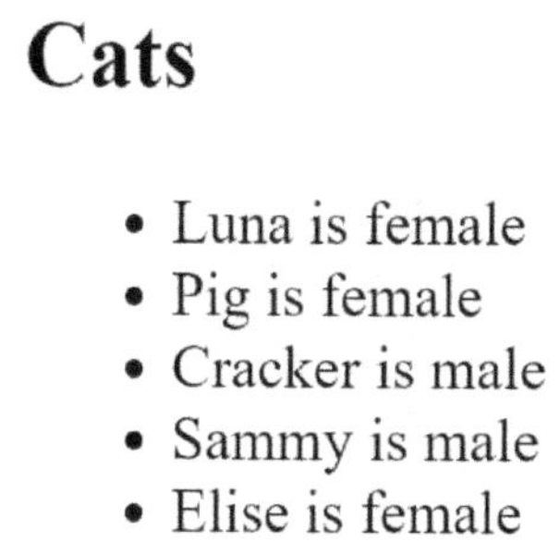

Cats

- Luna is female
- Pig is female
- Cracker is male
- Sammy is male
- Elise is female

Figure 10.7: Successfully displaying the data after login

> **NOTE**
>
> The solution to this activity can be found on page 708.

SUMMARY

In this chapter, you learned a pretty important use case for Vuex—working with remote APIs. Remote APIs can provide an incredible amount of additional functionality to your applications, sometimes for little to no additional cost to the developer. You saw how to use **Axios** to make network calls easier and how to combine that with the state management features of Vuex. Finally, you put it together with Vue Router to create a simple login/authorization demo.

In the next chapter, we are going to discuss how to build more complex Vuex stores using modules.

11

WORKING WITH VUEX — ORGANIZING LARGER STORES

OVERVIEW

In this chapter, you will learn how to better organize larger Vuex stores. As your applications grow in complexity and features, your store file may become harder to work with. Even simply finding things can become a difficult chore as the file grows larger and larger. This chapter will discuss two different approaches to making it easier to organize your stores for simpler updates. The first approach will have you splitting up your code across different files whereas the second will use a more advanced Vuex feature, modules.

INTRODUCTION

So far, the stores we have worked on have been simple and short. But, as everyone knows, even the simplest of applications tend toward complexity over time. As you have learned in the previous chapters, your store can contain a **state**, a block of **getters**, a block of **mutations** and **actions**, and as you will learn later in this chapter, **modules**.

As your application grows, having one file for your Vuex store could become hard to manage. Both bug fixing and updates for new functionality could become more difficult. This chapter will discuss two different ways to help manage this complexity and organize your Vuex stores. To be clear, these are *optional* things you can do to help manage your store. If your store is simple and you would like to keep it that way, that is fine. You can always use these approaches in the future, and the great thing is that no-one outside your store will need to be aware – they will continue to use Vuex data as they did before. You can keep these techniques in mind as a set of tools to help you when your application needs to level up. Let's start with the simplest of methods, file splitting.

APPROACH ONE – USING FILE SPLITTING

The first approach, and certainly the simplest one, involves simply taking the code of your various Vuex parts (the **state**, the **getters**, and so forth) and moving them into their own files. These files can then be imported by the main Vuex Store and used as normal. Let's consider a simple example:

```
import Vue from 'vue'
import Vuex from 'vuex'

Vue.use(Vuex)

export default new Vuex.Store({
  state: {
    name:"Lindy",
    favoriteColor: "blue",
    profession: "librarian"
  },
  mutations: {
  },
```

```
    actions: {
    },
    modules: {
    }
})
```

This is from the first exercise in *Chapter 9, Working with Vuex – State, Getters, Actions, and Mutations*, and is a store with only three state values. To migrate the state to a new file, you could create a new file in the **store** folder, called **state.js**, and set it up like so:

```
export default {
    name: 'Lindy',
    favoriteColor: 'blue',
    profession: 'librarian'
}
```

Then, back in your store, modify it to **import** and make use of the code:

```
import Vue from 'vue'
import Vuex from 'vuex'

Vue.use(Vuex)

import state from './state.js';

export default new Vuex.Store({
    state,
    mutations: {
    },
    actions: {
    },
    modules: {
    }
})
```

While this example ends up being *more* lines of code, you can see how we are beginning to separate out different parts of the store into different files to make it easier to update. Let's consider a slightly larger example, again taking earlier work from the second exercise in *Chapter 9, Working with Vuex – State, Getters, Actions, and Mutations*. Here is the original store:

```
import Vue from 'vue'
import Vuex from 'vuex'


Vue.use(Vuex)


export default new Vuex.Store({
  state: {
    firstName: "Lindy",
    lastName: "Roberthon"
  },
  getters: {
    name(state) {
      return state.firstName + ' ' + state.lastName;
    }
  },
  mutations: {
  },
  actions: {
  },
  modules: {
  }
})
```

This example only uses **state** values and a **getter**, but let's move both of them into new files. First, let's move the **state** into a file called **state.js**:

```
export default {
  firstName: 'Lindy',
  lastName: 'Roberthon'
}
```

And next, let's move the **getters** into a file called **getters.js**:

```
export default {
  name(state) {
    return state.firstName + ' ' + state.lastName;
  }
}
```

Now we can update the store:

```
import Vue from 'vue'
import Vuex from 'vuex'

Vue.use(Vuex)

import state from './state.js';
import getters from './getters.js';

export default new Vuex.Store({
  state,
  getters,
  mutations: {
  },
  actions: {
  },
  modules: {
  }
})
```

Applying the same type of update to **mutations** and **actions** would follow the exact same pattern, and obviously, you do not have to split everything. You could, for example, keep the state values in the main file but only split out your functions (**getters**, **mutations**, and **actions**).

EXERCISE 11.01: USING FILE SPLITTING

In this exercise, we are going to use file splitting across a slightly larger Vue store. Honestly, it is not very large at all, but we will use file splitting to handle **state**, **getters**, **mutations**, and **actions**.

To access the code files for this exercise, visit https://packt.live/32uwiKB:

1. Generate a new Vue application and add Vuex support.

2. Modify the default store's **index.js** file (located at **src/store/index.js**) to import the four files we will create to represent the store:

```
import Vue from 'vue'
import Vuex from 'vuex'


Vue.use(Vuex)


import state from './state.js';
import getters from './getters.js';
import mutations from './mutations.js';
import actions from './actions.js';


export default new Vuex.Store({
  state,
  getters,
  mutations,
  actions,
  modules: {

  }
})
```

3. Edit the new **state.js** file to add values for first and last names, numbers representing the amounts of cats and dogs possessed by the person in question, and a favorite film:

```
export default {
        firstName: 'Lindy',
        lastName: 'Roberthon',
        numCats: 5,
        numDogs: 1,
        favoriteFilm:''
}
```

4. Add a **getter.js** file that defines a **getter** for the full name and the total number of pets:

```
export default {
    name(state) {
        return state.firstName + ' ' +state.lastName
    },
    totalPets(state) {
        return state.numCats + state.numDogs
    }

}
```

5. Next, add a **mutations.js** file for adding the number of cats and dogs, setting the first and last name, and adding the favorite film:

```
export default {
    addCat(state) {
        state.numCats++;
    },
    addDog(state) {
        state.numDogs++;
    },
    setFirstName(state, name) {
        if(name !== '') state.firstName = name;
    },
    setLastName(state, name) {
        if(name !== '') state.lastName = name;
    },
    setFavoriteFilm(state, film) {
        if(film !== '') state.favoriteFilm = film;
    }

}
```

6. Finally, add **actions.js** to define one action, **updateFavoriteFilm**. This will make a network request to the **Star Wars** API to ensure that the new favorite film is only allowed if it is a Star Wars film:

```
export default {
    async updateFavoriteFilm(context, film) {
        try {
```

```
            let response = await fetch('https://swapi.dev/api/
films?search='+encodeURIComponent(film));
            let data = await response.json();
            if(data.count === 1) context.commit
                ('setFavoriteFilm', film);
            else console.log('Ignored setting non-Star Wars
                film '+film+' as favorite.');
        } catch(e) {
            console.error(e);
        }
    }
}
```

7. To see it in action, update **src/App.vue** to access various parts of the store. The only point of this step is to drive home the idea that how you use the store does not change:

```
<template>
  <div id="app">
    My first name is {{ $store.state.firstName }}.<br/>
    My full name is {{ $store.getters.name }}.<br/>
    I have this many pets - {{ $store.getters.totalPets }}.<br/>
    My favorite film is {{ $store.state.favoriteFilm }}.
  </div>
</template>

<script>
export default {
  name: 'app',
  created() {
    this.$store.dispatch('updateFavoriteFilm', 'A New Hope');
  }
}
</script>
```

The preceding code will generate an output as follows:

My first name is Lindy.
My full name is Lindy Roberthon.
I have this many pets - 6.
My favorite film is A New Hope.

Figure 11.1: Output from the newly organized store

You have now seen a (somewhat simple) example of using file splitting to manage the size of your Vuex store. While the functionality is no different than what you have seen before, as your application grows, you will probably find it much easier to make additions and fixes.

APPROACH TWO – USING MODULES

In the previous approach, we mainly just moved lines of code into other files. As we said, while this made it easier to work on the store itself, it changed nothing about how the store was used by Vue components. **Modules** help us deal with complexity at the level where components come in.

Imagine a large **state** object containing values representing many different things, such as this one:

```
state: {
  name:"Lindy",
  favoriteColor: "blue",
  profession: "librarian",
  // lots more values about Lindy
  books: [
    { name: "An Umbrella on Fire", pages: 283 },
    { name: "Unicorn Whisperer", pages: 501 },
    // many, many more books
  ],
  robots: {
    skill:'advanced',
    totalAllowed: 10,
    robots: [
```

```
    { name: "Draconis" },
    // so much robots
  ]
 }
}
```

This example contains information about a person, data related to books, and a set of values representing robots. That is a lot of data covering three uniquely different topics. Moving this into its own file does not necessarily make it easier to use or help keep things organized. This complexity would also spill over to **getters**, **mutations**, and **actions**. Given an action named **setName**, you could assume it applies to the state values representing the person, but if other state values had similar names, it could begin to get messy.

This is where modules come in. A module allows us to define a separate **bucket** in our store for a portion of our data. Each module can have a unique **state**, **getters**, **mutations**, and **actions** completely separated from the **root** or core store.

Here is an example store using a **resume** module:

```
import Vue from 'vue'
import Vuex from 'vuex'

Vue.use(Vuex)

export default new Vuex.Store({
  state: {
    firstName:'Raymond',
    lastName:'Camden'
  },
  getters: {
    name(state) {
      return state.firstName + ' ' + state.lastName;
    }
  },
  modules: {
    resume: {
      state: {
        forHire:true,
        jobs: [
          "Librarian",
```

```
        "Jedi",
        "Cat Herder"
      ]
    },
    getters: {
      totalJobs(state) {
        return state.jobs.length;
      }
    }
  }
}
})
```

Both the **root** store and the **module** define `state` and `getters` but could also expose **mutations** and **actions**. Notice how in the **resume** module `getters`, `totalJobs`, the `state` variable refers to its own state, not that of the parent. This is great as it ensures you can work within the module and not worry about modifying, by accident, another value in the root or some other module. You can access the root state in **getters** by using a new third argument, `rootState`:

```
totalJobs(state, anyArgument, rootState)
```

And actions can use **rootState** via the context object, `context.rootState`. In theory, though, your modules should concern themselves with their own data and only **reach out** to the root when necessary.

When using module values, your code must know the name of the module. Consider the following example:

```
first name {{ $store.state.firstName }}<br/>
for hire? {{ $store.state.resume.forHire }}<br/>
```

getters, **actions**, and **mutations** are *not* differentiated, though. This is how you would access both **getters**:

```
full name {{ $store.getters.name }}<br/>
total jobs {{ $store.getters.totalJobs }}<br/>
```

The idea behind this is to allow a module, or multiple modules, to potentially respond to the same calls. If this does not appeal to you, you can **namespace** your modules by passing in the **namespaced** option:

```
modules: {
  resume: {
    namespaced: true,
    state: {
      forHire:true,
      jobs: [
        "Librarian",
        "Jedi",
        "Cat Herder"
      ]
    },
    getters: {
      totalJobs(state) {
        return state.jobs.length;
      }
    }
  }
}
```

Then to refer to **getters**, **mutations**, and **actions** for this module, you must pass in the name of the module as part of the call. So, for example, the getter now becomes: **$store.getters['resume/totalJobs']**.

For the most part, that is the core of module support, but note there are more options for how modules can expose themselves globally that are outside the scope of this book. See the latter parts of the module documentation (https://vuex.vuejs.org/guide/modules.html) for examples of that. Finally, note that you can build modules within modules as deep as you like. Obviously, you want to put some thought into building incredibly deeply nested modules, but if you want to do that, Vuex allows it!

EXERCISE 11.02: MAKING USE OF MODULES

In this exercise, we'll work with a Vuex store that makes use of not one but two modules, and to make it more interesting, one of the modules will be stored in another file, showing that we can also use the first approach when using modules.

To access the code files for this exercise, visit https://packt.live/35d1zDv:

1. As usual, generate a new Vue application and ensure you add Vuex.

2. In the store file (**store/index.js**), add two **state** values for the first and last names and a getter to return both:

```
state: {
  firstName:'Raymond',
  lastName:'Camden'
},
getters: {
  name(state) {
    return state.firstName + ' ' + state.lastName;
  }
},
```

3. Next, add a **resume** module to the **store** file. It will have two **state** values, one representing an open-for-hire value and the other, an array of past jobs. Lastly, add a getter to return the total number of jobs:

```
modules: {
  resume: {
    state: {
      forHire:true,
      jobs: [
        "Librarian",
        "Jedi",
        "Cat Herder"
      ]
    },
    getters: {
      totalJobs(state) {
        return state.jobs.length;
      }
    }
  },
```

4. Now create a new file for the next module, **store/portfolio.js**. This will contain a **state** value representing an array of websites worked on and a mutation to add a value:

```
export default {
    state: {
        websites: [
            "https://www.raymondcamden.com",
            "https://codabreaker.rocks"
        ]
    },
    mutations: {
        addSite(state, url) {
            state.websites.push(url);
        }
    }
}
```

5. Back in the main store's **index.js** file, import **portfolio**:

```
import portfolio from './portfolio.js';
```

6. Then add **portfolio** to the list of modules, after **resume**:

```
modules: {
    resume: {
        state: {
            forHire:true,
            jobs: [
                "Librarian",
                "Jedi",
                "Cat Herder"
            ]
        },
        getters: {
            totalJobs(state) {
                return state.jobs.length;
            }
        }
    },
    portfolio
}
```

7. Now, let's make use of the modules in our main **src/App.vue** file. Modify the template to add calls to various parts of the store:

```
<p>
My name is {{ $store.getters.name }} and I
<span v-if="$store.state.resume.forHire">
    am looking for work!
</span><span v-else>
    am not looking for work.
</span>
</p>
<p>
  I've had {{ $store.getters.totalJobs }} total jobs.
</p>
<h2>Portfolio</h2>
<ul>
  <li
    v-for="(site,idx) in $store.state.portfolio.websites"
    :key="idx"><a :href="site" target="_new">{{ site }}</a></li>
</ul>
```

8. Then add a **form** so that we can add a **new website**:

```
<p>
  <input type="url" placeholder="New site for portfolio"
    v-model="site">
  <button @click="addSite">Add Site</button>
</p>
```

9. Define the method for **addSite**. It will commit the **mutation** and clear the site value. Be sure to add a local data value for site as well. Here is the complete script block:

```
export default {
  name: 'app',
  data() {
    return {
      site:''
    }
  },
  methods: {
    addSite() {
      this.$store.commit('addSite', this.site);
```

```
        this.site = '';
      }
    }
  }
```

The result will look as follows:

My name is Raymond Camden and I am looking for work!

I've had 3 total jobs.

Portfolio

- https://www.raymondcamden.com
- https://codabreaker.rocks

| New site for portfolio | Add Site |

Figure 11.2: The application making use of Vuex data with modules

Now you have seen yet another way to help manage your Vuex store. **Modules** provide a deeper, more complex way to organize your stores. As always, choose the method that best fits your application needs and the one you and your team are most comfortable with!

OTHER APPROACHES TO ORGANIZING YOUR VUEX STORES

While the previous two approaches should give you some good options for managing your Vuex store, there are a few other options you may wish to consider as well.

VUEX PATHIFY

Vuex Pathify (https://davestewart.github.io/vuex-pathify/) is a utility that makes it easier to access the Vuex store via a **path** API. So, for example, a store with a module called **resume** and a **state** value of **jobs** can be accessed like so: **store. get('resume/jobs')**. Basically, it creates a shortcut for reading and writing values to the store and simplifying synchronization. Fans of **XPath** will love this.

VUEX MODULE GENERATOR (VMG)

VMG is a library that adds basic **Create, Read, Update, Delete** (**CRUD**) operations to your store to save you from rewriting common logic. You can import the library's features and then add them to your **state**, **mutations**, and **actions**. Anyone who has been in web development for any amount of time is familiar with the CRUD pattern and will absolutely jump for joy at not having to write those functions again.

Check out the GitHub repository (https://github.com/abdullah/vuex-module-generator) for more details and sample applications.

VUEX ORM

Vuex ORM adds an ORM library to your Vuex store. **ORM** is short for **object-relational mapping** and is a pattern to help make object persistence simpler. Like VMG, Vuex ORM aims to simplify the rather common CRUD tasks web developers must write.

Vuex ORM lets you define classes that represent the structure of your store data. Once you have defined the structure of the data, Vuex ORM then provides utility functions to make storing and retrieving that data in the store much simpler. It even handles relationships between data, such as a **person** who has an array of **cat** objects that belong to it.

Here is an example of how you could define a type of data:

```
class Cat extends Model {
  static entity = 'cats'

  static fields () {
    return {
      id: this.attr(null),
      name: this.string(''),
      age: this.number(0),
      adoptable: this.boolean(true)
    }
  }
}
```

In the preceding class, four properties are defined for the **Cat** class: **id**, **name**, **age**, and **adoptable**. For each property, default values are specified. Once defined, asking for all the data is as simple as **Cat.all()**. There's a lot more to Vuex ORM, and you can check it out at https://vuex-orm.github.io/vuex-orm/.

ACTIVITY 11.01: SIMPLIFYING A VUEX STORE

This activity will be a bit different than the ones you have done before. In this activity, you are going to take an *existing* application making use of Vuex and apply some of the techniques you have learned in this chapter in order to simplify the store and make it easier to use in future updates. This could be most useful when needing to tweak or fix existing functionality.

Steps:

1. To begin this activity, you will use the completed example found at **Chapter11/activity11.01/initial** (https://packt.live/3kaqBHH).

2. Modify the store file to place the **state**, **getters**, and **mutations** into their own file.

3. Modify the **state** so that the **cat** values are in a **module**.

4. Migrate the cat-related **getter** to the **module**.

5. Update the **App.vue** file so that it still correctly displays the data it did initially.

   This is how it looks when built:

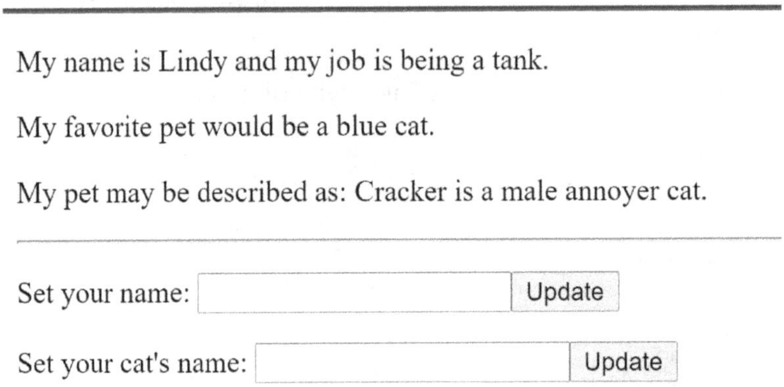

   My name is Lindy and my job is being a tank.

   My favorite pet would be a blue cat.

   My pet may be described as: Cracker is a male annoyer cat.

   Set your name: [   ] Update

   Set your cat's name: [   ] Update

Figure 11.3: Final output of the activity

NOTE

The solution to this activity can be found on page 714.

SUMMARY

In this chapter, you learned multiple different techniques to prepare your Vuex stores for growing complexity. You first learned how to move logic into separate files and include them within your store. You then learned about modules and how they are exposed to components using the store. Finally, you learned about some optional libraries that may make your Vuex use even more powerful.

In the next chapter, you are going to learn about an incredibly important aspect of development, unit testing.

12

UNIT TESTING

OVERVIEW

In this chapter, we will look at approaches to unit testing Vue.js applications in order to improve our quality and speed of delivery. We will also look at using tests to drive development using **Test-Driven Development** (**TDD**).

As we proceed, you will gain an understanding of why code needs to be tested and what kinds of testing can be employed on different parts of a Vue.js application. You will see how to unit test isolated components and their methods using shallow rendering and `vue-test-utils`, and you will learn how to test asynchronous component code. Throughout the course of the chapter, you will gain familiarity with techniques to write efficient unit tests for **mixins** and **filters**. Toward the end of the chapter, you will become familiar with approaches to testing a Vue.js applications that includes routing and Vuex, and you will learn about using snapshot tests to validate your user interface.

INTRODUCTION

In this chapter, we will look at the purpose and approaches to testing Vue.js applications effectively.

In previous chapters, we saw how to build reasonably complex Vue.js applications. This chapter is about testing them to maintain code quality and prevent defects.

Unit testing will allow us to write fast and specific tests that we can develop against and ensure that features don't exhibit unwanted behavior. We'll see how to write unit tests for different parts of a Vue.js application, such as components, mixins, filters, and routing. We will use tools supported by the Vue.js core team, such as `vue-test-utils`, and tools supported by the rest of the open source community, such as the Vue Testing library and the **Jest testing framework**. These different tools will serve to illustrate different philosophies and approaches to unit testing.

WHY WE NEED TO TEST CODE

Testing is crucial for ensuring that the code does what it's meant to do.

Quality production software is empirically correct. That means that for the enumerated cases that developers and testers have found, the application behaves as expected.

This lies in contrast with software that has *proven* to be correct, which is a very time-consuming endeavor and is usually part of academic research projects. We are still at the point where **correct software** (proven) is still being built to show what kinds of systems are possible to build with this constraint of correctness.

Testing prevents the introduction of defects such as bugs and regressions (that is, when a feature stops working as expected). In the next section, we will learn about the various types of testing.

UNDERSTANDING DIFFERENT TYPES OF TESTING

The testing spectrum spans from end-to-end testing (by manipulating the user interface) to integration tests, and finally to unit tests. End-to-end tests test everything, including the user interface, the underlying HTTP services, and even database interactions; nothing is mocked. For example, if you've got an e-commerce application, an end-to-end test might actually place a real order with a real credit card, or it might place a test order, with a test credit card.

End-to-end tests are costly to run and maintain. They require the use of full-blown browsers controlled through programmatic drivers such as **Selenium**, **WebdriverIO**, or **Cypress**. This type of test platform is costly to run, and small changes in the application code can cause end-to-end tests to start failing.

Integration or system-level tests ensure that a set of systems is working as expected. This will usually involve deciding on a limit as to where the **system under test** lies and allowing it to run, usually against mocked or stubbed upstream services and systems (which are therefore not under test). Since external data access is stubbed, a whole host of issues, such as timeouts and flakes, can be reduced (when compared to end-to-end tests). Integration test suites are usually fast enough to run as a continuous integration step, but the full test suite tends not to be run locally by engineers.

Unit tests are great at providing fast feedback during development. Unit testing paired with TDD is part of extreme programming practice. Unit tests are great at testing complicated logic or building a system from its expected output. Unit tests are usually fast enough to run that developers code against them before sending their code for review and continuous integration tests.

The following is an interpretation of the pyramid of testing. It can be interpreted as: you should have a high number of cheap and fast unit tests, a reasonable number of system tests, and a few end-to-end UI tests:

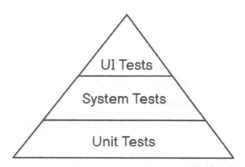

Figure 12.1: Pyramid of testing diagram

Now that we've looked at why we should be testing applications, let's start writing some tests.

YOUR FIRST TEST

To illustrate how quick and easy it is to get started with automated unit tests in a Vue CLI project, we will start by setting up and writing a unit test with Jest, @**vue-test-utils**. There is an official Vue CLI package that can be used to generate a setup that includes unit testing with Jest and **vue-test-utils**. The following command should be run in a project that has been set up with Vue CLI:

```
vue add @vue/unit-jest
```

Vue CLI adds Jest as the test runner, @**vue/test-utils**, the official **Vue.js** testing utilities, and **vue-jest**, a processor for .**vue** single-file component files in Jest. It adds a **test:unit** script.

By default, it creates a **tests/unit** folder, which we'll remove. Instead, we can create a **__tests__** folder and create an **App.test.js** file as follows.

We will use **shallowMount** to render the application and test that it displays the correct text. For the purposes of this example, we'll use the text: "**The Vue.js Workshop Blog**".

shallowMount does a **shallow render**, which means that only the top level of a component is rendered; all the child components are stubbed. This is useful for testing a component in isolation since the child components' implementations are not run:

```
import { shallowMount } from '@vue/test-utils'
import App from '../src/App.vue'

test('App renders blog title correctly', () => {
  const wrapper = shallowMount(App)
  expect(wrapper.text()).toMatch("The Vue.js Workshop Blog")
})
```

This test will fail when we run **npm run test:unit** because we do not have **The Vue.js Workshop Blog** in the **App** component:

```
) npm run test:unit --silent
 FAIL  __tests__/App.test.js
  × App renders blog title correctly (21ms)

  ● App renders blog title correctly

    expect(received).toMatch(expected)

    Expected substring: "The Vue.js Workshop Blog"
    Received string:    ""

      4 | test('App renders blog title correctly', () => {
      5 |   const wrapper = shallowMount(App)
    > 6 |   expect(wrapper.text()).toMatch(The Vue.js Workshop Blog )
        |                          ^
      7 | })
      8 |

      at Object.<anonymous> (__tests__/App.test.js:6:26)

Test Suites: 1 failed, 1 total
Tests:       1 failed, 1 total
Snapshots:   0 total
Time:
Ran all test suites.
```

Figure 12.2: Blog title heading failing the test at the command line

In order to get the test to pass, we can implement our blog title heading in the **App.vue** file:

```
<template>
  <div id="app" class="p-10">
    <div class="flex flex-col">
      <h2
        class="leading-loose pb-4 flex justify-center m-auto
          md:w-1/3 text-xl mb-8 font-bold text-gray-800 border-b"
      >
      The Vue.js Workshop Blog
      </h2>
    </div>
  </div>
</template>
```

Now that we have got the right heading, **npm run test:unit** will pass:

```
> npm run test:unit App --silent
PASS  __tests__/App.test.js
  ✓ App renders blog title correctly (26ms)

Test Suites: 1 passed, 1 total
Tests:       1 passed, 1 total
Snapshots:   0 total
Time:        2.097s
Ran all test suites matching /App/i.
```

Figure 12.3: Blog heading test passing

We can also check that it renders as expected in the browser:

```
The Vue.js Workshop Blog
```

You have just completed your first piece of TDD. This process started by writing a test that failed. This failure was followed by an update to the code under test (in this case the **App.vue** component), which made the failing test pass. The TDD process gives us confidence that our features have been tested properly since we can see that tests fail before they pass when we update the code that drives our feature.

TESTING COMPONENTS

Components are at the core of Vue.js applications. Writing unit tests for them is straightforward with **vue-test-utils** and Jest. Having tests that exercise the majority of your components gives you confidence that they behave as designed. Ideal unit tests for components run quickly and are simple.

We'll carry on building the blog application example. We have now built the heading, but a blog usually also needs a list of posts to display.

We'll create a **PostList** component. For now, it will just render a **div** wrapper and support a **posts Array** prop:

```
<template>
  <div class="flex flex-col w-full">
  </div>
</template>
<script>
export default {
  props: {
    posts: {
```

```
      type: Array,
      default: () => []
    }
  }
}
</script>
```

We can add some data in the **App** component:

```
<script>
export default {
  data() {
    return {
      posts: [
        {
          title: 'Vue.js for React developers',
          description: 'React has massive popularity here are the
            key benefits of Vue.js over it.',
          tags: ['vue', 'react'],
        },
        {
          title: 'Migrating an AngularJS app to Vue.js',
          description: 'With many breaking changes, AngularJS developers
            have found it easier to retrain to Vue.js than Angular 2',
          tags: ['vue', 'angularjs']
        }
      ]
    }
  }
}
</script>
```

Now that we have some posts, we can pass them as a bound prop to the **PostList** component from the **App** component:

```
<template>
  <!-- rest of template -->
      <PostList :posts="posts" />
  <!-- rest of template -->
</template>

<script>
```

```
import PostList from './components/PostList.vue'

export default {
  components: {
    PostList
  },
  // rest of component properties
}
```

Our **PostList** component will render out each post in a **PostListItem** component, which we'll create as follows.

PostListItem takes two props: **title** (which is a string) and **description** (also a string). It renders them in an **h3** tag and a **p** tag, respectively:

```
<template>
  <div class="flex flex-col m-auto w-full md:w-3/5 lg:w-2/5 mb-4">
    <h3 class="flex text-md font-semibold text-gray-700">
      {{ title }}</h3>
    <p class="flex leading-relaxed">{{ description }}</p>
  </div>
</template>
<script>
export default {
  props: {
    title: {
      type: String
    },
    description: {
      type: String
    }
  }
}
</script>
```

We now need to loop through the posts and render out a **PostListItem** component with relevant props bound in the **PostList.vue** component:

```
<template>
  !-- rest of template -->
    <PostListItem
      v-for="post in posts"
      :key="post.slug"
```

```
      :title="post.title"
      :description="post.description"
    />
  <!-- rest of template -->
</template>
<script>
import PostListItem from './PostListItem.vue'

export default {
  components: {
    PostListItem,
  },
  // rest of component properties
}
</script>
```

We can now see the heading and the post list in the application:

```
The Vue.js Workshop blog
```

To test the **PostListItem** component, we can shallow render with some arbitrary **title** and **description** props set, and check that they get rendered:

```
import { shallowMount } from '@vue/test-utils'
import PostListItem from '../src/components/PostListItem.vue'

test('PostListItem renders title and description correctly',
  () => {
  const wrapper = shallowMount(PostListItem, {
    propsData: {
      title: 'Blog post title',
      description: 'Blog post description'
    }
  })
  expect(wrapper.text()).toMatch("Blog post title")
  expect(wrapper.text()).toMatch("Blog post description")
})
```

The test output of **npm run test:unit __tests__/PostListItem.test. js** is as follows; the component passes the test:

```
> npm run test:unit __tests__/PostListItem.test.js --silent
PASS __tests__/PostListItem.test.js
  ✓ PostListItem renders title and description correctly (17ms)


Test Suites: 1 passed, 1 total
Tests:       1 passed, 1 total
Snapshots:   0 total
Time:        1.633s, estimated 2s
Ran all test suites matching /__tests__\/PostListItem.test.js/i.
```

Figure 12.4: PostListItem test output

Next, we'll see one of the pitfalls of shallow rendering. When testing the **PostList** component, all we can do is test the number of **PostListItem** components it's rendering:

```
import { shallowMount } from '@vue/test-utils'
import PostList from '../src/components/PostList.vue'
import PostListItem from '../src/components/PostListItem.vue'


test('PostList renders the right number of PostListItem',
  () => {
  const wrapper = shallowMount(PostList, {
    propsData: {
      posts: [
        {
          title: "Blog post title",
          description: "Blog post description"
        }
      ]
    }
  })
  expect(wrapper.findAll(PostListItem)).toHaveLength(1)
})
```

This passes, but we are testing something that the user will not directly interact with, the number of **PostListItem** instances rendered in **PostList**, as shown in the following screenshot:

```
) npm run test:unit __tests__/PostListItem.test.js --silent
 PASS  __tests__/PostListItem.test.js
  ✓ PostListItem renders title and description correctly (17ms)


Test Suites: 1 passed, 1 total
Tests:       1 passed, 1 total
Snapshots:   0 total
Time:        1.633s, estimated 2s
Ran all test suites matching /__tests__\/PostListItem.test.js/i.
```

Figure 12.5: PostList test output

A better solution is to use the **mount** function, which renders the full component tree, whereas the **shallow** function would only render out the children of the component being rendered. With **mount**, we can assert that the titles and descriptions are rendered to the page.

The drawback of this approach is that we're testing both the **PostList** component and the **PostListItem** component since the **PostList** component doesn't render the title or description; it renders a set of **PostListItem** components that in turn render the relevant title and description.

The code will be as follows:

```
import { shallowMount, mount } from '@vue/test-utils'
import PostList from '../src/components/PostList.vue'
// other imports and tests


test('PostList renders passed title and description for each
  passed post', () => {
  const wrapper = mount(PostList, {
    propsData: {
      posts: [
        {
          title: 'Title 1',
          description: 'Description 1'
        },
        {
          title: 'Title 2',
          description: 'Description 2'
        }
      ]
    }
```

```
  })
  const outputText = wrapper.text()
  expect(outputText).toContain('Title 1')
  expect(outputText).toContain('Description 1')
  expect(outputText).toContain('Title 2')
  expect(outputText).toContain('Description 2')
})
```

The new tests pass as per the following output of **npm run test:unit __ tests__/PostList.vue**:

```
> npm run test:unit __tests__/PostList.test.js --silent
 PASS  __tests__/PostList.test.js
  ✓ PostList renders the right number of PostListItem (18ms)
  ✓ PostList renders passed title and description for each passed post (8ms)


Test Suites:  1 passed, 1 total
Tests:        2 passed, 2 total
Snapshots:    0 total
Time:         3.405s
Ran all test suites matching /__tests__\/PostList.test.js/i.
```

Figure 12.6: Test run for PostList with both shallow and mounted tests

We have now seen how to write unit tests for Vue.js components using Jest and **vue-test-utils**. These tests can be run often, and test runs complete within seconds, which gives us near-immediate feedback while working on new or existing components.

EXERCISE 12.01: BUILDING AND UNIT TESTING A TAG LIST COMPONENT

When creating the fixture for **posts**, we populated a **tags** field with **vue**, **angularjs**, and **react** but did not display them. To make tags useful, we will display the tags in the post list.

To access the code files for this exercise, refer to https://packt.live/2HiTFQ1:

1. We can start by writing a unit test that will explain what we expect a **PostListItem** component to do when passed a set of tags as props. It expects that each tag will be rendered with a hashtag prepended to it; for example, the **react** tag will be shown as **#react**. In the **__tests__/PostListItem. test.js** file, we can add a new **test**:

```
// rest of tests and imports
test('PostListItem renders tags with a # prepended to
  them', () => {
```

```
  const wrapper = shallowMount(PostListItem, {
    propsData: {
      tags: ['react', 'vue']
    }
  })
  expect(wrapper.text()).toMatch('#react')
  expect(wrapper.text()).toMatch('#vue')
})
```

This test fails when run with **npm run test:unit __tests__/ PostListItem.test.js**:

```
> npm run test:unit __tests__/PostListItem.test.js --silent
FAIL __tests__/PostListItem.test.js
  ✓ PostListItem renders title and description correctly (20ms)
  ✗ PostListItem renders tags with a # prepended to them (7ms)

  ● PostListItem renders tags with a # prepended to them

    expect(received).toMatch(expected)

    Expected substring: "#react"
    Received string:    ""

      19 |     }
      20 |   })
    > 21 |     expect(wrapper.text()).toMatch(         )
         |                            ^
      22 |     expect(wrapper.text()).toMatch('#vue')
      23 | })
      24 |

      at Object.<anonymous> (__tests__/PostListItem.test.js:21:26)

Test Suites: 1 failed, 1 total
Tests:       1 failed, 1 passed, 2 total
Snapshots:   0 total
Time:        3.402s
Ran all test suites matching /__tests__\/PostListItem.test.js/i.
```

Figure 12.7: Tag test for PostListItem failing

2. Next, we should implement the tag list rendering in **src/components/
   PostListItem.vue**. We'll add tags as props of the **Array** type and use
   v-for to render out the tags:

```
<template>
    <!-- rest of template -->
    <div class="flex flex-row flex-wrap mt-4">
      <a
        v-for="tag in tags"
        :key="tag"
        class="flex text-xs font-semibold px-2 py-1 mr-2
          rounded border border-blue-500 text-blue-500"
      >
        #{{ tag }}
      </a>
    </div>
    <!-- rest of template -->
</template>
<script>
export default {
  props: {
    // rest of props
    tags: {
      type: Array,
      default: () => []
    }
  }
}
</script>
```

With the **PostListItem** component implemented, the unit test should
now pass:

```
> npm run test:unit __tests__/PostListItem.test.js --silent
 PASS  __tests__/PostListItem.test.js
  ✓ PostListItem renders title and description correctly (18ms)
  ✓ PostListItem renders tags with a # prepended to them (6ms)

Test Suites: 1 passed, 1 total
Tests:       2 passed, 2 total
Snapshots:   0 total
Time:
Ran all test suites matching /__tests__\/PostListItem.test.js/i.
```

Figure 12.8: PostListItem unit test passing

However, the tags are not displayed in the application:

The Vue.js Workshop blog

Vue.js for React developers
React has massive popularity here are the key benefits of
Vue.js over it.

Migrating an AngularJS app to Vue.js
With many breaking changes, AngularJS developers have found
it easier to retrain to Vue.js than Angular 2

Figure 12.9: PostList displaying without tags despite
the correct PostListItem implementation

3. We can write a unit test for **PostList** that would show this behavior. In
    essence, we'll be passing some tags in our **posts** list and running the same
    assertions as are already present in the **PostListItem.test.js** file. We'll do
    this in **__tests__/PostList.test.js**:

```
// rest of tests and imports
test('PostList renders tags for each post', () => {
  const wrapper = mount(PostList, {
    propsData: {
      posts: [
        {
          tags: ['react', 'vue']
        },
        {
          tags: ['html', 'angularjs']
        }
      ]
    }
  })
  const outputText = wrapper.text()
  expect(outputText).toContain('#react')
  expect(outputText).toContain('#vue')
  expect(outputText).toContain('#html')
  expect(outputText).toContain('#angularjs')
})
```

As per our application output, the test is failing when run with **npm run test:unit __tests__/PostList.test.js**:

```
> npm run test:unit __tests__/PostList.test.js --silent
 FAIL   __tests__/PostList.test.js
  ✓ PostList renders the right number of PostListItem (22ms)
  ✓ PostList renders passed title and description for each passed post (8ms)
  ✗ PostList renders tags for each post (8ms)

  ● PostList renders tags for each post

    expect(received).toContain(expected) // indexOf

    Expected substring: "#react"
    Received string:    ""

      53 |    })
      54 |    const outputText = wrapper.text()
    > 55 |    expect(outputText).toContain(       )
         |                       ^
      56 |    expect(outputText).toContain('#vue')
      57 |    expect(outputText).toContain('#html')
      58 |    expect(outputText).toContain('#angularjs')

      at Object.<anonymous> (__tests__/PostList.test.js:55:22)

Test Suites: 1 failed, 1 total
Tests:       1 failed, 2 passed, 3 total
Snapshots:   0 total
Time:        4.27s
Ran all test suites matching /__tests__\/PostList.test.js/i.
```

Figure 12.10: PostList tags test failing

4. In order to fix this test, we can find the issue in **src/components/ PostList.vue**, where the **tags** prop for **PostListItem** is not bound. By updating **src/components/PostList.vue** to bind the **tags** prop, we can fix the unit test:

```
<template>
  <!-- rest of template-->
    <PostListItem
      v-for="post in posts"
      :key="post.slug"
      :title="post.title"
      :description="post.description"
```

```
        :tags="post.tags"
    />
  <!-- rest of template -->
</template>
```

The failing unit test now passes, as shown in the following screenshot:

```
) npm run test:unit __tests__/PostList.test.js --silent
PASS  __tests__/PostList.test.js
  ✓ PostList renders the right number of PostListItem (24ms)
  ✓ PostList renders passed title and description for each passed post (9ms)
  ✓ PostList renders tags for each post (8ms)

Test Suites: 1 passed, 1 total
Tests:       3 passed, 3 total
Snapshots:   0 total
Time:        2.929s, estimated 3s
Ran all test suites matching /__tests__\/PostList.test.js/i.
```

Figure 12.11: PostList tags test passing

The tags also appear in the application, as shown in the following screenshot:

The Vue.js Workshop Blog

Vue.js for React developers
React has massive popularity here are the key benefits of
Vue.js over it.

Migrating an AngularJS app to Vue.js
With many breaking changes, AngularJS developers have found
it easier to retrain to Vue.js than Angular 2

Figure 12.12: Blog list rendering with tags

We have now seen how we can test rendered component output with both the shallow rendering and mounting of components. Let's briefly understand what each of these terms means:

- **Shallow rendering**: This renders at a depth of 1, meaning that if children are components, they will just be rendered as the component tag; their template will not be run.

- **Mounting**: This renders the full component tree in a similar fashion as would be rendered in the browser.

Next, we'll look at how to test component methods.

TESTING METHODS, FILTERS AND MIXINS

Since **filters** and **mixins** generate their output based solely on function parameters, they are straightforward to unit test. It is not recommended to test methods unless it's strictly necessary since the user doesn't call methods on the component directly. The users see the rendered UI, and their interactions with the application are manifested as events (for example, `click`, `input change`, `focus change`, and `scroll`).

For example, a filter that truncates its input to eight characters would be implemented as follows:

```
<script>
export default {
  filters: {
    truncate(value) {
      return value && value.slice(0, 8)
    }
  }
}
</script>
```

There are two options to test it. We could test it directly by importing the component and calling **truncate** on some input, as per the **truncate.test.js** file:

```
import PostListItem from '../src/components/PostListItem.vue'

test('truncate should take only the first 8 characters', () => {
  expect(
    PostListItem.filters.truncate('longer than 8 characters')
  ).toEqual('longer t')
})
```

The alternative is to check where it's being used in the **PostListItem** component:

```
<template>
  <!-- rest of template -->
    <h3 class="flex text-md font-semibold text-gray-700">
      {{ title | truncate }}
    </h3>
  <!-- rest of template -->
</template>
```

Now we can test **truncate** by checking what happens when we pass a long title into the **PostListItem** component in the **PostListItem.test.js** file, which we do in the following test:

```
// imports
test('PostListItem renders title and description correctly',
  () => {
  const wrapper = shallowMount(PostListItem, {
    propsData: {
      title: 'Blog post title',
      description: 'Blog post description'
    }
  })
  expect(wrapper.text()).toMatch("Blog post title")
  expect(wrapper.text()).toMatch("Blog post description")
})
// other tests
```

The preceding code will generate the output shown in the following screenshot:

```
> npm run test:unit __tests__/PostListItem.test.js --silent
FAIL __tests__/PostListItem.test.js
  × PostListItem renders title and description correctly (30ms)
  ✓ PostListItem renders tags with a # prepended to them (7ms)

  ● PostListItem renders title and description correctly

    expect(received).toMatch(expected)

    Expected substring: "Blog post title"
    Received string:    "Blog pos
      Blog post description"

       9 |      }
      10 |    })
    > 11 |    expect(wrapper text()) toMatch(               )
         |                                   ^
      12 |    expect(wrapper text()) toMatch("Blog post description")
      13 | })
      14 |

    at Object.<anonymous> (__tests__/PostListItem.test.js:11:26)

Test Suites: 1 failed, 1 total
Tests:       1 failed, 1 passed, 2 total
Snapshots:   0 total
Time:        3s
Ran all test suites matching /__tests__\/PostListItem.test.js/i.
```

Figure 12.13: PostListItem test for the title failing because
the content of the title is truncated

To fix this, we could update the failing test to expect **Blog pos** instead of **Blog post title**.

These two approaches are great for testing filters. As we saw before with **mount** versus **shallow** rendering, the difference is in the **tightness** of the unit test. The tighter unit test is the direct **filters.truncate()** test since it directly accesses the **truncate** filter. The looser unit test is the test using passed props and validating the component output. A tighter unit will usually mean tests are simpler, but it comes at the cost of sometimes testing functionality in a fashion that is very removed from how the end user perceives it. For example, the user would never call **filters. truncate()** directly.

We have seen how to test an arbitrary **truncate** filter. We will now implement an **ellipsis** filter and test it.

The **ellipsis** filter will be applied to the post description and will limit its length to **40** characters plus ....

EXERCISE 12.02: BUILDING AND TESTING AN ELLIPSIS FILTER

We have seen how to test an arbitrary **truncate** filter; we will now implement an **ellipsis** filter and test it.

To access the code files for this exercise, refer to https://packt.live/2UK9Mcs.

Now let's look at the steps to build and test an **ellipsis** filter:

1. We can start by writing a set of tests for the **ellipsis** filter (which will live in **src/components/PostListItem.vue**). One test should check that the filter does nothing if the passed value is less than **50** characters; another should check that if the passed value is more than **50** characters, it truncates to **50** and appends .... We will do this in a **__tests__/ellipsis.test.js** file:

```
import PostListItem from '../src/components/PostListItem.vue'


test('ellipsis should do nothing if value is less than 50
  characters', () => {
  expect(
    PostListItem.filters.ellipsis('Less than 50 characters')
  ).toEqual('Less than 50 characters')
})


test('ellipsis should truncate to 50 and append "..." when
  longer than 50 characters', () => {
  expect(
    PostListItem.filters.ellipsis(
      'Should be more than the 50 allowed characters by a
        small amount'
    )
  ).toEqual('Should be more than the 50 allowed characters by
    a...')
})
```

2. We can now implement the logic for **ellipsis** in **src/components/PostListItem.vue**. We will add a **filters** object with **ellipsis**, which will use **String#slice** if the passed value is longer than **50** characters and do nothing otherwise:

```
<script>
export default {
  // rest of component properties
  filters: {
    ellipsis(value) {
      return value && value.length > 50
        ? `${value.slice(0, 50)}...`
        : value
    }
  }
}
</script>
```

In this case, the test now passes **npm run test:unit __tests__/ellipsis.test.js**, as shown in *Figure 12.14*:

```
> npm run test:unit __tests__/ellipsis.test.js --silent
 PASS  __tests__/ellipsis.test.js
  ✓ ellipsis should do nothing if value is less than 50 characters (4ms)
  ✓ ellipsis should truncate to 50 and append "..." when longer than 50 characters

Test Suites: 1 passed, 1 total
Tests:       2 passed, 2 total
Snapshots:   0 total
Time:        1.503s
Ran all test suites matching /__tests__\/ellipsis.test.js/i.
```

Figure 12.14: The ellipsis filter unit test passing

3. We now need to integrate our **ellipsis** filter into the component. To check whether this will work, we can first write the test in **__tests__/PostListItem.test.js**:

```
// other tests and imports

test('PostListItem truncates long descriptions', () => {
  const wrapper = shallowMount(PostListItem, {
    propsData: {
      description: 'Very long blog post description that goes
        over 50 characters'
```

```
      }
    })
    expect(wrapper.text()).toMatch("Very long blog post description
      that goes over 50 ...")
  })
```

This test fails since we don't use the filter in the component template. The output will be as follows:

```
> npm run test:unit __tests__/PostListItem.test.js --silent
 FAIL  __tests__/PostListItem.test.js
  ✓ PostListItem renders title and description correctly (21ms)
  ✓ PostListItem renders tags with a # prepended to them (5ms)
  ✗ PostListItem truncates long descriptions (7ms)

  ● PostListItem truncates long descriptions

    expect(received).toMatch(expected)

    Expected substring: "Very long blog post description that goes over 50 ..."
    Received string:    "Very long blog post description that goes over 50 characters"

    29 |     }
    30 |   })
  > 31 |   expect(wrapper text()) toMatch(                                    )
       |                          ^
    32 | })
    33 |

    at Object.<anonymous> (__tests__/PostListItem.test.js:31:26)

Test Suites: 1 failed, 1 total
Tests:       1 failed, 2 passed, 3 total
Snapshots:   0 total
Time:        2.093s, estimated 3s
Ran all test suites matching /__tests__\/PostListItem.test.js/i.
```

Figure 12.15: PostListItem ellipsis test failing

4. To get the test to pass, we need to pipe the **description** property into the **ellipsis** filter in **src/components/PostListItem.vue**:

```
<template>
  <!-- rest of template -->
    <p class="flex leading-relaxed">{{ description | ellipsis }}
      </p>
  <!-- rest of template -->
</template>
```

Now, the test will pass, as displayed in the following screenshot:

```
> npm run test:unit __tests__/ellipsis.test.js --silent
PASS  __tests__/ellipsis.test.js
  ✓ ellipsis should do nothing if value is less than 50 characters (4ms)
  ✓ ellipsis should truncate to 50 and append "..." when longer than 50 characters

Test Suites: 1 passed, 1 total
Tests:       2 passed, 2 total
Snapshots:   0 total
Time:        1.503s
Ran all test suites matching /__tests__\/ellipsis.test.js/i.
```

Figure 12.16: PostListItem ellipsis test passing

We can see the descriptions being truncated in the application interface in the browser, as follows:

The Vue.js Workshop Blog

Vue.js for React developers
React has massive popularity here are the key bene...

#vue   #react

Migrating an AngularJS app to Vue.js
With many breaking changes, AngularJS developers h...

#vue   #angularjs

Figure 12.17: Blog post item descriptions being truncated to 50 characters

We have now seen how to test filters and other properties of a Vue.js component not only by testing directly against the object but also by testing the functionality where it is being used in component-level tests.

Next, we will see how to deal with an application that uses Vue.js routing.

TESTING VUE ROUTING

We have currently got an application that renders what is our blog home page or **feed view**.

Next, we should have post pages. To do this, we will use Vue Router, as covered in previous chapters, and ensure that our routing works as designed with unit tests.

Vue Router is installed using **npm**, specifically, **npm install vue-router**, and wiring it up in the **main.js** file:

```
// other imports
import router from './router'
// other imports and configuration
new Vue({
  render: h => h(App),
  router,
}).$mount('#app')
```

The **router.js** file registers **vue-router** with Vue using **Vue.use** and instantiates a **VueRouter** instance:

```
import Vue from 'vue'
import VueRouter from 'vue-router'

Vue.use(VueRouter)

export default new VueRouter({})
```

A router with no routes isn't very useful. We'll define the root path (**/**) to display the **PostList** component in the **router.js** file, as follows:

```
// other imports
import PostList from './components/PostList.vue'
// registering of Vue router
const routes = [
  {
    path: '/',
    component: PostList
  }
]
export default new VueRouter({
  routes
})
```

Now that we've got our initial route, we should update the **App.vue** file to leverage the component being rendered by the router. We'll render **render-view** instead of directly using **PostList**. The **posts** binding, however, stays the same:

```
<template>
  <!-- rest of template -->
      <router-view
        :posts="posts"
      />
  <!-- rest of template -->
</template>
```

Now, our posts in the **App.vue** file are missing a bit of core data to render a **SinglePost** component. We need to make sure to have the **slug** and **content** properties to render something useful on our **SinglePost** page:

```
<script>
export default {
  data() {
    return {
      posts: [
        {
          slug: 'vue-react',
          title: 'Vue.js for React developers',
          description: 'React has massive popularity here are the
            key benefits of Vue.js over it.',
          content:
            'React has massive popularity here are the key benefits
              of Vue.js over it.
            See the following table, we'll also look at how the is
              the content of the post.

            There's more, we can map React concepts to Vue and
              vice-versa.',
          tags: ['vue', 'react'],
        },
        {
          slug: 'vue-angularjs',
          title: 'Migrating an AngularJS app to Vue.js',
          description: 'With many breaking changes, AngularJS developers
            have found it easier to retrain to Vue.js than Angular 2',
          content:
            'With many breaking changes, AngularJS developers have
              found it easier to retrain to Vue.js than Angular 2
```

```
          Vue.js keeps the directive-driven templating style while
            adding a component model.

          It's performant thanks to a great reactivity engine.',
          tags: ['vue', 'angularjs']
        }
      ]
    }
  }
}
</script>
```

We can now start working on a **SinglePost** component. For now, we'll just have some placeholders in the template. Also, **SinglePost** will receive **posts** as a prop, so we can fill that in as well:

```
<template>
  <div class="flex flex-col w-full md:w-1/2 m-auto">
    <h2
      class="font-semibold text-sm mb-4"
    >
      Post: RENDER ME
    </h2>
    <p>Placeholder for post.content</p>
  </div>
</template>
<script>
export default {
  props: {
    posts: {
      type: Array,
      default: () => []
    }
  }
}
</script>
```

Next, we will register **SinglePost** in **router.js**, with the **/:postId** path (which will be available to the component under **this.$route.params.postId**):

```
// other imports
import SinglePost from './components/SinglePost.vue'
// vue router registration

const routes = [
  // other route
  {
    path: '/:postId',
    component: SinglePost
  }
]
// exports and router instantiation
```

If we switch back to implementing the **SinglePost** component, we've got access to **postId**, which will map to the slug in the **posts** array, and we've also got access to **posts** since it's being bound onto **render-view** by **App**. Now we can create a computed property, **post**, which finds posts based on **postId**:

```
<script>
export default {
  // other properties
  computed: {
    post() {
      const { postId } = this.$route.params
      return posts.find(p => p.slug === postId)
    }
  }
}
</script>
```

From this computed **post** property, we can extract **title** and **content** if **post** exists (we have to watch out for posts that don't exist). So, still in **SinglePost**, we can add the following computed properties:

```
<script>
export default {
  // other properties
  computed: {
    // other computed properties
```

```
    title() {
      return this.post && this.post.title
    },
    content() {
      return this.post && this.post.content
    }
  }
}
</script>
```

We can then replace the placeholders in the template with the value of the computed properties. So, our template ends up as follows:

```
<template>
  <div class="flex flex-col w-full md:w-1/2 m-auto">
    <h2
      class="font-semibold text-sm mb-4"
    >
      Post: {{ title }}
    </h2>
    <p>{{ content }}</p>
  </div>
</template>
```

Finally, we should make the whole post item a **router-link** that points to the right slug in the **PostListItem.vue** file:

```
<template>
  <router-link
    class="flex flex-col m-auto w-full md:w-3/5 lg:w-2/5 mb-4"
    :to="`/${slug}`"
  >
    <!-- rest of the template -->
  </router-link>
</template>
```

router-link is a Vue Router-specific link, which means that on the **PostList** page, upon clicking on a post list item, we are taken to the correct post's URL, as shown in the following screenshot:

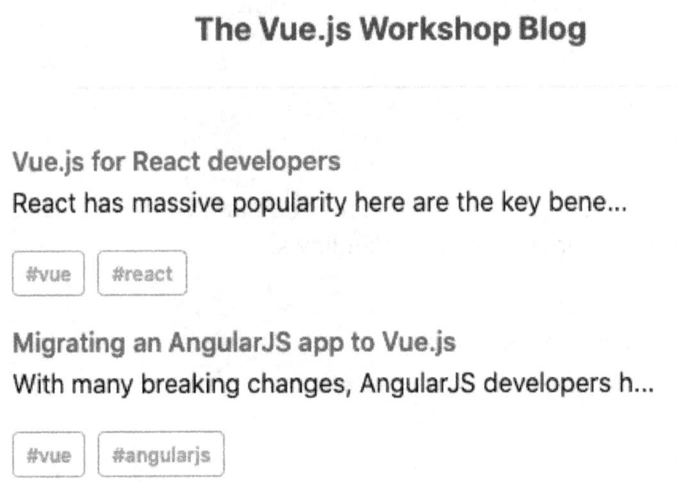

The Vue.js Workshop Blog
Vue.js for React developers
React has massive popularity here are the key bene...
#vue
#react
Migrating an AngularJS app to Vue.js
With many breaking changes, AngularJS developers h...
#vue
#angularjs

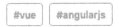

Figure 12.18: Post list view displayed in the browser

We'll be redirected to the correct URL, the post's slug, which will render the right post by **slug**, as shown in *Figure 12.19*.

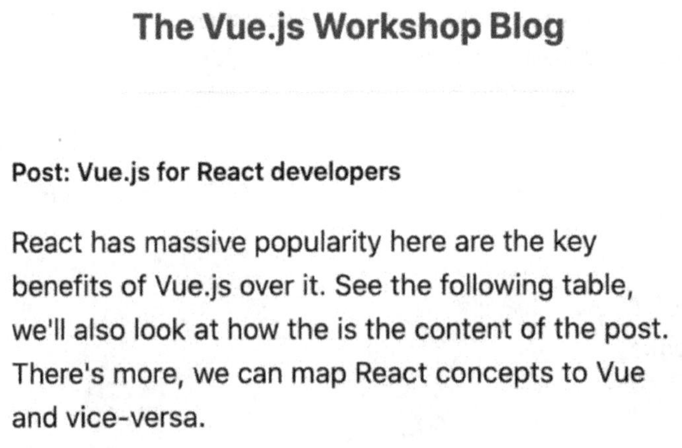

The Vue.js Workshop Blog
Post: Vue.js for React developers
React has massive popularity here are the key benefits of Vue.js over it. See the following table, we'll also look at how the is the content of the post. There's more, we can map React concepts to Vue and vice-versa.

Figure 12.19: Single post view displaying in the browser

To test **vue-router**, we will explore a new library that's better suited to testing applications with routing and a Vuex store, the Vue Testing library, which is accessible on **npm** as **@testing-library/vue**.

We can install it with **npm install --save-dev @testing-library/vue**.

To test **SinglePost** routing and rendering, we do the following. First of all, we should be able to access the **SinglePost** view by clicking on a post title in the **PostList** view. In order to do this, we check that we're on the home page by examining the content (we'll see two posts with the titles). Then we'll click a post title and check that the content from the home page is gone and the post content is displayed:

```
import {render, fireEvent} from '@testing-library/vue'
import App from '../src/App.vue'
import router from '../src/router.js'


test('Router renders single post page when clicking a post title',
    async () => {
    const {getByText, queryByText} = render(App, { router })
    expect(queryByText('The Vue.js Workshop Blog')).toBeTruthy()
    expect(queryByText('Vue.js for React developers')).toBeTruthy()
    expect(queryByText('Migrating an AngularJS app to Vue.js')).
        toBeTruthy()

    await fireEvent.click(getByText('Vue.js for React developers'))
    expect(queryByText('Migrating an AngularJS app to Vue.js')).
        toBeFalsy()
    expect(queryByText('Post: Vue.js for React developers')).
        toBeTruthy()
    expect(
        queryByText(
            'React has massive popularity here are the key benefits of
                Vue.js over it. See the following table, we'll also look at
                how the is the content of the post. There's more, we can
                map React concepts to Vue and vice-versa.'
        )
    ).toBeTruthy()
})
```

We should check that navigating directly to a valid post URL will yield the correct result. In order to do this, we'll use **router.replace('/')** to clear any state that's set, and then use **router.push()** with a post slug. We will then use the assertions from the previous code snippet to validate that we are on the **SinglePost** page, not the home page:

```
test('Router renders single post page when a slug is set',
  async () => {
  const {queryByText} = render(App, { router })
  await router.replace('/')
  await router.push('/vue-react')
  expect(queryByText('Migrating an AngularJS app to Vue.js')).
    toBeFalsy()
  expect(queryByText('Post: Vue.js for React developers')).
    toBeTruthy()
  expect(
    queryByText(
      'React has massive popularity here are the key benefits of
        Vue.js over it. See the following table, we'll also look at
        how the is the content of the post. There's more, we can map
        React concepts to Vue and vice-versa.'
    )
  ).toBeTruthy()
})
```

Those two tests work as expected when run with **npm run test:unit __tests__/SinglePost.test.js**. The following screenshot displays the desired output:

```
> npm run test:unit __tests__/SinglePost.test.js --silent
PASS  __tests__/SinglePost.test.js
  ✓ Router renders single post page when clicking a post title (66ms)
  ✓ Router renders single post page when a slug is set (36ms)

Test Suites: 1 passed, 1 total
Tests:       2 passed, 2 total
Snapshots:   0 total
Time:        2.203s
Ran all test suites matching /__tests__\/SinglePost.test.js/i.
```

Figure 12.20: Routing tests passing for SinglePost

We have now seen how to use the Vue.js Testing library to test an application that uses **vue-router**.

EXERCISE 12.03: BUILDING A TAG PAGE AND TESTING ITS ROUTING

Much like we have built a single-post page, we'll now build a tag page, which is similar to the **PostList** component except only posts with a certain tag are displayed and each post is a link to a relevant single-post view.

To access the code files for this exercise, refer to https://packt.live/39cJqZd:

1. We can start by creating a new **TagPage** component in **src/components/ TagPage.vue**. We know it will receive **posts** as a prop and that we will want to render a **PostList** component:

```
<template>
  <div class="flex flex-col md:w-1/2 m-auto">
    <h3
    class="font-semibold text-sm text-center mb-6"
    >
      #INSERT_TAG_NAME
    </h3>
    <PostList :posts="[]" />
  </div>
</template>

<script>
import PostList from './PostList'
export default {
  components: {
    PostList
  },
  props: {
    posts: {
      type: Array,
      default: () => []
    }
  },
}
</script>
```

2. Next, we want to wire the **TagPage** component into the router in **src/ router.js**. We'll import it and add it as part of **routes** with the **/ tags/:tagName** path:

```
// other imports
import TagPage from './components/TagPage.vue'
// Vue router registration
const routes = [
  // other routes
  {
    path: '/tags/:tagName',
    component: TagPage
  }
]
// router instantiation and export
```

3. We can now use **$route.params.tagName** in a computed property and create a **tagPosts** computed property that filters posts by tag:

```
<script>
// imports
export default {
  // rest of component
  computed: {
    tagName() {
      return this.$route.params.tagName
    },
    tagPosts() {
      return this.posts.filter(p => p.tags.includes(this.tagName))
    }
  }
}
</script>
```

4. Now that we have access to **tagPosts** and **tagName**, we can replace the placeholders in the template. We will render **#{{ tagName }}** and bind **tagPosts** to the **posts** prop of **PostList**:

```
<template>
  <div class="flex flex-col md:w-1/2 m-auto">
    <h3
      class="font-semibold text-sm text-center mb-6"
```

```
    >
      #{{ tagName }}
    </h3>
    <PostList :posts="tagPosts" />
  </div>
</template>
```

Now, the page displays as follows if we navigate, for example, to **/tags/ angularjs**:

The Vue.js Workshop Blog

#angularjs

Migrating an AngularJS app to Vue.js
With many breaking changes,
AngularJS developers h...

Figure 12.21: Tag page for angularjs

5. The next step is to convert the tag anchors (**a**) in **PostListItem** to **router-link** that points to **/tags/${tagName}** (in **src/components/ PostListItem.vue**):

```
<template>
  <!-- rest of template -->
    <router-link
      :to="`/tags/${tag}`"
      v-for="tag in tags"
      :key="tag"
      class="flex text-xs font-semibold px-2 py-1 mr-2
        rounded border border-blue-500 text-blue-500"
    >
      #{{ tag }}
    </router-link>
  <!-- rest of template -->
</template>
```

6. Now it is time to write some tests. We will first check that being on the home page and clicking on **#angularjs** puts us on the **angularjs** tag page. We'll write it as follows in **__tests__/TagPage.test.js**:

```
import {render, fireEvent} from '@testing-library/vue'
import App from '../src/App.vue'
import router from '../src/router.js'

test('Router renders tag page when clicking a tag in the post
    list item', async () => {
  const {getByText, queryByText} = render(App, { router })
  expect(queryByText('The Vue.js Workshop Blog')).
    toBeTruthy()
  expect(queryByText('Vue.js for React developers')).
    toBeTruthy()
  expect(queryByText('Migrating an AngularJS app to Vue.js')).
    toBeTruthy()

  await fireEvent.click(getByText('#angularjs'))
  expect(queryByText('Migrating an AngularJS app to Vue.js')).
    toBeTruthy()
  expect(queryByText('Vue.js for React developers')).toBeFalsy()
  expect(queryByText('React')).toBeFalsy()
})
```

7. We should also test that going directly to the tag URL works as expected; that is, we do not see irrelevant content:

```
// import & other tests
test('Router renders tag page when a URL is set', async () => {
  const {queryByText} = render(App, { router })
  await router.push('/')
  await router.replace('/tags/angularjs')
  expect(queryByText('Migrating an AngularJS app to Vue.js')).
    toBeTruthy()
  expect(queryByText('Vue.js for React developers')).
    toBeFalsy()
  expect(queryByText('React')).toBeFalsy()
})
```

The tests pass since the application is working as expected. Therefore, the output will be as follows:

```
> npm run test:unit __tests__/TagPage.test.js --silent
 PASS  __tests__/TagPage.test.js
  ✓ Router renders tag page when clicking a tag in the post list item (72ms)
  ✓ Router renders tag page when a URL is set (32ms)

Test Suites: 1 passed, 1 total
Tests:       2 passed, 2 total
Snapshots:   0 total
Time:        2.441s, estimated 3s
Ran all test suites matching /__tests__\/TagPage.test.js/i.
```

Figure 12.22: TagPage routing tests passing on the command line

We've now seen how to implement and test an application that includes
vue-router. In the next section, we will learn about testing Vuex in detail.

TESTING VUEX

To show how to test a component that relies on Vuex (Vue.js's official global state
management solution), we'll implement and test a newsletter subscription banner.

To start with, we should create the banner template. The banner will contain a
Subscribe to the newsletter call to action and a close icon:

```
<template>
  <div class="text-center py-4 md:px-4">
    <div
      class="py-2 px-4 bg-indigo-800 items-center text-indigo-100
      leading-none md:rounded-full flex md:inline-flex"
      role="alert"
    >
      <span
        class="font-semibold ml-2 md:mr-2 text-left flex-auto"
      >
        Subscribe to the newsletter
      </span>
      <svg
        class="fill-current h-6 w-6 text-indigo-500"
        role="button"
        xmlns="http://www.w3.org/2000/svg"
        viewBox="0 0 20 20"
      >
        <title>Close</title>
```

```
            <path
              d="M14.348 14.849a1.2 1.2 0 0 1-1.697 0L10 11.819l-2.651
              3.029a1.2 1.2 0 1 1-1.697-1.697l2.758-3.15-2.759-3.152a1.
                2
              1.2 0 1 1 1.697-1.697L10 8.183l2.651-3.031a1.2 1.2 0 1 1
              1.697 1.697l-2.758 3.152 2.758 3.15a1.2 1.2 0 0 1 0 1.
                698z"
            />
          </svg>
        </div>
      </div>
    </div>
</template>
```

We can display the **NewsletterBanner** component in the **App.vue** file as follows:

```
<template>
  <!-- rest of template -->
    <NewsletterBanner />
  <!-- rest of template -->
</template>
<script>
import NewsletterBanner from './components/NewsletterBanner.vue'

export default {
  components: {
    NewsletterBanner
  },
  // other component properties
}
</script>
```

We'll then install Vuex with the **npm install --save vuex** command. Once Vuex is installed, we can initialize our store in a **store.js** file as follows:

```
import Vue from 'vue'
import Vuex from 'vuex'

Vue.use(Vuex)

export default new Vuex.Store({
  state: {},
  mutations: {}
})
```

Our Vuex store is also registered in the **main.js** file:

```
// other imports
import store from './store'

// other configuration

new Vue({
  // other vue options
  store
}).$mount('#app')
```

In order to decide whether the newsletter banner should be displayed or not, we need to add an initial state to our store:

```
// imports and configuration
export default new Vuex.Store({
  state: {
    dismissedSubscribeBanner: false
  }
})
```

To close the banner, we need a mutation that will set **dismissedSubscribeBanner** to **true**:

```
// imports and configuration
export default new Vuex.Store({
  // other store configuration
  mutations: {
    dismissSubscribeBanner(state) {
      state.dismissedSubscribeBanner = true
    }
  }
})
```

We can now use the store state and the **dismissSubscribeBanner** mutation to decide whether to show the banner (using **v-if**) and whether to close it (binding to a click on the **close** button):

```
<template>
  <div v-if="showBanner" class="text-center py-4 md:px-4">
    <!-- rest of template -->
      <svg
        @click="closeBanner()"
        class="fill-current h-6 w-6 text-indigo-500"
        role="button"
        xmlns=http://www.w3.org/2000/svg
        viewBox="0 0 20 20"
      >
    <!-- rest of the template -->
  </div>
</template>
<script>
export default {
  methods: {
    closeBanner() {
      this.$store.commit('dismissSubscribeBanner')
    }
  },
  computed: {
    showBanner() {
      return !this.$store.state.dismissedSubscribeBanner
    }
  }
}
</script>
```

At this point, the banner looks like this in a browser:

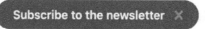

The Vue.js Workshop Blog

Vue.js for React developers
React has massive popularity here are the key bene...

`#vue`   `#react`

Migrating an AngularJS app to Vue.js
With many breaking changes, AngularJS developers h...

`#vue`   `#angularjs`

Figure 12.23: Newsletter banner displayed in a browser

To write unit tests, we will use the Vue Testing library, which provides a facility for injecting a Vuex store. We'll need to import the store and the **NewsletterBanner** component.

We can start with a sanity check that, by default, the newsletter banner is displayed:

```
import {render, fireEvent} from '@testing-library/vue'
import NewsletterBanner from '../src/components/
  NewsletterBanner.vue'
import store from '../src/store'


test('Newsletter Banner should display if store is initialised
  with it not dismissed', () => {
  const {queryByText} = render(NewsletterBanner, { store })
  expect(queryByText('Subscribe to the newsletter')).toBeTruthy()
})
```

The next check should be that if the store has **dismissedSubscribeBanner: true**, the banner should not be displayed:

```
// imports and other tests
test('Newsletter Banner should not display if store is initialised with
  it dismissed', () => {
  const {queryByText} = render(NewsletterBanner, { store: {
    state: {
```

```
      dismissedSubscribeBanner: true
    }
  } })
  expect(queryByText('Subscribe to the newsletter')).toBeFalsy()
})
```

The final test we'll write is to make sure that clicking the banner's close button commits a mutation to the store. We can do this by injecting a stub as the **dismissSubscribeBanner** mutation and checking that it is called when clicking the close button:

```
// imports and other tests
test('Newsletter Banner should hide on "close" button click',
  async () => {
  const dismissSubscribeBanner = jest.fn()
  const {getByText} = render(NewsletterBanner, {
    store: {
      ...store,
      mutations: {
        dismissSubscribeBanner
      }
    }
  })
  await fireEvent.click(getByText('Close'))
  expect(dismissSubscribeBanner).toHaveBeenCalledTimes(1)
})
```

The tests will now pass when run with **npm run test:unit __tests__/ NewsletterBanner.test.js**, as follows:

```
> npm run test:unit __tests__/NewsletterBanner.test.js --silent
 PASS  __tests__/NewsletterBanner.test.js
  ✓ Newsletter Banner should display if store is initialised with it not dismissed (34ms)
  ✓ Newsletter Banner should not display if store is initialised with it dismissed (4ms)
  ✓ Newsletter Banner should hide on "close" button click (32ms)


Test Suites: 1 passed, 1 total
Tests:       3 passed, 3 total
Snapshots:   0 total
Time:        2.825s, estimated 3s
Ran all test suites matching /__tests__\/NewsletterBanner.test.js/i.
```

Figure 12.24: Unit tests for NewsletterBanner passing on the command line

We've now seen how the Vue.js Testing library can be used to test application functionality driven by Vuex.

EXERCISE 12.04: BUILDING AND TESTING A COOKIE DISCLAIMER BANNER (VUEX)

We'll now look at how to implement a cookie disclaimer banner using Vuex and how to test it with the Vue.js Testing library.

We will store whether the cookie banner is showing in Vuex (the default is **true**); when the banner is closed, we will store it in Vuex.

Test this opening/closing with a mock Vuex store. To access the code files for this exercise, refer to https://packt.live/36UzksP:

1. Create a green cookie banner with a **Cookies Disclaimer** title in bold, the disclaimer, and an **I agree** button. We will create this in **src/components/ CookieBanner.vue**:

```
<template>
  <div
    class="flex flex-row bg-green-100 border text-center
      border-green-400
    text-green-700 mt-8 px-4 md:px-8 py-3 rounded relative"
    role="alert"
  >
    <div class="flex flex-col">
      <strong class="font-bold w-full flex">Cookies Disclaimer
      </strong>
      <span class="block sm:inline">We use cookies to improve your
experience</span>
    </div>
    <button
      class="ml-auto align-center bg-transparent
        hover:bg-green-500
      text-green-700 font-semibold font-sm hover:text-white
        py-2 px-4 border
      border-green-500 hover:border-transparent rounded"
    >
      I agree
    </button>
  </div>
</template>
```

2. Next, we will import, register, and render **CookieBanner** below **router-view** in **src/App.vue**:

```
<template>
  <!-- rest of template -->
      <CookieBanner />
  <!-- rest of template -->
</template>
<script>
// other imports
import CookieBanner from './components/CookieBanner.vue'

export default {
  components: {
    // other components
    CookieBanner
  },
  // other component properties
}
</script>
```

3. Add a **state** slice to control whether to display the cookie banner. In our Vuex store, we will initialize this **acceptedCookie** field as **false**:

```
// imports and configuration
export default new Vuex.Store({
  state: {
    // other state fields
    acceptedCookie: false
  },
  // rest of vuex configuration
})
```

4. We will also need an **acceptCookie** mutation to close the banner:

```
// imports and configuration

export default new Vuex.Store({
  // rest of vuex configuration
  mutations: {
    // other mutations
    acceptCookie(state) {
```

```
            state.acceptedCookie = true
        }
    }
})
```

5. Next, we will expose store state as an **acceptedCookie** computed
   property. We will create an **acceptCookie** function that triggers the
   acceptCookie mutation:

```
export default {
  methods: {
    acceptCookie() {
      this.$store.commit('acceptCookie')
    }
  },
  computed: {
    acceptedCookie() {
      return this.$store.state.acceptedCookie
    }
  }
}
</script>
```

6. We will use **v-if** to show the banner when cookies have not been accepted
   yet. The **I agree** button will close the banner when it's clicked by toggling
   acceptCookie:

```
<template>
  <div
    v-if="!acceptedCookie"
    class="flex flex-row bg-green-100 border text-center
      border-green-400
    text-green-700 mt-8 px-4 md:px-8 py--3 rounded relative"
    role="alert"
  >
    <!-- rest of template -->
    <button
      @click="acceptCookie()"
      class="ml-auto align-center bg-transparent
        hover:bg-green-500
      text-green-700 font-semibold font-sm hover:text-white
        py-2 px-4 border
      border-green-500 hover:border-transparent rounded"
    >
```

```
        I agree
      </button>
    </div>
</template>
```

We have now got a cookie banner that shows until **I agree** is clicked, as shown in the following screenshot:

Figure 12.25: Cookie banner displayed in the browser

7. We will now write a test that checks that the **CookieBanner** component is displayed by default:

```
import {render, fireEvent} from '@testing-library/vue'
import CookieBanner from '../src/components/CookieBanner.vue'
import store from '../src/store'

test('Cookie Banner should display if store is initialised with
  it not dismissed', () => {
  const {queryByText} = render(CookieBanner, { store })
  expect(queryByText('Cookies Disclaimer')).toBeTruthy()
})
```

8. We will also write a test to check that if **acceptedCookie** is true in the store, the cookie banner won't be displayed:

```
test('Cookie Banner should not display if store is initialised
  with it dismissed', () => {
  const {queryByText} = render(CookieBanner, { store: {
    state: {
      acceptedCookie: true
    }
  } })
  expect(queryByText('Cookies Disclaimer')).toBeFalsy()
})
```

9. Finally, we want to check that when the **I agree** button is clicked, the **acceptCookie** mutation is triggered:

```
test('Cookie Banner should hide on "I agree" button click',
  async () => {
  const acceptCookie = jest.fn()
  const {getByText} = render(CookieBanner, {
    store: {
      ...store,
      mutations: {
        acceptCookie
      }
    }
  })
  await fireEvent.click(getByText('I agree'))
  expect(acceptCookie).toHaveBeenCalledTimes(1)
})
```

The three tests we wrote pass when run with **npm run test:unit __tests__/CookieBanner.test.js**, as follows:

```
> npm run test:unit __tests__/CookieBanner.test.js --silent
 PASS  __tests__/CookieBanner.test.js
  ✓ Cookie Banner should display if store is initialised with it not dismissed (39ms)
  ✓ Cookie Banner should not display if store is initialised with it dismissed (5ms)
  ✓ Cookie Banner should hide on "I agree" button click (63ms)


Test Suites: 1 passed, 1 total
Tests:       3 passed, 3 total
Snapshots:   0 total
Time:        3.47s, estimated 5s
Ran all test suites matching /__tests__\/CookieBanner.test.js/i.
```

Figure 12.26: Tests for the cookie banner passing

We've now seen how to test components that rely on Vuex for state and updates.

Next, we'll look at snapshot testing and see how it simplifies the testing of render output.

SNAPSHOT TESTING

Snapshot tests provide a way to write tests for fast-changing pieces of code without keeping the assertion data inline with the test. They store snapshots instead.

Changes to a snapshot reflect changes to the output, which is quite useful for code reviews.

For example, we can add a snapshot test to the **PostList.test.js** file:

```
// imports and tests
test('Post List renders correctly', () => {
  const wrapper = mount(PostList, {
    propsData: {
      posts: [
        {
          title: 'Title 1',
          description: 'Description 1',
          tags: ['react', 'vue']
        },
        {
          title: 'Title 2',
          description: 'Description 2',
          tags: ['html', 'angularjs']
```

```
            }
        ]
    }
  })
  expect(wrapper.text()).toMatchSnapshot()
})
```

When we next run this test file, with **npm run test:unit __tests__/ PostList.test.js**, we will get the following output:

```
Snapshot Summary
  › 1 snapshot written from 1 test suite.

Test Suites: 1 passed, 1 total
Tests:       4 passed, 4 total
Snapshots:   1 written, 1 total
Time:        3.952s
Ran all test suites matching /__tests__\/PostList.test.js/i.
```

Figure 12.27: Snapshot test run for the first time

The snapshot was written to **__tests__/__snapshots__/PostList.test. js.snap**, as follows:

```
// Jest Snapshot v1, https://goo.gl/fbAQLP

exports[`Post List renders correctly 1`] = `
"Title 1 Description 1
      #react


      #vue
    Title 2 Description 2
      #html


      #angularjs"
`;
```

This makes it easy to quickly see what the changes mean in terms of concrete output.

We've now seen how to use snapshot tests. Next, we'll put all the tools we learned in the chapter together to add a new page.

ACTIVITY 12.01: ADDING A SIMPLE SEARCH BY TITLE PAGE WITH TESTS

We have already built a post list page, a single-post view page, and a posts-by-tag page.

A great way to resurface old content on a blog is by implementing a good search functionality. We will add search to the **PostList** page:

1. Create the search form with an input and a button in a new file at **src/components/SearchForm.vue**.

2. We'll now get the form to display by importing, registering, and rendering it in **src/App.vue**.

   We are now able to see the search form in the application, as follows:

The Vue.js Workshop Blog

Vue.js for React developers
React has massive popularity here are the key bene...

Migrating an AngularJS app to Vue.js
With many breaking changes, AngularJS developers h...

Figure 12.28: The post list view with a search form

3. We're now ready to add a snapshot test for the search form. In **__tests__/SearchForm.test.js**, we should add **SearchForm should match expected HTML**.

4. We want to track the contents of the search form input using **v-model** to two-way bind the **searchTerm** instance variable and the contents of the input.

5. When the search form is submitted, we'll need to update the URL with the right parameter. This can be done with **this.$router.push()**. We will store the search in a **q** query parameter.

6. We will want to reflect the state of the **q** query parameter in the search form input. We can do this by reading **q** from **this.$route.query** and setting it as the initial value for the **searchTerm** data field in the **SearchForm** component state.

7. Next, we'll want to filter the posts passed to **PostList** on the home page. We'll use **this.$route.query.q** in a computed property that filters posts by their title. This new computed property will then be used instead of **posts** in **src/App.vue**.

8. Next, we should add a test that changes the search query parameter and check that the app shows the right result. To do this, we can import **src/App.vue, src/store.js** and **src/router.js**, and render the app with the store and the router. We can then update the search field contents by using the fact that the placeholder for the field is **Search**. Finally, we can submit the form by clicking the element where **test id** is **Search** (which is the **search** button).

> **NOTE**
>
> The solution to this activity can be found on page 717.

SUMMARY

Throughout this chapter, we've looked at different approaches to testing different types of Vue.js applications.

Testing in general is useful for empirically showing that the system is working. Unit tests are the cheapest to build and maintain and should be the base of testing functionality. System tests are the next level up in the testing pyramid and allow you to gain confidence that the majority of features are working as expected. End-to-end tests show that the main flows of the full system work.

We've seen how to unit test components, filters, component methods, and mixins, as well as testing through the layers, and testing component output in a black box fashion instead of inspecting component internals to test functionality. Using the Vue.js Testing library, we have tested advanced functionality, such as routing and applications, that leverage Vuex.

Finally, we looked at snapshot testing and saw how it can be an effective way to write tests for template-heavy chunks of code.

In the next chapter, we will look at end-to-end testing techniques that can be applied to Vue.js applications.

13

END-TO-END TESTING

OVERVIEW

In this chapter, we will look at how to create an **End-to-End** (**E2E**) test suite for a Vue.js application with Cypress. In order to write robust tests, we'll look at common pitfalls and best practices such as intercepting HTTP requests and waiting for elements to appear without timeouts.

As we proceed, you will gain an understanding of E2E testing and its use cases. You will see how Cypress can be configured to test a Vue.js application and also interact with and inspect a user interface using it. Throughout the course of the chapter, you will gain familiarity with the pitfalls of arbitrary timeouts and how to avoid them with Cypress' waiting functionality. Toward the end of the chapter, you will also learn when, why, and how to intercept HTTP requests with Cypress.

INTRODUCTION

In this chapter, we'll write E2E tests for a highly asynchronous application.

In previous chapters, we've seen how to build complex Vue.js applications and how to write unit tests for them. This chapter will cover how to use Cypress to write E2E tests for a Vue.js application that is highly interactive and uses an HTTP API. We'll see how E2E testing gives you a high level of confidence that an application will work as designed by automating user flows.

UNDERSTANDING E2E TESTING AND ITS USE CASES

Most developers will have seen a version of the testing pyramid shown in the following figure:

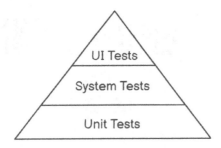

Figure 13.1: A diagram of the testing pyramid

E2E tests fall under the **User Interface** (**UI**) testing category. The type of test we'll be looking at in this chapter is automated E2E tests using Cypress.

E2E and UI tests provide a level of confidence higher than unit or integration tests. They're testing the application as used by the end user. The end user doesn't care why or where a bug is happening, just that there is a bug. The *where and why* of a bug tends to be the concern of unit and system-level tests. Unit and system-level tests check that the internals of a system work as the specification or code describes them. UI-level tests validate that application flows are working as expected.

A strong E2E test suite that runs fast, has few false negatives (where a test fails but the application works), and even fewer false positives (where all tests pass but the application is broken) enables **Continuous Deployment** (**CD**). CD, as its name entails, involves deploying a project or application continually. In this kind of setup, an application version is validated by the E2E suite and is then automatically deployed to production.

CONFIGURING CYPRESS FOR A VUE.JS APPLICATION

Cypress is a JavaScript E2E testing framework. It's designed to solve the very specific need of writing E2E tests using JavaScript. This is in contrast to other fully fledged **browser automation** solutions such as **WebDriverIO** (https://webdriver.io/), **Selenium Webdriver** (https://www.selenium.dev/), **Puppeteer** (https://developers.google.com/web/tools/puppeteer/), and **Playwright** (https://github.com/microsoft/playwright), which are commonly used to write E2E tests.

The big difference with Cypress compared to these other solutions is its singular focus on writing E2E tests (as opposed to generic browser automation). Tests can only be written using JavaScript (Selenium supports other languages), and up until recently, it only supported Chrome (Cypress 4.0 now has support for Firefox and Microsoft Edge as per https://www.cypress.io/blog/2020/02/06/introducing-firefox-and-edge-support-in-cypress-4-0/).

Cypress has a **Graphical User Interface** (**GUI**) to run and debug tests locally and comes with built-in assertion and stubbing/mocking libraries.

To add Cypress to a project using the Vue CLI, we can use the **e2e-cypress** plugin (https://cli.vuejs.org/core-plugins/e2e-cypress.html), whose install instructions guide us to run the following command at the command line. As part of adding the plugin, Cypress and its supporting packages are downloaded and unpacked, so it might take a while to complete:

```
vue add @vue/e2e-cypress
```

The plugin adds a **test:e2e** script that we can run using the following command. This command takes a while to start since it needs to run a production build of the application and then start the Cypress app:

```
npm run test:e2e
```

Eventually, we'll see the Cypress GUI as follows:

Figure 13.2: The Cypress GUI after plugin installation and the run test:e2e command

The plugin creates a default **test.js** file for us. The contents are as follows by default. The test goes to the application root (**/**) and checks that the **h1** on the page contains **Welcome to Your Vue.js App**:

```
// https://docs.cypress.io/api/introduction/api.html

describe('My First Test', () => {
  it('Visits the app root url', () => {
    cy.visit('/')
    cy.contains('h1', 'Welcome to Your Vue.js App')
  })
})
```

This works in an empty Vue CLI project.

We can try visiting **google.com** using **cy.visit(url)** and check that the **input** element that's synonymous with the Google home page is there by first selecting the input elements on the page with **cy.get('input')** and then using the **.should('exist')** assertion:

```
describe('My First Test', () => {
  it('Opens an arbitrary URL', () => {
    cy.visit('https://google.com')
    cy.get('input').should('exist')
  })
})
```

We can run the test by clicking on **test.js** in the Cypress UI (when **npm run test:e2e** is running) as follows:

Figure 13.3: The Cypress UI running test.js

When Cypress is running tests, a browser window is opened to run them:

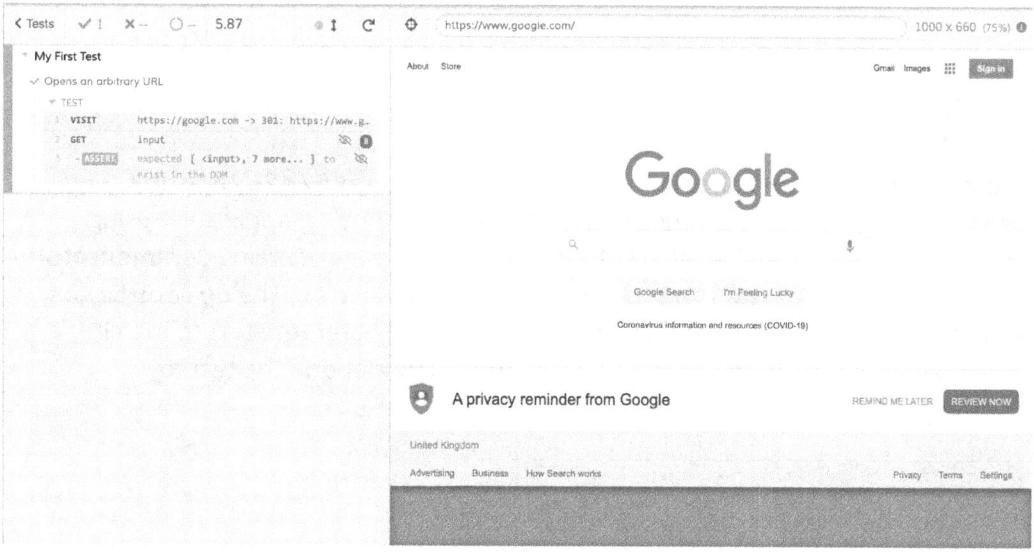

Figure 13.4: Cypress tests running in Chrome while visiting the Google home page

We've now seen how to install and use Cypress to visit web pages.

In the next section, we'll see how Cypress can be used to interact with and inspect a UI.

USING CYPRESS TO INTERACT WITH AND INSPECT A VUE.JS UI

In order to E2E test the **Commentator Pro** application, we should start by adding something to test. In this case, we'll have a heading (**h2**) with the name of the application. In the **App.vue** file, we'll have the following code:

```
<template>
  <div id="app" class="p-10">
    <div class="flex flex-col">
      <h2
        class="uppercase leading-loose pb-4 flex justify-center
          m-auto md:w-1/3 text-xl mb-8 font-bold text-gray-800
          border-b"
      >
        Commentator Pro
      </h2>
    </div>
  </div>
```

```
</template>

<script>

export default {}
</script>
```

In order to test this with Cypress, we can change the **tests/e2e/specs/
test.js** file with the following code. We'll go to the running application using
cy.visit('/') and then check that the **h2** on the page contains **Commentator
Pro** using **cy.contains('h2', 'Commentator Pro')**. The **cy.contains**
function is overloaded and can be used with one parameter (the text to match
against) or two parameters (the selector for the container and the text to
match against):

```
describe('Commentator Pro', () => {
  it('Has a h2 with "Commentator Pro"', () => {
    cy.visit('/')
    cy.contains('h2', 'Commentator Pro')
  })
})
```

We can then run **test.js** using the Cypress UI as seen in the following screenshot:

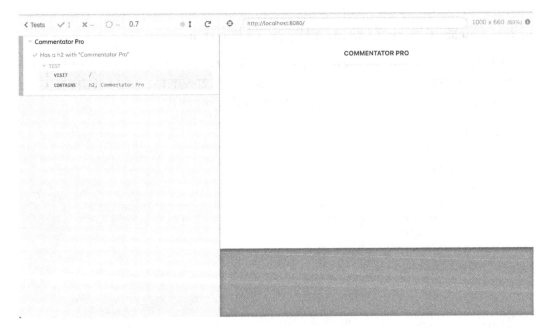

Figure 13.5: Heading content test running successfully in Chrome

Now that we've seen how to visit a page and assert on its content, we'll see how we can use Cypress to automate tests for a new feature in a Vue.js application.

EXERCISE 13.01: ADDING A "NEW COMMENT" BUTTON AND CORRESPONDING E2E TEST

In order for the **Commentator Pro** application to be useful, we should have an **Add a new comment** button to allow users to add comments.

We will add a blue jumbo button with the text **Add a New Comment** and write the corresponding E2E test with Cypress.

To access the code files for this exercise, refer to https://packt.live/36Pefjl.

To do this, perform the following steps:

1. To add a button in the app, we'll add a **button** element with some **TailwindCSS** classes in **src/App.vue**:

```
<template>
  <div id="app" class="p-10">
    <div class="flex flex-col">
      <!-- rest of template -->
      <button class="flex mx-auto bg-blue-500 hover:bg-blue-700
        text-white font-bold py-2 px-4 rounded">
        Add a New Comment
      </button>
    </div>
  </div>
</template>
```

The output should show as follows:

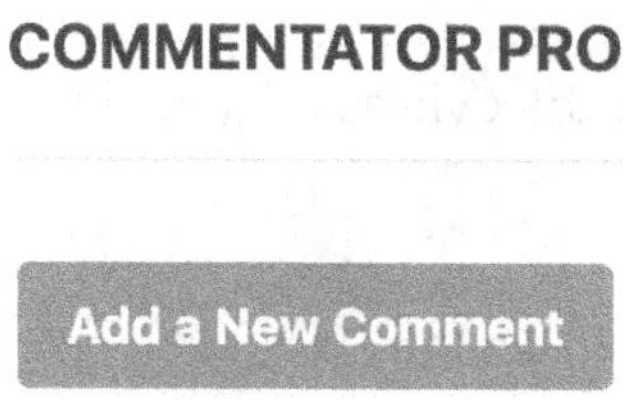

COMMENTATOR PRO

Add a New Comment

Figure 13.6: Commentator Pro application with the "Add a New Comment" button

2. Next, we'll create a new E2E test at **tests/e2e/specs/add-new-comment.**
   js. We'll set the name of the suite and description of the test to **Adding a**
   New Comment and **the homepage should have a button with the**
   right text respectively:

```
describe('Adding a New Comment', () => {
  it('the homepage should have a button with the right text',
    () => {
    // test will go here
  })
})
```

3. In order to test the home page, we'll have to navigate to it using
   cy.visit('/'):

```
describe('Adding a New Comment', () => {
  it('the homepage should have a button with the right text',
    () => {
    cy.visit('/')
  })
})
```

4. Finally, we can write the assertion that a **button** instance containing the text
   Add a New Comment is on the page:

```
describe('Adding a New Comment', () => {
  it('the homepage should have a button with the right text',
    () => {
    cy.visit('/')
    cy.contains('button', 'Add a New Comment')
  })
})
```

5. We can run this test using the Cypress UI (get it running using **npm run**
   test:e2e):

Figure 13.7: The "add-new-comment.js" test displaying in the Cypress UI

6. When we run the test, we'll get the following output in Chrome. The test passes since there is a button with the relevant text on the home page:

Figure 13.8: Cypress running our "add-new-comment" test in Chrome

We've now seen how to visit pages and assert against their content.

In the next section, we will look at using Cypress to test interactive behavior. Cypress has automatic selector retries, which make it a great fit for testing highly interactive Vue.js applications. We'll see how to use Cypress to interact with the UI and assert on the effect of our interactions.

TRIGGERING AND WAITING FOR UI UPDATES WITH CYPRESS

The tests we've written up until now are quite simple and only check that the application isn't crashing on load in the browser.

One of the strengths of E2E tests is testing with high fidelity that the UI behaves as expected when a user interacts with it. We'll use Cypress' selection (the `.get()` function), event triggering (the `.click()` function), and assertion (the `.should()` function) functionality to test a Vue.js application in this section. Cypress' automatic retries on DOM selection will allow us to write E2E tests without explicit wait/timeout conditions. Waits and timeouts are a staple of other E2E testing systems and tend to be a source of flakiness in tests.

To begin with, we will add a comment editor to our **Commentator Pro** application. Displaying the editor (a simple **textarea**) will be toggled by clicking on the **Add a New Comment** button.

In order to keep writing tests without wrangling complicated and brittle selectors, we'll start adding **data-test-id** attributes; to begin with, we can add one to the **Add a New Comment** button in the **App.vue** file:

```
<template>
  <div id="app" class="p-10">
    <div class="flex flex-col">
      <!-- rest of template -->
      <button
        class="flex mx-auto bg-blue-500 hover:bg-blue-700
          text-white font-bold py-2 px-4 rounded"
        data-test-id="new-comment-button"
      >

        Add a New Comment
      </button>
      <!-- rest of template -->
    </div>
  </div>
</template>
```

Next, we'll add a **showEditor** property to the Vue.js **data()** method on the **App** component. We'll use this expression in the **v-if** for the editor. We can also set the new comment button to toggle this instance property:

```
<template>
  <div id="app" class="p-10">
    <div class="flex flex-col">
      <!-- rest of template -->
      <button
        @click="showEditor = !showEditor"
        class="flex mx-auto bg-blue-500 hover:bg-blue-700
          text-white font-bold py-2 px-4 rounded"
        data-test-id="new-comment-button"
      >
        Add a New Comment
      </button>
      <!-- rest of template -->
    </div>
```

```
    </div>
  </template>
  <script>
  export default {
    data() {
      return {
        showEditor: false
      }
    }
  }
  </script>
```

We can add our editor with the **new-comment-editor data-test-id** that is toggled by **showEditor**:

```
<template>
  <div id="app" class="p-10">
    <div class="flex flex-col">
      <!-- rest of template -->
      <div v-if="showEditor">
        <textarea
          data-test-id="new-comment-editor"
          class="flex mx-auto my-6 shadow appearance-none
            border rounded py-2 px-3 text-gray-700 leading-tight
            focus:outline-none focus:shadow-outline"
        >
        </textarea>
      </div>
    </div>
  </div>
</template>
```

In order to test the toggling, we can add a test that opens that app and checks that the comment editor is not initially shown, as well as checking whether or not it shows depending on how many clicks are triggered on the **new-comment-button**:

```
describe('Adding a New Comment', () => {
  // other tests
  it('the Add a New Comment button should toggle the editor
    display on and off', () => {
    cy.visit('/')
    cy.get('[data-test-id="new-comment-editor"]').should
      ('not.be.visible')
```

```
    cy.get('[data-test-id="new-comment-button"]').click()
    cy.get('[data-test-id="new-comment-editor"]').should
      ('be.visible')

    cy.get('[data-test-id="new-comment-button"]').click()
    cy.get('[data-test-id="new-comment-editor"]').should
      ('not.be.visible')
  })
})
```

The preceding code will generate the following result:

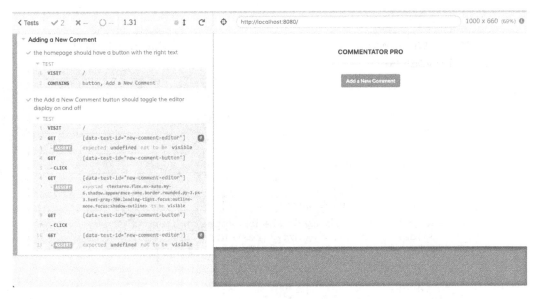

Figure 13.9: Cypress running "add-new-comment" tests, including the new editor-toggling test

We've now seen how to write Cypress tests that select and assert over DOM elements.

> **NOTE**
>
> **data-test-id** instances, as a convention, are a way to decouple tests from application and styling-specific selectors. This is especially useful if the people writing the tests aren't always the ones writing the code. In that situation, using **data-test-id** allows the markup structure and classes to change, but the tests will keep passing as long as the **test-id** instances remain on the correct element.

EXERCISE 13.02: ADDING NEW COMMENT EDITOR INPUT AND SUBMIT FUNCTIONALITY

To be able to send the new comment text to an API, we will need to store the text in a Vue.js state. The other prerequisite to adding a comment is to have a dummy "**submit**" button.

To access the code files for this exercise, refer to https://packt.live/2HaWanh.

To add these features and their corresponding tests, perform the following steps:

1. To store the **textarea** (editor) content in-memory, we'll use **v-model**. We'll create a new data (state) variable, **newComment**, that gets initialized to **""**. Now, **v-model** will two-way bind the **textarea** content and **newComment**:

```
<template>
  <div id="app" class="p-10">
      <!-- rest of template -->
      <textarea
        data-test-id="new-comment-editor"
        class="flex mx-auto my-6 shadow appearance-none
          border rounded py-2 px-3 text-gray-700 leading-tight
          focus:outline-none focus:shadow-outline"
        v-model="newComment"
      >
      </textarea>
      <!-- rest of template -->
  </div>
</template>
<script>
export default {
  data() {
    return {
      // other data properties
      newComment: ''
    }
  }
}
</script>
```

2. We'll add a **submit** button inside the editor, which should only show when the editor is toggled on. We also make sure to include a **data-test-id="new-comment-submit"** attribute in order to be able to select it with Cypress later:

```
<template>
  <div id="app" class="p-10">
    <!-- rest of template -->
    <div v-if="showEditor">
      <!-- rest of template -->
      <button
        data-test-id="new-comment-submit"
        class="flex mx-auto bg-blue-500 hover:bg-blue-700
          text-white font-bold py-2 px-4 rounded"
      >
      Submit
      </button>
      <!-- rest of template -->
    </div>
    <!-- rest of template -->
  </div>
</template>
```

3. It's now time to add an E2E test to test that **new-comment-editor** works as expected when we type text into it. In order to achieve this, we need to load up the application and click the **new comment** button so that the editor is displayed. We can then select **new-comment-editor** (by **data-test-id**) and use the Cypress .**type** function to add some text. We can chain .**should('have.value', 'Just saying...')** to validate that our interaction with **textarea** was successful:

```
describe('Adding a New Comment', () => {
  // other tests
  it('the new comment editor should support text input',
    () => {
    cy.visit('/')
    // Get the editor to show
    cy.get('[data-test-id="new-comment-button"]').click()
    cy.get('[data-test-id="new-comment-editor"]').should
      ('be.visible')

    cy.get('[data-test-id="new-comment-editor"]')
      .type('Just saying...')
```

```
            .should('have.value', 'Just saying...')
    })
})
```

When run using the Cypress UI, this **add-new-comment** test suite should yield the following result:

Figure 13.10: Cypress running "add-new-comment" tests, including
the new editor text input test

4. Finally, we can add an **E2E test** to check that the **submit** button does not appear by default but does appear when we click the **new comment** button. We can also check the text content of the **new-comment-submit** button:

```
describe('Adding a New Comment', () => {
  // other tests
  it('the new comment editor should have a submit button',
    () => {
    cy.visit('/')
    cy.get('[data-test-id="new-comment-submit"]').should
      ('not.be.visible')
    // Get the editor to show
    cy.get('[data-test-id="new-comment-button"]').click()
    cy.get('[data-test-id="new-comment-submit"]').should
      ('be.visible')
```

```
        cy.contains('[data-test-id="new-comment-submit"]', 'Submit')
    })
})
```

When this test is run through the Cypress UI, we see the following result:

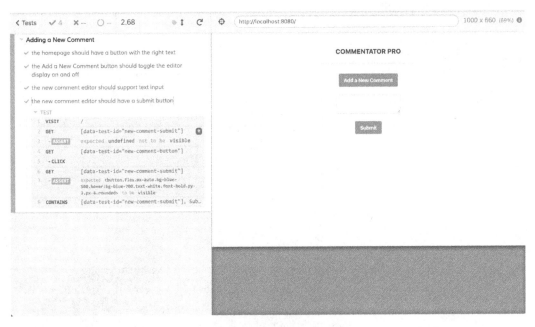

Figure 13.11: Cypress running "add-new-comment" tests, including
the new submit button test

5. One more feature we can add is to make the **submit** button disabled
    until there's text in the text editor. To do this, we can bind **:disabled** to
    !newComment on the **new comment submit** button. We'll make the button
    look disabled using reduced opacity. As an aside, one of the big reasons we
    added a two-way binding between **newComment** and **textarea** is to enable UI
    validations like this one:

```
<template>
        <!-- rest of template -->
        <button
            data-test-id="new-comment-submit"
            class="flex mx-auto bg-blue-500 hover:bg-blue-700
                text-white font-bold py-2 px-4 rounded"
            :disabled="!newComment"
```

```
        :class="{ 'opacity-50 cursor-not-allowed' : !newComment }"
      >
        Submit
      </button>
      <!-- rest of template -->
    </template>
```

6. The relevant test will look at whether or not the **new-comment-submit** button is disabled when the text editor content is empty using Cypress' **should('be. disabled')** and **should('not.be.disabled')** assertions:

```
describe('Adding a New Comment', () => {
  // other tests
  it('the new comment submit button should be disabled based
    on "new comment" content', () => {
    cy.visit('/')
    // Get the editor to show
    cy.get('[data-test-id="new-comment-button"]').click()
    cy.get('[data-test-id="new-comment-submit"]').should
      ('be.visible')

    cy.get('[data-test-id="new-comment-submit"]')
      .should('be.disabled')

    cy.get('[data-test-id="new-comment-editor"]')
      .type('Just saying...')

    cy.get('[data-test-id="new-comment-submit"]')
      .should('not.be.disabled')
  })
})
```

This yields the following output when run through Cypress UI and Chrome automation:

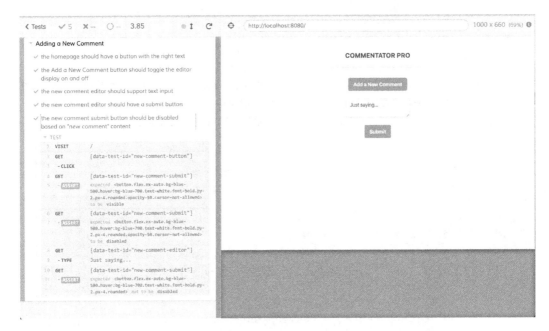

Figure 13.12: Cypress running "add-new-comment" tests, including the new comment submit button disabled test

We've now seen how to use Cypress to select, click, and input text. We've also seen approaches to check element visibility, text content, input values, and disabled states.

Anyone familiar with other automation frameworks will have noticed that in Cypress tests, there are no explicit waits or retries. This is because Cypress waits and retries assertions and selections automatically. Most of the tests we've written don't showcase this in a major way, but the next exercise, where we bring asynchronicity into the mix, will.

EXERCISE 13.03: ADDING A SUBMITTING STATE TO THE NEW COMMENT EDITOR

In order to showcase Cypress's impressive automatic retry/wait capability, we will look at adding and testing a **submitting** state for the new comment editor.

In effect, we'll be reacting to a click on the **submit** button and showing a spinner for **2.5s** to simulate a reasonably slow HTTP request to a backend API. This is an example that showcases Cypress' ability to automatically wait and retry selections. This feature reduces the need for arbitrary waits and that flakiness associated with them.

To access the code files for this exercise, refer to https://packt.live/2UzsYJU:

1. In order to show the spinner, we add the **tailwindcss-spinner** package to the project:

```
npm install --save-dev tailwindcss-spinner
# or
yarn add -D tailwindcss-spinner
```

2. We will need to configure it in the Tailwind config file (**tailwind.js**). It needs to be imported using **require('tailwindcss-spinner')**, added as a plugin, and the relevant variables need to be set in **theme**. Our spinner will be **gray** in color, use a Tailwind spacing of size **4**, and have a border width of **2px** and a duration of **500ms**:

```
module.exports = {
  theme: {
    extend: {},
    spinner: (theme) => ({
      default: {
        color: theme('colors.gray.400'),
        size: theme('spacing.4'),
        border: theme('borderWidth.2'),
        speed: theme('transitionDuration.500'),
      },
    }),
  },
  variants: {
    spinner: ['responsive'],
  },
  plugins: [require('tailwindcss-spinner')()],
}
```

3. Next, we need to add an **isSubmitting** state to the Vue.js application in **data()**, which will allow us to toggle the state for the **submit** button. We will initialize it to **false** since we are not submitting anything until the user clicks the **submit** button:

```
<script>
export default {
  data() {
    return {
      // other properties
```

```
        isSubmitting: false
      }
    }
  }
</script>
```

4. Next, we will add a click handler for the **submit** button (as **methods. submitNewComment**). It will simulate a **2.5s** load time using **setTimeout**:

```
<script>
export default {
  // other component properties
  methods: {
    submitNewComment() {
      this.isSubmitting = true
      setTimeout(() => {
        this.isSubmitting = false
      }, 2500)
    }
  }
}
</script>
```

5. Now that we've got a **fake submit** handler, we should bind it to click events on the **new-comment-submit** button:

```
<template>
  <div id="app" class="p-10">
    <div class="flex flex-col">
      <!-- rest of template -->
      <div v-if="showEditor">
        <!-- rest of editor -->
        <button
          data-test-id="new-comment-submit"
          class="flex mx-auto bg-blue-500 hover:bg-blue-700 text-
            white font-bold py-2 px-4 rounded"
          :disabled="!newComment"
          :class="{ 'opacity-50 cursor-not-allowed' : !newComment
            }"
```

```
        @click="submitNewComment()"
      >
        Submit
      </button>
    </div>
  </div>
</div>
</template>
```

6. Now comes the part where we need to react to the submit button. We'll be showing the spinner when **isSubmitting** is true. In order to do this, we simply need to set the **spinner** class to be added when **isSubmitting** is true. In addition to this, we'll set the button to be disabled when **isSubmitting** is true:

```
<template>
  <div id="app" class="p-10">
    <div class="flex flex-col">
      <!-- rest of template -->
      <div v-if="showEditor">
        <!-- rest of editor -->
        <button
          data-test-id="new-comment-submit"
          class="flex mx-auto bg-blue-500 hover:bg-blue-700
            text-white font-bold py-2 px-4 rounded"
          :disabled="!newComment || isSubmitting"
          :class="{
            'opacity-50 cursor-not-allowed' : !newComment,
            spinner: isSubmitting
          }"
          @click="submitNewComment()"
        >
        Submit
        </button>
      </div>
    </div>
  </div>
</template>
```

7. Finally, we can add a test to check that the loading spinner appears when the **submit** button is clicked. To begin with, we'll need to set up the text editor so that when clicking the **add new comment** button and setting a text value for the comment, the text editor is shown and enabled. Next, we can click the enabled **new-comment-submit** button and check that it is disabled and has the **spinner** class (using the **should()** function). After that, we should write another assertion that the button is not disabled anymore and does not show the spinner:

```
it('the new comment editor should show a spinner on submit',
  () => {
    cy.visit('/')
    // Get the editor to show
    cy.get('[data-test-id="new-comment-button"]').click()
    cy.get('[data-test-id="new-comment-submit"]').should
      ('be.visible')

    cy.get('[data-test-id="new-comment-editor"]')
      .type('Just saying...')

    cy.get('[data-test-id="new-comment-submit"]')
      .should('not.be.disabled')
      .click()
      .should('have.class', 'spinner')
      .should('be.disabled')

    // eventually, the spinner should stop showing
    cy.get('[data-test-id="new-comment-submit"]')
      .should('not.have.class', 'spinner')
      .should('not.be.disabled')
  })
```

Despite the **2.5s** during which the spinner shows, this test still passes due to Cypress' automatic retry/wait functionality:

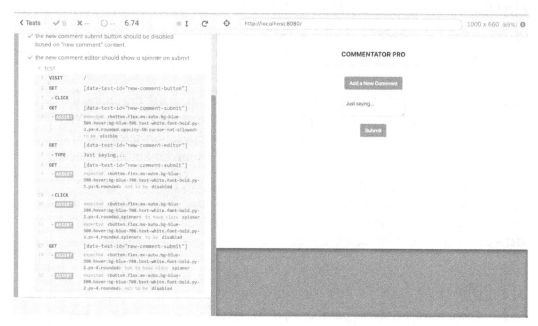

Figure 13.13: Cypress running "add-new-comment" tests, including the comment submission loading state test

We've now seen how Cypress allows us to seamlessly work around asynchronicity in the application by automatically waiting/retrying where an assertion or selection would fail.

INTERCEPTING HTTP REQUESTS

As mentioned in previous sections, Cypress is designed as a JavaScript E2E testing solution. This means that it comes with built-ins such as assertions, automatic wait/retries, sane defaults for running the application, and extensive mocking functionality.

HTTP requests can be slow and tend to introduce flaky behavior to tests. What's meant by flaky is intermittent false negatives, that is, failures that are not caused by an application issue but rather by connectivity issues (for example, between the server running the tests and the backend hosts).

We would also be testing the implementation of the backend system. When using **Continuous Integration** (**CI**), this would mean having to run the backend systems in whichever CI pipeline step needs to run E2E tests.

Usually, when the backend requests are intercepted and a mock response is sent, we also say that the HTTP requests are **stubbed**, in order to avoid tests flaking (meaning intermittent failures not linked to application changes).

Seeing that the requests do not go all the way through the stack (including the backend API), this is technically not a full E2E test of the system anymore. We can, however, consider it an E2E test of the frontend application since the whole application is made up of separate exercises and is not implementation-specific.

In order to mock requests in Cypress, we'll need to use `cy.server()` and `cy.route()`. The Cypress documentation also lets us know that in order to use the HTTP interception functionality, we currently need a client that uses `XMLHttpRequest` (and not the `fetch` API).

> **NOTE**
>
> There is work underway to support HTTP-level interception (which means `fetch`, **XHR**, and more will be supported eventually).

We'll use the **unfetch** library, which implements the `fetch` interface on top of `XMLHttpRequest`. We can install it using the following command:

```
npm install --save-dev unfetch
# or
yarn add -D unfetch
```

We can then import it into **src/App.vue** as follows.

```
<script>
import fetch from 'unfetch'
// rest of component
</script>
```

To showcase HTTP interception, we'll fetch a list of comments from **JSONPlaceholder** and store them under a **comments** reactive instance variable. We can use **fetch** (the name under which we imported **unfetch**) to do this in the **mounted()** life cycle event as follows:

```
<script>
// imports
export default {
  data() {
    return {
      // other data properties
      comments: []
    }
  },
  mounted() {
    fetch('https://jsonplaceholder.typicode.com/comments')
      .then(res => res.json())
      .then(comments => {
        this.comments = comments
      })
  }
  // other component properties
}
</script>
```

A sample comment includes an ID, a body, and an email, among other properties.

That means we can render the comments by creating a **ul** container, which only shows if there are comments (**comments.length > 0**). Inside the **ul** container, we can render a list of **li** elements with a card layout using **v-for**. Each card will render the body of the comment and the author's email inside a **mailto:** link.

Note how we set **comments-list** and **comment-card data-test-ids** for the list container and the list items respectively:

```
<template>
  <div id="app" class="p-10">
    <div class="flex flex-col">
      <!-- rest of template -->
      <ul
        v-if="comments.length > 0"
        class="flex flex-col items-center my-4 mx-auto
          md:w-2/3 lg:w-1/2"
```

```
      data-test-id="comments-list"
  >
    <li
      class="flex flex-col px-6 py-4 rounded overflow-hidden
        shadow-lg mb-6"
      v-for="(comment, index) in comments"
      :key="comment.id + index"
      data-test-id="comment-card"
    >
      <p class="flex text-gray-700 text-lg mb-4">
        {{ comment.body }}</p>
      <p class="flex text-gray-600 font-semibold text-sm">
        <a :href="'mailto:' + comment.email">
          {{ comment.email }}</a>
      </p>
    </li>
  </ul>
</div>
</div>
</template>
```

If we were to test this without HTTP interception, we would have to keep the assertions quite generic. For example, we can check that **comments-list** is visible and that there is a number (greater than 0) of **comment-card** instances in a new E2E test file:

```
describe('Loading Existing Comments', () => {
  it('should load & display comments', () => {
    cy.visit('/')
    cy.get('[data-test-id="comments-list"]')
      .should('be.visible')

    cy.get('[data-test-id="comment-card"]')
      .should('have.length.gt', 0)
  })
})
```

The following test run using the Cypress GUI passes but the tests are quite generic. We can't make any assertions about the specific number of comments or their content:

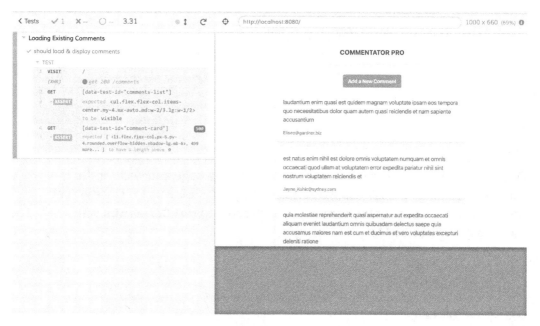

Figure 13.14: Cypress running "load-comments" tests, including a generic load and display test

To intercept the request, we have to initialize the Cypress mock server with **cy.server()**. We can then intercept specific requests using **cy.route()**, which yields the following new test. **cy.route**, when used with two parameters, takes the URL followed by the stub response, in our case an array of comments. We'll use a fictitious email address in our stubs:

```
describe('Loading Existing Comments', () => {
  // other tests
  it('should load and display comments correctly', () => {
    cy.server()
    cy.route('**/comments', [
      {
        body: 'Vue is getting great adoption',
        email: 'evan@vuejs.org',
        id: 100,
      },
      {
```

```
          body: 'Just saying...',
          email: 'evan@vuejs.org',
          id: 10
        },
        {
          body: 'The JS ecosystem is great',
          email: 'evan@vuejs.org',
          id: 1
        }
     ]).as('getComments')
   })
})
```

Once we've got our stub route set up, we can visit the page and wait for the comment fetching to finish using **cy.wait('@getComments')**, since we've previously set the alias of the comments fetch route to **getComments** with **.as('getComments')**:

```
describe('Loading Existing Comments', () => {
  // other tests
  it('should load and display comments correctly', () => {
    // test setup
    cy.visit('/')
    cy.wait('@getComments')

  })
})
```

We can then start asserting, first off, that **comments-list** is visible, and then assert on the number of **comment-card** cards:

```
describe('Loading Existing Comments', () => {
  // other tests
  it('should load and display comments correctly', () => {
    // test setup
    cy.get('[data-test-id="comments-list"]')
      .should('be.visible')

    cy.get('[data-test-id="comment-card"]')
      .should('have.length', 3)
  })
})
```

We can also assert on the specific contents of the cards using the
`.contains()` function:

```
describe('Loading Existing Comments', () => {
  // other tests
  it('should load and display comments correctly', () => {
    // test setup
    cy.contains('[data-test-id="comment-card"]', 'Vue is
      getting great adoption')
      .contains('evan@vuejs.org')
    cy.contains('[data-test-id="comment-card"]', 'Just saying...')
      .contains('evan@vuejs.org')
    cy.contains('[data-test-id="comment-card"]', 'The JS
      ecosystem is great')
      .contains('evan@vuejs.org')
  })
})
```

We can then run the suite with the Cypress GUI and see it passing:

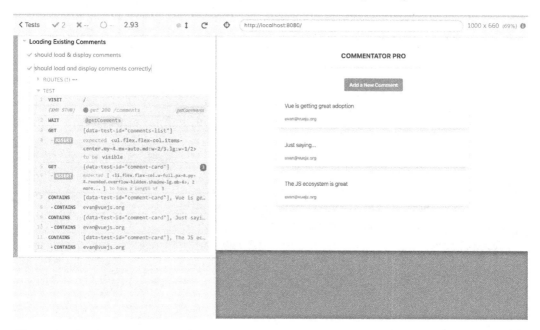

Figure 13.15: Cypress running "load-comments" tests, including our stubbed comments test

We've now seen how and why we might stub HTTP requests using Cypress.

EXERCISE 13.04: POST COMMENT TO API ON SUBMISSION

The **new comment** submit button currently only sets a loading state for a few seconds and then resets – the comment is not actually being sent anywhere.

Let's use the **JSONPlaceholder** API as the place to send our new comment.

When the POST request to the API succeeds, we'll add the comment to the top of the comments list.

To access the code files for this exercise, refer to https://packt.live/2IIWY3g.

To complete the exercise, we will perform the following steps:

1. Start by making the **submitNewComment** method actually post data to **c** using **fetch** (which is actually **unfetch**):

```
<script>
// imports
export default {
  // other component properties
  methods: {
    submitNewComment() {
      this.isSubmitting = true

      fetch('https://jsonplaceholder.typicode.com/comments', {
        method: 'POST',
        headers: {
          'Content-Type': 'application/json'
        },
        body: JSON.stringify({
          email: this.email,
          body: this.newComment
        })
      })
    }
  }
}
</script>
```

Unfortunately, the **fetch()** call by itself doesn't update the data or come out of the loading state. In order to do so, we need to chain some **.then()** function calls to handle the response, and a **.catch** function call in case we have an error. On success (**.then**), we should get the JSON output of the request and add it to the front of a copy of the **comments** array. We should also reset **isSubmitting**, **newComment**, and **showEditor**. On error (**.catch**), we will just reset the loading state, **isSubmitting**, to false; we won't clear the editor or close it since the user might want to try to submit it again:

```
<script>
// imports
export default {
  // other component properties
  methods: {
    submitNewComment() {
      this.isSubmitting = true

      fetch(
        // fetch params
      ).then(res => res.json())
      .then(data => {
        this.comments = [
          data,
          ...this.comments,
        ]
        this.isSubmitting = false
        this.newComment = ''
        this.showEditor = false
      }).catch(() => {
        this.isSubmitting = false
      })
    }
  }
}
</script>
```

We should now add new tests to the **tests/e2e/specs/add-new-comment.js** test suite.

2. First of all, to be good users of **JSONPlaceholder**, we'll stub out all the **GET** requests to **/comments** for the **add-new-comment** suite. In order to achieve this, we'll use a **beforeEach** hook that will start the Cypress stub server (**cy.server()**) and stub out **GET** requests to any URL matching the ****/comments** glob with the **[]** response (**cy.route('GET', '**/comments', [])**):

```
describe('Adding a New Comment', () => {
  beforeEach(() => {
    cy.server()
    // GET comments is not the concern of this test suite
    cy.route('GET', '**/comments', [])
  })
  // tests
```

3. We can then proceed to update the **the new comment editor should show a spinner on submit** test since we're not using a **setTimeout** anymore but an HTTP request. To start with, we need to stub out the **/comments** POST request, for which we'll use the configuration object syntax for **cy.route** in order to introduce some delay in the HTTP request so that it doesn't respond immediately. We alias this request with **.as('newComment')**:

```
describe('Adding a New Comment', () => {
  // setup & tests
  it('the new comment editor should show a spinner on submit',
    () => {
    cy.route({
      method: 'POST',
      url: '**/comments',
      delay: 1500,
      response: {}
    }).as('newComment')
    // rest of the test
  })
})
```

4. Instead of **// eventually, the spinner should stop showing**, we can now use **cy.wait()** to wait for the **newComment** HTTP request to complete before the check that the spinner is gone:

```
describe('Adding a New Comment', () => {
  // setup & tests
  it('the new comment editor should show a spinner on submit',
```

```
    () => {
      // test setup
      // click the "submit" button
      // check the spinner appears
      cy.wait('@newComment')
      // check that the spinner is gone
    })
  })
```

5. We've added new functionality to close the editor when the **submit** operation completes successfully, so we should add the relevant test. We'll use a similar skeleton to the updated **loading state** test with the setup of the POST comments route stubbing **cy.route('POST', '**/comments', {},** aliased as **.as('newComment')**. We can then get the new comment editor to display, add some text, and submit the form. We'll then proceed to wait for the **POST** request to complete before checking that the editor and submit button are not visible anymore:

```
describe('Adding a New Comment', () => {
  // other tests
  it('adding a new comment should close the editor', () => {
    cy.route(
      'POST',
      '**/comments',
      { body: 'Just saying...', email: 'hi@vuejs.org' }
    ).as('newComment')
    cy.visit('/')
    // Get the editor to show
    cy.get('[data-test-id="new-comment-button"]').click()
    cy.get('[data-test-id="new-comment-submit"]').should
      ('be.visible')

    cy.get('[data-test-id="new-comment-editor"]')
      .type('Just saying...')

    cy.get('[data-test-id="new-comment-submit"]')
      .should('not.be.disabled')
      .click()

    cy.wait('@newComment')
    cy.get('[data-test-id="new-comment-editor"]').should
      ('not.be.visible')
```

```
        cy.get('[data-test-id="new-comment-submit"]').should
          ('not.be.visible')
      })
    })
```

This test can now be run with the Cypress GUI and will pass:

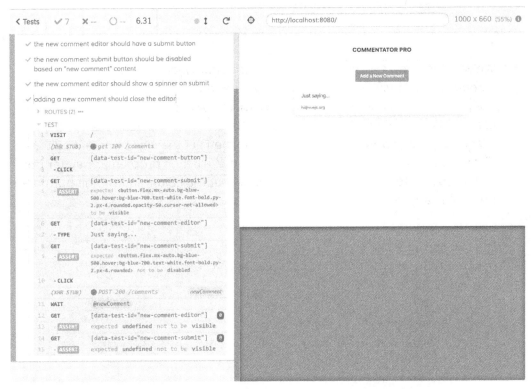

Figure 13.16: Cypress running "add-new-comment" tests, including
the editor closing on submission test

6. The second bit of functionality that we've added is that on completion of the HTTP request the new case is added to the front of the comments list. To test this, it's better to change the response of the comments' **GET** request to have at least one element (so that we can check that the new comment is added to the top of the list):

```
describe('Adding a New Comment', () => {
    // setup & other tests
    it('submitting a new comment should POST to /comments and
      adds response to top of comments list', () => {
      cy.route('GET', '**/comments', [
        {
          email: 'evan@vuejs.org',
```

```
                body: 'Existing comment'
              }
            ])
          })
        })
```

7. We can then stub the **POST** request with some mock data, add text to the editor, and submit the form:

```
describe('Adding a New Comment', () => {
  // setup & other tests
  it('submitting a new comment should POST to /comments and
     adds response to top of comments list', () => {
     // GET request stubbing
     cy.route({
       method: 'POST',
       url: '**/comments',
       response: {
         email: 'evan@vuejs.org',
         body: 'Just saying...',
       },
     }).as('newComment')
     cy.visit('/')

     cy.get('[data-test-id="comment-card"]').should
       ('have.length', 1)

     cy.get('[data-test-id="new-comment-button"]').click()

     cy.get('[data-test-id="new-comment-editor"]')
       .type('Just saying...')

     cy.get('[data-test-id="new-comment-submit"]')
       .should('not.be.disabled')
       .click()

     cy.wait('@newComment')
  })
})
```

8. Finally, we can assert on the fact that the first comment is the newly added comment using a combination of **cy.get()**, **.first()**, and **.contains()**:

```
describe('Adding a New Comment', () => {
  // setup & other tests
  it('submitting a new comment should POST to /comments and
    adds response to top of comments list', () => {
    // setup & wait for POST completion
    cy.get('[data-test-id="comments-list"]').should('be.visible')

    cy.get('[data-test-id="comment-card"]')
      .should('have.length', 2)
      .first()
      .contains('[data-test-id="comment-card"]', 'Just saying...')
      .contains('evan@vuejs.org')
  })
})
```

When running the **add-new-comment** suite with the Cypress GUI, we can see the new test passing:

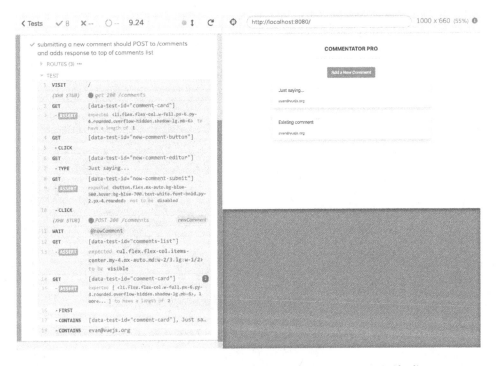

Figure 13.17: Cypress running "add-new-comment" tests, including the new comment added to the top of the list test

We've now seen how to use Cypress to intercept HTTP requests, so in the next section, we'll look at some of the reporting tools Cypress provides around visual regression (snapshot) testing.

VISUAL REGRESSION TESTING WITH CYPRESS SNAPSHOTS

The types of tests we've written with Cypress up to now have been functional tests, for the most part.

Functional tests check that the application *behaves* as expected. Visual tests check that the application *looks* as expected.

There are ways to inspect the rendered CSS, but that approach tends to be quite tedious and prone to breakage when the markup or styling is refactored (that is, the same visual output but with different rules or markup).

Fortunately, Cypress, with the **cypress-plugin-snapshots** plugin, allows us to take and compare snapshots of an application. First, it needs to be installed using the following command:

```
npm install --save-dev cypress-plugin-snapshots
# or
yarn add -D cypress-plugin-snapshots
```

The plugin adds the **.toMatchImageSnapshot** method on Cypress selections. For it to work, we need to register it in the plugin's initialization file.

We should import **cypress-plugin-snapshots/plugin** and run its export **initPlugin** with the plugin initialization data:

```
const { initPlugin } = require('cypress-plugin-snapshots/plugin');

module.exports = (on, config) => {
  initPlugin(on, config);
  // rest of plugin config, including return
}
```

We also need to register the relevant command from **cypress-plugin-snapshots/commands**, which can be done in the **commands.js** file:

```
import 'cypress-plugin-snapshots/commands'
```

We'll also need to add some config for **cypress-plugin-snapshots** to **cypress.json**:

```json
{
  "//": "other config",
  "env": {
    "cypress-plugin-snapshots": {
      "autoCleanUp": false,
      "autopassNewSnapshots": true,
      "diffLines": 3,
      "imageConfig": {
        "createDiffImage": true,
        "resizeDevicePixelRatio": true,
        "threshold": 0.01,
        "thresholdType": "percent"
      },
      "screenshotConfig": {
        "blackout": [],
        "capture": "fullPage",
        "clip": null,
        "disableTimersAndAnimations": true,
        "log": false,
        "scale": false,
        "timeout": 30000
      },
      "backgroundBlend": "difference"
    }
  }
}
```

Finally, we can add a snapshot test in the **test.js** file.

First, we'll clean up the file and stub out the **/comments** API call (this will be particularly useful for the snapshot test):

```
describe('Commentator Pro', () => {
  beforeEach(() => {
    cy.server()
    cy.route('GET', '**/comments', [
      {
        body: 'Just saying...',
        email: 'evant@vuejs.org'
      }
    ]).as('getComments')
  })
  // tests
})
```

Next, we can add the visual regression test. We'll get the editor open to maximize the single snapshot test, get the whole **app** using **#app**, and snapshot that:

```
describe('Commentator Pro', () => {
  // setup & other tests
  it('visual regression', () => {
    cy.visit('/')
    cy.get('[data-test-id="new-comment-button"]')
      .click()
    cy.wait('@getComments')
    cy.get('[data-test-id="new-comment-editor"]')
      .should('be.visible')
    cy.get('#app').toMatchImageSnapshot({
      threshold: 0.001,
    })
  })
})
```

When running the tests with the Cypress UI, we see the following output:

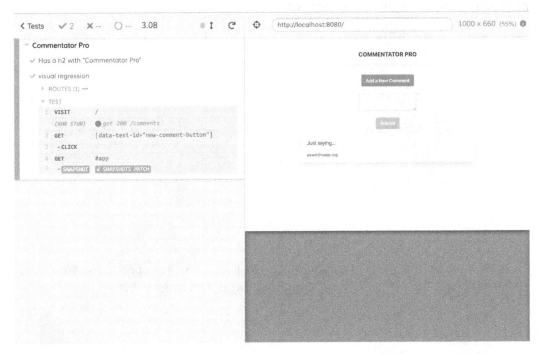

Figure 13.18: Cypress running tests, including the visual regression test

We can show the snapshots failing by changing the button color to red (from **bg-blue-500** to **bg-red-500**) in the **App.vue** file:

```
<template>
  <div id="app" class="p-10">
    <div class="flex flex-col">
      <!-- rest of template -->
      <button
        @click="showEditor = !showEditor"
        class="flex mx-auto bg-red-500 hover:bg-blue-700
          text-white font-bold py-2 px-4 rounded"
        data-test-id="new-comment-button"
      >
```

```
        Add a New Comment
      </button>
      <!-- rest of template -->
    </div>
  </div>
</template>
```

When we run the relevant set of tests, they're now failing (because, as we can see, the button is red instead of blue):

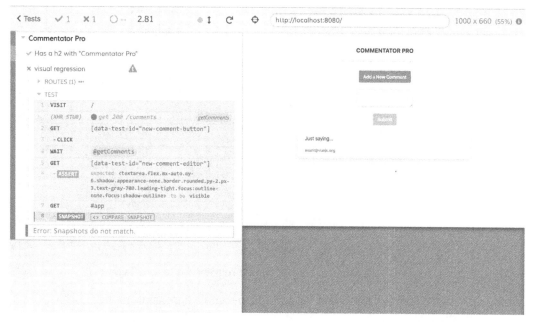

Figure 13.19: Cypress running tests, with a failing visual regression test

By clicking on **COMPARE SNAPSHOT**, we get a visual diff view, which allows us to update the snapshot:

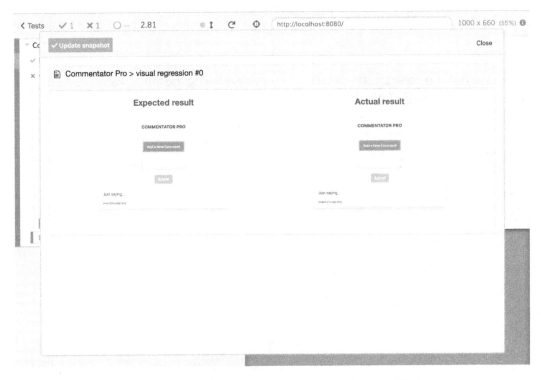

Figure 13.20: Cypress' failing visual regression test diff view

We've now seen how Cypress can be used to do visual regression testing.

We'll now look at adding a new feature and all the relevant tests for it.

ACTIVITY 13.01: ADDING THE ABILITY TO SET A USER'S EMAIL AND TESTS

You'll remember that we've hardcoded **evan@vuejs.org** as the email for any comments. What we'll do in this activity is add an email input that will set the **email** property on comments. We'll add the relevant tests in a new **tests/e2e/specs/ enter-email.js** suite:

1. In order to keep track of the email, we'll set it as a piece of reactive state in **data()** and add an email type input to the page, which will be two-way bound to **email** using **v-model**. We also add a label and corresponding markup. Note that we'll have a **data-test-id** attribute on the email input set to **email-input**.

2. We'll now add a **beforeEach** hook to set up the Cypress mock server and stub out the **GET** comments (list) request. The comments list request should be aliased as **getComments**.

3. We'll add our first test that checks whether typing into the email input works correctly. We'll go to the app, type an email, and check that what we typed is now the input value.

    When run using the Cypress UI, we should get the following passing test:

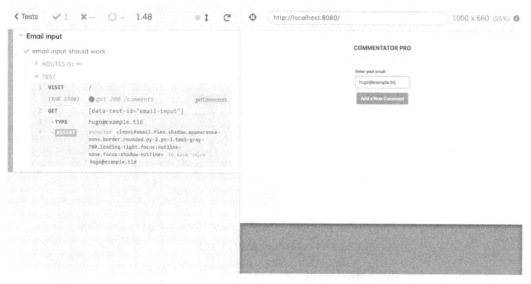

Figure 13.21: Cypress running "enter-email" tests, with the email input test

4. Having the **email** property is a pre-requisite to adding comments, so we'll disable the **Add a New Comment** button while **email** is empty (**!email**). We'll bind to the **disabled** attribute and toggle some classes based on whether or not the **email** field is populated.

5. With this new **disable add new comment button while email is empty** functionality, we should add a new E2E test. We'll load up the page and on initial load, we'll check that the email input is empty and that the **Add a New Comment** button is disabled. We'll then type an email into the email input field and check that the **Add a New Comment** button is now *not* disabled, which means it is enabled.

When run using the Cypress UI, we should see the new test passing with the following output:

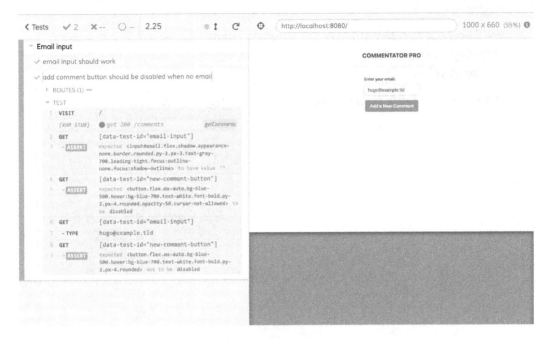

Figure 13.22: Cypress running "enter-email" tests, with the disabled add comment button test

6. Now that we've got a way to capture the email, we should pass it to the backend API when making the POST comments call (that is, when submitting a new comment). In order to do this, we should modify the spot in **methods. submitNewComment** where **email** is hardcoded as **evan@vuejs.org**.

7. Now that we're using the email that's been input by the user, we should write an E2E test to check that it's being sent. We'll stub out the POST request, alias it to **newComment**, and send back an arbitrary value. We can then visit the page, fill out the email input, open the comment editor, fill that out, and submit it. We'll then wait on the **newComment** request and assert on the request body that the body and email are as they were when we completed them.

> **NOTE**
>
> We could also opt to not stub out the **POST** request and instead check that the new comment card inserted on the page contains the right email and body.

When run using the Cypress UI, we get the following test run output:

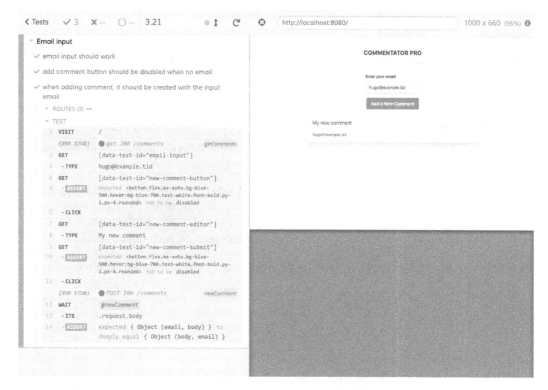

Figure 13.23: Cypress running "enter-email" tests, with the email input test

> **NOTE**
>
> The solution to this activity can be found on page 723.

SUMMARY

Throughout this chapter, we've looked at leveraging Cypress to test Vue.js applications from end to end.

E2E tests in general are useful to give us a high level of confidence that tested flows will work as expected, as opposed to unit or integration tests, which validate that our code works as expected at a much lower overhead.

We've seen how to use Cypress to inspect, interact with, and assert against a UI. We've also shown how Cypress' default wait/retry functionality is a great advantage while writing robust tests.

We leveraged Cypress' HTTP interception library to stub out HTTP requests and make tests more predictable and faster.

Finally, we looked at how to set up visual regression testing with Cypress.

In the next chapter, we'll look at how to deploy a Vue.js application to the web.

14

DEPLOYING YOUR CODE TO THE WEB

OVERVIEW

By the end of this chapter, you will be able to explain the benefits of a CI/CD workflow and how it ties into the release cycle, release cadence, and development workflows. To this end, you'll be able to articulate what the differences between Vue.js development and production builds are and what trade-offs are made. In order to test and deploy a Vue.js application, you'll configure GitLab CI/CD with pipelines, jobs, and steps. You'll become familiar with Netlify, AWS S3, and AWS CloudFront, and their key similarities and differences.

In this chapter, we will look at how to deploy a Vue.js application to be consumed over the World Wide Web and how to automate this deployment process to release often with ease and confidence.

INTRODUCTION

In this chapter, we will look at how you might leverage CI/CD tools and techniques to deliver applications to production with high confidence and at high frequency.

In previous chapters, we saw how to build and test complex Vue.js applications. This chapter is about leveraging all the techniques, including testing and automating them, in order to deliver software to production with minimal risk and time overhead.

THE BENEFITS OF CI/CD AS PART OF AN AGILE SOFTWARE DEVELOPMENT PROCESS

Continuous integration (**CI**) is the practice of integrating code multiple times a day. In order to support this, a modern **version control system** (**VCS**) such as Git that supports multiple working states (branches) in a single repository is necessary in order to allow developers to work on code independently, while still allowing them to collaborate and integrate their changes safely.

To augment the abilities of the VCS, hosting and collaboration tools around repositories (such as GitLab or GitHub) have been created and allow developers to view and manage code changes more efficiently through a web **user interface** (**UI**).

As part of, or in addition to, these hosting platforms and the collaboration tools they provide, automated checks are crucial to maintaining high confidence in the quality of the code before, during, and after integration. Adopting a CI approach often entails including additional code quality steps, such as unit or integration tests, coverage checks, and building artifacts on the mainline branches (branches into which changes are integrated) every time any new code is integrated.

The conventions that a team follows for using Git for code collaboration and CI are called a **Git workflow**, which is often shortened to **Git flow**.

A Git flow will predicate branch naming conventions, as well as how and when changes are integrated. For example, a team might decide that branches should be prefixed with ticket numbers followed by a short dash-cased description such as `WRK-2334-fix-ie-11-scroll`.

Other examples of conventions that are decided on and adhered to as part of a Git flow are commit message lengths and titles, the automated checks that should pass or are allowed to fail, and the number of reviewers required to merge a change request, which is a pull request or merge request in GitHub and GitLab parlance, respectively.

Git flows fall under two rough categories: trunk-based development and (feature) branch-based development. We'll cover branch-based development first since its limitations have become quite clear and the majority of projects tend to use trunk-based development.

In a branch-based Git workflow, multiple working branches are kept in the repository. Branch-based flows can be used to keep branches that mirror the state of environments.

For example, the following diagram shows three branches – **production, staging,** and **develop. production** does not contain any changes from **staging** or **develop. staging** is ahead of **production** but has no changes in common with **develop** other than the changes that are on **production. develop** is ahead of both **staging** and **production**: it's branched off of **production** at the same commit as **staging** is, but it doesn't share any further commits with **staging**:

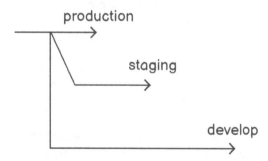

Figure 14.1: An example of a branch-based Git commit/branch tree with three environment branches

A branch-based workflow can also be used to keep track of changes going into release lines. This is useful in cases where a project has to maintain two versions of an application or library, but bug fixes or security patches need to be applied to both versions.

In the following example, we have got a similar branching example as the environment branch one. Release 1.0.0 contains some changes that are not present in 1.0.1 and 1.1.0 but does not share any of the newer code. Releases 1.0.1 and 1.1.0 are branched off of 1.0.0 at the same time, but they do not share further changes:

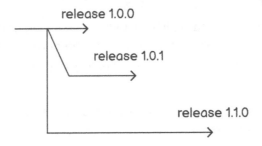

Figure 14.2: An example of a branch-based Git commit/branch tree with three release branches

In a trunk-based Git flow, each member of the team will create new branches off of a single branch, usually the "master" branch. This process is often referred to as "branching off of":

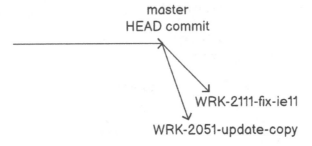

Figure 14.3: A sample trunk-based Git commit/branch tree with two feature branches branched off of the master

An extreme case of a trunk-based workflow is to have a *single* branch that everyone commits on.

> **NOTE**
>
> In a trunk-based environment, an alternative to "release branches" is to use Git tags to keep track of release snapshots. This gives the same advantages as maintaining branches with reduced branch noise and the added benefit of immutability since tags cannot be changed once they're created.

Continuous delivery (**CD**) is the ability of a team to deploy every good build to a production environment.

A pre-requisite to CD is CI, since CI provides some initial confidence in the quality of a build. As part of CD, new systems, tools, and practices are required beyond CI.

Refer to the following diagram for a look at the tools and practices that relate more to CI and those that relate more to CD:

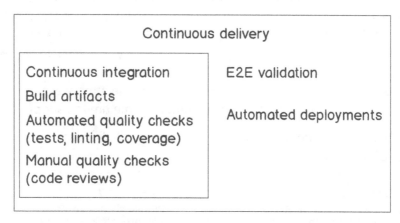

Figure 14.4: The relationship between CI and CD practices

The extra ingredient required to adopt CD is a high level of confidence that the application is going to keep working as expected (for the end user) and that new defects have not been unwittingly introduced. This means an additional end-to-end testing step is needed during or after the CI checks, to validate the build before being able to deploy it.

These end-to-end tests can be conducted manually, or they can be automated. In an ideal CD setup, the latter (automated end-to-end tests) is preferred since it means deployments do not include manual interaction. If the end-to-end tests pass, the build can automatically be deployed.

In order to facilitate CD, systems used to deploy software have had to be rethought. As part of CD, deployment cannot be a long-winded manual process. This has led to companies adopting cloud-native technologies, such as Docker, and infrastructure as code tools, such as HashiCorp's **Terraform**.

The emphasis on moving toward CD practices has led to the inception of ideas such as **GitOps** and **ChatOps**.

In GitOps and ChatOps, deployments and operational tasks are driven by the tools that developers and stakeholders interact with daily.

In GitOps, deployments can be done through GitHub/GitLab (or another Git-hosting provider), directly with GitHub Actions or GitLab CI/CD, or through CI/CD software (such as CircleCI or Jenkins), which have tight integrations and reporting with GitHub/GitLab.

In the case of ChatOps, conversational interfaces are used to deploy and operate software. Some flavors of ChatOps can be considered a subset of GitOps, for example, interacting with tools such as **Dependabot** (a tool that keeps a project's dependencies up to date) through comments on a GitHub pull request. ChatOps can also be implemented right into real-time chat tools, such as Slack or Microsoft Teams. Someone might send a message such as `deploy <service-name> <environment>`, which will deploy the service to the relevant environment. Note that chat interfaces are very reminiscent of command-line interfaces that developers might be used to but other stakeholders might take some time to adopt.

We've now looked at approaches to CI and CD; what we'll discuss next is the advantages of using CI and CD:

Continuous Integration	Continuous Delivery
Ensures the changeset being integrated is small (at most a couple days' worth of work).	Delivering value to production can be done more often and more safely.
Reduces the chance of huge sweeping changes across the codebase causing unforeseen bugs.	A small changeset (a couple of days' worth of work) can be rolled back without any issue.
Testing, code quality, and review steps give confidence in a clean integration.	A larger changeset due to a longer fixed (monthly, weekly, every sprint) release cadence (as opposed to CD) can have unforeseen consequences; the effect of rollback on a large release is complicated or difficult to grasp.

Figure 14.5: Advantages of CI and CD

Both practices also have an impact on the team's mindset and performance. Being able to see the changes you make integrated within a day and in production in less than a week means that contributors can see their work having an impact immediately.

CI/CD also helps promote agile principles, where changes are applied and deployed iteratively. This is as opposed to long timelines for projects, for which inaccuracies in estimations compound and can cause major delays.

BUILDING FOR PRODUCTION

Deploying applications to production starts with creating an artifact that can be deployed. In the case of Vue.js, we're building a client-side application, which means our build artifact will contain HTML, JavaScript, and CSS files.

The Vue CLI comes with a **build** command. This **build** command will take our Vue.js single-file components (.**vue** files) and compile them into render functions (JavaScript functions that the Vue runtime can use to render our application) that will be output to JavaScript.

As part of the build process, the Vue CLI will take JavaScript, Vue single-file components, and modules that are imported into each other and *bundle* them. Bundling means that related chunks of code that depend on each other will be output as a single JavaScript file.

Due to our use of the Vue CLI, the Vue.js library itself can also be slimmed down. The Vue.js runtime bundle can include a **runtime compiler** that takes string templates and turns them into render functions on the client side. Since we are compiling to render functions with the Vue CLI at build time, this part of Vue.js doesn't need to be included in our JavaScript.

The Vue CLI build step also includes a **dead code elimination** step. That means that it can analyze the code being generated and if any of it is obviously never used – for example, a statement such as **if (false) { /* do something */}** – then it will not be present in the build output.

By default, the Vue CLI builds for production when we call **vue service build**, which in Vue CLI projects is aliased to the **build** script, which can be run with **npm run build** or **yarn build**.

In a sample Vue CLI project, we'll see something along these lines:

```
) npm run build --silent

-  Building for production...


 DONE  Compiled successfully in 9453ms                      18:01:45

   File                              Size            Gzipped

   dist/js/chunk-vendors.bf9ee9a7.js    82.97 KiB        29.75 KiB
   dist/js/app.87c07e00.js              4.64 KiB         1.65 KiB
   dist/css/app.e2713bb0.css            0.33 KiB         0.23 KiB

   Images and other types of assets omitted.

   DONE  Build complete. The dist directory is ready to be deployed.
   INFO  Check out deployment instructions at https://cli.vuejs.org/guide/depl
 oyment.html
```

Figure 14.6: Output of "npm run build" in a fresh Vue CLI project

The **dist** folder is now ready to deploy using a static hosting solution such as Netlify or AWS S3 and CloudFront.

We have now seen how to build a Vue.js application for production using the Vue CLI with the **npm run build** command.

Next, we will see how to use GitLab CI/CD to test our code (before deploying it).

USING GITLAB CI/CD TO TEST YOUR CODE

GitLab has a built-in CI/CD tool called GitLab CI/CD.

In order to use GitLab CI/CD, you'll need a GitLab account.

To interact with Git repositories hosted on GitLab, you'll also need to associate an SSH key from your machine and to your GitLab account.

> **NOTE**
>
> Instructions to add an SSH key in the GitLab documentation can be found at https://docs.gitlab.com/ee/gitlab-basics/create-your-ssh-keys.html.

Once you've created an account, you can create a new repository using the **New Project** button at the top right of the **Projects** page, as shown in the following screenshot:

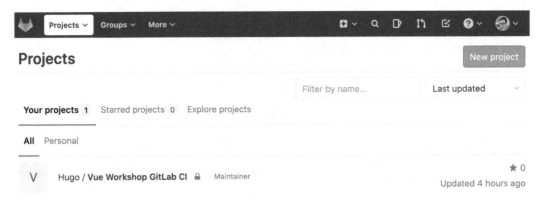

Figure 14.7: The GitLab "Projects" page with the New Project button

If you click the **New Project** button, you will be taken to the **New Project** page, where you can use the default **Blank Project** tab to create a project by giving it a name and a slug, as seen in the following screenshot:

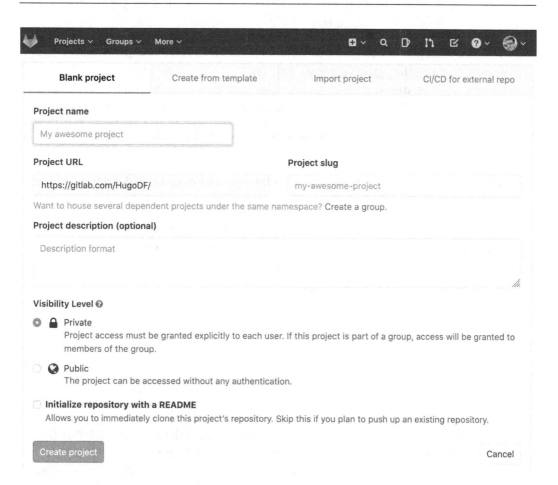

Figure 14.8: The GitLab New Project page with Blank Project selected

Once you click **Create Project**, the GitLab **Project** page will appear in an empty state that displays instructions on how to clone it. You should run the commands required to clone the repository, which probably boils down to an equivalent of the following (which you are expected to run on your machine):

> **NOTE**
>
> If you did not associate an SSH key with your account, at this stage GitLab should be showing you a warning with a link you can follow to set up an SSH key.

```
git clone <repository-url>
```

On your machine, you should then open the directory into which the repository was cloned. To add GitLab CI/CD, we need to add a `.gitlab-ci.yml` file into the root of the project. A sample `.gitlab-ci.yml` file that adds a `build` job to the `build` stage of the pipeline that installs dependencies (using `npm ci`), runs the production build (`npm run build`), and caches the output artifact is defined as follows.

The job name is defined by setting a top-level key in the YAML file – in this case, `build:`.

In YAML syntax, we'll then increase the indent to denote that the `build` key points to an object.

In the `build job` object, we will define which Docker image is used to run the job, using `image: node:lts`. This means we want this job to run on a Node.js **Long Term Support** (**LTS**) image, which will be Node.js 12 until October 20, 2020, at which point it will point to a Node.js 14 image.

> **NOTE**
>
> You can access the up-to-date Node.js LTS schedule at
> https://nodejs.org/en/about/releases/.

The other property we can define in our job is the stage. GitLab CI/CD pipelines by default have three stages: **build**, **test**, and **deploy**. These stages can be replaced using custom stages when a team's workflow doesn't fit into these three categories (for example, if there is more than one environment to deploy to). See the documentation (https://docs.gitlab.com/ee/ci/yaml/#stages).

> **NOTE**
>
> `stages` is used to define stages that can be used by jobs, and it is defined globally.
>
> The specification of `stages` allows for flexible multistage pipelines. The ordering of elements in stages defines the ordering of jobs' execution:
>
> a) Jobs of the same stage are run in parallel.
>
> b) Jobs of the next stage are run after the jobs from the previous stage complete successfully.

Our pipeline only has one stage and one job at the moment, so most of the preceding doesn't apply to us.

The final properties we set are **script**, which defines steps that should be run when the job is running, and **artifacts**, which configures artifact storage. In our case, we'll run **npm ci** to install all dependencies followed by **npm run build**, which will run the production Vue.js CLI build. Our artifact is set up to be held for a week and to contain the **dist** folder (which is where the Vue CLI **build** output is stored).

In full, we have the following:

```
build:
  image: node:lts
  stage: build
  script:
    - npm ci
    - npm run build
  artifacts:
    expire_in: 1 week
    paths:
      - dist
```

Once we push this **.gitlab-ci.yml** file to a repository containing a Vue CLI project, we will see the following in the repository view, where a pipeline with one step is running on the latest commit:

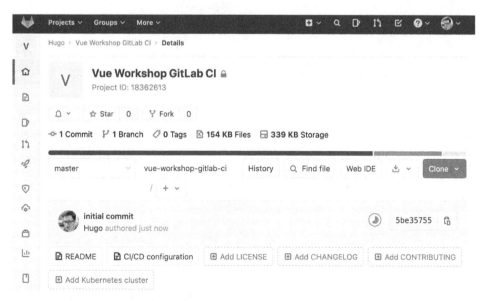

Figure 14.9: GitLab repository view with the build job running on the latest commit

If we click on the **Pipeline** icon (the blue in-progress indicator), we get the pipeline view. In the pipeline view, **Build** represents the **state** pipeline (which we set as **build**) and it represents the job name (which we defined as **build**). We see the same in-progress indicator until the job completes, as follows:

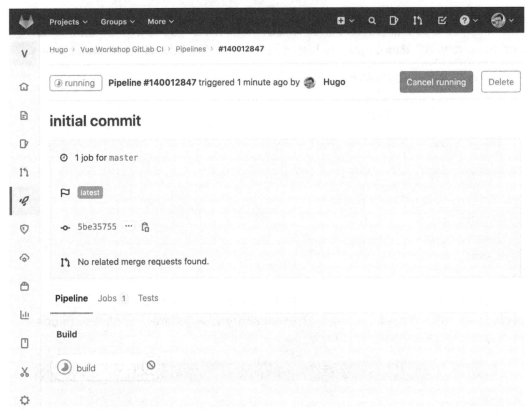

Figure 14.10: GitLab CI pipeline view with the build job running

Once the job completes, we see a **success** icon (green check-mark). We can click this icon or the job name to access the job view while the job is running or after it has completed (whether it has failed or succeeded). When a job has completed, we also see a **Retry** icon, which can be useful to retry a failed pipeline step. The following screenshot shows that the job ran successfully:

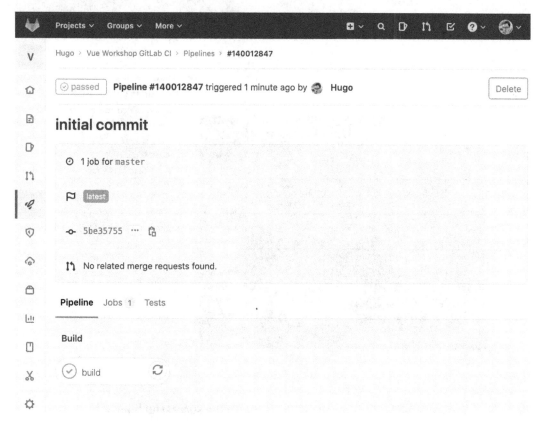

Figure 14.11: GitLab CI pipeline view with the build job passing

After clicking the job, we see the **Job** view, which shows us a detailed breakdown of all the steps in the job. Starting with the **Preparing the docker_machine executor** steps, which load up the Node.js Docker image, we see steps for running the script as well as cache and artifact restores, as follows:

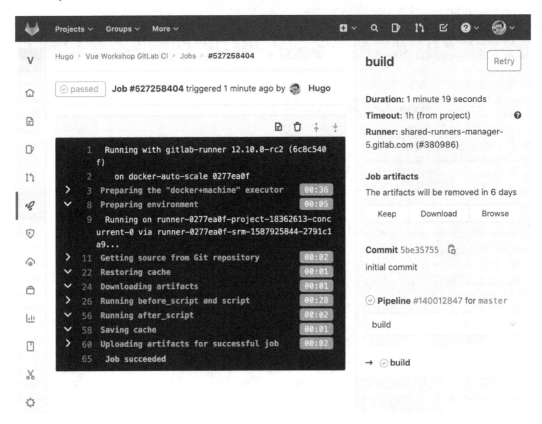

Figure 14.12: The GitLab CI job view with the successful build job

If we want to add a **test** step to our GitLab CI/CD runs, we need to be in a project that supports unit testing. This can be achieved using the Vue CLI, which is installed using **vue add @vue/unit-jest**. Installing and adding unit tests is covered in depth in *Chapter 12, Unit Testing*.

We will need to add a new job to the **.gitlab-ci.yml** file; we will call it **test**, use the **node:lts** image, and assign the job to the **test** state. In the job, we run **npm ci**, followed by **npm run test:unit** (which is the **npm** script added by the **unit-jest** CLI plugin):

```
# rest of .gitlab-ci.yml
test:
  image: node:lts
  stage: test
  script:
    - npm ci
    - npm run test:unit
```

Once we push this new **.gitlab-ci.yml** file up, we get the following view on the main repository page:

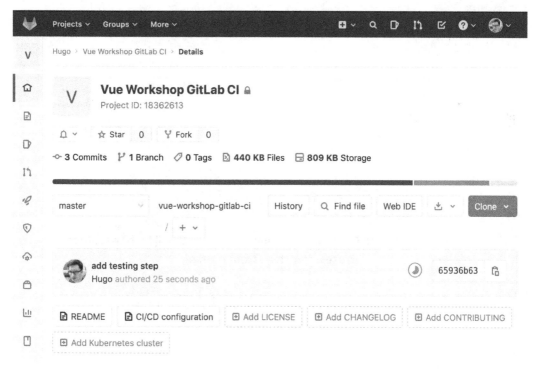

Figure 14.13: Repository view with GitLab CI/CD running the pipeline with the new test step

We can click through to the pipeline view. The reason GitLab CI/CD uses pipelines is that a failing step at a certain stage will mean steps in any subsequent stages will not run. For example, if we get a failing **build** job, the jobs that are part of the **test** stage will not run. The following screenshot explains this well:

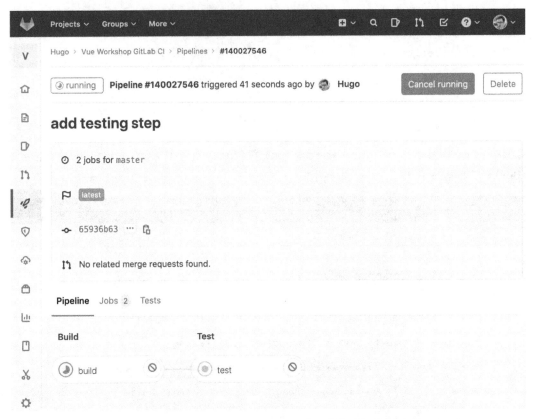

Figure 14.14: GitLab CI/CD pipeline view with a failed build job that stops the test job/stage from running

If we push another commit or retry the build step (if the failure is not caused by changes) and navigate to the pipeline view again, we'll see the following:

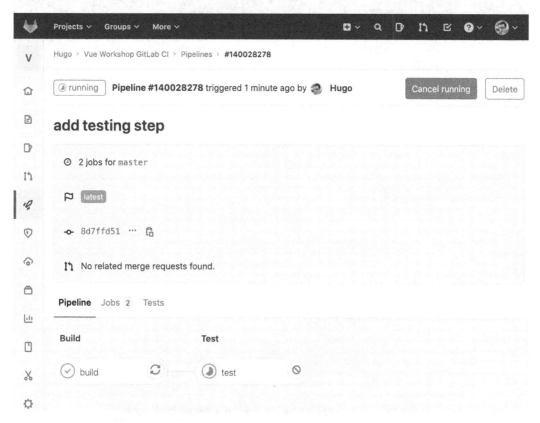

Figure 14.15: GitLab CI/CD pipeline view with the test job running
after the build stage jobs have all succeeded

Once the **test** job has succeeded, we'll see the following pipeline:

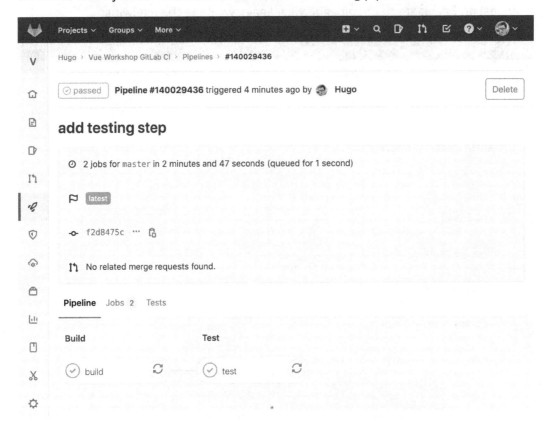

Figure 14.16: GitLab CI/CD pipeline view with all jobs
succeeding in the build and test stages

We've now added a GitLab CI/CD pipeline with the **build** and **test** stages that
will validate that on every push to the GitLab repository, the code still integrates
as expected.

EXERCISE 14.01: ADDING A LINT STEP TO YOUR GITLAB CI/CD PIPELINE

Linting is a way to get automated formatting and code style checks. Integrating it as part of CI makes sure that all code merged into the mainline branches adheres to a team's code style guide. It also reduces the number of code style review comments, which can be noisy and might detract from fundamental issues with the change request.

To access the code files for this exercise, refer to https://packt.live/2IQDFW0:

1. In order to add linting, we need to ensure that our **package.json** file includes the **lint** script. If it's missing, we'll need to add it and set it to **vue-cli-service lint**:

```
{
  "// other": "properties",
  "scripts": {
    "// other": "scripts",
    "lint": "vue-cli-service lint",
    "// other": "scripts"
  },
  "// more": "properties"
}
```

2. In order to run the lint on GitLab CI/CD, we need to add a new **lint** job that will run in a Node.js LTS Docker image at the **test** stage of the GitLab CI/CD pipeline. We will do this in **.gitlab-ci.yml**:

```
lint:
  image: node:lts
  stage: test
```

3. For the **lint** job to run the **lint** script as per **package.json**, we need to add a **script** section in the **.gitlab-ci.yml** file. It first needs to run **npm ci** to install the dependencies, and then **npm run lint** to run the linting:

```
lint:
  image: node:lts
  stage: test
  script:
    - npm ci
    - npm run lint
```

4. Finally, we need to commit and push the code to GitLab using the following commands:

```
git add .
git commit -m "add linting"
git push
```

Once the code is pushed, we can see the pipeline run using the GitLab CI/CD UI, as follows. Note how all the jobs at the **test** stage are run in parallel:

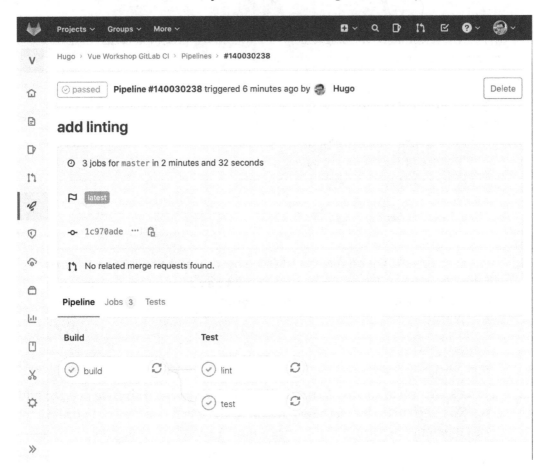

Figure 14.17: The GitLab CI/CD pipeline view with all the jobs succeeding, including "test" and "lint" running in parallel

We've now seen how to use GitLab CI/CD to run builds and tests on every commit.

Next, we'll see how to deploy a Vue.js application to Netlify.

DEPLOYING TO NETLIFY

Netlify is a hosting provider that specializes in static hosting and relevant supporting services in order to have a fully interactive site that uses static hosting. This includes offerings such as Netlify Functions (serverless functions), Netlify Forms (a no-backend form submission system), and Netlify Identity (an identity/authentication provider).

The following sections require you to have a Netlify account, which is free.

The simplest way to deploy a site to Netlify is to use the drag and drop interface. You'll find this at the bottom of the home page in the logged-in view: https://app.netlify.com. It looks as follows:

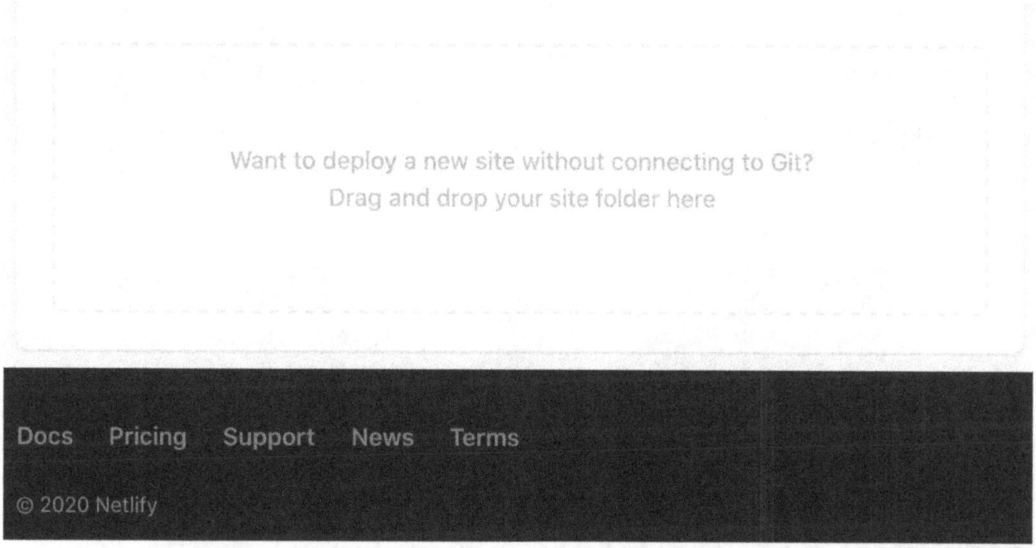

Want to deploy a new site without connecting to Git?
Drag and drop your site folder here

Docs   Pricing   Support   News   Terms

© 2020 Netlify

Figure 14.18: Netlify's drag and drop deployment section at the bottom of the App home page

We can, therefore, choose a project where we've run the **npm run build** command and deploy the **dist** folder by simply dragging it to the drag and drop deployment section, as shown in the following screenshot:

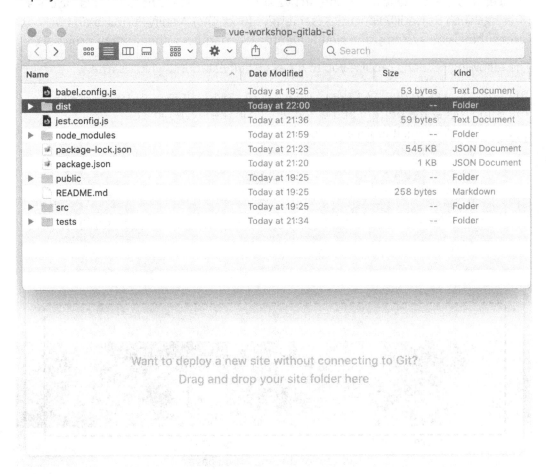

Figure 14.19: Dragging and dropping the dist folder onto the Netlify drag and drop deployment section

Once the upload has succeeded, Netlify redirects you to your new website's administration page. This will look as follows:

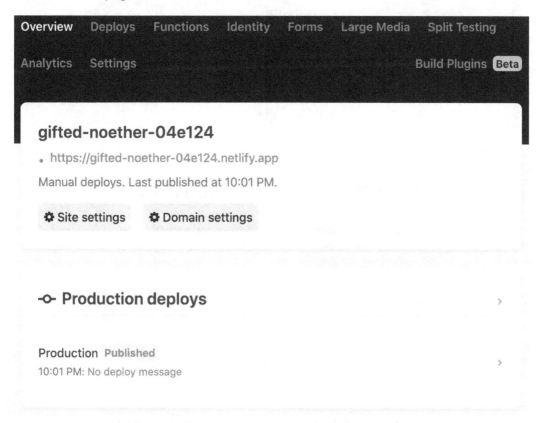

Figure 14.20: The Netlify new app page for the drag and drop site

We can click on the link to the site and we'll see the default Vue CLI home page template, as follows:

Welcome to Your Vue.js App

For a guide and recipes on how to configure / customize this project,
check out the vue-cli documentation.

Installed CLI Plugins

babel   eslint

Essential Links

Core Docs   Forum   Community Chat   Twitter   News

Figure 14.21: Netlify new app displaying a greeting message

We have now seen how to manually deploy a site to Netlify using the drag and drop interface.

Next, we will see how to deploy our site from GitLab to Netlify.

On the Netlify app home page, we need to click the `New site from Git` button, as displayed in the following screenshot:

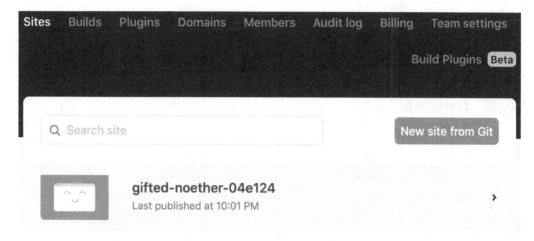

Figure 14.22: Netlify home page with the New site from Git button

We'll see a page asking us to choose a Git provider to connect to. For this example, we will use **GitLab**. The following screenshot represents how the screen will look:

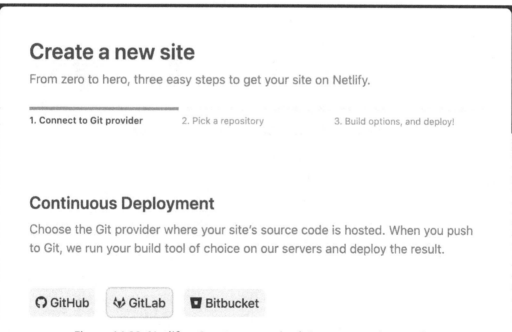

Figure 14.23: Netlify – Create a new site | Connect to Git provider

Upon clicking **GitLab**, we will get an OAuth authorization challenge from GitLab, which we need to accept by clicking on the **Authorize** button as shown in the following screenshot:

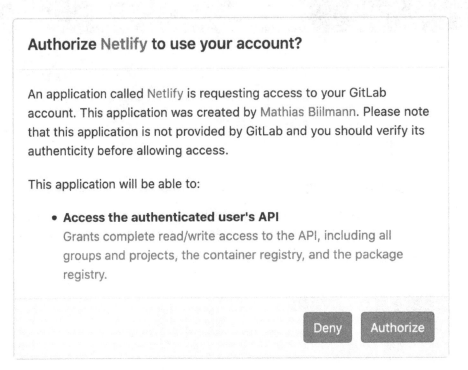

Figure 14.24: GitLab OAuth authorization modal

We will then be redirected to Netlify and asked to choose a repository to deploy, as follows:

Figure 14.25: Select a GitLab repository to deploy

We select the repository we want to deploy and are met with a configuration page. Since we're now building on Netlify's build servers, we need to configure Netlify to build the application and deploy the correct folder.

We fill out the **build** command as **npm run build** since that's our build script. The publish directory is **dist**.

We can then click the `Deploy site` button, which will start the deployment process, as follows:

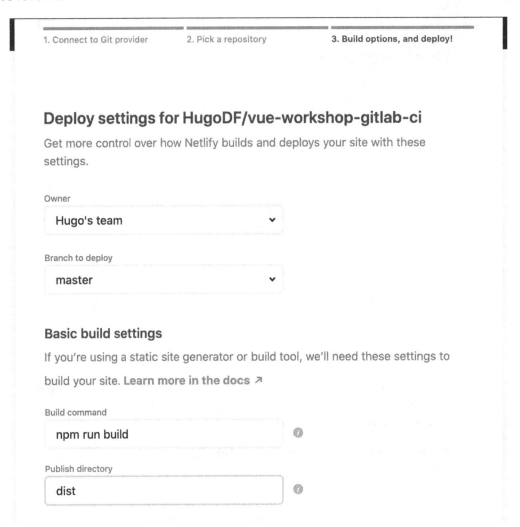

Figure 14.26: The Netlify build configuration tab, filled in with npm run build and dist for the build command and publish directory, respectively

We will then be redirected to the newly created app's page, as shown here:

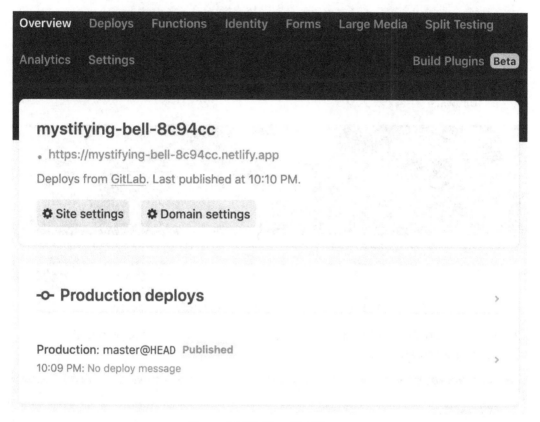

Figure 14.27: New Netlify app

We have now seen how to deploy an application to Netlify using the manual upload method and using GitLab as the Git hosting provider.

EXERCISE 14.02: DEPLOYING A SITE TO NETLIFY FROM GITHUB

We have seen how to deploy a site to Netlify from GitLab, but how different is it from deploying it from GitHub? The answer is that they are very similar; the only notable difference is the first step in the **Connect to Git provider** tab:

1. We'll begin by clicking the **New site from Git** button on the home page, as follows:

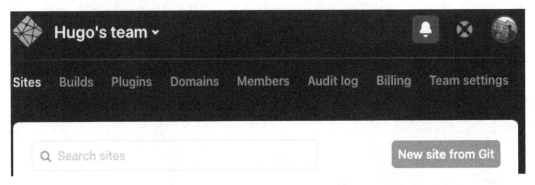

Figure 14.28: New site from Git on the Netlify dashboard

2. We will then choose **GitHub** as the Git hosting provider, as shown in the following screenshot:

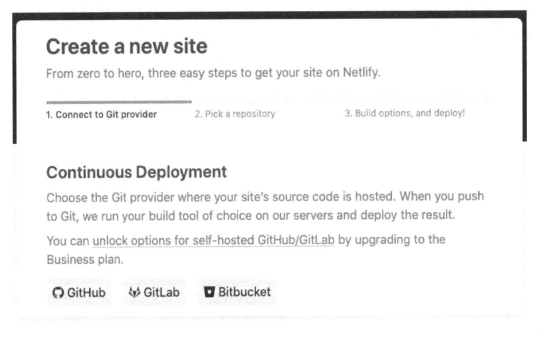

Figure 14.29: Continuous Deployment

3. When we get the GitHub OAuth authorization challenge, as shown in the following screenshot, we authorize Netlify:

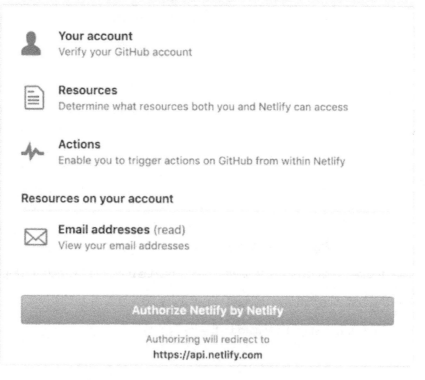

Figure 14.30: GitHub authorization challenge

4. We select the Vue CLI project we want to deploy from the repository list, as follows:

5.

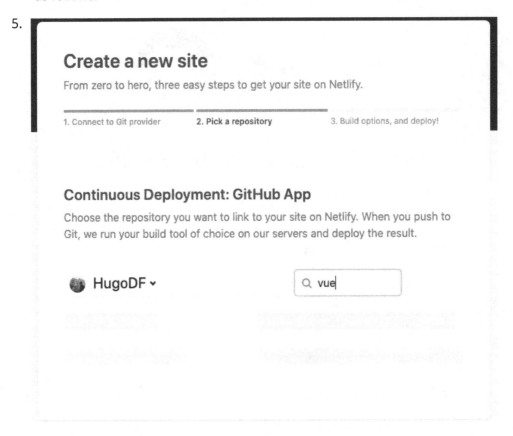

Figure 14.31: Selecting the correct repository

6. On the deployment options tab, we select **master** as the branch to deploy.

7. We set the build command as **npm run build**.

8. We set the publish directory as **dist**.

9. The completed deployment options look as follows:

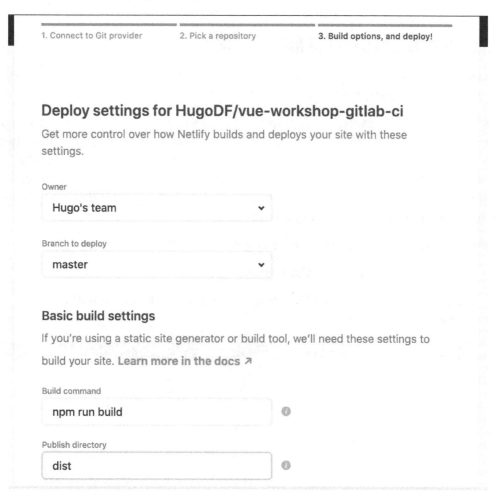

1. Connect to Git provider   2. Pick a repository   **3. Build options, and deploy!**

Deploy settings for HugoDF/vue-workshop-gitlab-ci

Get more control over how Netlify builds and deploys your site with these settings.

Owner

Hugo's team ⌄

Branch to deploy

master ⌄

Basic build settings

If you're using a static site generator or build tool, we'll need these settings to build your site. **Learn more in the docs** ↗

Build command

npm run build

Publish directory

dist

Figure 14.32: The Netlify build configuration tab filled in with npm run build and dist for the build command and publish directory, respectively

10. We click **Deploy site** to start the deployment process.

We've now seen how to deploy an application to Netlify using the manual upload method and using GitLab or GitHub as the Git hosting provider.

Next, we will see how to use **Amazon Web Services Simple Storage Service** (**AWS S3**) and AWS CloudFront to deploy a Vue.js application.

DEPLOYING TO AWS USING S3 AND CLOUDFRONT

Amazon S3 is a static storage offering that can be used as a host for static files, such as what is generated by the Vue CLI's `build` script.

CloudFront is AWS' **content delivery network** (**CDN**) offering. A CDN can improve a web application's performance by serving static content from an **edge** location. These servers are positioned around the world and are more likely to be geographically located close to the end user than the **origin** servers (the ones that actually serve the content). Edge servers in a CDN request resources from the origin if they don't have them cached but will serve subsequent requests.

A prerequisite for the following steps is an AWS account:

1. We will start by creating and configuring an S3 bucket.

    We begin by heading to the S3 product page. It will look similar to the following screenshot:

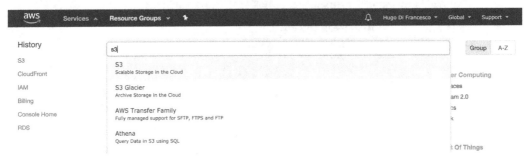

Figure 14.33: Select S3 from the AWS service list

2. On the S3 console home page, we can click the `Create bucket` button, which will take us to the bucket creation page, as seen here:

Figure 14.34: The Create bucket button on the AWS S3 console

3. To begin, we start by naming our bucket. For the purposes of this example, let's call it **vue-workshop**, as follows:

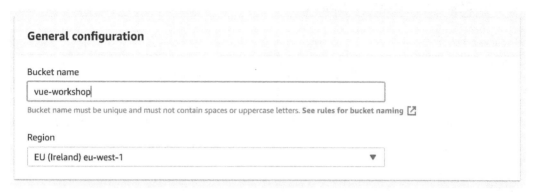

Figure 14.35: Entering the bucket name on the bucket creation page

4. We will also need to set the S3 bucket to be public. This is done by unselecting the **Block all public access** checkbox. Once this is done, we must check the acknowledgment checkbox, as seen here:

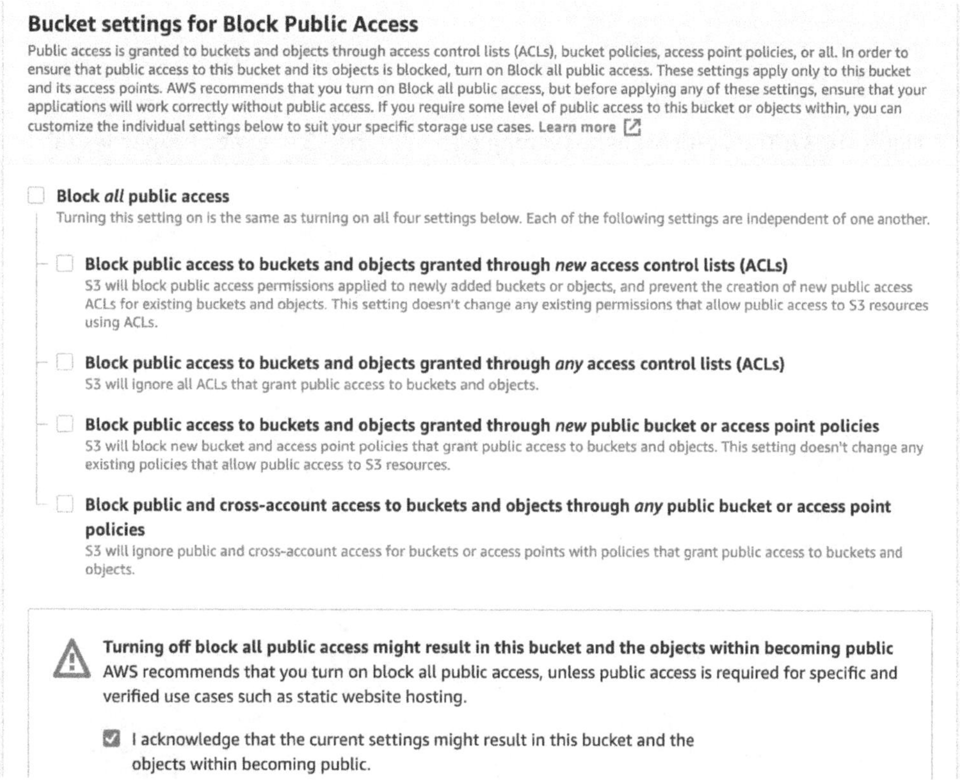

Bucket settings for Block Public Access

Public access is granted to buckets and objects through access control lists (ACLs), bucket policies, access point policies, or all. In order to ensure that public access to this bucket and its objects is blocked, turn on Block all public access. These settings apply only to this bucket and its access points. AWS recommends that you turn on Block all public access, but before applying any of these settings, ensure that your applications will work correctly without public access. If you require some level of public access to this bucket or objects within, you can customize the individual settings below to suit your specific storage use cases. Learn more ☑

☐ Block *all* public access
Turning this setting on is the same as turning on all four settings below. Each of the following settings are independent of one another.

☐ Block public access to buckets and objects granted through *new* access control lists (ACLs)
S3 will block public access permissions applied to newly added buckets or objects, and prevent the creation of new public access ACLs for existing buckets and objects. This setting doesn't change any existing permissions that allow public access to S3 resources using ACLs.

☐ Block public access to buckets and objects granted through *any* access control lists (ACLs)
S3 will ignore all ACLs that grant public access to buckets and objects.

☐ Block public access to buckets and objects granted through *new* public bucket or access point policies
S3 will block new bucket and access point policies that grant public access to buckets and objects. This setting doesn't change any existing policies that allow public access to S3 resources.

☐ Block public and cross-account access to buckets and objects through *any* public bucket or access point policies
S3 will ignore public and cross-account access for buckets or access points with policies that grant public access to buckets and objects.

⚠ **Turning off block all public access might result in this bucket and the objects within becoming public**
AWS recommends that you turn on block all public access, unless public access is required for specific and verified use cases such as static website hosting.

☑ I acknowledge that the current settings might result in this bucket and the objects within becoming public.

Figure 14.36: Set the S3 bucket to be public and acknowledge the warning

5. Once this is done, we are redirected to the bucket list page. We want to click into our new bucket. Then, we need to access the **Properties** tag in order to find the **Static website hosting** option:

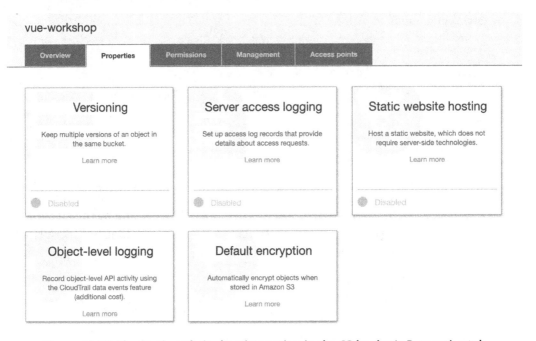

Figure 14.37: The Static website hosting option in the S3 bucket's Properties tab

7. We can fill out the `Static website hosting` S3 property, selecting `Use this bucket to host a website` and setting the index document and error document to `index.html`. It is a good idea to take note of the `Endpoint` URL, which we'll need to configure CloudFront, as follows:

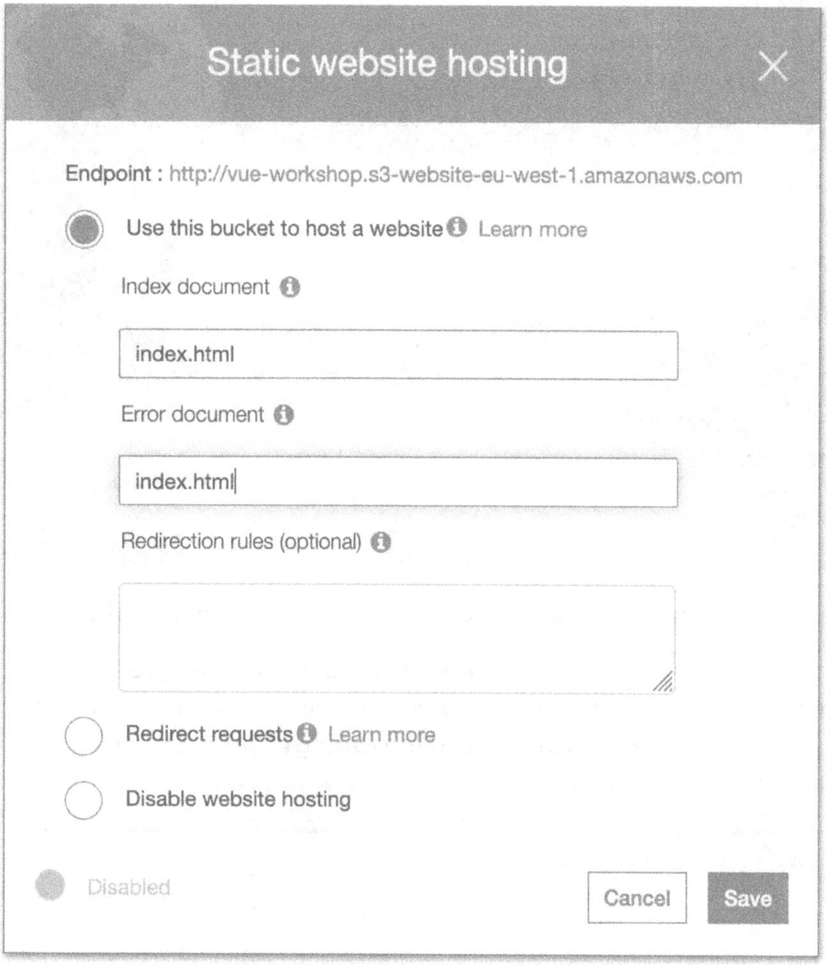

Figure 14.38: Filling out the Static website hosting S3 property

8. We can now go back to the **Overview** tab of the S3 bucket page, click **Upload**, and drag and drop the files from one of our **dist** folders, as seen in the following screenshot:

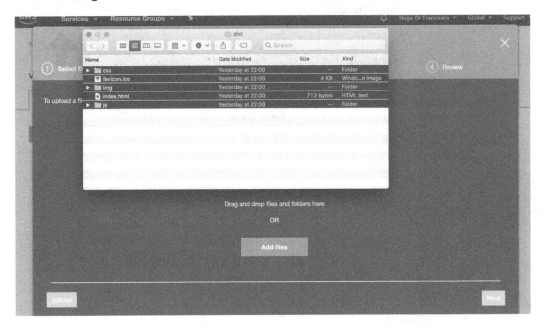

Figure 14.39: Adding files to the vue-workshop S3 bucket through drag and drop

10. Once files are dropped on the overview page, we click **Next** and need to make sure file permissions are set to **public** by selecting **Grant public read access to this object(s)** in the **Manage public permissions** section of the page. Once that is completed, we can complete the upload without any changes from the default values by clicking **Next** and **Upload**, after having reviewed the files being uploaded, as follows:

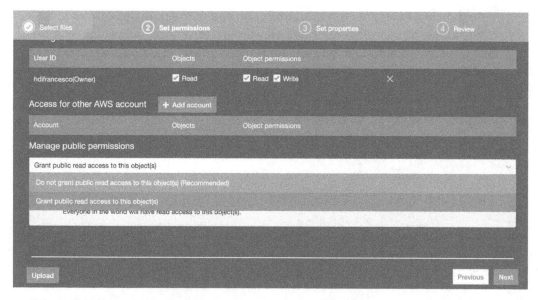

Figure 14.40: Setting file permissions to public on files being uploaded to the S3 bucket

12. Our S3 bucket should now be configured to host static content, and by visiting the website endpoint (which is available in **Properties | Static website hosting**), we see the following Vue.js application (which is what we uploaded):

Welcome to Your Vue.js App

For a guide and recipes on how to configure / customize this project,
check out the vue-cli documentation.

Installed CLI Plugins

babel   eslint

Essential Links

Core Docs   Forum   Community Chat   Twitter   News

Figure 14.41: The Vue.js application being served from our AWS S3 bucket

Note that S3 can only serve sites over HTTP, and domain names cannot be configured directly from S3 buckets. Beyond performance and robustness, being able to set custom domain names and HTTPS support are other reasons to set up AWS CloudFront as a CDN for our website.

13. We will start by navigating to the CloudFront console and clicking the **Create Distribution** button as follows:

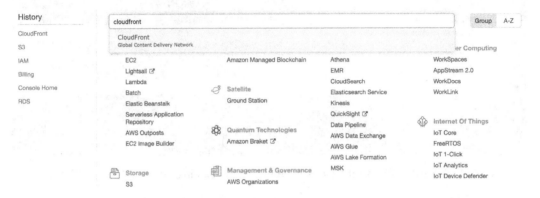

Figure 14.42: Select CloudFront from the AWS service list

15. When prompted for which type of distribution we want to create, we will select **Web** by clicking the relevant **Get Started** button, as seen in the following screenshot:

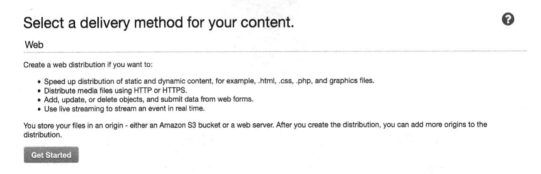

Figure 14.43: Choosing to create a Web CloudFront distribution

17. **Origin Domain Name** should be the S3 bucket website endpoint domain – in other words, the domain of the URL we used to access it earlier. It looks something like **example.s3-website.us-west-1.amazonaws.com** for the **example** bucket in the **us-east-1** region. The following screenshot displays this:

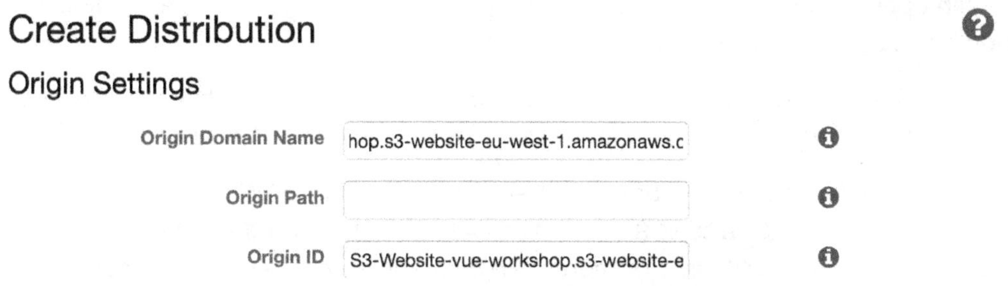

Create Distribution

Origin Settings

Origin Domain Name	hop.s3-website-eu-west-1.amazonaws.c
Origin Path	
Origin ID	S3-Website-vue-workshop.s3-website-e

**Figure 14.44: Enter the website endpoint domain in the CloudFront
distribution's "Origin Domain Name" field**

18. While we are setting up the distribution, it's a good idea to select the **Redirect HTTP to HTTPS** option for the **Default Cache Behavior** section's **Viewer Protocol Policy** field as follows:

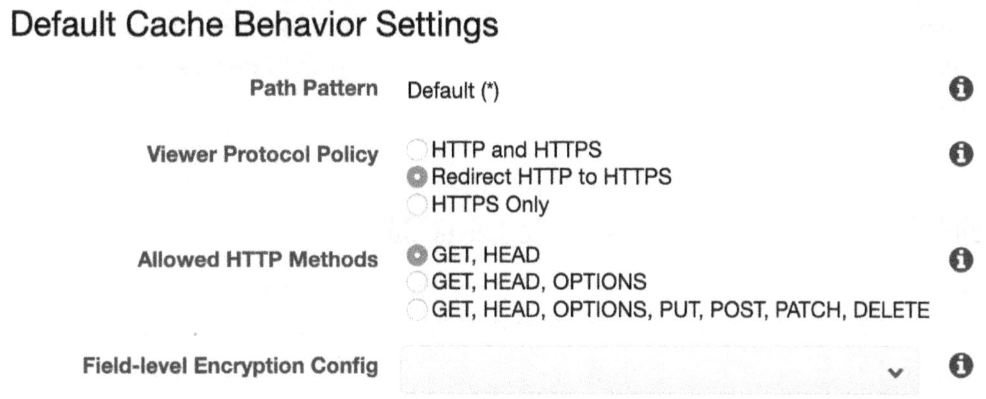

Default Cache Behavior Settings

Path Pattern	Default (*)
Viewer Protocol Policy	HTTP and HTTPS ⦿ Redirect HTTP to HTTPS HTTPS Only
Allowed HTTP Methods	⦿ GET, HEAD GET, HEAD, OPTIONS GET, HEAD, OPTIONS, PUT, POST, PATCH, DELETE
Field-level Encryption Config	

Figure 14.45: Select Redirect HTTP to HTTPS for the Viewer Protocol Policy field

We are now ready to click the **Create Distribution** button and wait for the changes to propagate.

> **NOTE**
>
> CloudFront distribution changes take a while to propagate since they are being deployed to servers around the world.

We can open the domain name for the CloudFront distribution once the console shows its status as **Deployed**.

We have seen how to set up S3 and CloudFront to serve a static website. We will now see how to use the AWS CLI to synchronize a local directory to the S3 bucket.

A prerequisite for the next section is a shell instance that has AWS credentials injected using the **AWS_ACCESS_KEY_ID**, **AWS_SECRET_ACCESS_KEY**, and **AWS_DEFAULT_REGION** environment variables. The access key and secret key need to be generated from the **Account** dropdown | **My Security Credentials** | **Access Keys**. It also requires the AWS CLI version 2.

If we're in a Vue CLI project, we can deploy the **dist** folder (which can be built using **npm run build**) to our **vue-workshop** bucket using an AWS S3 CLI command. We want to update an **s3** resource so that our command will start with **aws s3**. The command we want to issue is to synchronize files, so we will use the **aws s3 sync** command. We will sync **./dist** to the **vue-workshop** S3 bucket, using the AWS URI syntax – that is, **s3://vue-workshop**. We also want to make sure that the files we upload, just like the bucket configuration, allow **public-read**. In full, the command looks as follows:

```
aws s3 sync ./dist s3://vue-workshop --acl=public-read
```

EXERCISE 14.03: DEPLOYING TO S3 FROM GITLAB CI/CD

S3 is a very cost-effective and performant solution for storing static files at scale. In this exercise, we'll look at how to integrate GitLab CI/CD and AWS S3 to deploy a Vue.js application. This automates the deployment of the Vue.js application. The deployment will run on every push to GitLab without any manual intervention.

To access the code files for this exercise, refer to https://packt.live/3kJ1HPD.

In order to deploy to the S3 bucket from GitLab CI/CD, we will need to first set credential management:

1. Navigate to the **CI/CD** settings section of GitLab as follows:

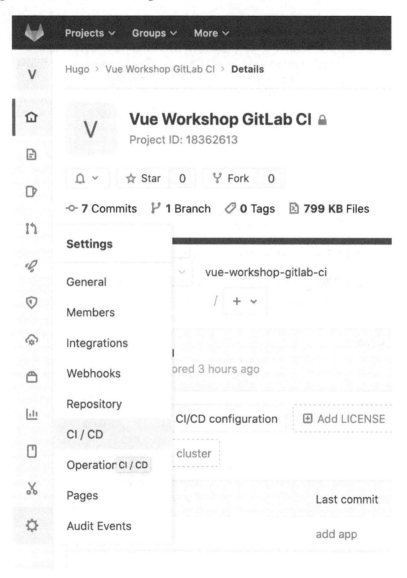

Figure 14.46: CI/CD in the Settings menu

2. We will want to add variables, so let's expand that section. You will see a message as shown in the following screenshot:

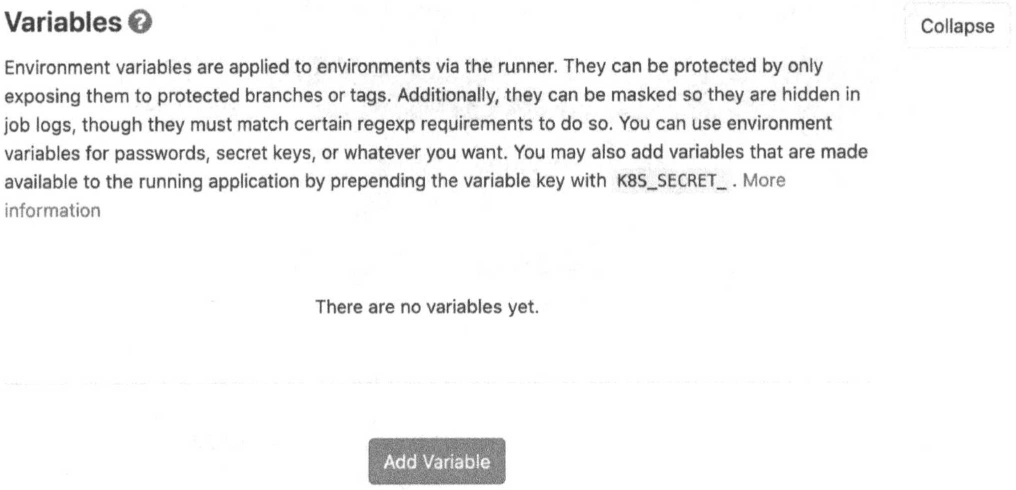

Variables ❓

Environment variables are applied to environments via the runner. They can be protected by only exposing them to protected branches or tags. Additionally, they can be masked so they are hidden in job logs, though they must match certain regexp requirements to do so. You can use environment variables for passwords, secret keys, or whatever you want. You may also add variables that are made available to the running application by prepending the variable key with `K8S_SECRET_`. More information

Collapse

There are no variables yet.

Add Variable

Figure 14.47: The Variables section of the GitLab CI/CD settings expanded

3. Next, we'll add **AWS_ACCESS_KEY_ID** and **AWS_SECRET_ACCESS_KEY** using the UI (values not shown since they're sensitive API keys), as follows:

4.

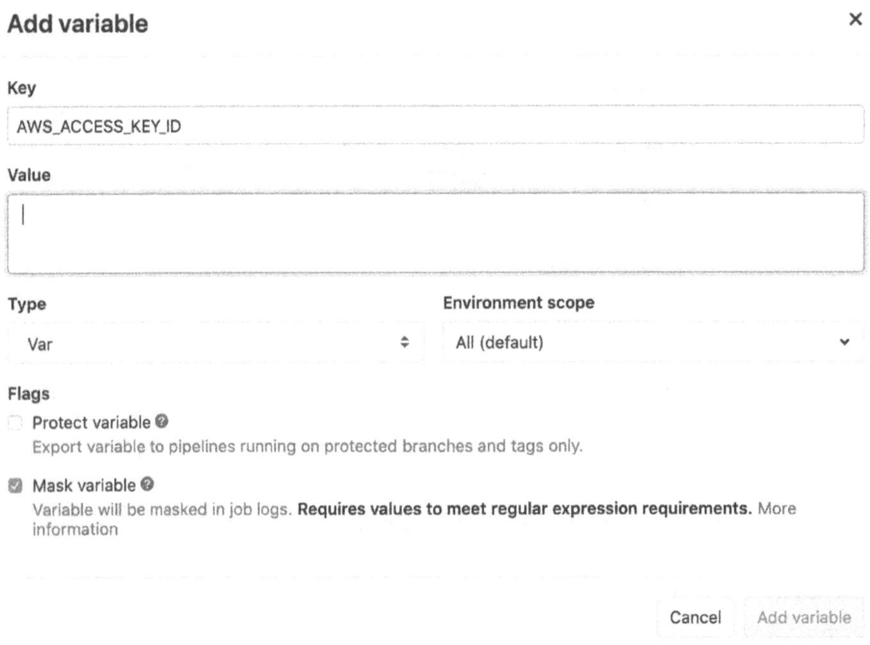

Add variable   ✕

Key

    AWS_ACCESS_KEY_ID

Value

    |

Type   **Environment scope**

    Var   ⇕   All (default)   ⌄

Flags

◌ Protect variable ❓
  Export variable to pipelines running on protected branches and tags only.

☑ Mask variable ❓
  Variable will be masked in job logs. **Requires values to meet regular expression requirements.** More information

                                          Cancel   Add variable

Figure 14.48: Entering the AWS_ACCESS_KEY_ID environment variable

5. We can then add the default **AWS_REGION** variable using the UI. This isn't so sensitive, so its value is shown in the following screenshot:

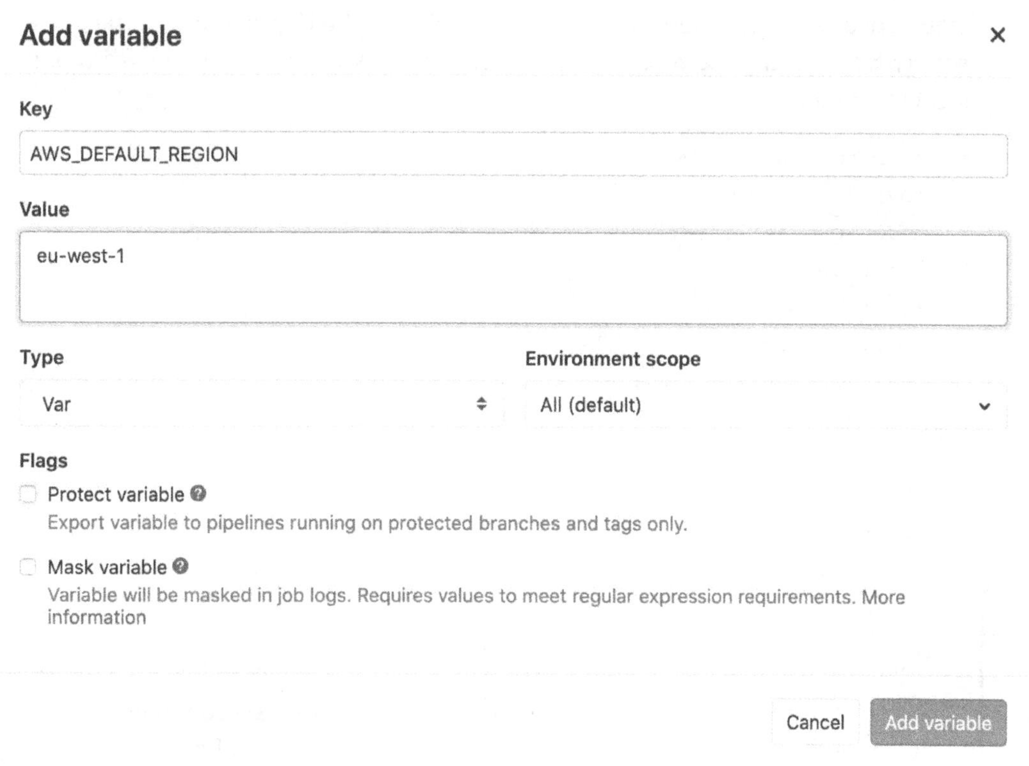

Add variable ✕

Key

| AWS_DEFAULT_REGION |

Value

| eu-west-1 |

Type		**Environment scope**
Var	⇕	All (default)	⌄

Flags

☐ Protect variable ❓
Export variable to pipelines running on protected branches and tags only.

☐ Mask variable ❓
Variable will be masked in job logs. Requires values to meet regular expression requirements. More information

Cancel   Add variable

Figure 14.49: Entering the AWS_DEFAULT_REGION environment variable

7. Now that we have set up our environment variables on GitLab CI/CD, we can start updating our **.gitlab-ci.yml** file. First, we want to start caching the **dist** directory after our **build** step. In order to do this, we need to add a **cache** property to the **build** job:

```
build:
  # other properties
  cache:
    key: $CI_COMMIT_REF_SLUG
    paths:
      - dist
  # other properties

# other jobs
```

8. We can now add our **deploy** job, which will be a part of the **deploy** stage. To access the AWS CLI, we will use a Python image (**python:latest**) and install the AWS CLI using **pip** (a Python package manager) in our **before_script** step. Once we've installed the AWS CLI, we will run the deployment in the **script** step using the **aws s3 sync** command we used to deploy from our local machine:

```
# other jobs
deploy:
  image: python:latest
  stage: deploy
  cache:
    key: $CI_COMMIT_REF_SLUG
    paths:
      - dist
  before_script:
    - pip install awscli
  script:
    - aws s3 sync ./dist s3://vue-workshop --acl=public-read
```

NOTE

We don't need to invalidate caches since the Vue CLI **build** command has built-in cache-busting through fingerprinting the contents of a file in the filename. Fingerprinting means that if the contents of a file change, its name/URL will change accordingly. When this new file is requested, it will be loaded from an un-cached URL and will therefore get the latest version of the file.

Once this update to the configuration is pushed to the GitLab repository, we can see the pipeline running three stages that all pass, as follows:

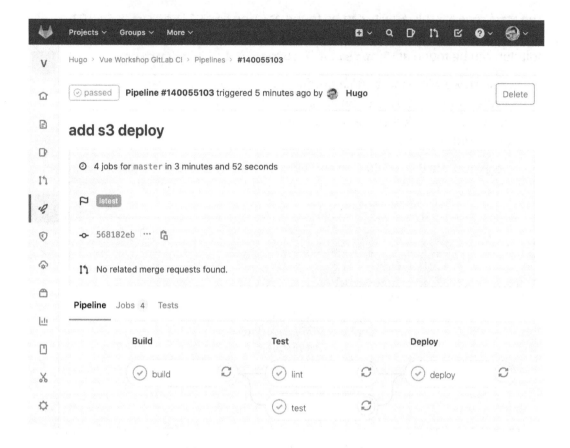

Figure 14.50: Passing build, test, and deploy jobs

We have now seen how to configure and deploy a Vue.js application to S3 and CloudFront using the AWS CLI and GitLab CI/CD.

ACTIVITY 14.01: ADDING CI/CD WITH GITLAB TO A BOOK SEARCH APP AND DEPLOYING TO AMAZON S3 AND CLOUDFRONT

Let's now take a fully built **book search** Vue.js application that loads data from the Google Books API and deploy it to S3/CloudFront using GitLab CI/CD. We will start by running the production build locally and checking the output. We will then switch to running the build and code quality steps (linting) on GitLab CI. Finally, we'll set up an S3 bucket and CloudFront distribution and integrate them with GitLab CI/CD to deploy on every push to the repository.

The start code for this activity can be found at **Chapter14/Activity14.01_ initial**; we start with a **book search** application build with the Vue CLI. The solution can be found at **Chapter14/Activity14.01_solution**:

1. To start, we will want to run a production build locally. We can use the regular command used to build all Vue CLI projects for production. We will also want to check that the relevant assets (JavaScript, CSS, and HTML) are generated correctly.

   We expect the **dist** folder to contain a similar structure, as follows:

   Figure 14.51: Sample contents of the dist folder (generated using the tree command) after a Vue CLI production build run

2. In order to run GitLab CI/CD, we will need a **.gitlab-ci.yml** file. We will add a job to **.gitlab-ci.yml** in which we run an install of the packages followed by the production build in a Node.js LTS Docker container, at the **build** stage. We will also make sure to cache the output of the production build.

   Once we use **git add .gitlab-ci.yml** and commit and push the changes, we should see the following GitLab CI/CD pipeline run, which includes the **build** job while it is in the running state:

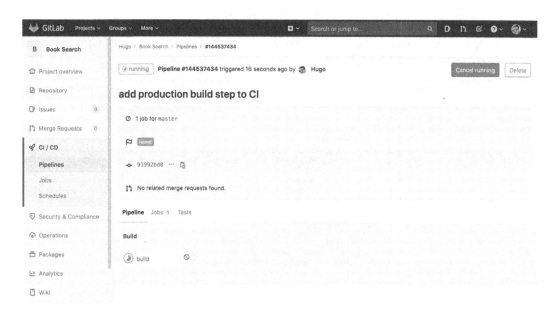

Figure 14.52: The GitLab CI/CD pipeline with the build job running

The following screenshot, on the other hand, represents the GitLab CI/CD pipeline when the **build** job has completed and is in the **passed** state:

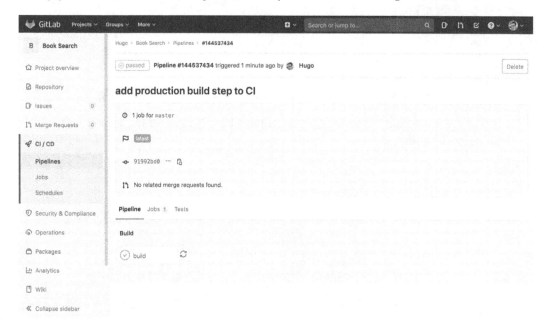

Figure 14.53: GitLab CI/CD pipeline with the build job passed

3. Next, we will want to add a code quality job to the **test** stage on GitLab CI/CD (by updating **.gitlab-ci.yml**). We'll call the job **lint** and it will run an install of the dependencies as well as linting through the Vue CLI.

    Once we use **git add .gitlab-ci.yml** and commit and push the changes, we should see the following GitLab CI/CD pipeline run, which includes the **lint** job while it is in the running state:

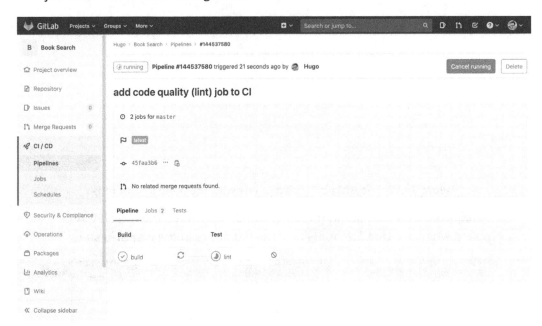

Figure 14.54: The GitLab CI/CD pipeline with the lint job running

The following screenshot displays the GitLab CI/CD pipeline with the **lint** job successfully completed:

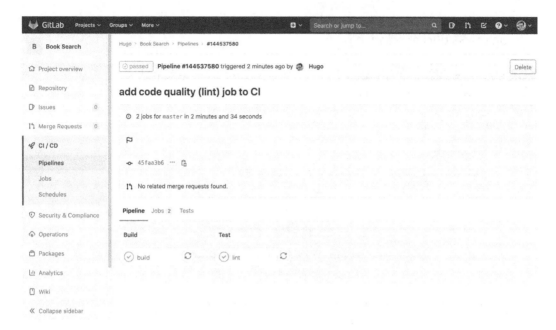

Figure 14.55: GitLab CI/CD pipeline with the lint job passed

4. In order to deploy our application, we'll need to create a **vue-workshop-book-search** S3 bucket with **public access** enabled using the S3 console.

    The S3 bucket creation page should look as follows:

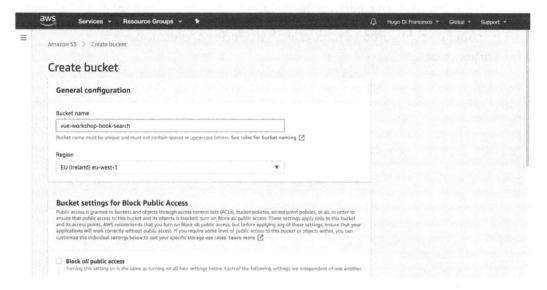

Figure 14.56: The S3 bucket creation page with vue-workshop-book-search entered as the bucket name

The following screenshot displays the public access and disclaimer information on the S3 bucket creation page:

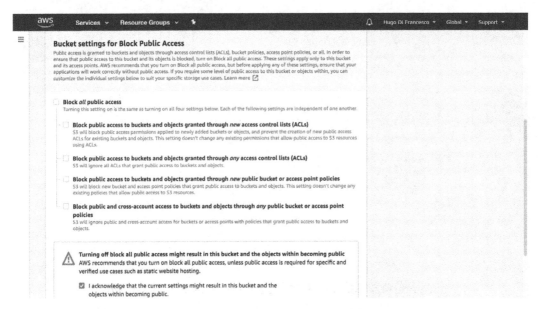

Figure 14.57: The S3 bucket creation page with public access enabled and the relevant disclaimer accepted

5. To access the S3 bucket contents over the web, we'll also need to configure it for web hosting. We can configure the web hosting property through the S3 console.

   It should be configured as follows, with the index and error page set to `index html`:

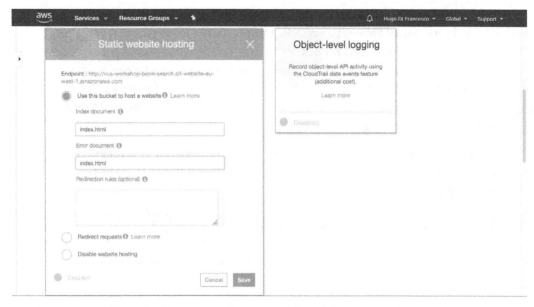

Figure 14.58: The S3 bucket properties page with web hosting enabled and configured with the index and error page set to index.html

6. For GitLab CI/CD to be able to create and update files on S3, we will need to add the relevant AWS secrets to our GitLab repo CI/CD settings. The secrets are found in the AWS management console at the **Username** dropdown | **My Security Credentials** | **Access keys** (access key ID and secret access key) | **Create New Access Key** (or pick a key to reuse). The following screenshot displays these details:

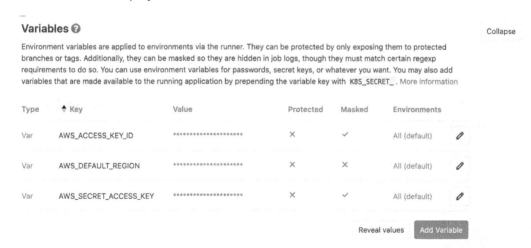

Figure 14.59: The GitLab CI/CD settings page with required the AWS environment variables added (with values masked)

8. Next, we will want to add a **deploy** job to the **deploy** stage on GitLab CI/CD (by updating **.gitlab-ci.yml**). We will call the job **deploy**; it will need to download the **awscli pip** package (Python package manager), which means the Docker image that makes the most sense is **python:latest**. The **deploy** job will load the built production build from cache, install **awscli** with **pip**, and run **aws s3 sync <build_directory> s3://<s3-bucket-name> --acl=public-read**.

Once we use **git add .gitlab-ci.yml** and commit and push the changes, we should see the following GitLab CI/CD pipeline run, which includes the **deploy** job in the running state:

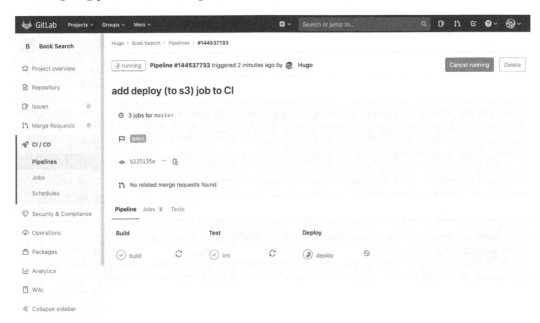

Figure 14.60: The GitLab CI/CD pipeline with the deploy job running

The following screenshot displays the GitLab CI/CD pipeline with the **deploy** job completed successfully:

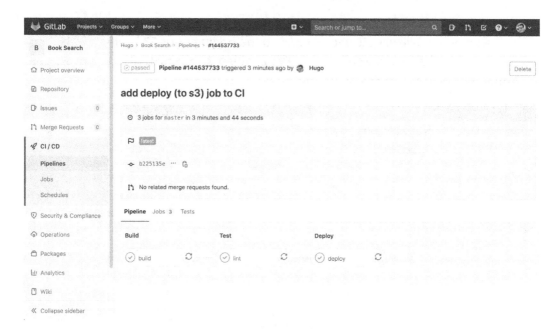

Figure 14.61: The GitLab CI/CD pipeline with the deploy job passed

Once the pipeline completes, our application should be available through the **web** S3 endpoint as in the following screenshot:

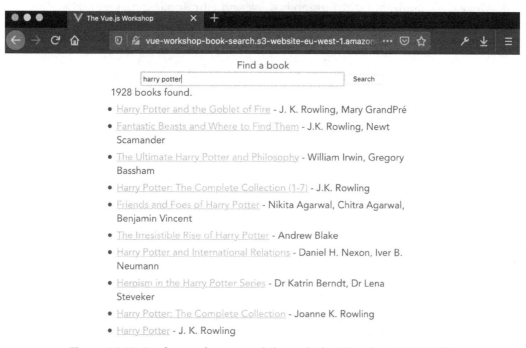

Figure 14.62: Book search accessed through the S3 web endpoint URL

9. Finally, we'll create a CloudFront distribution that acts as a CDN for the **web** S3 endpoint. We'll want to set **origin** to the origin of our S3 bucket's web endpoint and also make sure that we've enabled **Redirect HTTP to HTTPS**, as shown in the following screenshot:

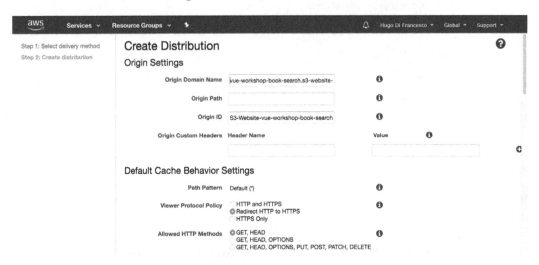

Figure 14.63: The CloudFront distribution creation page, displaying the origin and behavior settings

Once the CloudFront distribution is deployed, our application should be accessible through the CloudFront distribution's domain as shown in the following screenshot:

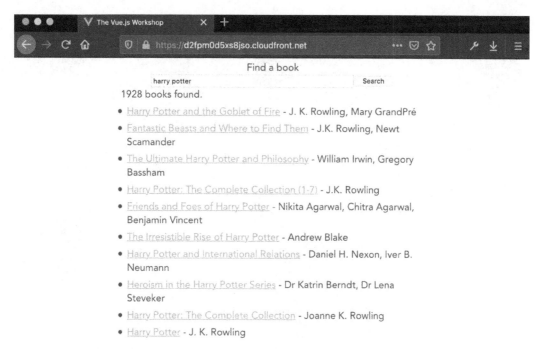

Figure 14.64: Book search accessed through the CloudFront domain displaying results for a "harry potter" query

> **NOTE**
>
> The activity solution can be found on page 730.

SUMMARY

Throughout this chapter, we've looked at how to introduce CI and CD practices to Vue.js projects in order to deploy to production safely and efficiently. We've seen how CI and CD are beneficial in the context of an agile delivery process. We used GitLab's CI/CD features to run tests, linting, and builds on every commit. We saw how to leverage Netlify to host a static website by connecting Netlify to our hosting provider. Finally, we looked at how to set up and deploy to AWS S3 and CloudFront.

Throughout this book, you have learned how to build, test, and deploy a Vue.js application that scales and performs for your team and your end users.

APPENDIX

CHAPTER 1: STARTING YOUR FIRST VUE PROJECT

ACTIVITY 1.01: BUILDING A DYNAMIC SHOPPING LIST APP USING VUE.JS

Solution:

To access the code files for this activity, refer to https://packt.live/35Tkzau.

1. Create a new Vue project using the Vue CLI by running the **vue create new-activity-app** command. Manually select the features via the command prompts for **dart-sass**, **babel**, and **eslint**.

2. Scaffold an input field with a placeholder, **Press enter to add new item**, which has a **v-model** bound to a data object called input and a **ref** attribute with the value of the input. Bind the *Enter* key to the **addItem** method, which will be created in the next step, by using @**keyup.enter** and referencing the **addItem** method:

```
<template>
  <div class="container">
    <h2>Shopping list</h2>
    <div class="user-input">
      <input
        placeholder="Press enter to add new item"
        v-model="input"
        @keyup.enter="addItem"
        ref="input"
      />
    </div>
  </div>
</template>

<script>
export default {
  data() {
    return {
      input: '',
    }
  },
}
</script>
```

```scss
<style lang="scss">
@import 'styles/global';

$color-green: #4fc08d;
$color-grey: #2c3e50;

.container {
  max-width: 600px;
  margin: 80px auto;
}
// Type
.h2 {
  font-size: 21px;
}

.user-input {
  display: flex;
  align-items: center;
  padding-bottom: 20px;
  input {
    width: 100%;
    padding: 10px 6px;
    margin-right: 10px;
  }
}
</style>
```

3. Introduce a button with a bound click event to **addItem** and include the corresponding method, **addItem()**, in the **methods** object. In the **addItem()** method, push the data prop **input** string into **shoppingList** and add a check to ensure the **input** prop exists. Optionally, add some styling to your buttons:

```
<template>
  <div class="container">
    <h2>Shopping list</h2>
    <div class="user-input">
      <input
        placeholder="Press enter to add new item"
        v-model="input"
        @keyup.enter="addItem"
```

```
        ref="input"
      /><button @click="addItem">Add item</button>
    </div>
  </div>
</template>

<script>
export default {
  data() {
    return {
      input: '',
      shoppingList: [],
    }
  },
  methods: {
    addItem() {
      // Don't allow adding to the list if empty
      if (!this.input) return
      this.shoppingList.push(this.input)
      // Clear the input after adding
      this.input = ''
      // Focus the input element again for quick typing!
      this.$refs.input.focus()
    },
  },
}
</script>
<style lang="scss">

...

// Buttons
button {
  appearance: none;
  padding: 10px;

  font-weight: bold;
  border-radius: 10px;
```

```scss
    border: none;
    background: $color-grey;
    color: white;
    white-space: nowrap;

    + button {
      margin-left: 10px;
    }
  }
}
</style>
```

4. Output the shopping list items in the DOM. When you click the **add item** button, it should be added to **shoppingList** and be displayed:

```
<template>
  <div class="container">
    ...

    <ul v-if="shoppingList">
      <li v-for="(item, i) in shoppingList" :key="i" class="item"
        ><span>{{ item }}</span>
        </li>
    </ul>
  </div>
</template>
<style lang="scss">
.item {
  display: flex;
  align-items: center;
}

ul {
  display: block;
  margin: 0 auto;
  padding: 30px;
  border: 1px solid rgba(0, 0, 0, 0.25);

  > li {
    color: $color-grey;
```

```
        margin-bottom: 4px;
    }
}

</style>
```

The following screenshot displays the shopping list:

Figure 1.44: The shopping list should be displayed based on user input

5. To match the last requirement to remove items from the list, create a new method called **deleteItem**, and allow one argument to be passed in, called **i**. If there is an argument passed into the method, filter out that array item and update the **shoppingList** prop; otherwise replace the data prop with an empty array:

```
...
<script>
export default {
  data() {
    return {
      input: '',
      shoppingList: [],
    }
  },
  methods: {
    addItem() {
      // Don't allow adding to the list if empty
      if (!this.input) return
      this.shoppingList.push(this.input)
```

```
        // Clear the input after adding
        this.input = ''
        // Focus the input element again for quick typing!
        this.$refs.input.focus()
      },
      deleteItem(i) {
        this.shoppingList = i
          ? this.shoppingList.filter((item, x) => x !== i)
          : []
      },
    },
  }
</script>
```

6. Create a **Delete all** button element and bind it to the **deleteItem** method using the click event, **@click**:

```
      <button class="button--delete" @click="deleteItem()">
        Delete all</button>


      ...


<style lang="scss">
...
.button--delete {
  display: block;
  margin: 0 auto;
  background: red;
}
</style>
```

7. Add a **remove** button in the list loop, which will delete individual shopping list items by passing in the **v-for** prop **i**:

```
<template>
  <div class="container">
      ...
    <ul v-if="shoppingList">
      <li v-for="(item, i) in shoppingList" :key="i" class="item"
        ><span>{{ item }}</span>
        <button class="button--remove"
          @click="deleteItem(i)">Remove</button>
      </li>
```

```
    </ul>
    <br />
    <button class="button--delete" @click="deleteItem()">
      Delete all</button>
  </div>
</template>

...

<style lang="scss">
...
.button--remove {
  background: none;
  color: red;
  text-transform: uppercase;
  font-size: 11px;
  align-self: flex-end;
}

</style>
```

Figure 1.45 displays the final output with all the details for the shopping list before adding the items:

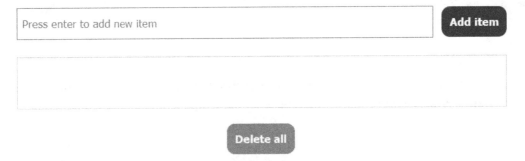

Figure 1.45: Final output

The following screenshot displays the output after adding items to the shopping list:

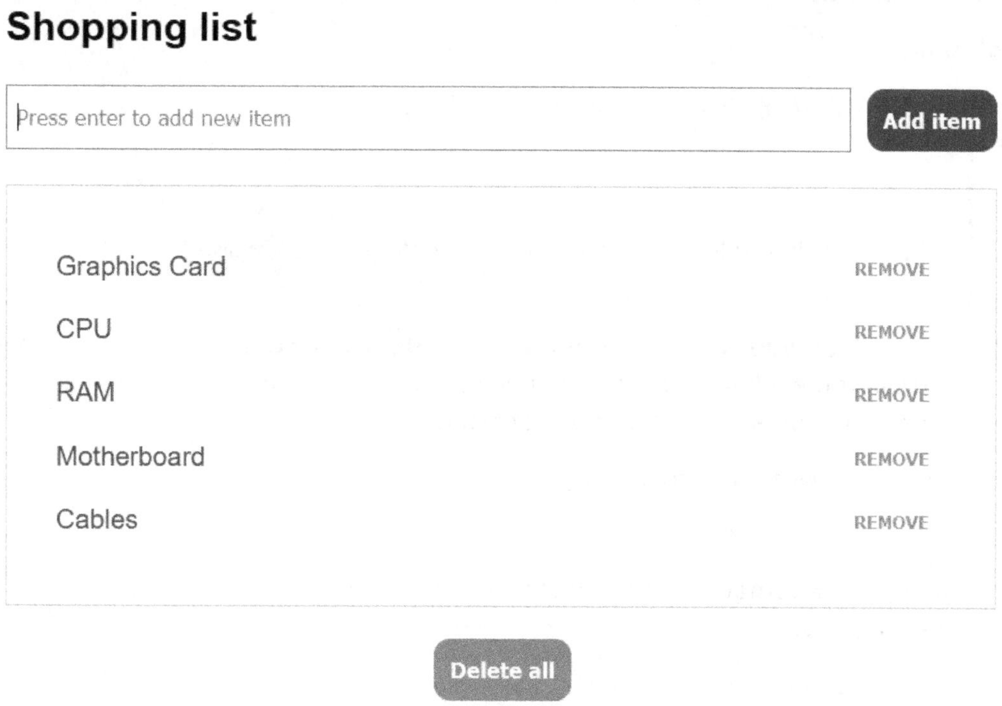

Shopping list

| Press enter to add new item | **Add item** |

Graphics Card — REMOVE

CPU — REMOVE

RAM — REMOVE

Motherboard — REMOVE

Cables — REMOVE

Delete all

Figure 1.46: Final output with items added to the shopping list

In this activity, you tested your knowledge of Vue by using all the basic functions of an **SFC**, such as expressions, loops, two-way binding, and event handling. You built a shopping list application that could let users add and delete individual list items or clear the total list in one click using Vue methods.

CHAPTER 2: WORKING WITH DATA

ACTIVITY 2.01: CREATING A BLOG LIST USING THE CONTENTFUL API

Solution:

Perform the following steps to complete the activity.

> **NOTE**
>
> To access the code files for this activity, refer to https://packt.live/33ao1f5.

1. Create a new Vue project using the Vue CLI **vue create activity** command and select the following presets: Babel, SCSS pre-processor (you can choose either of the pre-processor), and the prettier formatter.

2. Add a **contentful** dependency:

```
yarn add contentful
```

3. In **App.vue**, remove the default content and import **contentful** into the component:

```
<template>
  <div id=»app»>
  </div>
</template>

<script>
import { createClient } from 'contentful'

const client = createClient({
  space: ‹hpr0uushokd4›,
  accessToken: ‹jwEHepvQx-kMtO7_2ldjhE4WMAsiDp3t1xxBT8aDp7U›,
})

</script>
```

```scss
<style lang="scss">
#app {
  font-family: ‹Avenir›, Helvetica, Arial, sans-serif;
  -webkit-font-smoothing: antialiased;
  -moz-osx-font-smoothing: grayscale;
  text-align: center;
  color: #2c3e50;
  margin: 60px auto 0;
  max-width: 800px;
}
</style>
```

4. Add **async** methods to **getPeople** and **getBlogPosts** on the created life cycle, and assign the response of the calls to the **authors** and **posts** data props respectively in the template:

```
<template>
  <div id=»app»>
    <pre>{{ authors }}</pre>
    <pre>{{ posts }}</pre>
  </div>
</template>

<script>
import { createClient } from 'contentful'

const client = createClient({
  space: ‹hpr0uushokd4›,
  accessToken: ‹jwEHepvQx-kMtO7_21djhE4WMAsiDp3t1xxBT8aDp7U›,
})

export default {
  name: ‹app›,
  data() {
    return {
      authors: [],
```

```
      posts: {},
    }
  },
  async created() {
    this.authors = await this.getPeople()
    this.posts = await this.getBlogPosts()
  },
  methods: {
    async getPeople() {
      const entries = await client.getEntries({ content_type:
        'person' })
      return entries.items
    },
    async getBlogPosts() {
      const entries = await client.getEntries({
        content_type: <blogPost>,
        order: <-fields.publishDate>,
      })
      return entries.items
    },
  },
}
</script>
```

5. Loop over articles using the **posts** object, and output **publishDate**, **title**, **description**, and **image**:

```
<div class=»articles»>
  <hr />
  <h2>Articles</h2>
  <section v-if=»posts» class=»articles-list»>
    <article v-for=»(post, i) in posts» :key=»i»>
      <img
        class=»thumbnail»
        :src=»
          post.fields.heroImage.fields.file.url +
            '?fit=scale&w=350&h=196'
        «
```

```
                            />

     class=»article-text»>

   <div class="date">{{
            new Date(post.fields.publishDate).toDateString()
          }}</div>
          <h4>{{ post.fields.title }}</h4>
          <p>{{ post.fields.description }}</p>
        </div>
      </article>
    </section>
  </div>
```

6. Add some **scss** styling to **articles-list**:

```
.articles-list {
  article {
    display: flex;
    text-align: left;
    padding-bottom: 15px;

    .article-text {
      padding: 15px 0;
    }

    .thumbnail {
      margin-right: 30px;
    }
    .date {
      font-size: 12px;
      font-weight: bold;
      text-transform: uppercase;
    }
  }
}
```

7. Use computed props to output the author's information:

```
<template>
    ...

    <div v-if=»name» class=»author»>
      <h2
        >{{ name }} <br />
        <small v-if=»title» >{{ title }}</small></h2
      >

      <p v-if=»bio» >{{ bio }}</p>
    </div>
    ...
</template>

...
computed: {
    name() {
        return this.authors[0] && this.authors[0].fields.name
    },
    title() {
        return this.authors[0] && this.authors[0].fields.title
    },
    bio() {
        return this.authors[0] && this.authors[0].fields.shortBio
    },
},
...
```

The following screenshot displays the author information along with a list of their blog posts:

John Doe
Web Developer

Research and recommendations for modern stack websites.

Articles

MON DEC 30 2019

Hello world

Your very first content with Contentful, pulled in JSON format using the Content Delivery API.

SUN DEC 01 2019

Automate with webhooks

Webhooks notify you, another person or system when resources have changed by calling a given HTTP endpoint.

THU AUG 01 2019

Static sites are great

Worry less about security, caching, and talking to the server. Static sites are the new thing.

Figure 2.16: Expected outcome with Contentful blog posts

In this activity, you built a blog that lists articles from an API source using the basic functions of a Vue SFC, using **async** methods to fetch remote data from an API, and using computed properties to organize deep nested object structures.

CHAPTER 3: VUE CLI

ACTIVITY 3.01: BUILDING A VUE APPLICATION USING THE VUE-UI AND THE VUETIFY COMPONENT LIBRARY

Solution:

Perform the following steps to complete the activity.

> **NOTE**
>
> To access the code files for this activity, refer to https://packt.live/35WaCJG.

1. Open a command line, and run **vue create activity-app**.

2. Choose the last selection, **Manually select features**, by pressing the *Down arrow key* once and pressing *Enter*:

```
? Please pick a preset: (Use arrow keys)
  default (babel, eslint)
> Manually select features
```

3. Choose **Babel**, **CSS Pre-processors**, and **Linter / Formatter**:

```
? Check the features needed for your project:
 (*) Babel
 ( ) TypeScript
 ( ) Progressive Web App (PWA) Support
 ( ) Router
 ( ) Vuex
 (*) CSS Pre-processors
>(*) Linter / Formatter
 ( ) Unit Testing
 ( ) E2E Testing
```

4. Choose **Sass/SCSS (with dart-sass)**:

```
? Pick a CSS pre-processor (PostCSS, Autoprefixer and CSS Modules are
supported by default): (Use arrow keys)
> Sass/SCSS (with dart-sass)

  Sass/SCSS (with node-sass)

  Less

  Stylus
```

5. Next, we will choose **Eslint+ Prettier** to format the code as we proceed:

```
? Pick a linter / formatter config: (Use arrow keys)
 ESLint with error prevention only

 ESLint + Airbnb config

 ESLint + Standard config

> ESLint + Prettier
```

6. We will then choose the options **Lint on save** and **Lint and fix on commit** to pick additional lint features and save them:

```
? Pick additional lint features: (Press <space> to select,
 <a> to toggle all, <i> to invert selection)
 >(*) Lint on save

 (*) Lint and fix on commit
```

7. To place the configurations in the dedicated files, we will choose the **In dedicated config files** option:

```
? Where do you prefer placing config for Babel, PostCSS, ESLint,
 etc.? (Use arrow keys)
 > In dedicated config files

 In package.json
```

Skip saving by pressing *Enter*. **npm** packages will automatically be installed. You should see the following output in your terminal:

```
yarn install v1.16.0
info No lockfile found.
 [1/4] Resolving packages...
```

8. After the packages are installed, run the **yarn serve** command. Next, go to your browser and navigate to **http://localhost:8080**. You should see the output as follows:

Welcome to Your Vue.js App

For a guide and recipes on how to configure / customize this project,
check out the vue-cli documentation.

Installed CLI Plugins

babel   eslint

Essential Links

Core Docs   Forum   Community Chat   Twitter   News

Ecosystem

vue-router   vuex   vue-devtools   vue-loader   awesome-vue

Figure 3.43: The default Vue project screen

9. Stop the **serve** task, and run **vue ui** in the command line.

10. Inside the Vue-UI, go to the project selection screen (found at **http://localhost:8000/project/select**).

11. Click on the **Import** button and navigate to the folder your newly created Vue project is stored in. The following screenshot displays what your screen should look like:

Figure 3.44: The Vue-UI project manager

12. Click on the big green **Import this folder** button.

13. From the **Projects** dashboard, navigate to the **Plugins** tab.

14. Click on the **+ Add plugin** button. Your screen should look like the following screenshot:

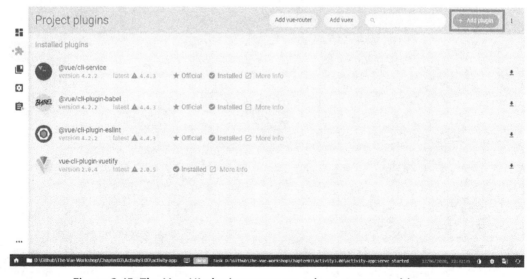

Figure 3.45: The Vue-UI plugins manager, where you can add, remove, and modify Vue plugins

15. Search for **vuetify** and install **vue-cli-plugin-vuetify**, then choose the default configuration settings, as shown in *Figure 3.46*:

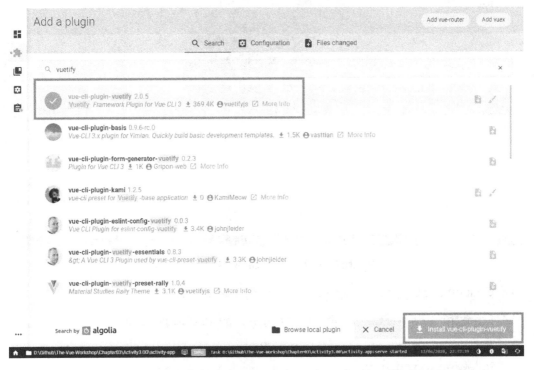

Figure 3.46: The App.vue default configuration when the Vuetify CLI is installed

16. Navigate to the **Tasks** page and click on **Start Tasks**. When the app initializes, click on the **Open App** button. On the localhost URL, you should see a Vuetify styled page as follows:

Figure 3.47: What you see in your browser when the Vuetify CLI plugin is installed

17. Click on the **Select a layout** hyperlink in your Vuetify page layout.

18. Click on the code link for the **Baseline** theme (or any other theme that interests you) from the options shown in the following screenshot:

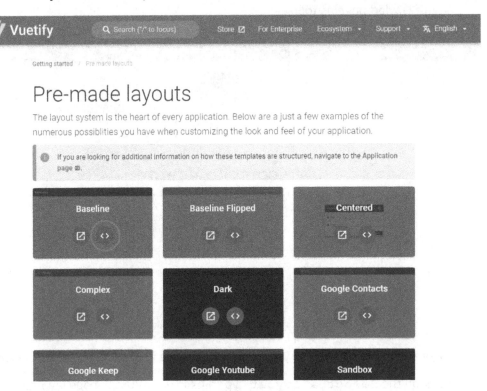

Figure 3.48: The Vuetify website has multiple premade layouts available

19. Copy the contents of the **baseline.vue** file from the Vuetify repo and replace your **App.vue** file content with this content. Your **localhost:8080** should reload with the new content you copied in and the browser should appear as follows:

Figure 3.49: The final outcome for the template as seen from your browser

By the end of this activity, you saw how to prepare a Vue.js project using the Vue-UI, selecting and organizing valuable presets used in the production of enterprise Vue applications. You installed and utilized the **Vuetify** framework utilizing Vuetify components to create a layout that you could then preview inside your browser.

CHAPTER 4: NESTING COMPONENTS (MODULARITY)

ACTIVITY 4.01: A LOCAL MESSAGE VIEW WITH REUSABLE COMPONENTS

Solution:

Perform the following steps to complete the activity.

> **NOTE**
>
> To access the code files for this activity, refer to https://packt.live/36ZxyH8.

First, we need a way to capture messages from the user:

1. Create a **MessageEditor** component that displays a **textarea**:

```
<template>
  <div>
    <textarea></textarea>
  </div>
</template>
```

2. Adding a reactive instance property can be done using the **data** component method:

```
<script>
export default {
  data() {
    return {
      message: ''
    }
  }
}
</script>
```

3. On **change** of **textarea**, we will store the state in a **message** reactive instance variable that we have set to null in the **data** component method:

```
<template>
  <!-- rest of the template -->
    <textarea
      @change="onChange($event)"
    >
```

```
    </textarea>
  </template>
  <script>
  export default {
    // rest of component properties
    methods: {
      onChange(event) {
        this.message = event.target.value
      }
    }
  }
  </script>
```

4. A **Send** operation should result in the latest content of the **textarea** being emitted as the payload of a **send** event:

```
<template>
  <!-- rest of the template -->
    <button @click="$emit('send', message)">Send</button>
  <!-- rest of the template -->
</template>
```

5. To display **MessageEditor**, we need to import it, register it in **components**, and reference it in the **template** section of **src/App.vue**:

```
<template>
  <div id="app">
    <MessageEditor />
  </div>
</template>
<script>
import MessageEditor from './components/MessageEditor.vue'
export default {
  components: {
    MessageEditor,
  },
}
</script>
```

6. To display messages, we will listen to **send** events using @**send** and add each payload to a new **messages** array reactive instance variable:

```
<template>
  <!-- rest of template -->
    <MessageEditor @send="onSend($event)" />
  <!-- rest of template -->
</template>
<script>
// rest of script
export default {
  // other component fields
  data() {
    return { messages: [] }
  },
  methods: {
    onSend(message) {
      this.messages = [...this.messages, message]
    }
  }
}
</script>
```

7. **MessageFeed** supports being passed through a **messages** array as a **prop**:

```
<template>
</template>
<script>
export default {
  props: {
    messages: {
      type: Array,
      required: true
    }
  }
}
</script>
```

8. We will use **v-for** to iterate through the **messages** array:

```
<template>
    <div>
    <p v-for="(m, i) in messages" :key="i">
      {{ m }}
    </p>
  </div>
</template>
```

9. To display the messages that we are storing, we will render **MessageFeed** in **App**, binding the **messages** app instance variable as the **messages** prop of **MessageFeed**:

```
<template>
  <!-- rest of template -->
    <MessageFeed :messages="messages" />
  <!-- rest of template -->
</template>
<script>
// other imports
import MessageFeed from './components/MessageFeed.vue'
export default {
  components: {
    // other components,
    MessageFeed
  }
}
</script>
```

10. In **MessageEditor**, we will refactor the **send** button click **handler** so that we also set **this.message** to ' ' when it's clicked:

```
<template>
  <!-- rest of template -->
    <textarea
      ref="textArea"
      @change="onChange($event)"
    >
```

```
      </textarea>
      <button @click="onSendClick()">Send</button>
    <!-- rest of template -->
</template>
<script>
export default {
  // rest of component
  methods: {
    // other methods
    onSendClick() {
      this.$emit('send', this.message)
      this.message = ''
      this.$refs.textArea.value = ''
    }
  }
}
</script>
```

The expected output is as follows:

Hello World!

Hello JavaScript!

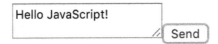

Figure 4.34: Message app with Hello World! and Hello JavaScript! sent

With that, we have learned how to use components, props, events, and refs to render a chat interface.

CHAPTER 5: GLOBAL COMPONENT COMPOSITION

ACTIVITY 5.01: BUILDING A VUE.JS APPLICATION WITH PLUGINS AND REUSABLE COMPONENTS

Solution:

Perform the following steps to complete the activity:

> **NOTE**
>
> To access the code files for this activity, refer to https://packt.live/35UIWpj.

1. Install **axios** into the project:

```
npm install --save axios
```

2. To inject **axios** as a property on **this** component instances, create a **src/plugins/axios.js** plugin file that, on **install**, will mean component instances have an **axios** property:

```
import axios from 'axios'
export default {
  install(Vue) {
    Vue.prototype.axios = axios
  }
}
```

3. For the plugin to work, import and register it in **src/main.js**:

```
// other imports
import axiosPlugin from './plugins/axios.js'

Vue.use(axiosPlugin)
// other initialisation code
```

4. We also want to inject our API's **baseUrl** into all our components. We will create a plugin inline of the **src/main.js** file to do this:

```
const BASE_URL = 'https://jsonplaceholder.typicode.com'
Vue.use({
  install(Vue) {
    Vue.baseUrl = BASE_URL
    Vue.prototype.baseUrl = BASE_URL
  }
})
```

> **NOTE**
>
> Those familiar with **axios** know we could have injected this URL as the **axios baseURL**.

5. Now, we need to fetch all **todos** from our **src/App.vue**. A good place to do this is inside the **mounted** life cycle method:

```
<script>
export default {
  async mounted() {
    const { data: todos } = await this.axios.get(
      `${this.baseUrl}/todos`)
    this.todos = todos
  }
}
</script>
```

6. To display the **todo** list, we will create a **TodoList** functional component in **src/components/TodoList.vue**. This will take a **todos** prop, loop through the items, and defer rendering of our **todo** under a **todo** scoped slot that binds it:

```
<template functional>
  <ul>
    <li v-for="todo in props.todos" :key="todo.id">
      <slot name="todo" :todo="todo" />
```

```
      </li>
    </ul>
</template>
```

7. We can now use the **TodoList** component to render out the **todos** prop we
    have already fetched in **src/App.vue**:

```
<template>
  <div id="app">
    <TodoList :todos="todos">
      <template #todo="{ todo }">
      {{ todo.title }}
      </template>
    </TodoList>
  </div>
</template>
<script>
import TodoList from './components/TodoList.vue'
export default {
  components: {
    TodoList
  },
  // other component methods
  data() {
    return { todos: [] }
  }
}
</script>
```

This will generate the following output:

- delectus aut autem
- quis ut nam facilis et officia qui
- fugiat veniam minus
- et porro tempora
- laboriosam mollitia et enim quasi adipisci quia provident illum
- qui ullam ratione quibusdam voluptatem quia omnis
- illo expedita consequatur quia in
- quo adipisci enim quam ut ab
- molestiae perspiciatis ipsa
- illo est ratione doloremque quia maiores aut
- vero rerum temporibus dolor
- ipsa repellendus fugit nisi
- et doloremque nulla
- repellendus sunt dolores architecto voluptatum
- ab voluptatum amet voluptas
- accusamus eos facilis sint et aut voluptatem
- quo laboriosam deleniti aut qui
- dolorum est consequatur ea mollitia in culpa
- molestiae ipsa aut voluptatibus pariatur dolor nihil
- ullam nobis libero sapiente ad optio sint
- suscipit repellat esse quibusdam voluptatem incidunt
- distinctio vitae autem nihil ut molestias quo
- et itaque necessitatibus maxime molestiae qui quas velit
- adipisci non ad dicta qui amet quaerat doloribus ea
- voluptas quo tenetur perspiciatis explicabo natus
- aliquam aut quasi
- veritatis pariatur delectus
- nesciunt totam sit blanditiis sit
- laborum aut in quam
- nemo perspiciatis repellat ut dolor libero commodi blanditiis omnis
- repudiandae totam in est sint facere fuga
- earum doloribus ea doloremque quis
- sint sit aut vero
- porro aut necessitatibus eaque distinctio

Figure 5.23: Todos loading and titles displaying

NOTE

The link to this dataset, which has been exposed as a JSON API, can be found at https://jsonplaceholder.typicode.com/.

8. Now, let's create a **TodoEntry** component where we will implement the majority of our todo-specific logic. A good practice for components is to have the props be very specific to the component's role. In this case, the properties of the **todo** object we will tackle are **id**, **title**, and **completed**, so those should be the props that our **TodoEntry** component receives. We will not make **TodoEntry** a functional component since we will need a component instance to create HTTP requests:

```
<template>
  <div>
    <label>{{ title }}</label>
    <input
      type="checkbox"
      :checked="completed"
    />
  </div>
</template>
<script>
export default {
  props: {
    id: {
      type: Number,
      required: true
    },
    title: {
      type: String,
      required: true
    },
    completed: {
      type: Boolean,
      default: false
    }
  }
}
</script>
```

9. Update **src/App.vue** so that it consumes **TodoEntry** as follows (make sure to bind **id**, **title**, and **completed**):

```
<template>
  <div id="app">
```

```
    <TodoList :todos="todos">
      <template #todo="{ todo }">
        <TodoEntry
        :id="todo.id"
        :title="todo.title"
        :completed="todo.completed"
      />
    </template>
  </TodoList>
 </div>
</template>
<script>
// other imports
import TodoEntry from './components/TodoEntry.vue'
export default {
  components: {
  // other components
    TodoEntry
 },
 // other component methods
}
</script>
```

We will get the following output:

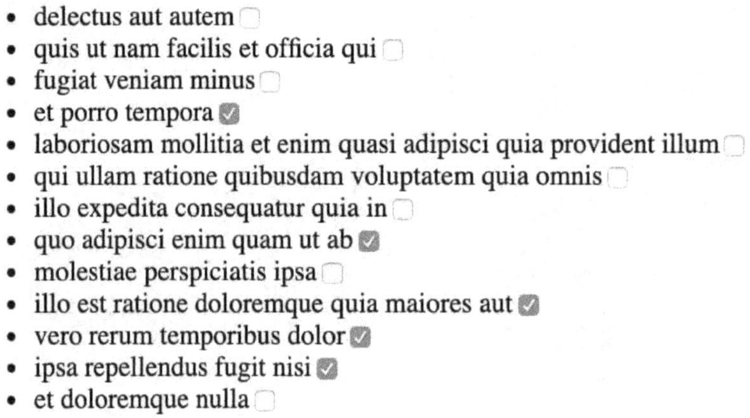

- delectus aut autem ⬜
- quis ut nam facilis et officia qui ⬜
- fugiat veniam minus ⬜
- et porro tempora ☑
- laboriosam mollitia et enim quasi adipisci quia provident illum ⬜
- qui ullam ratione quibusdam voluptatem quia omnis ⬜
- illo expedita consequatur quia in ⬜
- quo adipisci enim quam ut ab ☑
- molestiae perspiciatis ipsa ⬜
- illo est ratione doloremque quia maiores aut ☑
- vero rerum temporibus dolor ☑
- ipsa repellendus fugit nisi ☑
- et doloremque nulla ⬜

Figure 5.24: TodoEntry rendering data that has been fetched from the API

10. Now, we need to add the ability to toggle the **complete** status of a todo. We will implement the majority of this in **src/components/TodoEntry.vue**. We will listen to the **input** change event; on change, we will read the new value and send a **PATCH** request to **/todos/{todoId}** with an object containing **completed** set to the new value. We will also emit a **completedChange** event in Vue.js so that the **App** component can update the data that's in-memory:

```
<template>
  <!-- rest of the template -->
    <input
      type="checkbox"
      :checked="completed"
      @change="toggleCompletion()"
    />
  <!-- rest of the template -->
</template>
<script>
export default {
  // other component properties
  methods: {
    toggleCompletion() {
      const newCompleted = !this.completed
      this.$emit('completeChange', newCompleted)
      this.axios.patch(
        `${this.baseUrl}/todos/${this.id}`,
        { completed: newCompleted }
      )
    }
  }
}
</script>
```

11. In **App.vue**, we need to update the relevant **todo** when **completeChange** is triggered. Since **completeChange** does not include the ID of our **todo**, we will need to read that from the context when we set the **handleCompleteChange** function so that it listens to **completeChange**:

```
<template>
 <!-- rest of template -->
        <TodoEntry
          :id="todo.id"
          :title="todo.title"
          :completed="todo.completed"
          @completeChange="handleCompleteChange(todo.id, $event)"
        />
 <!-- rest of template -->
</template>
<script>
// imports
export default {
 // other component properties
  methods: {
    handleCompleteChange(id, newCompleted) {
      this.todos = this.todos.map(
        t => t.id === id
          ? { ...t, completed: newCompleted }
          : t
      )
    }
  }
}
</script>
```

At this stage, we should see the following output:

- delectus aut autem ☐
- quis ut nam facilis et officia qui ☐
- fugiat veniam minus ☐
- et porro tempora ☑
- laboriosam mollitia et enim quasi adipisci quia provident illum ☐
- qui ullam ratione quibusdam voluptatem quia omnis ☐
- illo expedita consequatur quia in ☐
- quo adipisci enim quam ut ab ☑
- molestiae perspiciatis ipsa ☐
- illo est ratione doloremque quia maiores aut ☑
- vero rerum temporibus dolor ☑
- ipsa repellendus fugit nisi ☑
- et doloremque nulla ☐
- repellendus sunt dolores architecto voluptatum ☑
- ab voluptatum amet voluptas ☑
- accusamus eos facilis sint et aut voluptatem ☑
- quo laboriosam deleniti aut qui ☑
- dolorum est consequatur ea mollitia in culpa ☐
- molestiae ipsa aut voluptatibus pariatur dolor nihil ☑
- ullam nobis libero sapiente ad optio sint ☑
- suscipit repellat esse quibusdam voluptatem incidunt ☐
- distinctio vitae autem nihil ut molestias quo ☑
- et itaque necessitatibus maxime molestiae qui quas velit ☐
- adipisci non ad dicta qui amet quaerat doloribus ea ☐
- voluptas quo tenetur perspiciatis explicabo natus ☑
- aliquam aut quasi ☑
- veritatis pariatur delectus ☑
- nesciunt totam sit blanditiis sit ☐
- laborum aut in quam ☐
- nemo perspiciatis repellat ut dolor libero commodi blanditiis omnis ☑
- repudiandae totam in est sint facere fuga ☐
- earum doloribus ea doloremque quis ☐
- sint sit aut vero ☐

Figure 5.25: Our to-do app using JSON placeholder data

With that, we have learned how to use plugins and reusable components to build a `todo` app that consumes **JSONPlaceholder** data.

CHAPTER 6: ROUTING

ACTIVITY 6.01: CREATING A MESSAGE SPA WITH DYNAMIC, NESTED ROUTING, AND LAYOUTS

Solution:

Perform the following steps to complete the activity:

> **NOTE**
>
> To access the code files for this activity, refer to https://packt.live/2ISxml7.

1. Create a new **MessageEditor.vue** file in the **src/views/** folder as the main component to interact with the user when writing a message. We use **textarea** as a message input field and attach the **listener** method **onChange** to the **DOM** event change to capture any input change regarding the message typed by the user. Also, we add **ref** to keep a pointer record to the rendered HTML **textarea** element for modifying our saved messages at a later stage.

   Besides this, we also attach another **listener** method, **onSendClick**, to the **click** event on the **Submit button** to capture the user's confirmation for sending the message. The actual logic implementation of both **onChange** and **onSendClick** is shown in *Step 3*.

2. The **<template>** section should look like the following:

```
<template>
  <div>
    <textarea
      ref="textArea"
      @change="onChange($event)"
    >
    </textarea>
    <button @click="onSendClick()">Submit</button>
  </div>
</template>
```

3. And in **script**, in addition to the previous code, we will also receive a **list** of messages to update with the new message after submitting, and emit the updated list back to the parent:

```
<script>
export default {
  props: {
    list: Array
  },
  data() {
    return {
      message: ''
    }
  },
  methods: {
    onChange(event) {
      this.message = event.target.value
    },
    onSendClick() {
      if (!this.message) return;
      this.list.push(this.message);
      this.$emit('list:update', this.list);
      this.message = ''
      this.$refs.textArea.value = ''
    }
  },
}
</script>
```

4. We need to define a parent route as a default route with the **path** of / and **name** of **messages** in the routes array in **./src/router/index.js**:

```
{
    path: '/',
    name: 'messages',
    component: () => import(/* webpackChunkName: "messages" */
      '../views/Messages.vue'),
}
```

Then add a new route as a nested route called **editor** under the **children** property of this route configuration:

```
{
    path: '/',
    name: 'messages',
    component: () => import(/* webpackChunkName: "messages" */
      '../views/Messages.vue'),
    children: [{
      path: 'editor',
      name: 'editor',
      component: () => import(/* webpackChunkName: "editor" */
        '../views/MessageList.vue'),
      props: true,
    }]
},
```

5. We create a new view component called **MessageList.vue** with **v-for** to render the list of messages into the **router-link** component:

```
<template>
  <div>
    <h2> Message Feed </h2>
    <div v-for="(m, i) in list" :key="i" >
      <router-link :to="`/message/${i}`">
        {{ i }}
        </router-link>
    </div>
  </div>
</template>
<script>
export default {
  props: {
    list: {
      type: Array,
      default: () => []
    }
  }
}
</script>
```

6. And, similarly to *Step 2*, register the **MessageList.vue** component with the **children** routes array of the **messages** route:

```
{
    path: '/',
    name: 'messages',
    component: () => import(/* webpackChunkName: "messages" */
        '../views/Messages.vue'),
    children: [{
        path: 'list',
        name: 'list',
        component: () => import(/* webpackChunkName: "list" */
            '../views/MessageList.vue'),
        props: true,
    }, {
        path: 'editor',
        name: 'editor',
        component: () => import(/* webpackChunkName: "editor" */
            '../views/MessageEditor.vue'),
        props: true,
    }]
},
```

7. Now our **messages** view needs a UI. We define the **Messages.vue** view with the use of **router-link** to allow navigation between **editor** and **list** and a **router-view** component for rendering the nested view:

```
<template>
  <div>
    <router-link :to="{ name: 'list', params: { list
      }}">List</router-link> |
    <router-link :to="{ name: 'editor', params: { list
      }}">Editor</router-link>
    <router-view :list.sync="list"/>
  </div>
</template>
<script>
```

And, of course, we need to receive a **list** of messages from **props**:

```
<script>
export default {
  props: {
    list: Array
  }
}
</script>
```

Since we don't have a global state or proper database, we need to mock a global list of messages in **./src/router/index.js**:

```
const messages = []
```

Then pass it as default **props** for the **messages** route, as follows:

```
{
    path: '/',
    name: 'messages',
    /* ... */
    props: {
      list: messages
    },
}
```

8. In order to catch whether the user is leaving the current editor view, we will add a Hook on the **beforeRouteLeave** in-component navigation guard, which will allow us to display a warning and abort or continue per the user's decision. This is done within **MessageEditor.vue** file:

```
beforeRouteLeave(to, from, next) {
      if (this.$refs.textArea.value !== '') {
        const ans = window.confirm(You have an unsaved message.
          Are you sure you want to navigate away?');

        next(!!ans);
      }
      else {
        next();
      }
    }
```

9. Creating **messageLayout.vue** is simple, with a header text, the **content** from **props**, and a **Back button**:

```
<template>
  <div class="message">
    <h2>Message content:</h2>
    <main>
      <slot/>
    </main>
    <button @click="goBack">Back</button>
  </div>
</template>
```

The **goBack** logic should be simple: if there is a previous route saved, let's go back one step in the navigation stack with **this.$routes.go(-1)**. Otherwise, we will just push the **messages** navigation route to the stack with **this.$router.push({ name: 'message'})**:

```
<script>
import MessageLayout from '../layouts/messageLayout.vue';
export default {
  props: {
    content: {
      type: String,
      default: ''
    },
  },
  methods: {
    goBack() {
      if (this.$route.params.from) {
        this.$router.go(-1)
      }
      else {
        this.$router.push({
          name: 'messages'
        })
      }
    }
  }
}
</script>
```

But then we still need to pass the previous route, **this.$route.params. from**, from the tracking. It should be done at the route registration.

10. We add the **message** route configuration inside **routes**, and we will use the **beforeEnter** component guard to save and pass the **from** previous navigation route to the **params** of the view.

Also, since it is a dynamic route with the **message/:id** pattern, we need to retrieve the content of the message and map that content to the related prop accordingly:

```
{
    path: '/message/:id',
    name: 'message',
    component: () => import(/* webpackChunkName: "message" */
        '../views/Message.vue'),
    props:true,
    beforeEnter(to, from, next) {
      if (to.params && to.params.id) {
        const id = to.params.id;

        if (messages && messages.length > 0 && id <
          messages.length) {
          to.params.content = messages[id];
        }
      }

      to.params.from = from;
      next()
    },
}
```

11. Finally, to code-split the UI layouts from **Message.vue** and **Messages.vue**, in the **./src/layouts** folder, we create both a **default.vue** layout and **messageLayout.vue** layout.

As we learned in this chapter, in **App.vue**, we will wrap **router-view** with a component that renders according to a layout variable. And, certainly, **router-view** needs to have a synchronous **layout** property to dynamically change the layout according to the current view:

```
<template>
  <div id="app">
    <component :is="layout">
```

```
        <router-view :layout.sync="layout"/>
      </component>
    </div>
  </template>
  <script>
  export default {
    data() {
      return {
        layout: () => import(/* webpackChunkName: "defaultLayout"
          */ './layouts/default.vue')
      }
    }
  }
  </script>
```

12. In **default.vue**, we will simply just have the header text for the **messages** section and a **slot**:

```
<template>
  <div class="default">
    <h1>Messages section</h1>
    <main>
      <slot/>
    </main>
  </div>
</template>
```

13. In **messageLayout.vue**, we will extract the header text and the button logic from **Message.vue**:

```
<template>
  <div class="message">
    <h2>Message content:</h2>
    <main>
      <slot/>
    </main>
    <button @click="goBack">Back</button>
  </div>
</template>
<script>
export default {
  methods: {
    goBack() {
```

```
        if (this.$route.params.from) {
          this.$router.go(-1)
        }
        else {
          this.$router.push({
            name: 'messages'
          })
        }
      }
    }
  }
}
</script>
```

And the final step is to make sure an **update:layout** event will be triggered to update the view layout upon component creation for both **Message.vue** and **Messages.vue**:

```
import MessageLayout from '../layouts/messageLayout.vue';
export default {
/*...*/
  created() {
    this.$emit('update:layout', MessageLayout);
  }
}
```

In **Messages.vue**, this will be as follows:

```
<script>
import DefaultLayout from '../layouts/default';

export default {
  props: {
    list: Array
  },
  created() {
    this.$emit('update:layout', DefaultLayout);
  }
}
</script>
```

14. Run the application using the following command:

```
yarn serve
```

To ensure you've completed the steps correctly, you will need to visit each route and ensure the content renders as shown in the corresponding figure. First, ensure that the **/list** view renders a message feed as shown in *Figure 6.47*:

Messages section

List | Editor

Message Feed

0
1
2

Figure 6.47: The /list view in the Messages app

15. Next, ensure that the **/editor** view allows a user to send a new message, as shown in *Figure 6.48*:

Messages section

List | Editor

Submit

Figure 6.48: The /editor view in the Messages app

16. Next, ensure the **/message/:id** dynamic route is working by going to the **/message/0** route. You should see message content similar to that shown in *Figure 6.49*:

Message content:

asfd

Back

Figure 6.49: The /message/0 view in the Message app

17. Ensure that when the user is composing a message, if they try to navigate away without having a saved message, an alert is triggered, as shown in *Figure 6.50*:

Figure 6.50: The /editor view when the user tries to navigate away with an unsaved message

> **NOTE**
>
> Our **messages** data is not saved upon refresh, as we don't have global state management. We can use **localStorage** to help to save the data while exploring the application.

In this activity, we put together several of the topics covered in this chapter, including setting up views, making use of templates and dynamic routes, and the use of Hooks to prompt a confirmation alert before the user navigates away with unsaved content. These tools can be used for many common SPA use cases and will be helpful in your future projects.

CHAPTER 7: ANIMATIONS AND TRANSITIONS

ACTIVITY 7.01: BUILDING A MESSAGES APP WITH TRANSITION AND GSAP

Solution:

Perform the following steps to complete the activity:

> **NOTE**
>
> To access the code files for this activity, visit https://packt.live/399tZ3Y.

1. We will reuse the code created in *Chapter 6, Routing* for the **Message** app so we have all the routing setup accordingly.

   The **template** section of **src/views/MessageEditor.vue** will be as follows:

```
<template>
  <div>
    <textarea
      ref="textArea"
      @change="onChange($event)"
    >
    </textarea>
    <button @click="onSendClick()">Submit</button>
  </div>
</template>
```

2. Next, the **script** section of **src/views/MessageEditor.vue** should contain logic for both clicking on and leaving the route:

```
<script>
export default {
  props: {
    list: Array
  },
  data() {
    return {
      message: ''
    }
  },
```

```
  methods: {
    onChange(event) {
      this.message = event.target.value
    },
    onSendClick() {
      if (!this.message) return;
      this.list.push(this.message);
      this.$emit('list:update', this.list);
      this.message = ''
      this.$refs.textArea.value = ''
    }
  },
  beforeRouteLeave(to, from, next) {
    if (this.$refs.textArea.value !== '') {
      const ans = window.confirm('You have unsaved message.
        Are you sure to navigate away?');

      next(ans);
    }
    else {
      next();
    }
  }
}
</script>
```

3. Next, we will need our **template** code for **MessageList.vue**. The code will be as follows:

```
<template>
  <div>
    <h2> Message Feed </h2>
    <transition-group
      @appear="enter"
      tag="div"
      move-class="flip"
      :css="false"
    >
      <div v-for="(m, i) in list" :key="m">
        <router-link :to=""`/message/${i}`">
```

```
            {{ i }}
          </router-link>
        </div>
      </transition-group>
    </div>
</template>
```

4. Next, we will need a **script** section in our **MessageList.vue** file. To add the **script** section, the code will be as follows:

```
<script>
import { TimelineMax } from 'gsap';

export default {
  props: {
    list: {
      type: Array,
      default: () => []
    }
  },
  methods: {
    enter(el, done) {
      const tl = new TimelineMax({
        onComplete: done,
        stagger: 1.2,
        duration: 2,
      });
      tl.fromTo(el, {opacity: 0}, {opacity: 1})
        .to(el, {rotation: -270, duration: 1, ease: "bounce"})
        .to(el, {rotation: -360})
        .to(el, {rotation: -180, opacity: 0})
        .to(el, {rotation: 0, opacity: 1});
    }
  }
}
</script>
```

5. We'll also create a **style** section in **MessageList.vue** and define the **.flip-move** class with the following code:

```
<style>
.flip-move {
  transition: transform 1s;
}
</style>
```

6. **Message.vue** should contain the rendered content inside a **p** element. We'll also define the **content** prop and emit an update signal:

```
<template>
  <div>
    <p>{{content}}</p>
    <router-view/>
  </div>
</template>
<script>
import MessageLayout from '../layouts/messageLayout.vue';

export default {
  props: {
    content: {
      type: String,
      default: ''
    }
  },
  created() {
    this.$emit('update:layout', MessageLayout);
  }
}
</script>
```

7. Ensure your **src/router/index.js** file is the same as the one created in *Activity 6.01, Creating a Message SPA with Dynamic, Nested Routing, and Layouts* in *Chapter 6, Routing*, which can be found at https://packt.live/2ISxml7:

```
import Vue from 'vue'
import VueRouter from 'vue-router'
import Messages from '@/views/Messages.vue'
```

```
Vue.use(VueRouter)

const messages = []

export const routes = [
  {
    path: '/',
    name: 'messages',
    component: () => import(/* webpackChunkName: "messages" */
      '../views/Messages.vue'),
    props: {
      list: messages
    },
    children: [{
      path: 'list',
      name: 'list',
      component: () => import(/* webpackChunkName: "list" */
        '../views/MessageList.vue'),
      props: true,
    }, {
      path: 'editor',
      name: 'editor',
      component: () => import(/* webpackChunkName: "list" */
        '../views/MessageEditor.vue'),
      props: true,
    }]
  },
  {
    path: '/message/:id',
    name: 'message',
    component: () => import(/* webpackChunkName: "message" */
      '../views/Message.vue'),
    props:true,
    beforeEnter(to, from, next) {
      if (to.params && to.params.id) {
        const id = to.params.id;

        if (messages && messages.length > 0 && id <
          messages.length) {
          to.params.content = messages[id];
        }
      }
```

```
        to.params.from = from;
        next()
      },
    }
  ]


const router = new VueRouter({
  mode: 'history',
  base: process.env.BASE_URL,
  routes
})


export default router
```

8. We will now wrap **router-view** in the **<template>** section of **App.vue** with a **transition** component that has two attributes, **name="fade"** and **mode="out-in"**:

```
<component :is="layout">
    <transition name="fade" mode="out-in">
      <router-view :layout.sync="layout"/>
    </transition>
  </component>
Create CSS stylings for the related classes, inside App.vue:
<style>
.fade-enter-active, .fade-leave-active {
  transition: opacity 2s, transform 3s;
}
.fade-enter, .fade-leave-to {
  opacity: 0;
  transform: translateX(-20%);
}
</style>
```

9. In **src/views/Messages.vue**, we will wrap **router-view** with a **transition** component. This time, we will use a custom **enter-active-class** transition class attribute in addition to the **fade** name:

```
<transition name="fade" enter-active-class="zoom-in">
  <router-view :list.sync="list"/>
</transition>
```

10. Add the **zoom-in** and **fade-enter** animation effects in the **style** section of
    src/views/Messages.vue:

```
<style>
.zoom-in {
  animation-duration: 0.3s;
  animation-fill-mode: both;
  animation-name: zoom;
}

.fade-enter-active {
  transition: opacity 2s, transform 3s;
}
.fade-enter {
  opacity: 0;
  transform: translateX(-20%);
}
</style>
```

11. Add **transition-group** as the wrapper for the list of message links in
    src/views/MessageList.vue, with JavaScript hooks for programmatic
    animation. But we have to specify that transition on the initial render of the
    page, as the list is supposed to animate when appearing. We will add the
    appear attribute and bind **enter** to **appear**, as well as add the **move-class**
    flip (an animation to be created later in the **style** section):

```
<transition-group
  appear
  @appear="enter"
  tag="div"
  move-class="flip"
  :css="false"
>
  <div v-for="(m, i) in list" :key="m">
    <router-link :to="`/message/${i}`">
      {{ i }}
    </router-link>
  </div>
</transition-group>
```

12. Add GSAP as a dependency and implement the bounce-in effect on the **appear** transition event handler (hook) in **src/views/MessageList.vue**:

```
<script>
import { TimelineMax } from 'gsap';

export default {
  props: {
    list: {
      type: Array,
      default: () => []
    }
  },
  methods: {
    enter(el, done) {
      const tl = new TimelineMax({
        onComplete: done,
        stagger: 1.2,
        duration: 2,
      });
      tl.fromTo(el, {opacity: 0}, {opacity: 1})
        .to(el, {rotation: -270, duration: 1, ease: "bounce"})
        .to(el, {rotation: -360})
        .to(el, {rotation: -180, opacity: 0})
        .to(el, {rotation: 0, opacity: 1});
    }
  }
}
</script>
```

13. Next, we need to create the **flip-move** class that we defined in our HTML. We'll do that by adding a **style** section with our new **flip-move** class:

```
<style>
.flip-move {
  transition: transform 1s;
}
</style>
```

14. Run the application using the **yarn serve** command and you should see the following in your browser at **localhost:8080**:

Messages section

List | Editor

Message Feed

0
1

[   ] Submit

Figure 7.19: Fade out when navigating from message list view to editor view

You should now see a fade out when navigating from the message list view to the editor view, as shown in *Figure 7.19*, and also a fade out when going from the editor view to the list view, as shown in *Figure 7.20*:

Messages section

List | Editor

[   ] Submit

Message Feed

Figure 7.20: Fade out when navigating from editor view to message list view

When the messages are in the feed, you should see a bouncing effect during the flipping motion, as shown in *Figure 7.21*:

Messages section

List | Editor

Message Feed

0
1

Figure 7.21: Bouncing effect when displaying the message feed in the message list view

Finally, when clicking on a specific message in the list, it should render the content as shown in *Figure 7.22*:

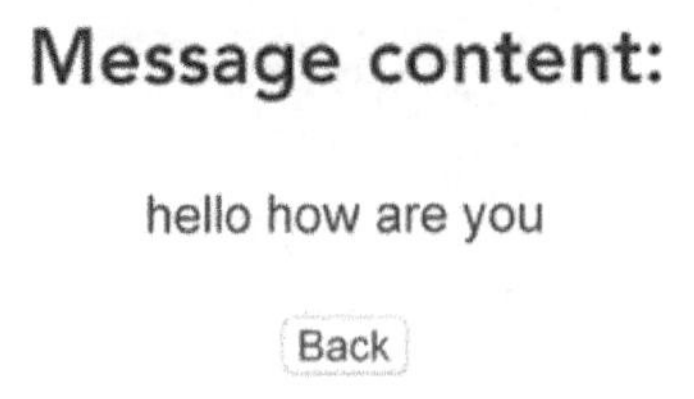

Message content:

hello how are you

Back

Figure 7.22: Single message view

In this activity, we put together several different animations and combined them with routing to create custom page transitions. We used several different animation types to demonstrate the many possibilities animations can provide.

CHAPTER 8: THE STATE OF VUE.JS STATE MANAGEMENT

ACTIVITY 8.01: ADDING EMAIL AND PHONE NUMBER TO A PROFILE CARD GENERATOR

Solution:

Perform the following steps to compete the activity:

> **NOTE**
>
> To access the code files for this activity, refer to https://packt.live/3m1swQE.

1. We can start by adding a new **email** input field and label to **src/components/AppProfileForm** for the **Email** field:

```
<template>
  <!-- rest of template -->
    <div class="flex flex-col mt-2">
      <label class="flex text-gray-800 mb-2" for="email">Email
      </label>
      <input
        id="email"
        type="email"
        name="email"
        class="border-2 border-solid border-blue-200 rounded
          px-2 py-1"
      />
    </div>
  <!-- rest of template -->
</template>
```

2. We can then add a new **phone** input field (of type **tel**) and a label to **AppProfileForm** for the **Phone Number** field:

```
<template>
  <!-- rest of template -->
    <div class="flex flex-col mt-2">
      <label class="flex text-gray-800 mb-2" for="phone">Phone
        Number</label>
      <input
        id="phone"
        type="tel"
        name="phone"
```

```
        class="border-2 border-solid border-blue-200 rounded
          px-2 py-1"
      />
    </div>
    <!-- rest of template -->
  </template>
```

The new fields look as follows:

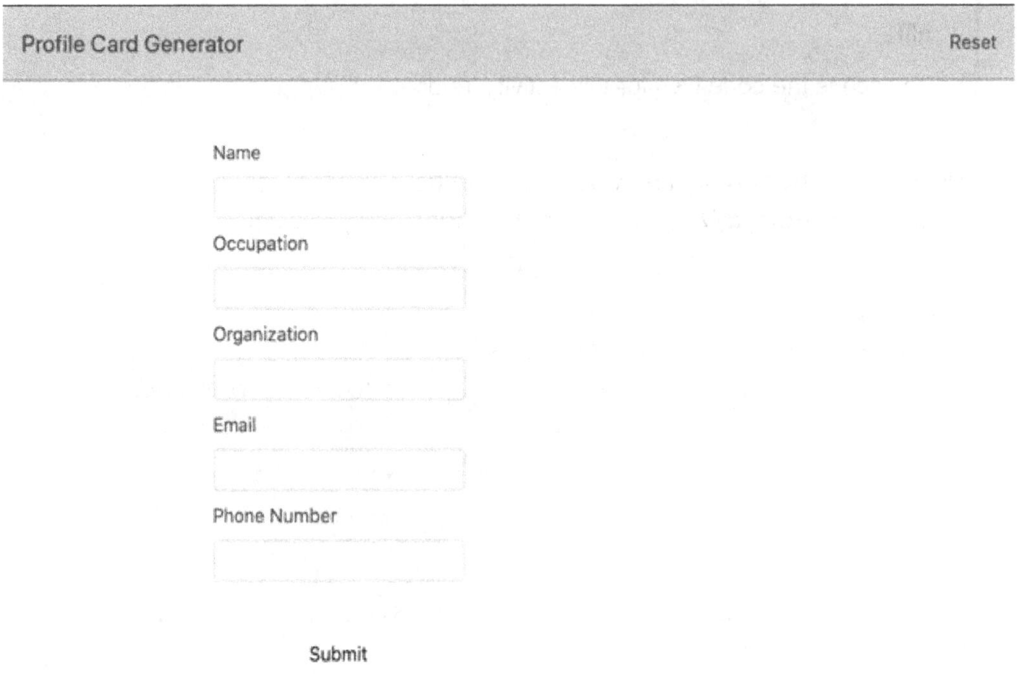

Figure 8.35: Application with new Email and Phone Number fields

3. We can then add the **email** and **phone** fields to the initial state and mutations
    in **src/store.js** so that **organization** gets initialized, set during
    profileUpdate, and reset during **profileClear**:

```
// imports & Vuex setup
export default new Vuex.Store({
  state: {
    formData: {
      // rest of formData fields
      email: '',
      phone: '',
    }
  },
```

```
mutations: {
  profileUpdate(state, payload) {
    state.formData = {
      // rest of formData fields
      email: payload.email || '',
      phone: payload.phone || '',
    }
  },
  profileClear(state) {
    state.formData = {
      // rest of formData fields
      email: '',
      phone: '',
    }
  }
}
})
```

4. We need to track **email** in the local state of the **src/components/
    AppProfileForm.vue** component using **v-model** and initialize it in the
    data() function:

```
<template>
  <!-- rest of template -->
    <div class="flex flex-col mt-2">
      <label class="flex text-gray-800 mb-2" for="email">Email
      </label>
      <input
        id="email"
        type="email"
        name="email"
        v-model="email"
        class="border-2 border-solid border-blue-200 rounded
          px-2 py-1"
      />
    </div>
  <!-- rest of template -->
</template>
<script>
export default {
  // rest of component
  data() {
```

```
      return {
        // other data properties
        email: ''
      }
    }
  }
</script>
```

5. We need to track **phone** in the local state of the **src/components/ AppProfileForm.vue** component using **v-model** and initialize it in the **data()** function:

```
<template>
  <!-- rest of template -->
    <div class="flex flex-col mt-2">
      <label class="flex text-gray-800 mb-2" for="phone">Phone
        Number</label>
      <input
        id="phone"
        type="tel"
        name="phone"
        v-model="phone"
        class="border-2 border-solid border-blue-200 rounded
          px-2 py-1"
      />
    </div>
  <!-- rest of template -->
</template>
<script>
export default {
  // rest of component
  data() {
    return {
      // other data properties
      phone: ''
    }
  }
}
</script>
```

6. For the payload of the mutation to contain **email** and **phone**, we'll need to add it to the **$store.commit('profileUpdate')** payload. We'll also want to reset it on the form when a component triggers a **profileClear** mutation:

```
<script>
export default {
  // rest of component
  methods: {
    submitForm() {
      this.$store.commit('profileUpdate', {
        // rest of payload
        email: this.email,
        phone: this.phone
      })
    },
    resetProfileForm() {
      // other resets
      this.email = ''
      this.phone = ''
    }
  }
}
</script>
```

7. For **email** to display, we need to render it in **src/components/AppProfileDisplay.vue** using a conditional paragraph (to hide the **Email** label when there is no email set):

```
<template>
  <!-- rest of template -->
    <p class="mt-2" v-if="formData.email">
      Email: {{ formData.email }}
    </p>
  <!-- rest of template -->
</template>
```

8. For **phone** to display, we need to render it in **src/components/ AppProfileDisplay.vue** using a conditional span (to hide the **Phone Number** label when there is no phone set):

```
<template>
  <!-- rest of template -->
    <p class="mt-2" v-if="formData.phone">
      Phone Number: {{ formData.phone }}
    </p>
  <!-- rest of template -->
</template>
```

The application should look as follows when the form is filled out and submitted:

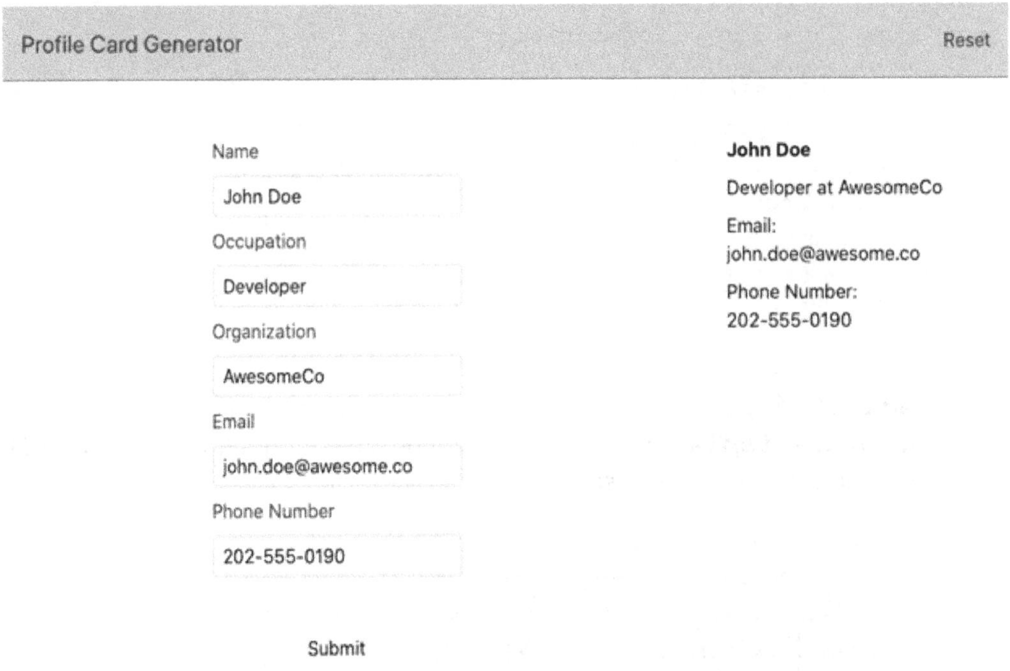

Profile Card Generator   Reset

Name

John Doe

Occupation

Developer

Organization

AwesomeCo

Email

john.doe@awesome.co

Phone Number

202-555-0190

Submit

John Doe

Developer at AwesomeCo

Email:
john.doe@awesome.co

Phone Number:
202-555-0190

Figure 8.36: Application with Email and Phone Number fields

We have now seen how to add new fields to a Vuex-managed application. Next, we will see how to decide whether to put something into global or local state.

CHAPTER 9: WORKING WITH VUEX – STATE, GETTERS, ACTIONS, AND MUTATIONS

ACTIVITY 9.01: CREATING A SIMPLE SHOPPING CART AND PRICE CALCULATOR

Solution:

Perform the following steps to complete the activity:

> **NOTE**
>
> To access the code files for this activity, refer to https://packt.live/2KpvBvQ.

1. Create a new Vue application with Vuex support via the CLI.

2. Add the products and empty **cart** to the store located in **store/index.js**. Note that the product names and prices are arbitrary:

```
state: {
  products: [
    { name: "Widgets", price: 10 },
    { name: "Doodads", price: 8 },
    { name: "Roundtuits", price: 12 },
    { name: "Fluff", price: 4 },
    { name: "Goobers", price: 7 }
  ],
  cart: [
  ]
```

3. Create a new **Products** component (**components/Products.vue**) that iterates over each product and includes the name and price for each product. It will also include buttons to add or remove items from the cart:

```
<h2>Products</h2>
<table>
  <thead>
    <tr>
      <th>Name</th>
      <th>Price</th>
      <th> </th>
    </tr>
  </thead>
```

```
    <tbody>
        <tr v-for="(product, idx) in products" :key="idx">
        <td>{{ product.name }}</td>
        <td>{{ product.price }}</td>
        <td>
            <button @click="addToCart(product)">Add to Cart
                </button>
            <button @click="removeFromCart(product)">Remove from
                Cart</button>
        </td>
        </tr>
    </tbody>
    </table>
```

4. In order for products to be used without prepending **$store**, include **mapState** and define its use within the **computed** property of the **Products** component:

```
import { mapState } from 'vuex';


export default {
  name: 'Products',
  computed: mapState(['products']),
```

5. Next include the methods for adding and removing items from the cart. This will simply call the mutations in the store:

```
methods: {
    addToCart(product) {
        this.$store.commit('addToCart', product);
    },
    removeFromCart(product) {
        this.$store.commit('removeFromCart', product);
    }
}
```

6. Define your mutations to handle working with the cart in the **store/index.js** file. When adding a new item to the cart, you first need to see if it was previously added and if so, simply increment the quantity. When removing items from the cart, if the quantity hits 0, the item should be removed completely:

```
mutations: {
  addToCart(state, product) {
    let index = state.cart.findIndex(p => p.name ===
      product.name);
    if(index !== -1) {
      state.cart[index].quantity++;
    } else {
      state.cart.push({ name: product.name, quantity: 1});
    }
  },
  removeFromCart(state, product) {
    let index = state.cart.findIndex(p => p.name ===
      product.name);
    if(index !== -1) {
      state.cart[index].quantity--;
      if(state.cart[index].quantity === 0) state.cart.splice
        (index, 1);
    }
  }
}
```

7. Define a **Cart** component (**components/Cart.vue**) that iterates over the cart and shows the quantity of each item:

```
<h2>Cart</h2>
<table>
  <thead>
    <tr>
      <th>Name</th>
      <th>Quantity</th>
    </tr>
  </thead>
  <tbody>
    <tr v-for="(product, idx) in cart" :key="idx">
```

```
        <td>{{ product.name }}</td>
        <td>{{ product.quantity  }}</td>
      </tr>
    </tbody>
  </table>
```

8. As with the previous component, add **mapState** and alias the cart:

```
import { mapState } from 'vuex';

export default {
  name: 'Cart',
  computed: mapState(['cart'])
}
```

9. Define the final component, **Checkout** (**components/Checkout.vue**), and have it display a property named **cartTotal**. This will be defined via a getter that will be created in the store:

```
<h2>Checkout</h2>
Your total is ${{ cartTotal }}.
```

10. Map the getter in the script block:

```
import { mapGetters } from 'vuex';

export default {
  name: 'Cart',
  computed: mapGetters(['cartTotal']),
```

11. Add a checkout button. It should only show up when there is a total and should run a method named **checkout**:

```
    <button v-show="cartTotal > 0" @click="checkout">Checkout
      </button>
```

12. Define **checkout** to simply alert the user:

```
methods: {
  checkout() {
      alert('Checkout process!');
    }
  }
}
```

13. Back in the Vuex store, define the getter for **cartTotal**. It needs to iterate over the cart and determine the sum by multiplying price by quantity:

```
getters: {
  cartTotal(state) {
    return state.cart.reduce((total, item) => {
      let product = state.products.find(p => p.name ===
        item.name);
      return total + (product.price * item.quantity);
    }, 0);
  }
},
```

14. Use all three components in the main **App.vue** component:

```
<template>
  <div id="app">
    <Products />
    <Cart />
    <Checkout />
  </div>
</template>

<script>
import Products from './components/Products.vue'
import Cart from './components/Cart.vue'
import Checkout from './components/Checkout.vue'

export default {
  name: 'app',
  components: {
    Products, Cart, Checkout
  }
}
</script>
```

Start your application as you have done before (**npm run serve**) and open the URL in your browser. You should get the following output initially, showing an empty cart:

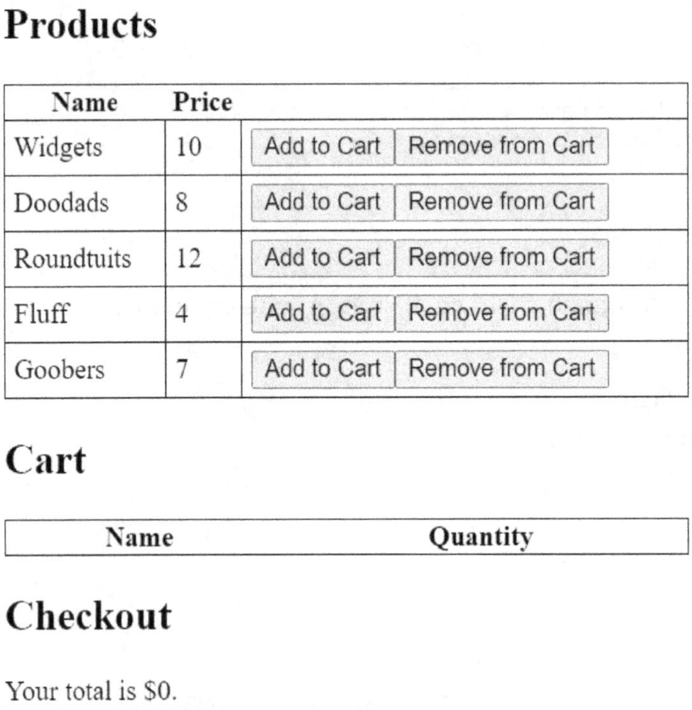

Products

Name	Price		
Widgets	10	Add to Cart	Remove from Cart
Doodads	8	Add to Cart	Remove from Cart
Roundtuits	12	Add to Cart	Remove from Cart
Fluff	4	Add to Cart	Remove from Cart
Goobers	7	Add to Cart	Remove from Cart

Cart

Name	Quantity

Checkout

Your total is $0.

Figure 9.9: Initial display of the cart

As you add and remove items, you'll see the cart and totals update in real time:

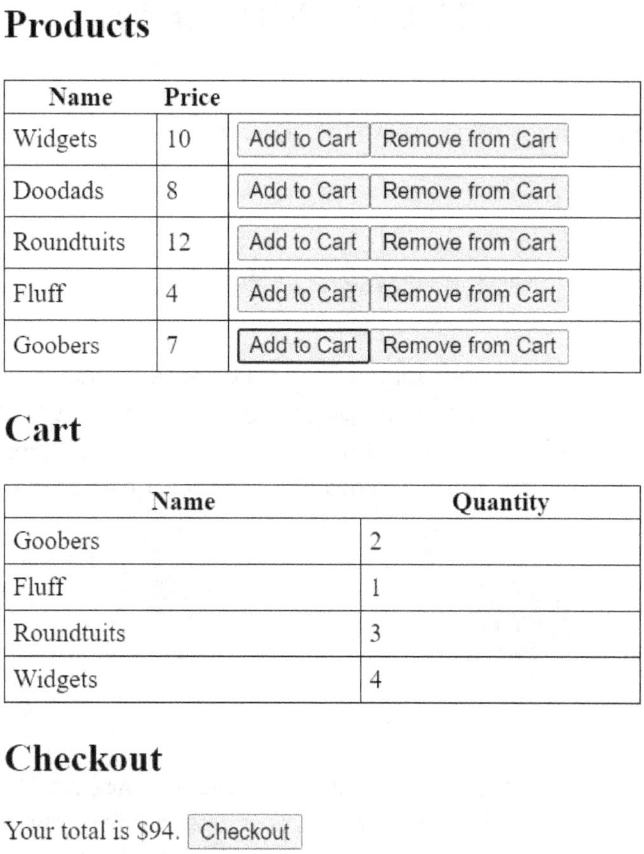

Products

Name	Price		
Widgets	10	Add to Cart	Remove from Cart
Doodads	8	Add to Cart	Remove from Cart
Roundtuits	12	Add to Cart	Remove from Cart
Fluff	4	Add to Cart	Remove from Cart
Goobers	7	Add to Cart	Remove from Cart

Cart

Name	Quantity
Goobers	2
Fluff	1
Roundtuits	3
Widgets	4

Checkout

Your total is $94. Checkout

Figure 9.10: The cart with items of multiple quantities added

The preceding figure displays the products and their prices, along with a cart containing multiple quantities of different products and the final checkout amount. You've now got a fully built, albeit simple, e-commerce cart product driven by Vue and Vuex.

CHAPTER 10: WORKING WITH VUEX — FETCHING REMOTE DATA

ACTIVITY 10.01: USING AXIOS AND VUEX WITH AUTHENTICATION

Solution:

Perform the following steps to complete the activity.

> **NOTE**
>
> To access the code files for this activity, refer to https://packt.live/3kVox6M.

1. Use the CLI to scaffold a new application and be sure to enable both Vuex and Vue Router. When done, then use **npm** to install **Axios**. Now that you have got the app scaffolded, let's begin building it. First, open **App.vue**, the core component in the application, and modify it so that the entire template is the view:

```
<template>
  <div id="app">
    <router-view/>
  </div>
</template>
```

2. By default, the CLI will scaffold two **views**: **Home** and **About**. We are going to change **About** to be the view that displays cats, but for now, open **Home. vue** and add the login form. Use a button to run a method to perform the (fake) login:

```
<template>
  <div>
    <h2>Login</h2>
    <form>
      <div>
        <label for="username">Username: </label>
        <input type="text" id="username" v-model="username"
          required>
      </div>
      <div>
        <label for="password">Password: </label>
        <input type="password" id="password" v-model="password"
          required>
      </div>
```

```
        <div>
            <input type="submit" @click.prevent="login" value=
                "Log In">
        </div>
    </form>
  </div>
</template>
```

3. Add the **data** for the login form and a **handler** for the login button. This will then fire off a dispatch to the store. On a successful login (and it will always be successful), **$router.replace** is used to navigate to the next page. This is done instead of **$router.go** so that the user cannot hit their back button to return to the login form:

```
<script>

export default {
  name: 'home',
  data() {
    return {
      username:'',
      password:''
    }
  },
  methods: {
    async login() {
      let response = await this.$store.dispatch('login',
      { username:this.username,
        password:this.password
      });
      if(response) {
        this.$router.replace('cats');
      } else {
        // handle a bad login here..
      }
    }
  }
}
</script>
```

4. Now let's build the **Cats** component in **views/Cats.vue**. This will simply iterate over the cats from the store and dispatch a call to the store to load them:

```
<template>
  <div>
    <h2>Cats</h2>
    <ul>
    <li v-for="(cat,idx) in cats" :key="idx">
      {{cat.name}} is {{cat.gender}}
    </li>
    </ul>
  </div>
</template>


<script>
import { mapState } from 'vuex';

export default {
  created() {
    this.$store.dispatch('loadCats');
  },
  computed: {
    ...mapState(["cats"])
  }
}
</script>
```

5. Now build the Vuex store by editing **store/index.js**. Begin by importing Vuex and defining constants for the two endpoints. Remember that we are *faking* a real API here, so the endpoints just return static JSON:

```
import Vue from 'vue'
import Vuex from 'vuex'
Vue.use(Vuex)

import axios from 'axios';
const LOGIN_URL = 'https://api.jsonbin.io/b/
    5debc045bc5ffd04009563cd';
const CATS_URL = 'https://api.jsonbin.io/b/
    5debc16dcb4ac6042075d594';
```

6. The store needs to keep two things: the authentication **token** and **cats**. Set up the **state** and define **mutations** for them:

```
export default new Vuex.Store({
  state: {
    token:'',
    cats:[]
  },
  mutations: {
    setCats(state, cats) {
      state.cats = cats;
    },
    setToken(state, t) {
      state.token = t;
    }
  },
```

7. Now add the **actions**. The login action stores the result as a **token** and the **cats** action passes the **token** as an **authorization** header:

```
actions: {
  loadCats(context) {
    axios.get(CATS_URL,
      {
        headers: {
          'Authorization': 'bearer '+context.state.token
        }
      })
      .then(res => {
        context.commit('setCats', res.data);
      })
      .catch(error => {
        console.error(error);
      });
  },
  async login(context, credentials) {
    return axios.get(LOGIN_URL, {
      params:{
        username: credentials.username,
        password: credentials.password
      }
```

```
      })
        .then(res => {
          context.commit('setToken', res.data.token);
          return true;
        })
        .catch(error => {
          console.error(error);
        });
    }
  }
})
```

8. The final piece of the application is the router, and there is a pretty interesting aspect to it. Think about the **cats** page. What happens if a user goes to that page first? With no token, the call to the endpoint will fail to return valid data. (Again, in a *real* server, that is.) Luckily, Vue Router provides a very simple way to handle this—route guards. Make use of **beforeEnter** to handle this call in the **cats** route. Edit your **router/index.js** file to look like the following code:

```
import Vue from 'vue'
import VueRouter from 'vue-router'
import Home from '../views/Home.vue'

import store from '../store';

Vue.use(VueRouter)

const routes = [
  {
    path: '/',
    name: 'home',
    component: Home
  },
  {
    path: '/cats',
    name: 'cats',
    component: () => import(/* webpackChunkName: "cats" */ '../views/
Cats.vue'),
    beforeEnter: (to, from, next) => {
      if(!store.state.token) {
        next('/');
      }
```

```
      next();
    }
  }
]

const router = new VueRouter({
  mode: 'history',
  base: process.env.BASE_URL,
  routes
})

export default router
```

9. Start the application with **npm run serve**, copy the URL to your browser, and you should get the following output initially:

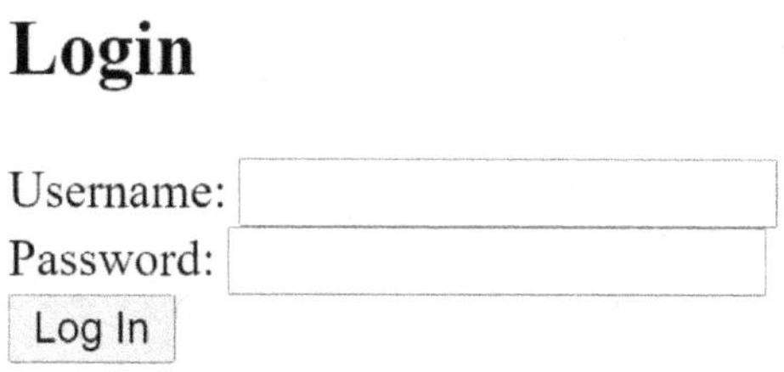

Login

Username: [   ]
Password: [   ]
[Log In]

Figure 10.8: Initial login screen

After logging in, you will see the data displayed as in the following screenshot:

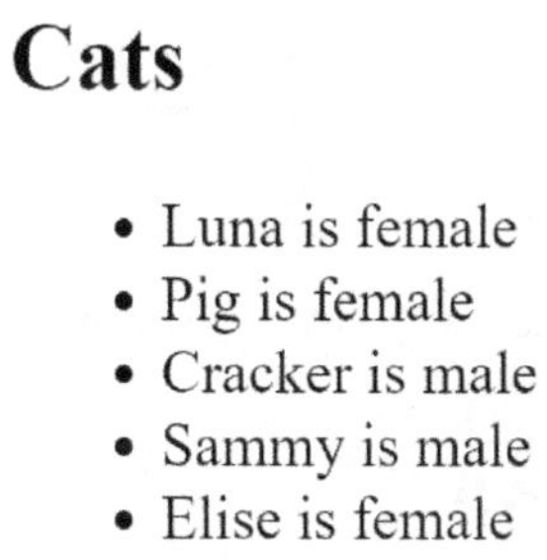

Cats

- Luna is female
- Pig is female
- Cracker is male
- Sammy is male
- Elise is female

Figure 10.9: Successfully displaying the data after login

In this activity, you have seen what an authentication system would look like when using Vuex and **Axios**. While the backend was fake, the code used here could easily be connected to a real authentication system.

CHAPTER 11: WORKING WITH VUEX — ORGANIZING LARGER STORES

ACTIVITY 11.01: SIMPLIFYING A VUEX STORE

Solution:

Perform the following steps to complete the activity.

> **NOTE**
>
> To access the initial code file for this activity, visit https://packt.live/3kaqBHH.

1. Begin by creating a new file, **src/store/state.js**, that will store the state values for everything but the **cat** object:

```
export default {
    name:'Lindy',
    job:'tank',
    favoriteColor:'blue',
    favoriteAnimal:'cat'
}
```

2. Make a new file, **src/store/getters.js**, and move the getter for **desiredPet** into it:

```
export default {
    desiredPet(state) {
        return state.favoriteColor + ' ' + state.favoriteAnimal;
    }
}
```

3. Next, make **src/store/mutations.js** and copy over the **mutations** not related to the cat name:

```
export default {
  setName(state, name) {
    state.name = name;
  },
  setJob(state, job) {
    state.job = job;
  },
  setFavoriteColor(state, color) {
    state.color = color;
```

```
  },
  setFavoriteAnimal(state, animal) {
    state.animal = animal;
  }
}
```

4. Update the store (**src/store/index.js**) file to import the new files:

```
import state from './state.js';
import getters from './getters.js';
import mutations from './mutations.js';
```

5. Edit the existing **state**, **mutations**, and **getters** block to use the included values:

```
export default new Vuex.Store({
  state,
  getters,
  mutations,
```

6. Now move the cat-related values into the **modules** block of the store. Create a **state**, **getters**, and **mutations** block and move all the values over, updating them to refer to the state values, not **state.cat**:

```
    cat: {
      state: {
        name:'Cracker',
        gender:'male',
        job:'annoyer'
      },
      getters: {
        petDescription(state) {
          return state.name + ' is a ' + state.gender +
          ' ' + state.job + ' cat.';
        }
      },
      mutations: {
        setCatName(state, name) {
          state.name = name;
        },
        setCatGender(state, gender) {
          state.gender = gender;
        },
```

```
        setCatJob(state, job) {
            state.job = job;
        }
    }
}
```

7. Run the application and confirm that the **App.vue** component continues to work as it did before.

   Your output will be as follows:

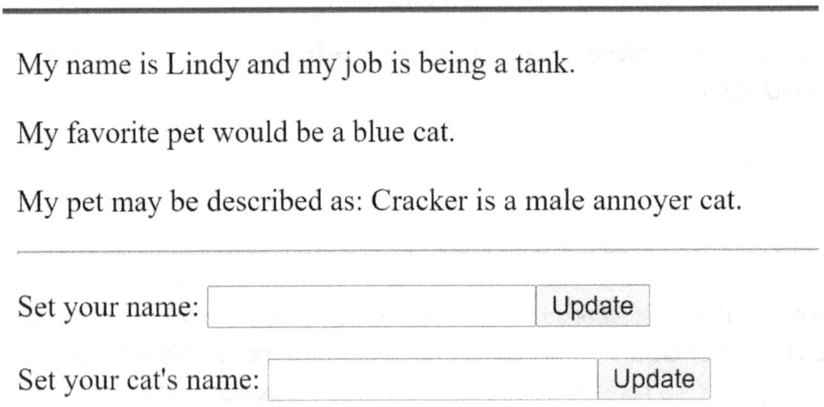

My name is Lindy and my job is being a tank.

My favorite pet would be a blue cat.

My pet may be described as: Cracker is a male annoyer cat.

Set your name: [   ] Update

Set your cat's name: [   ] Update

Figure 11.4: Final output of the activity

You now have a Vuex store modified to be more approachable, easier to edit, and simpler to debug in the future. To access the solution for this activity, visit https://packt.live/3l4Lg0x.

CHAPTER 12: UNIT TESTING

ACTIVITY 12.01: ADDING A SIMPLE SEARCH BY TITLE PAGE WITH TESTS

Solution:

Perform the following steps to complete the activity:

> **NOTE**
>
> To access the code files for this activity, refer to https://packt.live/2UVF28c.

1. Create the search form with an input and a button in a new file in **src/components/SearchForm.vue**:

```
<template>
  <form class="flex flex-row m-auto mb-10">
    <input
      placholder="Search"
      class="bg-white focus:outline-none focus:shadow-outline
        border
      border-gray-300 rounded py-2 px-4 flex
      appearance-none leading-normal"
      type="text"
    />
    <button
      type="submit"
      class="flex bg-blue-500 hover:bg-blue-700
      text-white font-semibold font-sm hover:text-white
        py-2 px-4 border
      border-blue-500 hover:border-transparent rounded"
    >
      Search
    </button>
  </form>
</template>
```

2. We'll now get the form to display by importing, registering, and rendering it in **src/App.vue**:

```
<template>
  <!-- rest of template -->
    <div class="flex flex-col">
      <SearchForm />
      <!-- rest of template -->
    </div>
  <!-- rest of template -->
</template>
```

3. We're now ready to add a snapshot test for the search form. In **__tests__/ SearchForm.test.js**, we should add **SearchForm should match expected HTML**:

```
import {render} from '@testing-library/vue'
import SearchForm from '../src/components/SearchForm.vue'

test('SearchForm should match expected HTML', () => {
  const {html} = render(SearchForm)
  expect(html()).toMatchSnapshot()
})
```

4. We want to track the contents of the search form input using **v-model** to two-way bind the **searchTerm** instance variable and the contents of the input:

```
<template>
  <!-- rest of template -->
    <input
      v-model="searchTerm"
      placeholder="Search"
      class="bg-white focus:outline-none focus:shadow-outline border
        border-gray-300 rounded py-2 px-4 flex
        appearance-none leading-normal"
      type="text"
    />
  <!-- rest of template -->
</template>
<script>
export default {
  data() {
```

```
    return {
      searchTerm: ''
    }
  }
}
</script>
```

5. When the search form is submitted, we'll need to update the URL with the right parameter. This can be done with **this.$router.push()**. We will store the search in a **q** query parameter.

```
<template>
  <form
    @submit="onSubmit()"
    class="flex flex-row m-auto mb-10"
  >
  <!-- rest of template -->
  </form>
</template>
<script>
export default {
  // other properties
  methods: {
    onSubmit() {
      this.$router.push({
        path: '/'
        query: {
          q: this.searchTerm
        }
      })
    }
  }
}
</script>
```

6. We will want to reflect the state of the **q** query parameter in the search form input. Read **q** from **this.$route.query** and set it as the initial value for the **searchTerm** data field in the **SearchForm** component state:

```
<script>
export default {
  data() {
```

```
        return {
          searchTerm: this.$route.query.q || ''
        }
      },
      // other properties
    }
  </script>
```

7. Next, we'll want to filter the posts passed to **PostList** on the home page. We'll use **this.$route.query.q** in a computed property that filters posts by their title. This new computed property will then be used instead of **posts** in **src/App.vue**:

```
<template>
  <!-- rest of template -->
    <router-view
      :posts="relevantPosts"
    />
  <!-- rest of template -->
</template>
<script>
export default {
  // other properties
  computed: {
    relevantPosts() {
      const { q } = this.$route.query
      if (!q) {
        return this.posts
      }
      return this.posts.filter(
        p => p.title.toLowerCase().includes(q.toLowerCase())
      )
    }
  }
}
</script>
```

8. Next, we should add a test that changes the search query parameter and check that the app shows the right result. To do this, we can import **src/App.vue**, **src/store.js**, and **src/router.js**, and render the app with the store and the router. We can then update the search field contents by using the fact that the placeholder for the field is **Search**. Finally, we can submit the form by clicking the element where **test id** is **Search** (which is the **search** button):

```
// imports and other tests
test('SearchForm filter by keyword on submission',
  async () => {
  const {getByPlaceholderText, getByText, queryByText} =
    render(App, {
    router,

    store

  })
  expect(queryByText('Migrating an AngularJS app to Vue.js')).
    toBeTruthy()
  expect(queryByText('Vue.js for React developers')).
    toBeTruthy()
  await fireEvent.update(getByPlaceholderText('Search'), 'react')

  await fireEvent.click(getByText('Search'))

  expect(queryByText('Vue.js for React developers')).
    toBeTruthy()
  expect(queryByText('Migrating an AngularJS app to Vue.js')).
    toBeFalsy()
})
```

We are now in a state where we have passing tests. The following screenshot shows this:

```
> npm run test:unit __tests__/SearchForm.test.js --silent
 PASS  __tests__/SearchForm.test.js
  ✓ SearchForm should match expected HTML (40ms)
  ✓ SearchForm filter by keyword on submission (113ms)
```

Figure 12.29: Passing tests for routing

We have also got an application that is able to filter by search term, as follows:

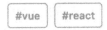

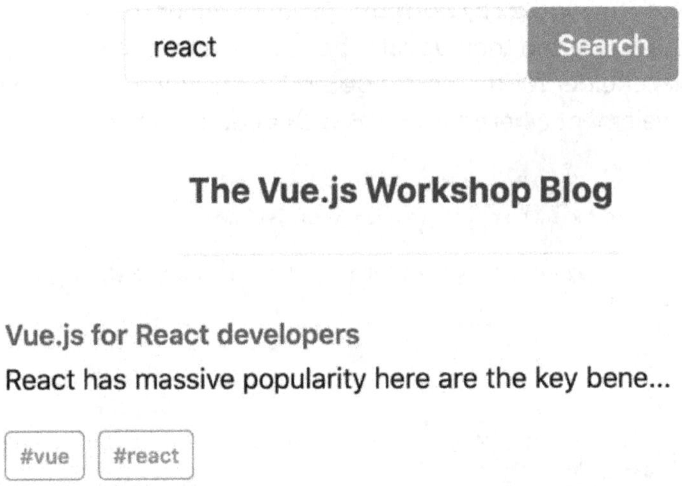
react
Search
The Vue.js Workshop Blog
Vue.js for React developers
React has massive popularity here are the key bene...
#vue
#react

Figure 12.30: Searching for "react" filters posts relevant to that search term

We've seen how to create and test a Vue.js application with multiple pages, Vuex, and a slew of components.

CHAPTER 13: END-TO-END TESTING

ACTIVITY 13.01: ADDING THE ABILITY TO SET A USER'S EMAIL AND TESTS

Solution:

Perform the following steps to complete the activity:

> **NOTE**
>
> To access the code files for this activity, refer to https://packt.live/2IZP4To.

1. In order to keep track of the email, we'll set it as a piece of reactive state in **data()** and add an email type input to the page, which will be two-way bound to **email** using **v-model**. We also add a label and the corresponding markup. Note that we'll have a **data-test-id** attribute on the email input set to **"email-input"**:

```
<template>
  <div id="app" class="p-10">
    <div class="flex flex-col">
      <!-- rest of template -->
      <div class="flex flex-col mx-auto mb-4">
        <label
          class="flex text-gray-700 text-sm font-bold mb-2"
          for="email"
        >
          Enter your email:
        </label>
        <input
          v-model="email"
          id="email"
          type="email"
          data-test-id="email-input"
          class="flex shadow appearance-none border
            rounded py-2 px-3 text-gray-700 leading-tight
            focus:outline-none focus:shadow-outline"
          required
        />
      </div>
      <!-- rest of template -->
```

```
</template>
<script>
// imports
export default {
  data() {
    return {
      email: '',
      // other data properties
    }
  },
  // other component properties
}
</script>
```

2. We'll now add a **beforeEach** hook to set up the Cypress mock server and stub out the **GET** comments (list) request. The comments list request should be aliased as **getComments**:

```
describe('Email input', () => {
  beforeEach(() => {
    cy.server()
    cy.route('GET', '**/comments', []).as('getComments')
  })
})
```

3. We'll add our first test that checks whether typing into the email input works correctly. We'll go to the app, type an email, and check that what we typed is now the input value:

```
describe('Email input', () => {
  // setup
  it('email input should work', () => {
    cy.visit('/')
    cy.get('[data-test-id="email-input"]')
      .type('hugo@example.tld')
      .should('have.value', 'hugo@example.tld')
  })
})
```

When run using the Cypress UI, we get the following passing test:

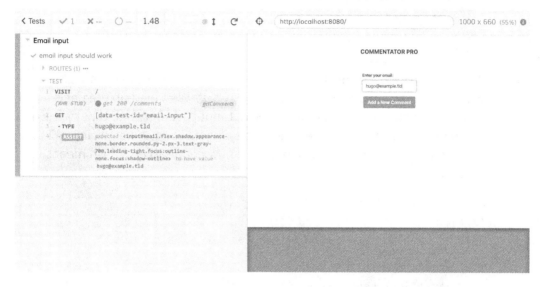

Figure 13.24: Cypress running "enter-email" tests, with the email input test

4. The **email** property existing is a pre-requisite to adding comments, so we'll disable the **add new comment** button while **email** is empty (**!email**). We'll bind to the **disabled** attribute and toggle some classes based on whether or not the **email** field is populated:

```
<template>

  <div id="app" class="p-10">
    <div class="flex flex-col">
      <!-- rest of template -->
      <button
        @click="showEditor = !showEditor"
        class="flex mx-auto bg-blue-500 hover:bg-blue-700
          text-white font-bold py-2 px-4 rounded"
        data-test-id="new-comment-button"
        :disabled="!email"
        :class="{ 'opacity-50 cursor-not-allowed' : !email }"
      >
        Add a New Comment
```

```
      </button>
      <!-- rest of template -->
    </div>
  </div>
</template>
```

5. With this new **disable add new comment button while email is empty** functionality, we should add a new E2E test. We'll load up the page and on initial load, we'll check that the **email** input is empty and that the **new comment** button is disabled. We'll then type an email into the email input field and check that the **new comment** button is now *not* disabled, which means it is enabled:

```
describe('Email input', () => {
  // setup & other tests
  it('add comment button should be disabled when no email',
    () => {
    cy.visit('/')
    cy.get('[data-test-id="email-input"]')
      .should('have.value', '')

    cy.get('[data-test-id="new-comment-button"]')
      .should('be.disabled')

    cy.get('[data-test-id="email-input"]')
      .type('hugo@example.tld')

    cy.get('[data-test-id="new-comment-button"]')
      .should('not.be.disabled')
  })
})
```

The output from the test run after the updates is as follows:

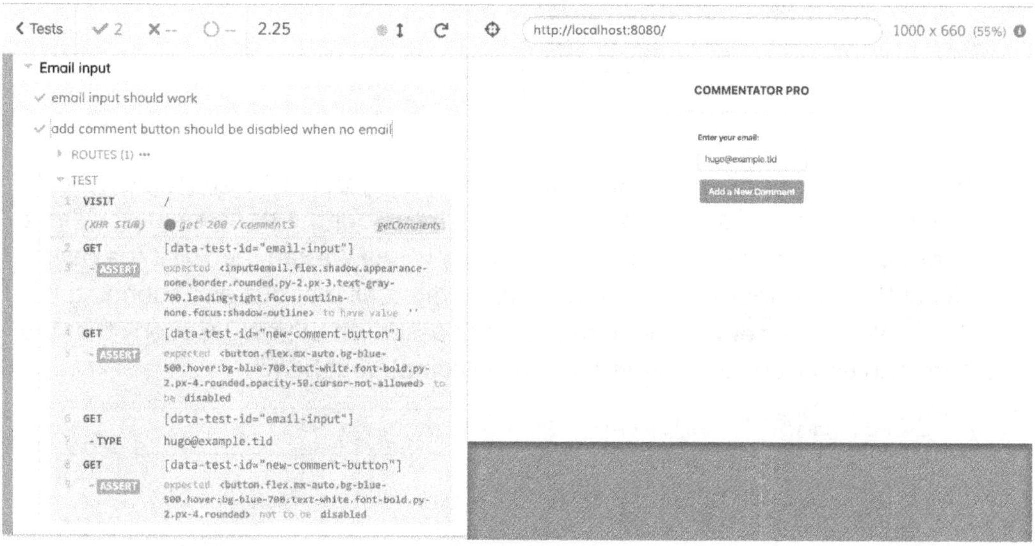

Figure 13.25: Cypress running "enter-email" tests, with the disabled add comment button test

6. Now that we've got a way to capture the email, we should pass it to the backend API when making the POST comments call (that is, when submitting a new comment). In order to do this, we should modify the spot in **methods. submitNewComment** where **email** is hardcoded as **evan@vuejs.org**:

```
<script>
// imports
export default {
  // other component properties
  methods: {
    submitNewComment() {
      // rest of method
      fetch('https://jsonplaceholder.typicode.com/comments', {
        // other fetch options
        body: JSON.stringify({
          email: this.email,
          body: this.newComment
        })
```

```
        }).then(res => res.json())
        // rest of promise chain
    }
  }
}
</script>
```

7. Now that we're using the email that's been input by the user, we should write an E2E test to check that it's being sent. We'll stub out the **POST** request, alias it to **newComment**, and send back an arbitrary value. We can then visit the page, fill out the email input, open the comment editor, fill that out, and submit it. We'll then wait on the **newComment** request and assert on the request body that the body and email are as they were when we completed them:

```
describe('Email input', () => {
  // setup & other tests
  it('when adding comment, it should be created with the
    input email', () => {
    cy.route('POST', '**/comments', {
      body: 'My new comment',
      email: 'hugo@example.tld'
    }).as('newComment')

    cy.visit('/')

    cy.get('[data-test-id="email-input"]')
      .type('hugo@example.tld')

    cy.get('[data-test-id="new-comment-button"]')
      .should('not.be.disabled')
      .click()

    cy.get('[data-test-id="new-comment-editor"]')
      .type('My new comment')

    cy.get('[data-test-id="new-comment-submit"]')
      .should('not.be.disabled')
      .click()

    cy.wait('@newComment')
      .its('request.body')
      .should('deep.equal', {
```

```
            body: 'My new comment',
            email: 'hugo@example.tld'
        })
    })
})
```

When run using the Cypress UI, we get the following test run output:

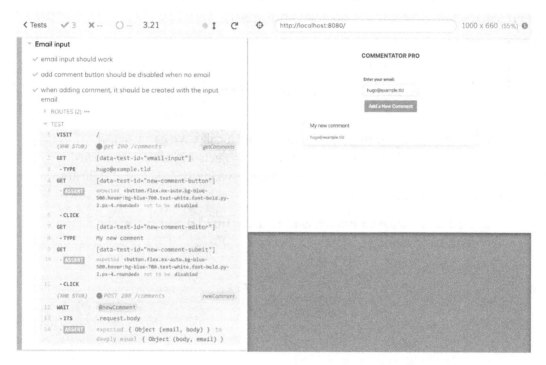

Figure 13.26: Cypress running "enter-email" tests, with the email input test

We've now seen how to effectively build and test (with an E2E test) a Vue.js application with Cypress.

CHAPTER 14: DEPLOYING YOUR CODE TO THE WEB

ACTIVITY 14.01: ADDING CI/CD WITH GITLAB TO A BOOK SEARCH APP AND DEPLOYING TO AMAZON S3 AND CLOUDFRONT

Solution

Perform the following steps to complete the activity:

> **NOTE**
>
> To access the code files for this activity, refer to https://packt.live/36ZecBT.

1. To start, we'll want to run a production build locally. We can use the regular command used to build all Vue CLI projects for production. We'll also want to check that the relevant assets (JavaScript, CSS, and HTML) are generated correctly.

    The production build command is **npm run build**, as seen in the following screenshot:

```
> npm run build --silent

  Building for production...

  DONE  Compiled successfully in 9430ms                                 18:00:16

  File                                  Size              Gzipped

  dist/js/chunk-vendors.42c7f7f4.js     88.54 KiB         31.15 KiB
  dist/js/app.ea91d572.js               4.09 KiB          1.81 KiB
  dist/css/app.c6bb8d4a.css             0.91 KiB          0.37 KiB

  Images and other types of assets omitted.

  DONE  Build complete. The dist directory is ready to be deployed.
  INFO  Check out deployment instructions at https://cli.vuejs.org/guide/deployment.html
```

Figure 14.65: The npm run build output for the initial book-search Vue CLI project

The **npm run build** command builds a **dist** directory with contents as in the following screenshot. It contains **CSS**, **JavaScript**, and **HTML** assets, as well as **sourcemaps** (**.js.map** files) and **favicon**:

```
> tree dist
dist
├── css
│   └── app.c6bb8d4a.css
├── favicon.ico
├── index.html
└── js
    ├── app.ea91d572.js
    ├── app.ea91d572.js.map
    ├── chunk-vendors.42c7f7f4.js
    └── chunk-vendors.42c7f7f4.js.map

2 directories, 7 files
```

Figure 14.66: Sample contents of the dist folder (generated using the tree command) after a Vue CLI production build run

2. In order to run GitLab CI/CD, we will need a **.gitlab-ci.yml** file. We will add a job to **.gitlab-ci.yml** in which we run an install of the packages followed by the production build in a Node.js LTS Docker container, at the **build** stage. We'll also make sure to cache the output of the production build:

```
build:
  image: node:lts
  stage: build
  script:
    - npm ci
    - npm run build
  cache:
    key: $CI_COMMIT_REF_SLUG
    paths:
      - dist
  artifacts:
    expire_in: 1 week
    paths:
      - dist
```

Once we use `git add .gitlab-ci.yml` and commit and push the changes, we should see the following GitLab CI/CD pipeline run, which includes the **build** job in the running state:

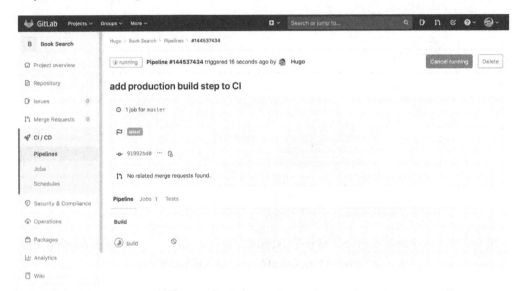

Figure 14.67: The GitLab CI/CD pipeline with the build job running

The following screenshot displays the GitLab CI/CD pipeline with the **build** job completed successfully:

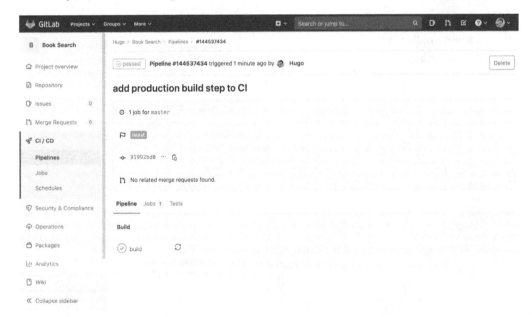

Figure 14.68: The GitLab CI/CD pipeline with the build job passed

3. Next, we will want to add a code quality job to the **test** stage on GitLab CI/CD (by updating **.gitlab-ci.yml**). We'll call the job **lint** and it will run an install of the dependencies as well as linting through the Vue CLI:

```
# other jobs
lint:
  image: node:lts
  stage: test
  script:
    - npm ci
    - npm run lint
```

Once we use **git add .gitlab-ci.yml** and commit and push the changes, we should see the following GitLab CI/CD pipeline run, which includes the **lint** job in the running state:

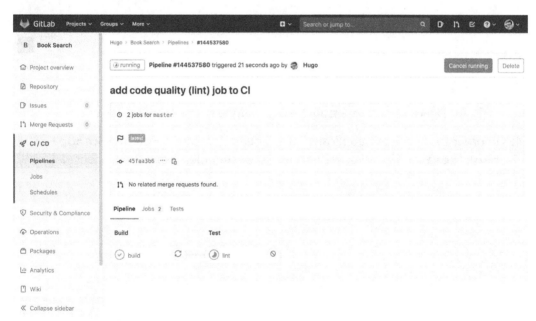

Figure 14.69: The GitLab CI/CD pipeline with the lint job running

The following screenshot displays the GitLab CI/CD pipeline with the **lint** job completed successfully:

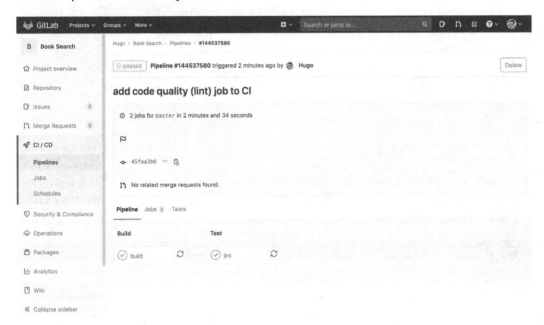

Figure 14.70: The GitLab CI/CD pipeline with the lint job passed

4. In order to deploy our application, we'll need to create a **vue-workshop-book-search** S3 bucket with public access enabled using the S3 console.

The S3 bucket creation page should look as shown in the following screenshots:

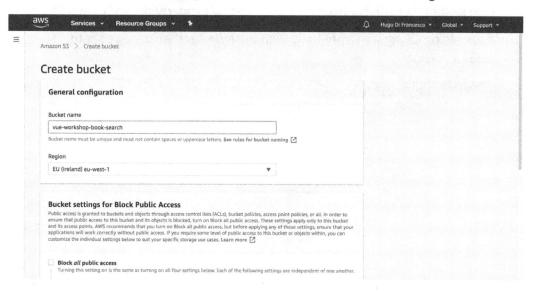

Figure 14.71: The S3 bucket creation page with vue-workshop-book-search entered as the bucket name

Figure 14.72 displays the S3 bucket creation page with the public access and disclaimer information:

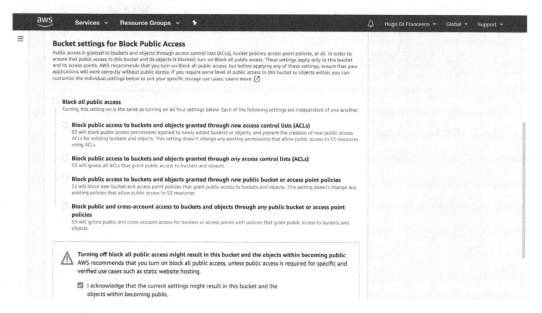

Figure 14.72: The S3 bucket creation page with public access enabled and the relevant disclaimer accepted

5. To access the S3 bucket contents over the web, we'll also need to configure it for web hosting. We can configure the web hosting property through the S3 console.

It should be configured as follows, with the index and error page set to `index.html`:

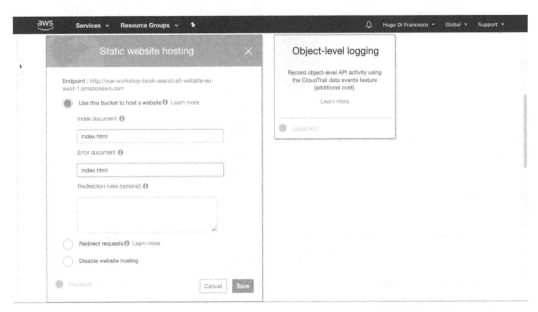

Figure 14.73: The S3 bucket properties page with web hosting enabled and configured with the index and error page set to index.html

6. For GitLab CI/CD to be able to create and update files on S3, we'll need to add the relevant AWS secrets to our GitLab repo CI/CD settings. The secrets are found in the AWS management console at the **Username** dropdown | **My Security Credentials** | **Access keys** (access key ID and secret access key) | **Create New Access Key** (or pick a key to reuse). The following screenshot displays the **CI/CD Settings** page:

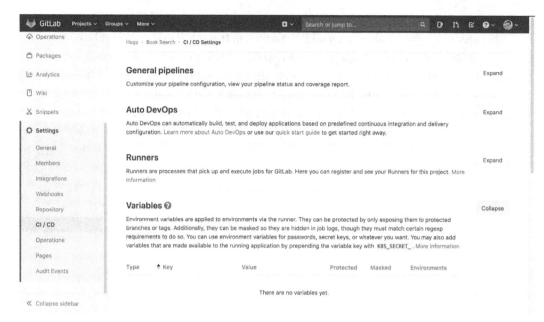

Figure 14.74: The GitLab CI/CD Settings page with the Variables section open

Once the **Expand** button is clicked for the **Variables** section, we add the relevant AWS environment variables: **AWS_ACCESS_KEY_ID**, **AWS_DEFAULT_REGION**, and **AWS_SECRET_ACCESS_KEY**. The **Variables** section will then look as follows:

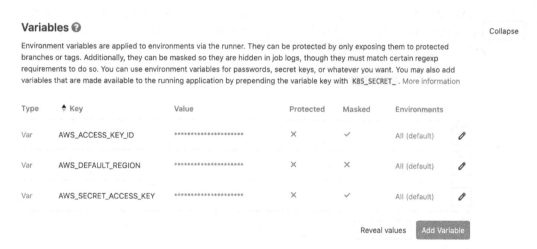

Figure 14.75: The GitLab CI/CD Settings page with the required AWS environment variables added (with values masked)

7. Next, we will want to add a **deploy** job to the **deploy** stage on GitLab CI/CD (by updating **.gitlab-ci.yml**). We will call the job **deploy**; it will need to download the **awscli pip** package (Python package manager), which means the Docker image that makes the most sense is **python:latest**. The **deploy** job will load the built production build from cache, install **awscli** with **pip**, and run **aws s3 sync <build_directory> s3://<s3-bucket-name> --acl=public-read**:

```
# other jobs

deploy:
  image: python:latest
  stage: deploy
  cache:
    key: $CI_COMMIT_REF_SLUG
    paths:
      - dist
  before_script:
    - pip install awscli
  script:
    - aws s3 sync ./dist s3://vue-workshop-book-search
      --acl=public-read
```

Once we use **git add .gitlab-ci.yml** and commit and push the changes, we should see the following GitLab CI/CD pipeline run, which includes the **deploy** job in the running state:

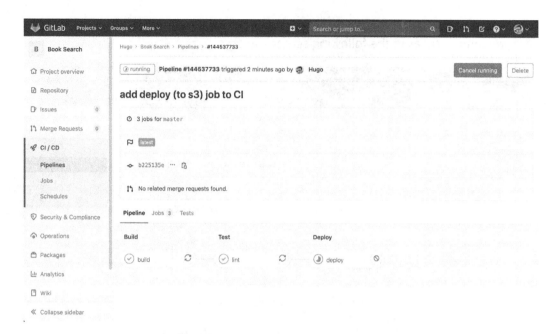

Figure 14.76: The GitLab CI/CD pipeline with the deploy job running

Figure 14.77 displays the GitLab CI/CD pipeline with the **deploy** job completed successfully:

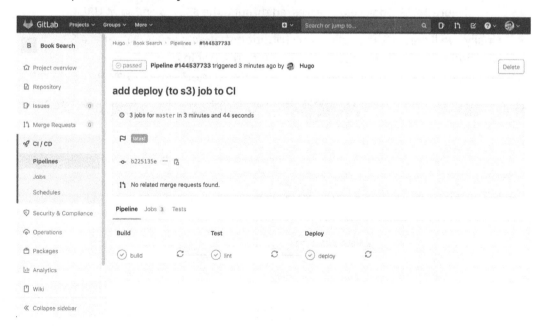

Figure 14.77: The GitLab CI/CD pipeline with the deploy job passed

Once the pipeline completes, our application should be available through the S3 web endpoint, as in the following screenshot:

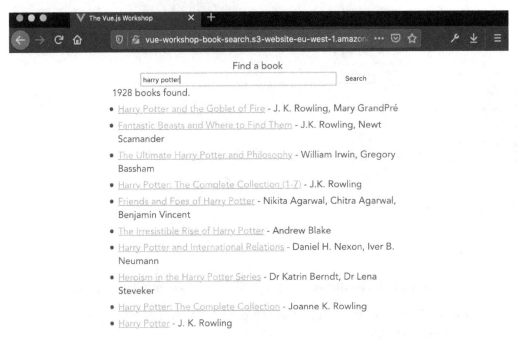

Figure 14.78: Book search accessed through the S3 web endpoint URL

8. Finally, we'll create a CloudFront distribution that acts as a CDN for the S3 web endpoint. We'll want to set **origin** to the origin of our S3 bucket's web endpoint and also make sure that we've enabled **Redirect HTTP to HTTPS**:

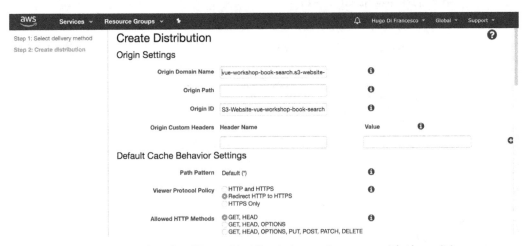

Figure 14.79: The CloudFront Distribution creation page with the origin domain set to the S3 bucket

Once the CloudFront distribution is deployed, our application should be accessible through the CloudFront distribution's domain, as shown in the following screenshot:

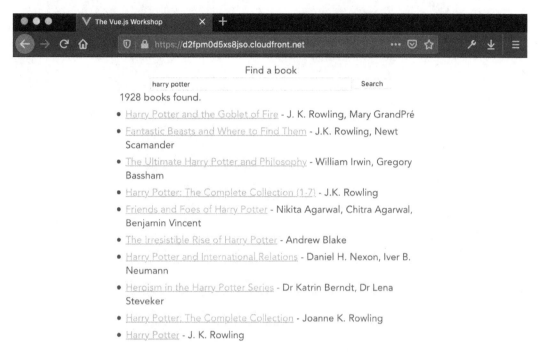

Figure 14.80: Book search accessed through the CloudFront domain, displaying results for a harry potter query

With that, we've used GitLab CI/CD to add CI/CD to an existing Vue CLI project. We then deployed it to S3 using CloudFront as our CDN.

INDEX

CPSIA information can be obtained
at www.ICGtesting.com
Printed in the USA
LVHW101958280821
696355LV00006B/361